TREATING ALCOHOL PROBLEMS

MARITAL AND FAMILY INTERVENTIONS

THE GUILFORD SUBSTANCE ABUSE SERIES

HOWARD T. BLANE and THOMAS R. KOSTEN, Editors

Treating Alcohol Problems
Marital and Family Interventions

Edited by
TIMOTHY J. O'FARRELL
Harvard Medical School
Veterans Affairs Medical Center
Brockton and West Roxbury, Massachusetts

Foreword by WILLIAM R. MILLER

THE GUILFORD PRESS
New York London

© 1993 The Guilford Press
A Division of Guilford Publications, Inc.
72 Spring Street, New York, NY 10012

Printed in the United States of America

This book is printed on acid-free paper.

Last digit is print number: 9 8 7 6 5 4 3 2

Library of Congress Cataloging-in-Publication Data

Treating alcohol problems: marital and family interventions /
    edited by Timothy J. O'Farrell: foreword by William Miller.
        p.   cm.
    Includes bibliographical references and index.
    ISBN 0-89862-195-X
    1. Alcoholism—Treatment.   2. Family psychotherapy.
3. Marital psychotherapy.   4. Alcoholics—Family relationships.
I. O'Farrell, Timothy J. II.   Series.
    [DNLM: 1.   Alcoholism—therapy. 2.   Family Therapy.
3. Marital Therapy.   WM 274 T7835   1993]
    RC565.T725   1993
    616.86'10651—dc20
    DNLM/DLC
    for Library of Congress   93-3061
                                                            CIP

To My Family

My wife, Jayne Sara, and son, Colin Robert

My sister and brothers,
Anne, Pat, and Mike

In memory of
my parents, Robert and Helen O'Farrell

—T. J. O'Farrell

Contributors

Richard D. Ager, Ph.D., The University of Michigan Alcohol Research Center, Ann Arbor, Michigan

Nathan H. Azrin, Ph.D., Department of Psychology, Nova University, Ft. Lauderdale, Florida

Richard Bale, Ph.D., Veterans Affairs Medical Center, Menlo Park, California, and Department of Psychiatry and Behavioral Sciences, Stanford University School of Medicine, Palo Alto, California

David Barrett, M.S., Drinking Check-up Project, Southeastern Wisconsin Medical and Social Services, Milwaukee, Wisconsin

Joan E. Dittrich, Ph.D., Private Practice of Psychology, Napa, California

Patrick Duggan, M.S., L.C.D.C., Parkside Recovery Center, Memorial Southwest Hospital, Houston, Texas

Larry M. Gentilello, M.D., Department of Surgery, Harborview Medical Center, University of Washington School of Medicine, Seattle, Washington

J. Clark Laundergan, Ph.D., Department of Sociology and Center for Addiction Studies, University of Minnesota, Duluth, Minnesota

Robert A. Lewis, Ph.D., Family Studies Program, Department of Child Development and Family Studies, Family Research Institute, Purdue University, West Lafayette, Indiana

Michael R. Liepman, M.D., Department of Psychiatry, University of Massachusetts Medical School, Worcester, Massachusetts

Eric R. McCollum, Ph.D., Marriage and Family Therapy Program, Department of Family and Child Development, Virginia Polytechnic Institute and State University at Falls Church, Falls Church, Virginia

Barbara S. McCrady, Ph.D., Center of Alcohol Studies, Rutgers–The State University of New Jersey, Piscataway, New Jersey

Thorana S. Nelson, Ph.D., Marriage and Family Therapy Program, Department of Family and Child Development, Utah State University, Logan, Utah

Nora E. Noel, Ph.D., Department of Psychology, University of North Carolina at Wilmington, Wilmington, North Carolina

Timothy J. O'Farrell, Ph.D., Department of Psychiatry, Harvard University Medical School, Boston, Massachusetts, and Alcohol and Family Studies Laboratory, Veterans Affairs Medical Center, Brockton and West Roxbury, Massachusetts

Deborah J. Ossip-Klein, Ph.D., Department of Community and Preventive Medicine, University of Rochester School of Medicine, Rochester, New York

Fred P. Piercy, Ph.D., Department of Child Development and Family Studies, Purdue University, West Lafayette, Indiana

Robert G. Rychtarik, Ph.D., Research Institute on Alcoholism, New York Sate Division of Alcoholism and Alcohol Abuse, Buffalo, New York

Robert W. Sisson, Ph.D., Bristol County Sheriff's Office, North Dartmouth, Massachusetts

Douglas H. Sprenkle, Ph.D., Department of Child Development and Family Studies, Purdue University, West Lafayette, Indiana

Edwin J. Thomas, Ph.D., School of Social Work and Department of Psychology, The University of Michigan, Ann Arbor, Michigan

Terry S. Trepper, Ph.D., Marriage and Family Therapy Program, Family Studies Center, Department of Behavioral Sciences, Purdue University Calumet, Hammond, Indiana

Robert J. Volk, Ph.D., Department of Family Medicine, The University of Texas Medical Branch at Galveston, Texas

Joseph L. Wetchler, Ph.D., Marriage and Family Therapy Program, Family Studies Center, Department of Behavioral Sciences, Purdue University Calumet, Hammond, Indiana

Terence Williams, M.A., Family Center, Hazelden Foundation, Center City, Minnesota

Allen Zweben, D.S.W., School of Social Welfare, University of Wisconsin-Milwaukee, Milwaukee, Wisconsin

Foreword

Imagine the following situation. Medical care in your society is largely unregulated. Virtually anyone can proclaim herself or himself to be a medical practitioner and offer health care services for those with cancer, heart disease, injury, infectious diseases, or any health problem. There are no federal regulatory agencies overseeing and approving medications or other medical treatments. If you are ill, the treatment that you receive depends upon the practitioner you happen to see. Medical practitioners make little or no use of the large body of existing research on what methods are and are not effective in treating specific illnesses. Instead they offer whatever methods they happen to have learned and believe in, and charge whatever the market will bear for their services. There are no professional standards requiring practitioners to use those treatments which have been shown to be medically effective, or to refrain from unsupported or disproved methods. There is no accountability for unsuccessful outcomes. In fact, the general view is that those who fail to recover weren't sufficiently motivated to get better, didn't try hard enough, hadn't yet hit bottom.

Most would regard this to be a shocking and unacceptable state of affairs in a scientific age. Yet this has been largely the situation with regard to the treatment of alcoholism through the latter half of the 20th century. Practitioners and programs have tended to prescribe whatever approach they happen to offer (Hansen & Emrick, 1983). There has been little or no overlap between the list of therapeutic modalities supported by scientific evidence and those employed as standard practice in alcoholism treatment (Miller & Hester, 1986). Economic interests have played a major role in shaping the treatment delivery system, and the costliness of treatment modalities has been, at best, unrelated to their effectiveness (Holder et al., 1991; Institute of Medicine, 1990).

That is why it is more than encouraging to witness the gradual emergence in this field of practice informed and guided by science. This volume represents a step in that direction. In nearly every recent review of the effectiveness of alcoholism treatment, marital and family therapy has been identified as a promising well-substantiated therapeutic component. Yet not every form of treatment that includes the spouse or family will be helpful in overcoming alcohol problems. Some approaches practiced under the name of marital/family intervention may well be harmful. An important challenge for the future is to define more clearly those ways of working with couples and families which lead to beneficial outcomes.

In this volume, written for practitioners, the authors conclude each clinical chapter with a summary of current research knowledge regarding the approaches they have described. In some areas there is already a substantial base of empirical support; in others this knowledge is relatively new and limited. Yet the message is clear: We must be willing to put our cherished but fallible beliefs and especially our treatment practices to the test, to see whether they hold up under scientific evaluation. Our clients, after all, entrust to us their very lives. We owe them nothing less.

WILLIAM R. MILLER, Ph.D.
University of Mexico

REFERENCES

Hansen, J., & Emrick, C. D. (1983). Whom are we calling "alcoholic"? *Bulletin of the Society of Psychologists in Addictive Behaviors, 2,* 164–178.

Holder, H., Longabaugh, R., Miller, W. R., & Rubonis, A. V. (1991). The cost effectiveness of treatment for alcoholism: A first approximation. *Journal of Studies of Alcohol, 52,* 517–540.

Institute of Medicine, National Academy of Sciences (1990). *Broadening the base of treatment for alcohol problems.* Washington, DC: National Academy Press.

Miller, W. R., & Hester, R. K. (1986). The effectiveness of alcoholism treatment methods: What research reveals. In W. R. Miller & N. Heather (Eds.), *Treating addictive behaviors: Processes of change* (pp. 121–174). New York: Plenum.

Preface

Marital and family therapy in alcoholism treatment has been called "one of the most outstanding current advances in the area of psychotherapy of alcoholism" by a 1974 report from the National Institute on Alcohol Abuse and Alcoholism (NIAAA) to the United States Congress. Case reports and uncontrolled treatment studies that presented favorable results were the basis for this enthusiastic appraisal. NIAAA also recommended that controlled outcome studies be conducted to evaluate these promising treatment methods. In the nearly 20 years since that report, considerable progress has been made in the development of the rationale, clinical applications, and outcome research related to marital and family therapy in alcoholism treatment.

The *rationale* for the use of marital and family therapy in alcoholism treatment has developed from several converging lines of research and clinical findings. Many alcoholics have extensive marital and family problems, and positive marital and family adjustment is associated with better alcoholism treatment outcomes at follow-up. Further, growing clinical and research evidence describes reciprocal relationships between marital–family interactions and abusive drinking. Problem drinking leads to marital and family discord, including separation, divorce, and child and spouse abuse. At the same time, marital and family problems may stimulate excessive drinking, and family interactions often help to maintain alcohol problems once they have developed. Even when recovery from the alcohol problem has begun, marital and family conflicts may often precipitate renewed drinking by abstinent alcoholics. Finally, marital and family therapy can help not only the alcoholic but also the "other victims" of alcoholism because it has been estimated that each alcoholic affects at least four other persons, with family members being affected most frequently.

The *clinical applications* of marital and family therapy in alcoholism treatment have grown considerably in the past 20 years. Most of the methods described in this book were developed and refined during this period. The clinical situations for which marital or family intervention is deemed appropriate also have expanded substantially. Formerly, such interventions often were seen as most useful for only a subset of alcoholics with acknowledged serious marital and family problems. Currently, clinical guidelines suggest that such interventions should not be reserved solely for alcoholics who have serious marital and family problems secondary to, preceding, or coexisting with the alcohol problem. With therapy, couples and families with less serious problems often are better able to work together to support the alcoholic's sobriety and to enrich the marital–family relationships that have been strained by alcoholism-related stressors. Further, even when marital-family factors do not play an important role in triggering or maintaining the abusive drinking, involving the spouse or family in treatment may strengthen the alcoholic's ability to refrain from drinking while learning to deal with nonmarital factors and may help support alternative nondrinking behaviors. The field has left behind the days when most treatment centers provided little or no marital or family involvement. Currently, the only justifiable reason for not including family members in the alcoholic's treatment is refusal by the alcoholic or the family to consent to such contact. In fact, the Joint Commission on Accreditation of Healthcare Organizations' (JCAHO) standards for accrediting alcoholism treatment programs in the United States now require that the spouse or other adult family members who live with the alcoholic be included in at least the assessment process for all alcoholics who seek help.

Research on the effectiveness of marital and family therapy in alcoholism treatment has accumulated over the past 20 years. This body of research indicates that various specific marital and family therapy interventions can be used effectively at different stages of the alcoholism recovery process to initiate change when the alcoholic is unwilling to seek help, to stabilize sobriety and relationships once the alcoholic has sought help, and to maintain long-term recovery. Although many studies have been completed, the marital and family therapy methods that have shown promise in outcome research are not widely used by practitioners who treat alcoholics and their families. The gap between research and practice, which has been noted with concern by many, exists for a number of reasons. For one, the outcome studies are scattered throughout various research journals that often are not read by practitioners. Further, research articles do not provide the procedural details of clinical application that are needed by the practitioner who wishes to use up-to-date effective methods.

The purpose of this book is to provide practical guidelines for clinicians who wish to learn and use marital and family therapy methods that have shown promise in recent outcome research. Each stage of change in the alcoholism recovery process is considered separately because alcoholics and their families have different needs and require different therapeutic approaches at different stages in the recovery process. Part I provides marital and family therapy methods for initiating change and helping the family when the alcoholic is unwilling to seek help. Three chapters describe somewhat different methods for getting reluctant alcoholics to stop drinking and to enter treatment. These methods include Unilateral Family Therapy (Thomas and Ager), Community Reinforcement Training for Families (Sisson and Azrin), and the Johnson Institute Intervention approach (Liepman). In the final chapter in this section, Dittrich describes a group program that is designed to help wives of treatment-resistant alcoholics decrease their emotional distress and consider their own options for change rather than try to influence the alcoholic to change.

Part II provides methods for stabilizing sobriety and marital and family relationships when the alcoholic has sought help at a treatment center. Methods for use in both inpatient and outpatient settings, drawn from a variety of theoretical approaches, are included. Inpatient programs include Bale's eclectic approach to family treatment in short-term detoxification and Laundergan and Williams's psychoeducational disease-model program for family members of alcoholics in a residential rehab program. Outpatient approaches include two behavioral marital therapy (BMT) programs, O'Farrell's Antabuse Contract plus BMT couples group program and Noel and McCrady's work combining BMT with alcohol-focused spouse involvement to change spouse behaviors that trigger or reinforce drinking by the alcoholic. Two final chapters in this section from the Purdue University Family Therapy Program present outpatient methods drawn from a family systems approach for use with women alcoholics (Wetchler and colleagues) and with adolescent alcohol abusers (Trepper and colleagues).

Part III describes methods for maintaining long-term recovery and preventing relapse. Two chapters describe methods to maintain recovery after the alcoholic has completed an intensive treatment program: behavioral contracts between alcoholics and family members after an inpatient rehab program (Ossip-Klein and Rychtarik), and couples relapse-prevention sessions after a BMT couples group program (O'Farrell). In the final chapter in this section, McCrady presents an outpatient couples therapy program based on Marlatt and Gordon's model of the relapse process.

Part IV suggests future directions for work in this area and presents concluding comments. Methods to deal with alcohol problems encountered by practitioners outside the alcoholism treatment setting, including brief treatment for less serious alcohol problems (Zweben and Barrett) and family intervention in the trauma center (Gentilello and Duggan), are presented as examples of future directions that are explored in some depth in the final chapter by O'Farrell.

Each chapter on a specific marital or family therapy method includes several sections. Chapters begin with an overview of the specific method under consideration to give a general idea of how the treatment works. Special clinical considerations about characteristics of clients, therapists, and settings for which the method is most likely to work come next. The majority of each chapter provides specific guidelines for implementing the method and an extended case study of the successful application of the method. A final section summarizes current knowledge regarding the method's effectiveness based on outcome research. A reference list provides further readings on clinical and research aspects of the treatment method.

This book is intended to give you, the practitioner, clinical methods to use in your work with alcoholics and the families. Each chapter is written by a clinical researcher who has subjected his or her work on marital and family therapy with alcoholics to empirical scrutiny. Not all authors have used well-controlled, randomized clinical trials to evaluate the methods presented in their chapters. In fact, a few chapters present therapy models currently being tested in research projects by experienced researchers who have provided earlier outcome studies. Further research will no doubt clarify the effectiveness of these methods and others that have not yet been developed or fully evaluated.

This book gives you descriptions of carefully developed, well-conceived marital and family therapy methods for which promising scientific evidence exists. Each chapter is written by an outstanding clinician researcher with extensive experience treating alcoholics and their families. The ultimate value of this book will come from your own attempts to apply the methods presented here in your day-to-day work to help alcoholics and their families. May you and your clients benefit from what is written here.

Acknowledgments

Many have contributed to this volume. I am grateful to all of the authors who contributed their invaluable clinical and research expertise to this project. Thanks to William Miller and Reid Hester for inspiring this book by their many efforts to bring research-tested methods to alcoholism practitioners, to Henry Cutter for his insightful collaboration in my own research that led me to this volume, and to Stephen Maisto and Dennis Upper for their encouragement and helpful comments on the initial outline for this book. Sharon Panulla and Susan Marples at Guilford Press were extremely helpful with all aspects of the writing, editing, and publishing process. Patricia DeVaux of DFA Office Services and Susan Taylor provided much appreciated assistance with the word processing and correspondence involved in preparing this volume. My work on this volume was supported in part by grant R01 AA08637 from the National Institute on Alcohol Abuse and Alcoholism and by a grant from the Smithers Foundation. Finally, I am grateful to my wife, Jayne, and son, Colin, for their support and tolerance during this undertaking; the joy and strength I derive from the warm and loving family they provide has inspired and sustained my efforts to help alcoholics and their families.

TIMOTHY J. O'FARRELL

Contents

Part III

MAINTAINING LONG TERM RECOVERY AND PREVENTING RELAPSE

Part IV

FUTURE DIRECTIONS AND CONCLUDING COMMENTS

Part I

INITIATING CHANGE AND HELPING THE FAMILY WHEN THE ALCOHOLIC IS UNWILLING TO SEEK HELP

Chapter 1

Unilateral Family Therapy with Spouses of Uncooperative Alcohol Abusers

Edwin J. Thomas
Richard D. Ager

OVERVIEW

Unilateral Family Therapy (UFT) for alcohol abuse assists cooperative, non-alcohol-abusing spouses to influence their uncooperative alcoholic partners to stop drinking, enter treatment, or both (Thomas, 1989; Thomas & Santa, 1982; Thomas, Santa, Bronson, & Oyserman, 1987). The alcohol-abusing partners do not (and, at least initially, will not) participate in the treatment. This approach does not assume that the cooperative spouse is to blame for the difficulties. However, the alcoholic's spouse is viewed as a vital and potentially crucial point of leverage who may be the main or only rehabilitative influence accessible to the therapist.

With spouses of uncooperative alcohol abusers the unilateral approach to family therapy has three foci of intervention. The *individual focus* emphasizes assisting the cooperative spouse with his or her coping by reducing stress and anxiety about the abuser's drinking, and channeling the spouse's efforts toward specific ways to address the drinking problem. The *interactional focus* entails mediating changes in marital and family functioning by reducing marital discord through unilateral relationship enhancement, reducing nagging and other customary drinking control efforts, and decreasing the spouse enabling of the alcohol abuse. The *third-party focus* involves work with the spouse or other family members to bring about change in the uncooperative family member by inducing the alcohol abuser to seek treatment or other assistance, to stop drinking, or both.

In the unilateral treatment program, major emphasis is placed on assisting the spouse to become a positive rehabilitative influence with the resistant drinker. In this connection, there are three main phases of treatment. The first phase involves preparing the spouse to assume a rehabilitative role. The second phase consists of conducting abuser-directed interventions to actively influence the alcohol abuser to enter treatment, stop drinking, or both. The third phase involves maintaining spouse and abuser treatment gains.

Beneficial outcomes were reported in two studies of this treatment program. The results for the spouses included reductions of dysfunctional drink-related behaviors, such as enabling, and increases in personal and marital adjustment. At the final follow-up for the alcohol abusers in an experimental evaluation, three-quarters had entered treatment and/or maintained clinically meaningful reductions of drinking levels, including abstinence. These findings provided support for the effectiveness of the UFT treatment program and for the conclusion that the unilateral approach to alcohol abuse can assist the spouse to become a positive rehabilitative influence with an uncooperative drinker.

SPECIAL CONSIDERATIONS

The treatment program presented here was conducted as part of clinical research. Some of the research conditions of this treatment program are indicated below with implications for the provision of service.

Use of Spouses and Others as Mediators

Although the treatment methods described here were developed for spouses, some of the abuser-directed interventions employed the abuser's parents and/or children in addition to the spouse. These treatment methods should also be generally applicable in work with family members other than the spouse in trying to reach an unmotivated drinker.

Treatment Setting

Alcohol treatment for the abusers was provided in community agencies outide of the research clinic in which the spouses were seen. This necessitated making intervening arrangements that often set up additional obstacles to getting the abusers into treatment. Use of UFT in settings that can readily accept the abuser into treatment should greatly facilitate the abuser's treatment entry. Such an arrangement also could facilitate coordination of the abuser's treatment with the therapy provided earlier for the spouse.

Abusers and Spouses Most Likely to Benefit

The eligibility criteria employed in the research have relevance for selecting participants for this type of treatment. Criteria for the spouse included recognition that the partner had a drinking problem, willingness to receive help to try to do something about that problem, and absence of a drinking problem for the spouse. Criteria for the abuser included a drinking problem for which he or she was unwilling to receive treatment. Additional criteria for both partners were absence of domestic violence, no other problem of drug abuse, no history of severe emotional disorder, no immediate plans for marital dissolution, and no other concurrent professional counseling. In addition to the spouse's consent to participate in the research, abusers also gave consent to allow their spouses to disclose information about them and to participate in spouse treatment that could influence their drinking. Although aspects of this treatment program might well apply to cases not meeting these criteria (e.g., abuse of other drugs in addition to alcohol), the use of confrontive interventions in cases in which these criteria are not met could increase the risk of failure and precipitate such adverse complications as domestic violence, marital estrangement, and self-destructive acts by the abuser.

To function as an intermediary for change, the spouse ideally should have capabilities to be a good treatment mediator. Thomas and Ager (1992) have identified a number of areas as important for the spouse as treatment mediator. These include motivation for spouse treatment, compliance with the treatment regimen, and skills to perform treatment-related tasks. Power and influence over the alcohol abuser and a strong investment in improving the marriage also are important. Research by Ager (1991) has indicated that spouse psychopathology and high levels of marital conflict conspire against good treatment mediation.

DESCRIPTION OF TREATMENT METHOD

Using eligibility criteria such as those described above, selection of suitable spouses and of abusers through their spouses should be carried out beforehand by telephone screening, as was done in these research studies, or by interview with the spouse. Assessment is carried out as appropriate for each component of the treatment program when it comes up in the program. Table 1.1 presents an outline of the content of the UFT program that is described in detail next.

Preparing the Spouse for a Rehabilitative Role (Phase I)

Treatment Orientation

The treatment orientation, given at the outset, emphasizes the distinctive aspects of the UFT program for spouses. The orientation information includes such factors as the following: (1) the rights of the spouse to receive treatment and likewise the right of the abuser to refuse treatment; (2) the importance of not disclosing to others, particularly the abuser, what transpires in the treatment; (3) the assumption that the spouse is not to blame for the excessive drinking of a partner; (4) the potential of the spouse to become a positive rehabilitative influence with the alcohol abuser; and (5) the steps of the treatment program. Finally, the responsibilities of the spouse in unilateral treatment are

TABLE 1.1. Overview of Unilateral Family Therapy (UFT) for Spouses of Alcohol Abusers

---

   I. Preparing the spouse to assume a rehabilitative role: Phase I (3–8 weekly sessions)
      A. Treatment orientation
      B. Spouse role induction
         1. Alcohol monitoring
         2. Alcohol education
         3. Unilateral relationship enhancement
         4. Modification of the spouse's customary drinking control
         5. Disenabling

  II. Conducting abuser-directed interventions: Phase II (5–18 weekly sessions)
      A. Intervention assessment
      B. Nonconfrontive interventions
         1. Sobriety support
         2. Physician's appointment
      C. Confrontive interventions
         1. Programmed confrontation
         2. Programmed request
         3. Supplements and variations (e.g., agreements/contracts, heart letters)
      D. Follow-up interventions
      E. Special problems

 III. Maintaining spouse and abuser treatment gains: Phase III (3–6 weekly sessions)

---

reviewed, The spouse's responsibilities are to provide needed information as frankly as possible, to cooperate in gathering data and in formulating the intervention plan, to intervene only as planned with the
therapist at the agreed-upon time, and to follow the agreed-upon plan
as stipulated.

As treatment progresses, the spouse learns further that this is not
conventional talk therapy. The spouse's coping is handled largely
through gains made by participation in each of the spouse role-
induction components. The primary focus is on working with the spouse
to reach the drinker. This is done through careful planning and problem
solving with the therapist. Along with the descriptions of the program
components provided below, further details on the specific treatment
procedures are provided in the case application presented later.

After the orientation, the therapist conducts a brief *assessment of
the alcohol abuser's drinking problem* through a careful interview with the
spouse. This interview covers the abuser's drinking pattern, withdrawal
history, and duration of the drinking problem. Problems due to drinking also are covered including neurological problems, physical problems,
emotional and psychological drinking-related consequences, and moral
deterioration. In addition, treatment history and past success at attempting to control the drinking are reviewed. The implications of this history for UFT with the spouse and for interventional possibilities are
considered as the treatment progresses.

Spouse Role Induction

Spouse role induction experiences prepare the spouse to assume a positive rehabilitative role. These experiences shape and enhance the
spouse's influence potential and the favorability of the marital conditions for subsequently engaging in abuser-directed interventions. The
five program components are introduced more or less in the order
given, with each preceded by a brief description and justification.

Alcohol Monitoring

The spouse is asked to monitor the abuser's alcohol consumption using a form on which the type and amount of alcohol consumed are
recorded each day. When the spouse has no way to determine the
amount of alcohol consumed, he or she records whether the abuser
was drunk that day, was abstinent, or drank alcohol of an undetermined
amount. Such recording helps to highlight the seriousness of the
abuser's problem for the spouse and provides the spouse and therapist
with current, specific data on the amount of drinking.

Alcohol Education

Although the spouses of alcohol abusers recognize that their partners had a drinking problem, most underestimate its seriousness and are insufficiently informed about the nature and effects of excessive alcohol use. It is therefore necessary to provide most spouses with some individualized education concerning aspects of their partner's alcohol problem. This can be done as necessary at various points, particularly following the alcohol abuse assessment just described. Assigning reading materials such as *I'll Quit Tomorrow* (Johnson, 1973) or *Chemical Dependence and Recovery: A Family Affair* (Johnson Institute) can also be helpful.[1]

Unilateral Relationship Enhancement

Relationships in alcoholic marriages commonly involve conflict, anger, mistrust, resentment, and poor communication, as has been frequently described in the literature (Bailey, 1961; Ghodse, 1982; Jacob & Krahn, 1988; Paolino & McCrady, 1977). Discordant relationships provide a poor basis for spouse mediation. Therefore, unilateral relationship enhancement (URE) is introduced as an important step to help prepare the spouse to function as a positive rehabilitative influence. Enhancing behaviors of the spouse may be "pleasers," such as making special meals, initiating enjoyable activities, and showing affection in various other ways. Enhancing behaviors of the spouse also include not engaging in "displeasers," such as being critical, leaving the bathroom in a mess, or coming home late from work.

To enhance the relationship, the spouse is requested to carry out behaviors when the abuser is sober that the abuser would find enjoyable and that the spouse is willing and able to carry out. The objective is not to provide marital therapy but rather to improve the marital relationship, given the motivation and response capability of the spouse at that time. Drawing from a list of potential pleasers based on an assessment with the spouse, from three to ten behaviors are typically included in the program. Each of these behaviors is recorded daily on a form and monitored in the treatment session by the therapist. Spouses are encouraged to see their enhancing efforts as an "investment" that promises to enhance the marital relationship now and to facilitate the success of more active interventions to be introduced later.

Client reports to date indicate that such enhancement provides for more harmonious interactions and facilitates later mediational efforts of the spouse. Even so, however, for a few spouses there may be problems. Occasionally, a spouse will claim that there is no room for improvement in their relationship. Nevertheless, the therapist can explore and often identify "extras" that might enhance the relationship. Some abusers drink so heavily and consistently that there are few opportunities for the spouse to engage in URE activities when the drinker is sober. Then the spouse can be asked to choose times for enhancement when there is little or no drinking. The spouse also can select enhancers that do not require interpersonal contact such as buying special foods or doing other small favors. Further information on clinical procedures, cases, clinical results, and problems related to URE can be found in Thomas, Adams, Yoshioka, & Ager (1990).

Modification of the Spouse's Customary Drinking Control

Most spouses attempt to get their alcohol abusing-partners to reduce their drinking through such aversive techniques as nagging, complaining, and threatening (Homila, 1985; Orford et al., 1975; Wiseman, 1980). The spouse's previous efforts to bring about change typically have been carried out on an occasional, brief, and nonsystematic basis. These efforts generally have consisted of strongly ingrained responses that are generally ineffective, produce negative abuser reactions, and perpetuate existing patterns of marital conflict and disagreement. Modification of this "old drinking-influence system" is important for a number of reasons. Such change can reduce or eliminate the aversiveness of the spouse's efforts to change the abuser's drinking. Changed spouse behavior interrupts or eliminates old interaction and influence patterns that otherwise could interfere with the abuser-directed intervention. Finally, altering these coercive influence attempts can create an atmosphere conducive to enhancing the effectiveness of various program components.

In the program to modify drinking control, spouses are requested to stop all "old system" efforts to reduce the abuser's drinking. Particular emphasis is placed on eliminating the most frequently employed drinking-control behaviors of the spouse as identified by interview assessment or by use of the Drink Control Scale (DCS) of the Spouse Sobriety Influence Inventory (SSII) (Thomas, Yoshioka, & Ager, 1993c). See Table 1.2 for illustrative items of the SSII. Baseline and monitoring may be carried out by interview or use of the SSII.

Some spouses worry that not criticizing or not attempting to control the drinking may be read by the abuser as condoning alcohol abuse, and result in increased drinking. The therapist can point out that despite his or her drinking-control efforts, the partner continues to have an alcohol problem. Further, continuing coercive control efforts will tend to increase marital discord and can interfere with the abuser-directed interventions to follow.

TABLE 1.2. Selected Items from Spouse Sobriety Influence Inventory (SSII)

---

2. Expressed disapproval of the drinking
5. Spoke to the drinker before he or she went out in order to get him or her to drink less or not at all in that situation
8. Hid or threw out alcohol
27. Prevented drinking friend from coming to the house
38. Refused to talk to the drinker when he or she was drunk or had been drinking
39. Said that if the drinker loved you or the children he or she would stop drinking
42. Made sarcastic remarks about the drinking
44. Withheld sex or other forms of affection because of the drinker's drinking
46. Threatened divorce or separation if the drinker did not stop drinking
49. Tried to get even because of the drinking

Note. Of the 52 items, 45 are from the DCS and seven are from the Sobriety Support Scale (SSS)

Even when successfully reducing overt control behavior, a few spouses sometimes continue to be preoccupied with negative thoughts about the drinking or anxiety or anger related to the alcohol abuse. If these thoughts or emotions do not abate over several weeks of program operation, as they usually do, the therapist can consider addressing detachment directly and more broadly. In effect, the therapist can assist the spouse to "back off" and "let go" so as to achieve greater distance from the drinking and its effects (Leite, 1987). Further information on clinical procedures, cases, problems, and clinical results related to modifying the spouse's customary drinking control efforts can be found in Yoshioka, Thomas, and Ager (1992).

Disenabling

Most spouses, as is well recognized in the field of alcohol treatment, help to make the abuser's drinking possible, that is, "enable" it (Cermak, 1986; Johnson, 1973; Orford et al., 1975). For example, it is not uncommon to find that the spouse drinks with the abuser, buys the alcohol, delays meals while the abuser drinks, and hosts social engagements where the abuser characteristically drinks too much. To counter spouse enabling, a tailor-made program of "disenabling" is embarked upon, with emphasis on the most frequent enabling behaviors. Such behaviors can be identified through interview or, more readily, by use of the Spouse Enabling Inventory (SEI), developed especially to assess spouse enabling behaviors (Thomas, Yoshioka, & Ager, 1993a). See Table 1.3 for illustrative items. Baseline and monitoring can also be carried out by interview or use of the SEI.

It is important for the therapist to recognize that reducing enabling

TABLE 1.3. Selected Items from the Spouse Enabling Inventory (SEI)

8. Invited friends over to drink
9. Went to bars with drinker
10. Bought alcohol and kept it in the home
11. Served alcohol with meals and snacks
16. Made hangover remedies
27. Made excuses for the drinker's behavior when he or she was drunk or had been drinking
37. Comforted the drinker about his or her feelings of guilt about drinking
40. Minimized the seriousness of the drinking (ignored it, said it was not a problem, said the drinker could control it when he or she could not)
42. Concealed his or her drinking from others
45. Consumed alcoholic beverages with the drinker

behaviors can easily stir up marital discord, as may happen when the spouse refuses to drink with the abuser or to buy the booze for him or her. Disenabling also may risk harming the abuser or others, as in not bringing the abuser inside from the freezing cold where he or she has passed out. Disenabling alternatives need to be carefully planned and implemented on an individual basis to minimize marital disruption and potentially dangerous consequences.

Further, enabling behaviors may be very reinforcing for the spouse. Some spouses complain, for example, that they feel punished by having to stop their own occasional drinking or not hold parties where alcohol is served. Other spouses are reluctant to give up enabling inasmuch as it has come to represent a major way in which affection and closeness are communicated in the marriage (e.g., comforting the abuser when he or she expresses guilt about drinking). The therapist can acknowledge what the spouse is giving up but point out that continuing the enabling can support the drinking and retard the spouse's later efforts to get the abuser to stop drinking and/or enter treatment. Further information on clinical procedures, cases, problems, and clinical results related to disenabling can be found in Thomas, Yoshioka, and Ager (1993b).

Conducting Abuser-Directed Interventions (Phase II)

Interventions expressly for the abuser, as indicated, are aimed at influencing the abuser to enter treatment for his or her alcohol abuse, to reduce the drinking, or both. Ideally, the reduced drinking should take the form of abstinence but, in some cases, moderated drinking short of abstaining is the best outcome that can be achieved at the time, with abstinence being the ultimate goal. Such interventions tend to be stronger and more intrusive than most conventional treatment methods and should be undertaken only after sufficient progress has been made in otherwise preparing the spouse to assume a positive rehabilitative role.

Just as recovery from alcoholism is a process not an event (Prochaska & DiClemente, 1986), the interventions that may help initiate or sustain recovery likewise are part of the change process. The interventive process involved in seeking help and recovery may include many events for the uncooperative alcohol abuser. These include some or all of the following: (1) an induction to seek help by a spouse or others, (2) an agreement to seek help, (3) action to receive help, (4) continuation of the treatment or help, (5) avoidance of relapse, and (6) establishment of an alcohol-free lifestyle. At the same time, the abuser (1) may now come to recognize that there is a drinking problem, if not recognized before; (2) may decide to do something about it, which may or may not include seeking outside help; and (3) may reduce or stop drinking, again alone or with help.

Given the complexity and potential diversity of these events, it should be clear that a single intervention for an uncooperative drinker, however well planned, may be insufficient. Rather, interventions for abusers should be prepared in light of the diversity of the phenomena that may need to be targeted. Accordingly, abuser-directed interventions are (1) employed as an individualized configuration of specific interventions prepared to address various aspects of the help-seeking and change process, and (2) implemented as necessary depending upon the problems presented by the abuser in changing toward recovery.

Among the abuser-directed interventions described below are nonconfrontive interventions, confrontive interventions with and without supplements and variations, and follow-up treatment techniques.

Intervention Assessment

Intervention assessment aims at determining the suitability and feasibility of different interventive alternatives. This assessment generally begins during the first or second session and addresses a number of areas. Individuals other than the spouse who might also be involved as mediators (family members, friends, physicians, religious officials, or employers) should be considered. The spouse's potential to carry out an intervention, including ability and willingness to firmly confront the abuser about the drinking and to recommend treatment, are important to assess; and the Spouse Treatment Mediation Inventory (STMI) (Ager & Thomas, 1993) may be of use here (see Table 1.4).

The therapist must evaluate what the spouse is willing to do if the abuser continues to drink and whether contingencies for failure to enter

TABLE 1.4. Selected Items from the Spouse Treatment Mediation Inventory (STMI)

13. My spouse sees me as competent and knowledgeable
20. I often forget or put off things I promise to do
22. When it comes to change, my spouse is inflexible
23. I am willing to work hard to make my marriage work
26. I am fed up with trying to help my spouse change
29. I am highly motivated to make changes through participating in this treatment program
34. There is a lot of conflict in my marriage
35. I make most of the decisions about how the family money is used
40. I am not able to confront my spouse when I have concerns about him or her
41. I am able to get my spouse to do things that he or she would not otherwise do

treatment are feasible (e.g., if divorce is considered as a possible contingency, whether the spouse can handle the emotional and financial changes that may be required). The consequences of such contingencies for the abuser, including the anticipated degree of abuser compliance with the recommended action, and the risks of suicide, psychological decompensation, and violence also must be considered. Appropriate treatment options for the abuser must be assessed using the information gathered in the alcohol abuse assessment about the seriousness of the drinking problem. Finally, it is important to evaluate the abuser's current readiness for treatment, which may include consideration of the success of any past treatment, attitudes about treatment (rigidity, resistance, openness), and recognition of having a drinking problem.

The therapist needs to determine whether treatment will adversely affect the abuser's job security and what the treatment options are. With regard to financing, the therapist should investigate specific insurance coverage, financial resources, and whether the abuser qualifies for other medical treatment (e.g., veterans' services), sliding scales, or social service payment for treatment. The therapist also should examine whether the abuser has access to an employee assistance program for alcohol abuse and, if so, whether information about the abuser's treatment should be kept from the employer to avoid possible adverse consequences.

Nonconfrontive Interventions

Because they tend to be less intrusive than confrontive interventions, nonconfrontive interventions are generally to be preferred as starting points when the intervention assessment indicates their suitability.

Sobriety Support

Prior to treatment, most spouses do not respond to the drinker so as to support sobriety, or, if they do, their supporting responses tend to be occasional or otherwise nonsystematic. In contrast to the spouse's customary drinking control behaviors, such as nagging about the drinking, sobriety support by the spouse consists of spouse behaviors that serve to strengthen nondrinking responses for the abuser, to weaken abuser inducements to drinking, or both. For example, the spouse may try to initiate a non-alcohol-related activity (e.g., serving nonalcoholic beverages or suggesting a movie) at times when the abuser commonly drinks. Other examples of sobriety support by the spouse might include efforts to shorten a drinking session, reduce the amount consumed when the abuser is actively drinking, or reinforce abstinence or moderate drinking. When employed as an initial intervention, sobriety support is particularly appropriate when the abuser's drinking is not heavy, and causes no psychological, physical, social, or work-related difficulties, even though the spouse considers it a problem. Although it can be used prior to confrontive interventions, sobriety support has been used most commonly following a confrontive intervention when it was implemented along with other techniques intended to strengthen recovery.

Physician's Appointment

For the physician's appointment, the spouse is helped to arrange an alcoholism examination for the abuser that can be followed by a doctor's recommendation for alcohol abuse treatment. If the physician agrees to cooperate, this intervention can be less distressing to the marriage than a confrontative intervention. If expert advice is given to the alcoholic in the presence of the spouse, it may be as effective in recovery as more intensive treatment (see Orford, 1986). Other sources of expert advice are therapists, pastors, rabbis, or employer representatives.

Confrontive Interventions

In situations where nonconfrontive interventions are inappropriate or insufficient, the stronger confrontive interventions with their several variations are implemented.

Programmed Confrontation

With the primary aim of influencing the drinker to enter alcohol abuse treatment, the programmed confrontation entails training the spouse and sometimes other family members to confront the abuser firmly but compassionately, generally in the presence of a therapist in the therapist's office. The confrontation is carried out only if the spouse is willing to follow through with a strong contingent consequence in the event that the abuser refuses to get treatment or change the drinking. Possible contingencies include separation, divorce, development of a separate life for the spouse outside the marriage, or alteration of the domestic or household maintenance arrangements (e.g., preparing and eating meals separately). The confrontation is a powerful induction that should be used with considerable care and only when the spouse is willing and able to carry out the consequences.

An outline of the recommended steps to follow in the development of a programmed confrontation, along with examples, is presented in Table 1.5. The steps are intended to be carried out systematically to help ensure that the confrontation is properly structured and staged. The spouse must be scripted and rehearsed adequately. Possible outcomes of the confrontation session should be anticipated. Following these recommended steps should help to reduce the risk of negative surprises. Further details about clinical procedures are given in the case application and in Thomas and Yoshioka (1989), where clinical results and other cases related to the programmed confrontation are also reported.

The programmed confrontation bears some similarities to other confrontive interventions, including the "Intervention" of the Johnson approach (Johnson, 1973, 1986; see also Liepman, Chapter 3, this volume). However, there are also some important differences. For example, in the unilateral approach, the programmed confrontation is preceded by a detailed assessment, and it is one of several abuser-directed interventions, which include sobriety support, that are generally conducted. The abuser-directed interventions are also only one portion, albeit a critical one, of the more comprehensive treatment of the UFT approach. In UFT, spouses also are assisted to increase their skills in coping with some of the personal distress and marital dysfunctions associated with living with an uncooperative alcohol abuser and more generally are helped to assume a positive rehabilitative role.[2]

Programmed Request

The programmed request differs from an ordinary request in that, like the programmed confrontation, it is carefully selected, planned, and implemented following a set of systematic clinical procedures (see Table 1.5). The programmed request differs from the programmed confrontation in that there is some evidence of readiness on the part of the abuser to respond favorably to such a request, and, in general, an un-

TABLE 1.5. Selected Steps in a Programmed Confrontation or Request

1. Determining suitability (assessing which intervention is most appropriate for the spouse to use to reach the abuser)
2. Determining feasibility (assessing spouse confrontational skills and the feasibility of using a spouse-invoked contingency)
3. Modeling a spouse confrontation (giving a verbal description, playing an exemplar audio or video tape)
4. Preparing the spouse's script:
   a. Introductory statements (that the purpose is to discuss the abuser's drinking and request the abuser to allow the spouse to be heard and to remain silent until the spouse is finished)
   b. Statement of concern about the abuser's drinking problem ("I am doing this because I care" or "... because I love you")
   c. Specification of drinking level and pattern (duration, quantity and frequency of alcohol consumption, frequency of drunkenness)
   d. Itemization of drinking-related events, problems caused thereby, and effects (a few salient incidents involving danger, embarrassment, extreme behavior, loss of self-respect or friendship)
   e. Specification of recommended action (to enter treatment for alcohol abuse)
   f. Specification of contingent consequences if action is not taken (fewer enjoyable activities together, greater spouse detachment, separation, divorce)
5. Rehearsing the presentation (use of therapist–spouse role plays with audio recording)
6. Staging the confrontation (getting the drinker to the office sober and without conflict; seating)
7. Planning postconfrontation (arranging drinker's appointment with an alcoholism counselor; implementation of contingent consequences, if and when appropriate)
8. Conducting the confrontation (outlining the therapist's nonparticipatory role, including the therapist's introductory and closing remarks)
9. Monitoring postconfrontation and following through (initiating contingent consequences, if appropriate, and planning further spouse intervention, if necessary)

Note. From E. J. Thomas (1989) with revisions. Copyright 1989 by Charles C. Thomas. Adapted by permission.

---

willingness of the spouse to carry out a strong consequence if the abuser fails to comply with the request. When appropriately made, the programmed request can be strong enough to accomplish its objective. For further details and case examples of a programmed request, the reader is referred to Thomas and Yoshioka (1989).

Supplements and Variations

Some abusers will refuse flatly to comply with the action recommendation, insisting that they can quit on their own. We have found it helpful to be prepared for such a response with a "what if" statement drafted before conducting the intervention. The "what if" statement is a written *agreement/contract* between the spouse and abuser that includes what the abuser agrees to do (e.g., not consume even one drink) and what action the abuser agrees to carry out if the agreement is broken (e.g., immediately enter a specific treatment program). It may sometimes be necessary for the abuser to remain under a physician's supervision during the early stages of abstention if there is any physical danger associated with withdrawal.

More generally, agreements and contracts between the spouse and abuser provide an important addition to the initial confrontive intervention. Such agreements address possible problems posed by the abuser's reluctance in the confrontation session to agree to seek help, or to continue receiving help. Agreements or contracts, such as the "what if" statement, also may be employed as an initial interventive induction, particularly if the abuser has expressed a strong interest in reducing or abstaining from drinking. However, we did not have occasion to use agreements or contracts in this way, finding them to be more suitable for use after the stronger confrontive interventions already described.

The *heart letter,* prepared by a child, family member, or other person close to the abuser, is written "from the heart" and read by the spouse during the confrontation. After selecting the appropriate person to prepare the letter, that person is informed by the spouse of the purpose of the confrontation and asked if he or she would help by preparing a heart letter. Brief instructions of topics to cover in preparing the letter should include a "caring statement," and a statement about the extent and severity of the problem as the letter writer sees it. The letter also can describe a few alcohol-related incidents that clearly demonstrate the seriousness of the drinking problem, and a statement affirming that the drinker needs help because of the drinking. After receiving a draft of the letter, the therapist and spouse edit the letter to exclude blame, lectures, or statements that could incite needless aversive reactions from the drinker. The letter is then integrated into the script with a brief introductory statement such as "Cathy [the daughter] has written a letter about your drinking that I would like to read. It says 'Dear Dad: I love you and I write because I have been concerned about your drinking. . . .' "

Another variation is *inclusion of family members and significant others,* such as friends, clerics, or employers, as participants in the confrontation. In addition to preparing written or nonwritten statements, participants also may add contingencies to their statements. All participants in the confrontation meet for one or several sessions in which the plan and organization of the confrontation are discussed. These preparatory meetings consider the order of presentation, potential problems, and revisions and editing of participants' statements. Finally, the individuals involved are given an opportunity to practice and refine their delivery.[3]

Other supplements that may be effective are *letters* from the therapist, physician, or other health professional. Rather than appealing to the abuser's emotions, these statements should focus on concrete evidence indicating the seriousness of the alcohol problem and the need for treatment.

Follow-Up Interventions

If the abuser agrees to the action recommendation, the contingency is generally not stated. However, the abuser may consent to the action recommendation, yet not follow through with it. Consequently, the contingency can be used later at home in a brief follow-up intervention in which the spouse reminds the abuser of having agreed to the recommendation, and states the contingency, as prepared earlier and rehearsed. If the drinker still does not follow the recommended action, the spouse then carries out the contingency with or without the further assistance of the therapist.

Follow-up interventions can include the statement or restatement of contingencies, invocation of contingent consequences, or other actions of the spouse. Such interventions represent an integral part of the treatment program, and should be prepared when the spouse has contingent consequences he or she is willing to invoke. They can be carried out during treatment, if needed, or programmed to be carried out following treatment, in case the abuser should relapse or discontinue the treatment he or she has agreed to attend. Like the others, these interventions should be planned and rehearsed carefully.

Special Problems

As the time of the programmed confrontation approaches, the spouse may become apprehensive and express reluctance to follow through with the plan. If this occurs, the therapist should explore the basis for the apprehension. If appropriate, the therapist should discuss alterations in the script or other program adjustments that may make it easier to proceed. Often, therapist reassurance that the spouse can carry it out successfully is sufficient to sustain further work. With more practice in giving the presentation, the spouse's confidence generally increases.

Likewise, a spouse may become so anxious or distraught during the actual presentation that he or she is temporarily unable to continue (cries, gets confused, forgets). The therapist can first suggest that the spouse take a few moments to collect her or his thoughts and, if necessary, give a gentle reminder of what comes next in the script. If the therapist can detect potential problems of this type earlier in therapy, a back-up audio tape of the spouse's presentation can be made and then played, if needed.

Despite the fact that the therapist has emphasized earlier that ad hoc confrontations should be avoided, a few spouses may conduct them anyway. Such confrontations generally are not successful; but if they are, the therapist and spouse should try to build on them by facilitating the abuser's entry into treatment. If the ad hoc confrontation is not successful, the spouse can be assisted to try to soften any negative impact it may have caused, and to help establish better conditions for a planned confrontation to follow.

Some abusers become angry with the spouse following a confrontation. The therapist always should assess the potential for violence to protect the spouse against possible retaliations. We have found it helpful for the therapist to request that the couple not talk about the confrontation on the way home afterwards and to avoid doing anything that might be considered "rash" or "extreme" following the confrontation. If it is anticipated prior to the confrontation that there is a potential for violence, the spouse should arrange for a safe place to stay after the confrontation and/or for a less volatile confrontation.[4]

If at all possible, it is best to get the abuser into treatment directly after the confrontation. Unfortunately, however, some treatment centers do not allow such an arrangement. For example, they may require that an appointment or a bed be scheduled a few days or more after the confrontation, refuse to schedule until after the confrontation to avoid a no-show, or require the abuser to arrange the appointment him- or herself. To meet these potential barriers, the therapist may need to direct the spouse to less restrictive facilities or to advocate for the spouse with a treatment facility to make treatment entry easier.

Maintaining Spouse and Abuser Treatment Gains (Phase III)

Two additional interventive areas serve to foster maintenance and generalization of the positive changes achieved by the spouse and to help prevent abuser relapse during the remainder of treatment and thereafter. The first is *spouse support* in which the spouse is helped to refrain from enabling and patterns of customary drink control, and to continue relationship enhancement and sobriety support.

The second area involves *spouse-mediated relapse prevention training*, which includes the following as applied to the abuser: (1) identification of high-risk situations for drinking, (2) temptation resistance training, (3) acceleration of nondrinking behaviors, (4) handling of relapses, (5) education concerning the nature of relapses and how they may be prevented, and (6) restoration of balance in lifestyle. A description of the procedures for these areas goes beyond the scope of this chapter. For details on direct work with the abuser, the reader is referred to such sources as Gorski and Miller (1986), Marlatt and Gordon (1985), McCrady (1989), and O'Farrell (1986).

CASE APPLICATION

Both in their late 50s and employed full-time, Mr. and Mrs. C. had three children in their late 20s and early 30s, two of whom still lived at home. Mrs. C. sought help because Mr. C.'s drinking problem had become increasingly worse over the past 6 years. His Michigan Alcoholism Screening Test (MAST) score was 16, which is considerably higher than the recommended cut-off score of 5 (Selzer, 1971).

Preparing the Spouse for a Rehabilitative Role

Treatment Orientation

Early in the orientation and at several later points, Mrs. C. brought up personal and marital problems not specifically related to the alcohol abuse. The therapist gently reminded her that she would need to "put these problems on the shelf" during the work here on assisting her with her husband's alcohol problem.

The therapist learned from the alcohol history that the husband's tolerance had decreased markedly over the years. He now had frequent memory problems, a long-standing hand tremor, frequent blackouts, and poor coordination. He had drunk alcohol persistently, almost on a daily basis, since the drinking problem became severe 6 years before. He had had a 2-week period when he was on medication incompatible with alcohol during which he did not drink and evidently experienced no major withdrawal symptoms.

Spouse Role Induction

Alcohol Monitoring and Alcohol Education

Mrs. C. agreed to begin monitoring her husband's alcohol consumption after the first session, using the appropriate forms presented by the therapist. During the following sessions, alcohol data were monitored and reviewed, disclosing that Mr. C. was drunk about half of the days monitored, with an occasional day in which Mrs. C. did not detect any drinking. Mrs. C. was given alcohol education materials on blackouts, medical complications, and enabling over the following weeks. After she read the materials at home, they were briefly reviewed and discussed as needed in the early sessions, which she found helpful.

Unilateral Relationship Enhancement

Identifying behaviors for unilateral relationship enhancement involved the following process. During the second session, the therapist introduced the concept of relationship enhancement. Mrs. C. was asked to think of behaviors that would be pleasing to her husband that she might be willing to increase or behaviors that were displeasing to him that she might be willing to decrease. It was emphasized that the behaviors should be those pleasing for the drinker, not necessarily for her. However, no item should be included that she was not willing to change for purposes of the program. With the assistance of an illustrative list of pleasers and displeasers that the therapist provided, Mrs. C. identified several potential enhancers.

Treatment planning for relationship enhancement proceeded in the following way. The therapist listed the identified pleasing activities, and reviewed each to determine whether it was an appropriate and feasible target of change. The surviving behaviors were then specified and a retrospective baseline was taken. Items selected for enhancement were (1) to initiate with him or respond to sexual advances from him; (2) to engage in special activities, such as outings, going to movies, attending church, and watching TV together; (3) to serve oatmeal; and (4) to perform household chores, such as sewing and picking up things.

Implementation, monitoring, and outcome of activities for relationship enhancement proceeded as follows. Mrs. C. indicated that she was willing to undertake the enhancement program and record relevant data on a monitoring form. She was told that there were no performance quotas and that she should do her best to increase the activities selected within her "comfort zone." The therapist explained that this procedure was not intended to correct any major marital problems or reduce the drinking, but was designed to help prepare the marital system for later changes. It could be viewed as an "investment" made now, to be realized later, so that the chances of getting her husband to change would be better.

At the following session, Mrs. C.'s relationship enhancement monitoring data revealed increases in some activities, which the therapist commended. Mrs. C. requested that one of the categories, serving oatmeal, be expanded to include serving other foods that Mr. C. liked such as stuffed cabbage, burritos, and roasts. This was agreed upon and a new baseline taken for this category. During the following weeks, Mrs. C. made moderate improvements in most of the areas targeted, with some lapses, acknowledged as understandable, during times when she experienced heavy demands in her work. Over the course of treatment, Mrs. C. demonstrated increases above baseline in 51% of the areas targeted.[5]

Modification of Customary Drinking Control

Identifying behaviors related to drinking control came next. Sometime during the fourth session, the therapist introduced the concept of the "old drinking-influence system." This was illustrated with an incident described by Mrs. C. in which she angrily told her husband to get into treatment after he became particularly drunk. Using the SSII Inventory, 21 old drinking-control behaviors were identified as commonly employed by Mrs. C.—a fairly large number.

Treatment planning for changes in drinking-control methods was done by the therapist and Mrs. C. After reviewing and further specifying these items, five were removed because they either did not relate to the drinking or its control, were general complaints about the marriage or efforts to change it, or Mrs. C. reported that she no longer engaged in the behavior. Most of the remaining items reflected drinking-related reprisals, recommendations to enter treatment, and cautions against drinking. The therapist and Mrs. C. came up with alternative responses that could be used in place of these behaviors.

Implementation, monitoring, and outcome of changes in drinking control behaviors proceeded as follows. Mrs. C. was willing to try to change the control behaviors thus selected but, rather than taking on a few at a time, she preferred to target all of them at once, which was done. In the monitoring, it was learned that she had some difficulties limiting comments about her husband's drinking during the early weeks of the program, although these soon diminished. Her score on the DCS of the SSII was $M = 2.7$ before treatment, 1.9 posttreatment, and 1.8 6 months after treatment ended (potential scores ranged from a low of 1 to a high of 5).

Disenabling

Identifying behaviors related to enabling was the next step. At the sixth session, the concept of enabling was introduced in connection with Mrs.

C.'s comment that she had drinks with her husband while on vacation. Nine items from the SEI that Mrs. C. had endorsed as behaviors she commonly employed were listed on a separate piece of paper.

Treatment planning for decreasing enabling was a collaborative effort. Each item selected from the SEI was reviewed, with Mrs. C. providing examples. Four were removed from the list because they either did not fit the definition of enabling or Mrs. C. indicated that she did not engage in the behavior. Through further specification of the behaviors and discussion of the abuser's anticipated responses to a reduction of these behaviors, the therapist learned that eliminating these behaviors would not result in any harm to a family member or in any notable marital conflict. The items were: (1) suggesting alcohol-related social activities, (2) helping the drinker find things lost while drunk, (3) giving something to eat to cushion the effects of the alcohol, (4) making excuses to the drinker for his drinking, and (5) making excuses to others for the drinking. Drinking alcohol herself was added to the list, as was done in disenabling with all the spouses.

Implementation, monitoring, and outcome of changes in enabling behavior proceeded as follows. Regarding the item about helping the drinker find things lost while drunk, Mrs. C. expressed concern about the potential negative consequences of refusing to help her husband look for his car keys. After agreeing to help the drinker in this way only in an emergency, Mrs. C. indicated that she was willing to begin the program. In monitoring, she reported that she had drunk a champagne toast while celebrating once with friends but was otherwise successful in stopping the targeted behaviors. In monitoring potential negative responses to the disenabling, Mrs. C. reported only one — namely, that her husband gave her a "dirty look" once when she declined to have a drink with him. In general, the program proceeded without any particular marital distress or danger to anyone. Based on the SEI scores, Mrs. C. demonstrated a reduction in enabling from $M = 1.8$ before treatment, to 1.1 posttreatment with an increase to 1.5 six months after treatment was completed (again scores ranged from 1 to 5).

Conducting Abuser-Directed Interventions

Intervention Assessment

In the assessment conducted periodically over the first 10 sessions, the therapist discussed with Mrs. C. appropriate treatment for Mr. C. and which alternatives for abuser-directed intervention might be suitable. Although inpatient treatment appeared to be the most appropriate, Mrs. C. thought that her husband would emphatically reject that alternative, partly because she thought it would jeopardize his employment. However, Mrs. C. indicated that he might be receptive to intensive out-patient treatment that took place after work in the evenings over several weeks. In assessing Mr. C.'s potential responses to a strong intervention, it appeared that there was no notable danger of Mr. C.'s physical retaliation, psychological decompensation, or suicide.

As directed by the therapist, Mrs. C. contacted her insurance company and received specific information about her husband's coverage. She discovered the insurance would pay for most of the costs of any inpatient or outpatient alcoholism treatment. Further, she indicated that the family could afford the additional costs that they might have to pay for such treatment.

The therapist inquired about family members or close friends who had a positive relationship with Mr. C., were aware of the drinking problem, and might be open to help in directing him to treatment. Mrs. C. mentioned her three adult children, whom the therapist noted as potential participants for a confrontation, if one was conducted.

Physician's Appointment

In response to the alcohol education materials discussed in the third session, Mrs. C.'s expressed concern about some alcohol-related medical complications she had observed in her husband. The therapist took this as an opportunity to broach the subject of a physician's appointment. Mrs. C. was receptive to the idea, and later suggested it to Mr. C. when he was sober and not upset. Mr. C. refused to get a physical examination, claiming he was concerned that insurance forms would be sent to his place of employment and put his job in jeopardy. Mrs. C. agreed to contact the insurance company to inquire about confidentiality relating to medical exams. During the interim, Mr. and Mrs. C. attended a charity event where Mr. C. had his cholesterol level checked and found it to be quite high. Soon after, a family friend advised Mr. C. to follow up on the test with a physical. Mrs. C. took this as an opportunity to ask her husband more firmly to get a medical examination, and he agreed.

As decided in therapy, when Mrs. C. telephoned to schedule the physician's appointment, she mentioned her husband's level of drinking and the need for him to have tests for alcohol-related problems. The physician ordered the tests and the results indicated liver dysfunction. The physician stated his concerns about the liver dysfunction in a letter to Mr. C. along with the recommendation that Mr. C. stop drinking. Although Mr. C. failed to follow this advice, information from the letter was included as a supplement in the programmed confrontation conducted later.

Programmed Confrontation

Determining Suitability

Because Mr. C. was strong-willed and had been stubbornly resistant to Mrs. C.'s earlier efforts to get him help for the drinking problem, it was decided that a potent intervention was required.

Determining Feasibility

It was clear that Mrs. C. was quite capable of making direct requests of Mr. C. She could speak to him about his alcohol use, and could do so in a firm and calm manner. With regard to contingencies for the confrontation, Mrs. C. was not prepared to consider divorce or separation if Mr. C. didn't follow the action recommendations. However, she was prepared to stop or reduce a number of companionable activities that were a particular source of pleasure for Mr. C. Contingencies she was prepared to implement if Mr. C. refused to enter treatment included: not sleeping in the same bedroom, not waking up Mr. C. or sharing the mornings with him, not eating with him, and not participating with him in outside activities.

Preparing Spouse's Script and Supplements

During the fifth session, an audio tape of a model confrontation was played for Mrs. C. She was given an outline and summary of the different parts of a confrontation script. Script preparation continued over the next several weeks. After she drafted a given section, the therapist reviewed the draft and suggested changes, as necessary, and Mrs. C. then prepared alterations for the following week. To help generate ideas for the various sections of the script, the therapist showed Mrs. C. illustrative statements (with identities disguised) taken from other scripts (for further details on script content, see Table 1.5). In addition, all three of Mr. and Mrs. C.'s children, who agreed to prepare heart letters, were given guidelines about what to include, and these letters, along with references to the physician's letter, were included in the script.

Rehearsing the Presentation

Over the next six sessions, Mrs. C. rehearsed the script with the therapist playing the role of her husband and providing feedback about the delivery. The material was tape-recorded for training purposes. In the role-plays, the therapist systematically introduced more problematic abuser reactions to the action recommendation or to facts presented in the script. This helped Mrs. C. become prepared for possible alternative reactions and plan appropriate responses. Mrs. C. and the therapist also prepared a short "what if" statement to be used if Mr. C. insisted on trying to stop the drinking on his own. The script was practiced by Mrs. C. alone, outside of treatment, and in the therapy session until she and the therapist were confident about her preparation. The therapist cautioned that the script needed to be followed as rehearsed and that Mrs. C. should avoid any last minute changes. Finally, the therapist helped Mrs. C. prepare for potential problems that might occur during the confrontation, such as Mr. C. exploding with anger or attempting to leave in the middle.

Staging the Confrontation

Mrs. C. asked her husband to come to a treatment session "because we need your help on a matter." She was told to say nothing further about what was to be discussed. The time of the appointment was chosen to minimize the chance that Mr. C. would be drunk. Mrs. C. was enjoined to avoid any marital conflict, particularly during the days immediately before confrontation. Mr. C. consented to come for a meeting without having asked questions about it. Mrs. C. was asked to have her husband sit in the easy chair farthest from the therapist's office door while she would sit in an upright chair between the abuser and the door. The therapist would also sit in an upright chair, also situated between Mr. C. and the door without being too close to either Mr. or Mrs. C.

Planning Postconfrontation

Planning for the period following the intervention covered a number of issues. It included prearranging treatment for Mr. C. It also was recommended that Mrs. C. not enter into any discussion of the content of the script or revert to old system behaviors after the confrontation occurred. The therapist helped prepare Mrs. C. to follow through on the contingent consequences in the event that Mr. C. failed to comply with agreements made at the time of the confrontation. Mrs. C. also clarified the specific costs of treatment (which would be important to Mr. C.), and spoke with the alcohol clinic evaluator who was to see Mr. C.

Conducting the Confrontation

After greeting Mr. and Mrs. C. and seating everyone according to the plan, the therapist introduced the session. The therapist thanked Mr. C. for coming and indicated that Mrs. C. would do most of the talking.

Mr. C. was visibly angry with the therapist, refusing to shake the therapist's hand when he first arrived and avoiding eye contact.

Mrs. C. delivered the script with care, confidence, and, aside from some early uneasiness, a steady voice that conveyed genuine concern. Mr. C. listened intently, particularly to the heart letters. In response to the action recommendation of intensive outpatient treatment, Mr. C. said he could not decide. Following a period of waiting, Mrs. C. indicated, as scripted, that we needed a decision now. After more silence, Mr. C. insisted that he would not consent to inpatient treatment. Mrs. C. again described the recommended intensive outpatient program, distinguishing it from inpatient treatment. Eventually Mr. C. consented to attend the initial evaluation appointment that had been arranged. The therapist closed the meeting by thanking Mr. C. for coming. The therapist also tactfully suggested that the two not discuss the matter after leaving and that they refrain from doing anything that might be considered rash or extreme following the meeting.

Monitoring Postconfrontation and Following Through

At the subsequent treatment session now near the end of treatment, Mrs. C. indicated that her husband had attended his alcohol evaluation appointment. An alcohol problem requiring treatment had been diagnosed, and an additional appointment had been scheduled. We have no record of whether Mr. C. attended the second appointment, although he did begin attending AA meetings one or more times per week.

Providing for Stabilization and Maintenance

During this session and some earlier sessions, the therapist discussed the subject of sobriety support. This was now the end of the 6 months of treatment. The therapist suggested that Mrs. C. continue her relationship enhancement activities, disenabling, and reduction of customary drinking-control behaviors. She also was instructed to increase her efforts to support sobriety, such as being pleasant when Mr. C. was not drinking, avoiding needless aversive interactions, and providing some reinforcement for sobriety and AA meeting attendance. The appropriate nature and frequency of such reinforcement were discussed. Mrs. C. also was advised to respond calmly to possible slips and to say, for example, "It's not too late to stop again." In the event of a more extended relapse, the therapist and Mrs. C. planned a brief follow-up intervention. This included the contingency that was not stated during the confrontation and that could be invoked if Mr. C. discontinued treatment before resolving the alcohol problem. In closing, Mrs. C. indicated that she was a "satisfied customer" with the therapy.

Outcome

During the follow-up assessment 6 months after treatment ended, Mr. C. showed a marked decrease in his drinking. As indicated above, he also maintained regular attendance at AA meetings. In addition, Mrs. C. increased her support for sobriety, based on scores from the SSS of the SSII Inventory which increased from $M = 2.5$ posttreatment to $M = 4.33$ at the 6-month follow-up (potential scores ranged from 1 to 5).

RESEARCH SUMMARY

Two studies provide results bearing on the effectiveness of the treatment program. In both studies, a cooperative, non-alcohol-abusing spouse was employed as a mediator in treatment to influence the uncooperative, alcohol-abusing partner to enter treatment, reduce drinking, or both.

Pilot Study

In a 3½-year pilot study, 25 spouses were recruited by newspaper advertisements to receive free professional treatment in an experimental treatment program to help them do something about their partner's drinking. Subjects were selected by the eligibility criteria described earlier. The mean age was 43 with the large majority currently employed and having had at least some college education. The median household income was $27,000. All but one spouse was white and there was one male. The average MAST score of the abusers on a spouse-rated version was 23, which is considerably higher than the recommended cutoff score for alcoholism of 5 (Selzer, 1971).

Of the 25 spouses, 15 received 4–6 months of treatment and 10 were classified in a nontreatment category because they had had limited treatment contact for one reason or another. There was a 53% reduction in alcohol consumption from before to after treatment for the abusers whose spouses had received UFT treatment, and a slight increase in alcohol consumption for abusers whose spouses had not received the treatment. In a related analysis, abusers for whom relevant data were available were classified as "improved" if they reduced their drinking by 53% or greater, entered alcoholism treatment, or both. Of the 13 abusers whose spouses were in the treatment group, 8 (or 61%) improved, whereas none of the 6 abusers whose spouses did not receive treatment showed improvement ($p = .02$ by Fisher's Exact Test). There were also reductions in life distress for the spouses and increases in affectional expression and sexual satisfaction in the marriages. The reader is referred elsewhere for further description of these results (Thomas, Santa, Bronson, & Oyserman, 1987).

Experimental Evaluation

In a 4-year experimental evaluation, one in each successive pair of eligible spouses was randomly assigned to either an immediate ($n = 27$) or Delayed ($n = 28$) treatment condition in which spouses received 6 months of unilateral treatment. A no-treatment condition consisted of 14 otherwise eligible spouses whose alcohol-abusing partners were unwilling to give consent for their spouses to receive this type of treatment. Research assessments were given to all spouses before treatment and subsequently at 6-, 12-, and 18-month intervals. The research assessment battery consisted of a number of instruments, including new spouse assessment inventories developed on this project (the SEI, the SSII, and the STMI).

Of the 69 spouses, 65 were female, two were African-American, two Hispanic, and the rest white. The mean MAST score for abusers as rated by the spouse was 20.3, indicating again a high level of problematic drinking. The subjects were also otherwise generally similar to those involved in the pilot study.

Treatment outcomes summarized here were statistically significant at $p \leq .05$ by repeated-measures analysis of variance or, for categorical data, by χ^2 tests, unless indicated otherwise. Positive changes relating to the spouse role induction were associated directly and clearly with spouse participation in the treatment program. For example, spouse enabling and the spouses' customary drink control were significantly reduced following treatment. Other positive changes for spouses included reductions in psychopathology and life distress, and improvements in marital adjustment and satisfaction.

There were likewise significant changes in drink-related outcomes for the abusers associated with the treatment program. For example, treatment entry of the abuser was significantly higher immediately following spouse treatment. And, at the time of the last assessment, 57% of the abusers in the spouse treatment conditions had entered treatment as compared with 31% of the abusers in the no-treatment condition: χ^2 (1, $N = 55$) = 2.76, $p < .095$. Abusers reduced their drinking from time 1–4 by 68% in the treatment conditions versus 20% in the no-treatment condition. Thus, although there were some improvements through time in drink-related outcomes for all abusers, these and other results indicated that the improvements associated with the spouse treatment were notably greater (for further details, see Thomas, Yoshioka, Ager, & Adams, 1993).

CONCLUSIONS

There were at least three important features of the method for reaching the uncooperative drinker presented here. The first is that unilateral family therapy was employed as the approach to treatment, which was made possible by the treatment mediation provided by the cooperative spouse. Major emphasis in the treatment program was placed on assisting the spouse to become a positive rehabilitative influence with the resistant drinker. Treatment was pursued in three main phases: preparing the spouse to assume a positive rehabilitative role (Phase I); conducting abuser-directed interventions to actively influence the alcohol abuser to enter treatment, stop drinking, or both (Phase II); and maintaining spouse and abuser treatment gains (Phase III).

A second aspect was the conception of recovery from alcoholism as a complex process consisting of diverse events and changes that call for an individualized configuration of treatment efforts to reach the resistant drinker. The interventions implemented through the spouse depended upon the problems presented by the abuser and the related changes that occurred in the process of the abuser's recovery. The spouse was assisted to mediate one or more interventions, engage diverse participants in the interventive effort (physicians, family members, others) and, if success were not achieved with the initial intervention, to conduct follow-up interventions, depending upon the problems presented.

The third feature was that in the two studies conducted on the unilateral approach, positive outcomes were obtained for the spouses and abusers that correspond with the distinctive interventional foci of unilateral family therapy. Thus, in regard to the individual focus of UFT, spouse coping was increased for the spouses, as indicated by reductions of spouse life distress and psychopathology following spouse treatment. Changes relating to the interactional focus included increases for the spouses in marital happiness and adjustment. Finally, in regard to the third-party focus, positive changes for the alcohol abusers associated with treatment for their spouses consisted of the abusers' entry into treatment for alcohol abuse, and/or reduced drinking, including abstinence. The findings provide support for the effectiveness of the UFT treatment program and, through this application, for the conclusion that a cooperative, nonalcohol-abusing spouse can be assisted to become a positive rehabilitative influence with an uncooperative alcohol abuser.

ACKNOWLEDGMENTS

The research reported in this chapter was supported in part by grants 1 R01 AA04163-03 and 5 R01 AA04163-07 of the National Institute on Alcohol Abuse and Alcoholism, Edwin J. Thomas, Principal Investigator. We wish to acknowledge the contributions of Denise Bronson, Cathleen Santa, Joanne Yaffe, and Daphna Oyserman in the pilot phase of the research, and of Kathryn Betts Adams, David Moxley, and, particularly, of Marianne Yoshioka in the evaluation phase.

NOTES

1. Among the many sources of alcohol education materials are the Johnson Institute, Al-Anon Family Group Headquarters, Alateen, the Hazelden Foundation, the National Clearing House for Alcohol/Drug Information, the National Council on Alcoholism, and the National Institute on Alcohol Abuse and Alcoholism (NIAAA).

2. Although the programmed confrontation may include other family members or significant others, our research was focused mainly, as indicated, on development of UFT for spouses of uncooperative alcohol abusers. The Johnson approach has emphasized use of additional family members and sometimes others (Johnson, 1987). The Johnson model is an important early approach that was one of several developments drawn on when the UFT framework was evolved.

3. Use of employers in a confrontation generally requires additional assessment and planning in light of the many potential complications involving risks to the abuser's job, and so forth. Involvement of the abuser's employee assistance program (EAP), if available, in such planning would generally be highly desirable. Intervention concurrently through an EAP may also be used.

4. Recall that all spouses and abusers were screened initially for domestic violence by telephone interview with the spouse. No instances of violence became known to us following any of the interventions employed in these studies.

5. The percentage is based on the Relationship Enhancement Index score, which equals the average of the weekly number of items that showed improvement from baseline divided by the total number of URE items assigned.

REFERENCES

Ager, R. D. (1991). *A validation study of the Spouse Treatment Mediation Inventory.* Unpublished doctoral dissertation, University of Michigan, Ann Arbor, Michigan.

Ager, R. D., & Thomas, E. J. (1993). The Spouse Treatment Mediation Inventory. In K. Corcoran & J. Fischer (Eds.), *Measures for clinical practice: A sourcebook* (2nd. ed.). New York: Free Press.

Bailey, M. B. (1961). Alcoholism and marriage (a review of research and professional literature). *Quarterly Journal of Studies on Alcohol, 22,* 81–97.

Cermak, T. L. (1986). Diagnostic criteria for codependency. *Journal of Psychoactive Drugs, 18,* 15–20.

Chemical Dependence and Recovery: A Family Affair. Minneapolis, MN: Johnson Institute Books.

Ghodse, A. M. (1982). Living with an alcoholic. *Postgraduate Medical Journal, 58,* 636–640.

Gorski, T. T., & Miller, M. (1986). *Staying sober: A guide for relapse prevention.* Independence, MO: Independence Press.

Homila, M. (1985). *Wives, husbands and alcohol: A study of informal drinking control within the family.* Helsinki: Finnish Foundation for Alcohol Studies.

Jacob, T., & Krahn, G. L. (1988). Marital interaction of alcoholic couples: Comparison with depressed and nondepressed couples. *Journal of Consulting and Clinical Psychology, 56,* 73–79.

Johnson, V. E. (1973). *I'll quit tomorrow.* New York: Harper.

Johnson, V. E. (1986). *Intervention: How to help someone who doesn't want help.* Minneapolis, MN: Johnson Institute Books.

Johnson, V. E. (1987). *How to use intervention in your professional practice.* Minneapolis, MN: Johnson Institute Books.

Leite, E. (1987). *Detachment: The art of letting go while living with an alcoholic* (rev. ed.). Minneapolis, MN: Johnson Institute Books.

McCrady, B. (1989). Extending relapse prevention models to couples. *Addictive Behaviors, 14,* 69–74.

Marlatt, G. A., & Gordon, J. R. (Eds.). (1985). *Relapse prevention: Maintenance strategies in the treatment of addictive behaviors.* New York: Guilford Press.

O'Farrell, T. J. (1986). Marital therapy in the treatment of alcoholism. In N. S. Jacobson & A. S. Gurman (Eds.), *Clinical handbook of marital therapy.* New York: Guilford Press.

Orford, J. (1986). Critical conditions for change in the addictive behaviors. In W. R. Miller & N. Heather (Eds.), *Treating addictive behaviors.* New York: Plenum Press.

Orford, J., Guthrie, S., Nicholls, P., Oppenheimer, E., Egert, S., & Hensman, C. (1975). Self-reported coping behavior of wives of alcoholics in association with drinking outcome. *Journal of Studies on Alcohol, 36,* 1254–1267.

Paolino, T. J., & McCrady, B. S. (1977). *The alcoholic marriage: Alternative perspectives.* New York: Grune & Stratton.

Prochaska, J. O., & DiClemente, C. C. (1986). Toward a comprehensive model of change. In W. R. Miller & N. Heather (Eds.), *Treating addictive behaviors: Processes and change.* New York: Plenum Press.

Selzer, M. L. (1971). The Michigan Alcoholism Screening Test (MAST): The quest for a new diagnostic instrument. *American Journal of Psychiatry, 3,* 176–181.

Thomas, E. J. (1989). Unilateral family therapy to reach the uncooperative alcohol abuser. In B. A. Thyer (Ed.), *Behavioral Family Therapy.* Springfield, IL: Charles C. Thomas.

Thomas, E. J., Adams, K. B., Yoshioka, M. R., & Ager, R. D. (1990). Unilateral relationship enhancement in the treatment of spouses of uncooperative alcohol abusers. *American Journal of Family Therapy, 18,* 334–344.

Thomas, E. J., & Ager, R. D. (1992). Treatment mediation and the spouse as treatment mediator. *American Journal of Family Therapy, 19,* 315–326.

Thomas, E. J., & Santa, C. A. (1982). Unilateral family therapy for alcohol abuse: A working conception. *American Journal of Family Therapy, 10, 49–58.*

Thomas, E. J., Santa, C., Bronson, D., & Oyserman, D. (1987). Unilateral family therapy with the spouses of alcoholics. *Journal of Social Service Research, 10,* 145–162.

Thomas, E. J., & Yoshioka, M. R. (1989). Spouse interventive confrontations in unilateral family therapy for alcohol abuse. *Social Casework, 70,* 340–347.

Thomas, E. J., Yoshioka, M. R., & Ager, R. D. (1993a). The Spouse Enabling Inventory. In K. Corcoran & J. Fischer (Eds.), *Measures for clinical practice: A sourcebook* (2nd ed.). New York: Free Press.

Thomas, E. J., Yoshioka, M. R., & Ager, R. D. (1993b). *Spouse enabling of alcohol abuse: Assessment and modification.* Manuscript submitted for publication.

Thomas, E. J., Yoshioka, M. R., & Ager, R. D. (1993c). The Spouse Sobriety Influence Inventory. In K. Corcoran & J. Fischer (Eds.), *Measures for clinical practice: A sourcebook* (2nd ed.). New York: Free Press.

Thomas, E. J., Yoshioka, M., Ager, R. D., & Adams, K. B. (1993). *Experimental outcomes of spouse intervention to reach the uncooperative alcohol abuser: Preliminary report.* Manuscript submitted for publication.

Wiseman, J. P. (1980). The "home treatment": The first steps in trying to cope with an alcoholic husband. *Family Relations, 29,* 541–549.

Yoshioka, M. R., Thomas, E. J., & Ager, R. D. (1992). Nagging and other drinking-control efforts of spouses of uncooperative alcohol abusers: Assessment and modification. *Journal of Substance Abuse, 4,* 309–318.

Chapter 2

Community Reinforcement Training for Families
A Method to Get Alcoholics into Treatment

Robert W. Sisson
Nathan H. Azrin

OVERVIEW

Traditional Concepts

A traditional concept of alcoholism states that the drinker is the first to know that he or she has an alcohol problem, but that the drinker immediately denies it. Family, friends, and employers become aware of the problem only after the disease has progressed to the point that the drinker has lost the ability to cover up the problems caused by the drinking. Family members suffer from a state of codependency in which they ostensibly try to help the drinker to stop; but unwittingly, simultaneously satisfy their own needs to have the drinker continue to drink heavily. Family members are considered coaddicts and are termed "enablers" or "controllers."

This dilemma—an alcoholic who denies the drinking problem and family members as coaddicts who need the drinker to have a problem but think they are helping—forms the rationale of traditional counseling approaches for families of alcoholics. The most common traditional approach is Al-Anon. Al-Anon helps family members identify their codependent needs and lead their lives detached from the drinker's self-destructive behavior. The coaddicts can begin their recovery only by assuming responsibility for the care of themselves and not the addict.

This "hands off" approach avers that drinkers must decide to seek help on their own for their treatment to be successful.

Behavior Analysis

A perspective of family behavior based on function is that a family member's response to the alcoholic is governed by the principles of learning. A family member's reaction either may help to deter the drinking or may inadvertently increase it. Family members learn by negative reinforcement to avoid serious consequences of their drinker's behavior. Negative reinforcement is a process in which the occurrence of a behavior is increased if the behavior is followed by the escape from or avoidance of an aversive stimulus. In the alcoholic's family, family members call the boss with excuses for the alcoholic's absences so they can avoid the problems they would face if the alcoholic lost his job; they bail the drinker out of jail to avoid embarrassment; and they make supper at one o'clock in the morning to avoid a beating. Unfortunately, in an attempt to avoid aversive events, family members also make it easier for the drinking to continue. If family members can be trained to recognize the relationship between their behavior and the alcoholic's drinking behavior, they may be able to obtain the desired reduction or elimination of the alcoholic's drinking.

This rationale then suggests the utility of training the spouse, or other family member, in reinforcement therapy techniques as a means of decreasing or terminating the drinking of an alcoholic, and getting the drinker into treatment.

This approach is somewhat comparable to behavior therapy programs in other settings in which the individual whose behavior is being changed is not the client seeing the therapist. For example, behavioral consultants are assigned the task of helping children to stop wetting the bed, get along better in school, and act less violent. Mentally ill and mentally retarded patients in institutions and group homes are helped to overcome disabilities and to have a more rewarding life. These techniques are applied frequently without the involvement of the individual whose behavior is to change. At other times, people change their behavior as a result of a life crisis or the demands of another. Individuals with eating disorders, obesity, high blood pressure, or nicotine addiction often seek help after a serious health problem with or without the insistence of a loved one. For many years in the field of alcohol and drug addiction, it was generally accepted that the individual with the addiction problem should not be tampered with, but should be left alone until he or she came to the realization (by hitting bottom) of the need for help. More recently, interventions have been developed to help the addicted individual become motivated to change.

Community Reinforcement Approach

Behavioral psychology has developed several methods of treating alcoholic dependent people. In some, the spouse or other family members are included in the treatment as with the Community Reinforcement Approach (CRA) treatment method (Hunt & Azrin, 1973; Azrin, 1976; Azrin, Sisson, Meyers, & Godley, 1982). In this approach, family members are an integral part of the program that includes: (1) a prescription for disulfiram (Antabuse), (2) a family program to encourage the client to continue to take disulfiram, (3) reciprocity marriage counseling, (4) a job club for unemployed, (5) social skills training, (6) advice on social and recreational activities, and (7) help with controlling urges to drink. The CRA is an intensive program; intervention is rapid and is accomplished in a short period of time in order to take advantage of the client's motivation.

An unexpected development during an evaluation of this approach (Azrin et al., 1982) was that a number of family members of active drinkers contacted the agency where the study was being performed, in order to get the alcoholic in their family involved in the CRA program. Many of these family members typically had heard of the program from friends whose alcoholism had been successfully treated by the CRA. Unfortunately, the alcoholics in these families refused to come to the CRA program for treatment. Typically, wives contacted the program, many of whom had been abused by their intoxicated husbands.

A Community Reinforcement Training (CRT) program for families, based on behavioral psychology, was developed and evaluated. This program was designed to teach the family member, usually, and here described as, the wife: (1) how to reduce physical abuse to herself, (2) how to encourage sobriety, (3) how to encourage seeking professional treatment, and (4) how to assist in treatment. To reduce physical abuse, wives were taught how to react to the earliest sign of impending violence as well as to the violence itself. To encourage sobriety, wives learned how to reinforce the alcoholic for periods of sobriety and how to arrange negative consequences of drinking through requiring the drinker to take responsibility for correcting the disruption caused by drinking. To encourage the drinker to seek treatment, wives learned to identify moments when the drinker was most motivated. To assist in the treatment, wives attended the professional sessions and helped the drinker to engage in prescribed activities thereafter. The present chapter describes this CRT program for families.

SPECIAL CONSIDERATIONS

Before beginning this program for helping family members of abusive drinkers, a counselor must first decide whether he or she is able to make the commitment required by the program. The family member will rely on the counselor a great deal and may call upon the counselor during nonworking hours. As described below, the procedures direct the family to call the counselor at a crisis point when the drinker requests help. This may happen late on a Saturday night and the counselor must be ready to respond.

A second prerequisite is that arrangements must be made ahead of time to implement the CRA when the drinker has decided to enter counseling. The drinker's motivation for change will be greatest at the start of counseling. At the first counseling session, the drinker's tolerance for Antabuse must be assessed medically, a prescription written, and the first dose administered. In addition, counselors should be skilled in all aspects of the CRA and have the necessary flexibility in their schedule to implement it as rapidly as possible. In addition, a separate "job club" program is quite useful in assisting unemployed clients to find work.

A final consideration is that the counselor must be aware of the cultural heritage of the family and the historical role each family member plays in that culture. Despite advances in the women's movement, there are still men from a variety of different cultures around the world who believe that a wife or child has no legitimate basis for concern about a husband's drinking. Some men will use violence in order to maintain their role as head of the family. This violence is intensified by the use of alcohol and the threat posed by other family members asserting themselves. A counselor must be prepared to deal with some degree of violence without imposing his or her own cultural and personal perspective. For example, a counselor, after seeing a badly beaten wife for the first time, may feel that the wife would be served best by leaving the husband. However, the wife may not want to leave the husband, but instead may want the alcoholic husband to stop drinking. Although marital violence that is potentially life threatening generally would preclude the use of the present approach, at least until the worst danger is eliminated (e.g., police removing weapons), lesser degrees of violence often are part of the clinical picture for families treated with this method. Specific procedures to evaluate and reduce the risk of violence are described below.

DESCRIPTION OF THE TREATMENT METHOD

The Community Reinforcement Training for families is a standardized training program to teach individuals how to encourage their family member to stop drinking and to enter counseling. Table 2.1 provides an overview of this treatment method. It is a description of these procedures in the order they are presented to the family member. This section is a manual for counselors. It is written as a series of directives for the counselor in order to simplify the understanding of the procedures. Each situation will present different challenges and some families may be better prepared emotionally and financially than others to implement the procedures. The time required to get the drinker into counseling will also vary.

General Guidelines

Clients should be seen the first day they contact the clinic. Usually a family member has thought about seeking help for a period of time and most often something has just happened, usually the night before, that has motivated them to seek help. It is important to take advantage of this motivation by seeing them immediately. All of the following procedures are first discussed, then role-played with the client. Whenever possible, activities are written down to remind the family member of how to behave. The long-term effects of these procedures are discussed and compared to the short-term problems they might cause. After the intake session, these procedures may be taught in a group. In this way family members who have had successes may discuss how they handled various situations and encourage the newcomers.

The First Session: Awareness of the Problem

The first session is extremely important because it provides the family member, usually the wife, with motivation to continue counseling and hope that the husband may change his drinking habits. For the sake of clarity, we will assume that a wife has contacted the program and is concerned about her husband's drinking, although this obviously is not always the case.

When the client enters the counseling center, she should be greeted by the counselor and given two forms to fill out while waiting. The first is a Family Inconvenience Review Checklist (see Table 2.2) consisting of a list of possible problems caused by the husband's drinking. The items include problems ranging from "embarrassing you in public" and "having money problems" to "being slapped around" and "being beat-

TABLE 2.1. Overview of Community Reinforcement Training for Families

A. Determination of severity of the alcohol problems
   1. Measuring quantity and frequency
   2. Discussing problems caused to the family—Family Inconvenience Review Checklist
   3. Allowing the family member to vent

B. Motivation of the family member
   1. Describing the community reinforcement approach
   2. Describing Antabuse and its benefits for the family member
   3. Describing briefly the procedures and how the family member will be helped to perform the procedures
   4. Keeping record with daily calendar of drinking behavior

C. Family-initiated alcohol treatment procedures
   1. Positive consequences for not drinking
     a. Positive communication techniques
     b. Discussion of the problem with the drinker
       − choosing time and place
       − telling them how you feel
     c. Reinforcement for not drinking
       − dismissing the notion of bribery
       − making a list
       − stressing the importance of immediacy
       − telling why the reinforcement is given
   2. Schedule of competing events: enjoyable, not associated with heavy drinking, family oriented
   3. Awareness of drinking
     a. being present at times of drinking
     b. offering alternatives
     c. avoiding violence
   4. Negative consequences for intoxiation
     a. withholding reinforcements and explaining why
     b. ignoring
   5. Help for the drinker to be responsible for his or her actions
     a. no help
     b. examples of correction and overcorrection
     c. boundaries of common sense
   6. Dangerous situations
     a. assessing the risk
     b. evaluating the behavior chain
     c. teaching when and how to leave—have a plan
   7. Outside activities for the client
     a. decreasing the stress on the family member
     b. establishing new friends
     c. joining job club
     d. group counseling
   8. Counseling as an option
     a. the "I promise I'll stop drinking" litany
     b. the window of opportunity when drinkers are most motivated
     c. joint counseling—rapid implementation

D. Community Reinforcement Approach: Antabuse rehearsals, reciprocity marriage counseling, job club

TABLE 2.2. Family Inconvenience Review Checklist

Below is a listing of situations that may have happened to you as a result of your family member's drinking. Please place an "x" next to each of the following situations that you have experienced.

_____ 1. Bailing your family member out of jail.
_____ 2. Paying high-risk insurance due to alcohol-related arrests.
_____ 3. Being embarrassed in public while your family member was drinking.
_____ 4. Being afraid of your family member when he or she drinks.
_____ 5. Having your children afraid of your family member when he or she drinks.
_____ 6. Calling work with an excuse for a family member's absence when he or she is hungover.
_____ 7. Being physically struck by your drinking family member.
_____ 8. Having financial problems due to your family member's drinking.
_____ 9. Being hospitalized due to injuries caused by your family member while drinking.
_____ 10. Bringing your family member to a detoxification center or hospital due to drinking.
_____ 11. Worrying about your family member's drinking.
_____ 12. Having emotional problems due to your family member's drinking.
_____ 13. Having friends avoid you and your family members due to drinking.
_____ 14. Being separated due to drinking or thinking about it.
_____ 15. Seeing your children struck by your family member while drinking.

---

en so badly that hospitalization was necessary." A second form is a questionnaire about the drinking habits of the problem-drinking spouse for the past 30 days. This gives the counselor an idea of the severity of the alcohol problem.

The counselor reviews these forms in detail with the client and allows the client to reveal the full extent of how the drinker's behavior has affected her life. At this point the counselor should listen sympathetically and allow her the opportunity to fully express her pent-up anger and/or sadness. Failure to let the wife thoroughly vent at this time can result in her doing so much later in counseling when the drinker is in treatment, which can impede progress.

Review of her answers to the second questionnaire about the quantity and frequency of her husband's drinking leads into asking her to describe her husband's drinking from the time she first met him. Next the counselor asks the wife what attempts she has made in the past to get her husband to cut back or stop his drinking. This, with her responses to the other questions, provides some insights into her living situation. Finally, the client is asked if her husband has ever stated or promised that he would stop drinking. Frequently, many drinkers will state that they will stop drinking right after they have done something that is very contrary to their self-image. The wife is told that the counseling will teach her how to take advantage of such situations.

Motivation of the Spouse or Family Member

Now the counselor takes over the session by telling the wife that he/she is going to speak for awhile and she should listen and hold on to her questions. The tone of the session changes from sympathetic listening to didactic education and forms the basis for future counseling sessions.

First the counselor explains to her the goals and potential benefits of her participation in the CRT program. Examples from the description of problems she has listed are used. The counselor says something like,

> "The purpose of the program is to help your husband to stop drinking and come into counseling with you. From what you've told me, your husband was a drinker when you were first dating, but would drink heavily only once a week. During the past couple of years, he has become a daily drinker, has lost jobs and, as a result, caused you financial problems. More recently, you've noticed personality changes and he has become much more difficult to get along with. Last week he got stopped for drunk driving and promised not to drink again. Last night he came home intoxicated, and when you confronted him it turned into a terrible argument, and he slapped you several times. Our attempt is going to be to get him to stop drinking and enter counseling, so you can get some stability in your life and not be afraid of him becoming violent.
>
> "When he comes into counseling we are going to want him to take a pill called Antabuse. Antabuse is a small white pill that, if taken daily, prevents an individual from drinking even small amounts of alcohol. If a person drinks on Antabuse, they become violently ill. An important characteristic of Antabuse that can really help you is that once your husband is taking Antabuse regularly, even if he decides to stop taking it and go back to drinking, he can't for approximately 5 to 14 days because it stays in the system. We'll set up a procedure where you dissolve the pill in a small amount of water and watch him take it. You will know far ahead of time if he's going to drink so you won't have to worry daily if he is going to drink and get violent again. In addition, we have marriage counseling to help you learn to communicate better, and we have a job program to help your husband find a better job."

The counselor asks her now if she has any questions and explains her role in the "Antabuse Contract." Objections her husband may have to Antabuse are discussed and the importance of her encouraging her husband to take it once he attends counseling is stressed, as is being involved in administering it to him every day. She is told not to bring it up to him until then.

Next the counselor describes the training program briefly. She is told that the counselor is going to teach her to encourage her husband not to drink by being nicer to him when not drinking, communicating to him that she prefer he doesn't drink, and scheduling activities in which he doesn't drink. She is told she will learn to not be so nice when he is drinking and to let him be responsible for his own actions when he drinks. She is also told she will learn how to avoid violent situations. When he does state that he would like to stop drinking, she will immediately take advantage of that and call the counselor to bring her husband in at once. Also, the counselor will be available 24 hours a day to answer any questions and help with any crisis.

The wife is given a 30-day calendar. On it she should write down if and how much her husband drinks as best she can determine. She should also mark down if anything unusual happens—if he misses work, gets arrested, becomes violent. This typically will end the first session. The client is seen the next day to get started and take advantage of her motivation.

Reinforcement Procedures

The following is a description of the procedures that are taught to the wives. The counselor should first discuss the procedure in a general way, then specifically tell her how and when she might use it. The situation is role-played with her until she feels comfortable. She may feel incapable of doing some procedures and may not want to do others. Other women will be very assertive and do the procedures quickly. Some women have gone home after their first session and told their husbands that they are going to go to counseling, and brought them in the next day. On the other hand, one woman was so afraid of her husband that she was afraid to return to counseling for fear he might see her car there; so we practiced the procedures over the phone. The counselor starts where the client is most comfortable and works at her pace.

Positive Consequences for Not Drinking

The clients are taught to be nice when the husband is not drinking. Words like "positive reinforcement" or "reward" are avoided. A list is made of things enjoyed by the husband. The list usually includes favorite foods, discussing topics he enjoys, gifts, sexual activities, and generally being pleasant. She also is instructed to tell him that she is being pleasant because she enjoys being with him when he is not drinking.

At a time when her husband is not drinking and "in a good mood" and when they are feeling close to one another, the counselor instructs her to have a discussion about his drinking. Using positive communication techniques, she is told to tell her husband that she feels better when he is not drinking. She should be specific, for example, "I feel so much closer to you when you're not drinking. I love being with you and going to the movies and out to dinner together or just sitting around playing cards." She should be sympathetic by using an "understanding statement." She should say something like, "I understand that you have a very hard job and we have a lot of financial problems that cause you a lot of stress." She is taught to be very specific in her request. "I wish you wouldn't go out to the bar on Friday night and instead would stay home with me and not drink." If the drinker at this time states that he is willing to try to stop drinking, then she is instructed to suggest counseling at this time. If he does not respond well then, she does not bring up counseling, but continues to be supportive of his not drinking.

Being nice to the drinker when he is not drinking is frequently hard for the wife to do. Her feelings of resentment for past drinking episodes can make her reluctant to be pleasant at all. If this is the case, the counselor explores alternatives such as divorce or separation, and suggests she should decide whether she would want to live with him if he stops drinking altogether. This discussion can help deter subsequent problems in the conjoint marriage counseling when and if she refuses to participate in a positive way, because she feels the drinker should in some way "pay" for the hurt he has caused her. She is told she may be happier with a divorce, that it is her choice, but if she decides to give her marriage one last try before ending it the counselor is willing to work with her.

Competing Activities

The wife is instructed to schedule activities that her husband would enjoy and at which it is very unlikely that heavy drinking would occur. Examples are individual but often include taking the children to an amusement park, dinner with friends who don't drink, visiting relatives, and becoming active in organizations that are not settings for heavy drinking. The counselor has a discussion about any friends who are supportive of trying to help her husband stop drinking and are aware of the problem. The wife can schedule time with these friends and less time with her husband's drinking buddies. Early morning activities on Sunday are good because it helps the drinker by reminding him that he has to get up early after a traditionally heavy drinking night. In general, the counselor encourages the spouse to interest her husband in activities that interfere with his drinking.

Awareness of Drinking

The counselor teaches the wife what to do when her husband is drinking and to try to be present when he begins drinking. In this way, she can attempt to discourage his drinking by reminding him of how pleasant things are when he's not drinking. She can remind him of scheduled activities that he may miss or have to attend with a hangover. She should suggest other activities such as eating, dancing, or going someplace else. She also should tell the drinker how many he is having. When it is clear that her husband intends to continue drinking, she should leave. She also should leave at the first sign or threat of violence.

Negative Consequences for Intoxication

If the drinker becomes intoxicated or comes home intoxicated, instruct the wife to ignore him as much as possible and provide none of the extra pleasantries that she provides for him when he is sober. She is to tell him in a neutral manner that she does not like his drinking and that she would rather not be around him when he is drunk. If she can, she should not be in the same room with him and should busy herself with other activities.

Responsibility of Alcoholic for Self-Correction

The counselor teaches the wife that when her husband becomes intoxicated, she is to hold him responsible for his own actions. She is instructed not to hold missed meals for him, not to make him comfortable if he passes out in odd places, not to bail him out of jail without an agreement for counseling, nor call his employer with excuses for lateness or absence from work. She also should have him clean up after himself if he vomits or becomes incontinent, and should definitely not clean up such messes herself, but rather should have him correct these situations. Each wife will be able to identify with the counselor activities she has done to help hide the husband's drinking and the counselor will show her how not to do this anymore.

These guidelines are, of course, to be followed within the boundaries of common sense. If the drinker is in a life-threatening situation or one that is potentially very damaging to his health, the wife should take prompt and immediate action. An example would be passing out outside in the middle of winter.

Dangerous Situations

The spouse and other family members often find themselves in situations in which the husband, especially while intoxicated, becomes physically violent toward them. Frequently, this is one of the reasons the wife contacts a counseling center for help. The purpose of this part of the program is to help the wife identify potentially violent situations so that she can take immediate action before getting hurt. To do this, the counselor helps to construct the usual sequence of events that typically lead to violence, write the sequence down, and teach her to identify "cues" before the physical violence begins. Usually, the physical violence is a behavior in a long chain of events with cues that can be identified indicating when violence is going to occur. Teach her to recognize cues such as "the way he closed the car door," or a "certain glint in his eye," as well as the obvious cues of intoxication, arguing, and throwing things.

At the earliest recognized sign of impending violence, direct the wife not to argue or threaten, but calmly to tell her husband he has obviously been drinking and appears upset, and that she feels uncomfortable being around him and she will be leaving until he feels better and is sober. If he is not present, she should leave a note. She then leaves (taking the children) and goes to a previously arranged, nearby relative, friend, motel, or women's center until the drinker is sober and there is no longer any danger of violence. Make these arrangements with all your clients, even if violence has not been a problem in the past. Typically, except in the cases of very violent men, the wife should tell her husband where she will be.

If the drinker actually does become violent, the client is instructed to leave and to call the police. The importance of filing charges is explained to the client. This is essential because it makes the drinker aware that violent behavior will not be tolerated. It also reassures the police that the wife is serious, so they will go out when she calls again. It provides a situation in which the drinker may decide to stop drinking and to enter the counseling program. The counselor suggests to the wife that she not return to her husband unless he agrees to counseling.

Outside Activities For the Wife

The counselor will help the wife find outside activities and interests that she can have for herself so her life is not so dependent on her husband. When appropriate, she is helped to find a job by using the job club so that she can reduce her feeling of being trapped by reducing her financial dependence on her husband. In a group therapy setting, a few group members can try outside activities and organizations together so they feel less isolated. Frequently, violent men will try to isolate their wives from the rest of the world. This gives the wife a feeling of loneliness and dependence upon the drinker and of being trapped and unable to do anything about the situation. Coming to the group can make a woman feel less alone with this problem and encourage her to be more assertive.

Suggestion of Counseling for Alcoholic

People with alcohol problems frequently state that they want to stop drinking. Sometimes this can appear manipulative as their declaration is generally short-lived and lasts long enough to get them out of a problem. Another way of looking at this behavior is to recognize that verbal behavior and short-lived attempts at stopping drinking are governed by the principles of behavioral psychology. The wife is taught to take advantage of this behavior rather than viewing it as another manipulation.

People with drinking problems appear to be most motivated to stop drinking after specific incidents in which their problem has caused them some major inconvenience, or they feel ashamed because they have done something seriously at odds with their self-image. Examples of such occasions are after having a physically debilitating drinking episode, spending a huge amount of money drinking, having a car accident, or having some contact with the law. The drinker may be embarrassed or ashamed after something as minor as acting like a fool at a party, or something as serious as being violent with a family member. These are moments of higher motivation for the drinker. At this time, teach the wife to suggest stopping drinking and entering counseling. The wife may now be ready to demand that he attend counseling or she will seek a divorce.

When the drinker agrees and states he needs help, the wife calls the counselor immediately, regardless of time of day or day of the week. They all meet at the clinic or center as soon as possible. This "window of motivation" is closing quickly. A few hours of sleep and a couple of more beers may change the drinker's mind.

This approach is different from more confrontational approaches in which family members and friends meet to discuss their concerns with the drinker. It is designed to take advantage of the drinker's motivation by implementing the CRA in an outpatient setting very rapidly. This is particularly useful in working with violent men who may become agitated in a confrontational situation. The use of Antabuse makes it possible to start treatment safely in an outpatient setting when the drinker cannot afford a residential stay due to a lack of insurance.

The First Conjoint Session: Starting the CRA Treatment

The Initial Greeting of Couple and Preparations for Couple Session

This first conjoint session is very important. It is similar to the intake session of the CRA described elsewhere (e.g., Sisson & Azrin, 1989) except the counselor already knows much about the drinker from working with their spouse. The counselor greets the couple in a friendly manner and makes sure to shake hands with the husband. He may be feeling quite suspicious and anxious about dealing with the incident that caused him to come in at this time. An intake package, which includes the Inconvenience Review Checklist for drinkers (see Table 2.3) and a drinking questionnaire covering the past 30 days, is given to the drinker. He is told to fill out the package while the counselor speaks to the wife.

The counselor asks the spouse to describe the incident that caused her husband to come in at this time. It is important for the counselor to understand why he decided to come in now. Was he motivated because his wife demanded it or threatened to leave him? Was he arrested or is he tired of drinking? The wife is reminded about the Antabuse and her role. The counselor confirms that she will be supportive of her husband taking Antabuse. In some cases, she may decide to make it a requisite for her staying in the marriage.

Starting the Couple Session

Next, the husband is asked to come into the office to begin the conjoint couple session. A statement is made acknowledging that the counselor has been providing counseling to his wife and that the counselor is very happy that he came in. The responses to the intake package are carefully reviewed with the husband and wife. The wife can respond to any underreporting he may have done about his drinking and the problems it has caused. The drinker is asked why he decided to come into treatment now. His answer is very important because you need to know what the client sees as being his or her immediate needs in order to provide him the necessary reinforcement.

The counselor explains to the couple that the counselor is going to speak for a moment. During this talk, the counselor should restate the problems alcohol is causing the drinker and his family. Then Antabuse is explained and how the counselor feels it would specifically help them is discussed. The counselor describes the Antabuse protocol—the spouse being involved in helping the drinker take the Antabuse.

TABLE 2.3. Drinker Inconvenience Review Checklist

Do you have an alcohol problem? This program is not only for the full-fledged alcoholic, but also for the person experiencing problems with alcohol. The situations listed below are commonly agreed upon by others as alcohol problems and reasons for counseling. Please indicate which of the following situations apply to you by placing an "x" in the space in front of the number that applies. Remember, the questionnaire concerns only those situations you feel involve problems with alcohol, and the reasons why you would like counseling.

_____ 1. Being hospitalized for alcohol-related problems.
_____ 2. Being physiologically addicted to alcohol and unable to stop drinking without a physician's help or the help of a hospital or detox center.
_____ 3. Being in jail for alcohol-related arrests.
_____ 4. Suffering severe withdrawal symptoms (i.e., tremors, hallucinations, stomach cramps, nausea, vomiting, etc.).
_____ 5. Having an automobile accident while under the influence of alcohol.
_____ 6. Being sent home or fired because of hangovers or drinking.
_____ 7. Being arrested for driving while under the influence of alcohol.
_____ 8. Missing work or school because of hangovers or drinking.
_____ 9. Acting foolish and/or aggressive at parties or in bars.
_____ 10. Having financial difficulties as a result of drinking.
_____ 11. Not being able to remember what you did while drunk.
_____ 12. Having difficulty sleeping due to drinking.
_____ 13. Having family problems due to drinking.
_____ 14. Not getting promoted at work due to drinking.
_____ 15. Losing driving privileges due to alcohol-related arrests.
_____ 16. Suffering severe hangovers after drinking.
_____ 17. Having lapses of memory due to drinking (blackouts).
_____ 18. Being committed to a detoxification center, hospital, or alcoholism treatment program because of drinking.
_____ 19. Having decreased ambition since drinking.
_____ 20. Having decreased sexual drive or impotency due to drinking.
_____ 21. Feeling guilty about drinking.
_____ 22. Having poor health or alcohol-related health problems.
_____ 23. Being disowned by friends or family over drinking.
_____ 24. Losing trust and respect of family, friends, fellow employees, or relatives due to drinking.
_____ 25. Being divorced or separated due to drinking.
_____ 26. Having severe shakes or tremors (DT's) due to alcoholism.
_____ 27. Feeling sad, depressed, or unhappy over drinking.
_____ 28. Having suicidal thoughts because of alcohol problems.
_____ 29. Being arrested for doing things while drinking (e.g., assault, disorderly conduct, battery).
_____ 30. Having to pay for high-risk insurance because of alcohol-related traffic arrests.
_____ 31. Dropping out or not doing well in school because of drinking.
_____ 32. Having a poor reputation due to being a heavy drinker.
_____ 33. Needing a drink in the morning to overcome hangover or shakes.
_____ 34. Getting violent or into fights while drinking.
_____ 35. Having friends, family, or your children afraid of you when you are drinking.

(cont.)

TABLE 2.3. (cont.)

_____ 36. Not being able to get a good job due to a reputation as a heavy drinker.
_____ 37. Spending money foolishly while drinking.
_____ 38. Experiencing fear of becoming an alcoholic (unable to control your drinking or worrying about drinking too much).
_____ 39. Suffering personal injury or hurting others while drinking.
_____ 40. Having emotional problems due to drinking (i.e., anxieties).
_____ 41. Others (Specify) _____

The counselor says something like,

"To review your situation, your use of alcohol has caused you a number of problems with your work, your health, and your family. Over the past couple of years, your drinking has increased from once or twice a week to usually daily. You've had blackouts, you've lost a couple of jobs, and you've spent money foolishly. More recently, you've gotten a ticket for driving while intoxicated that helped you cut down for awhile. Now, last night you and your wife had an argument when you came home intoxicated and it ended by your striking her and her leaving you and going to stay with her sister.

"I would recommend that you consider taking Antabuse. Antabuse is a small white pill that prevents you from drinking alcohol by making you very ill if you drink even small amounts. Antabuse really can help you. Once you're taking it regularly, even if you decide to stop taking it and resume drinking, you can't go back to drinking for 5 to 14 days. During those few days, a lot can happen to change your mind. We set up an early warning system by having your wife administer the Antabuse to you every day. This way, if you feel like drinking again you'll have to let someone know who cares about you. In addition, your wife is going to be less afraid of you because, if she has given you the Antabuse in the morning, she doesn't have to worry that you're going to come home and maybe hit her again. Also you have an upcoming court appearance for your drunk driving charge. Taking Antabuse and staying sober is something to demonstrate to the court."

Generally, a counselor can tell, by watching the drinker, what his reaction to this is going to be. Even if the counselor is sure the drinker will want to take Antabuse, the wife is asked how she feels about him taking the medication. She should state directly to her husband why she would like him to stop drinking and take Antabuse. This is generally a very emotional time for both of them. Most of the time the drinker will comply. If he doesn't, the counselor asks him to try to take it for a month or even less. If he still refuses, discuss openly with his wife what her options may be; this is seldom necessary.

At this point, the client will see necessary medical staff for a prescription of Antabuse. In the case of very heavy drinking, the medical staff may determine that a supervised detoxification is necessary to monitor withdrawal. In this case, begin the planned CRA treatment as soon as the client has been detoxified.

Antabuse Assurance

In either case, the client should begin the Antabuse program with the spouse helping to dispense the medication. This can be done as soon as the physician medically clears the client, usually 12–24 hours after the last drink. (Note that individuals cannot take Antabuse until they have a blood alcohol level of zero.) The couple does not leave the clinic until they have been instructed in this regimen and you have watched him take the Antabuse.

This is done by taking out the Antabuse tablet and showing it to the couple. It is placed in a ceramic coffee cup and a couple of ounces of water are added. The water partially dissolves the pill and, when gently tapped, the pill dissolves completely. It is given to the drinker and he is told to drink it in one gulp. He is praised for his decision to stop drinking and the wife is asked to state how she feels. This can be a very emotional moment for them. Allow them to discuss how they feel.

Next the counselor asks them to agree on a set time and place every day to take Antabuse. Generally, it is tied to a regular occurring event such as breakfast, dinner, or bedtime. They are instructed to bring the Antabuse to each counseling session because each session will start by the couple performing the "Antabuse rehearsal" procedure.

The couple usually goes home after this first session surprisingly happy and relaxed. This may be the first time they have made a concrete step in reestablishing their relationship and having the husband stop drinking.

The next task is to continue the CRA with the alcoholic and spouse. Begin by rehearsing the "Antabuse refusal" procedures to prepare for situations when the alcoholic refuses to take Antabuse, and "Reciprocity marriage counseling" procedures to teach the couple how to communicate better. Practice "job finding" if he is out of work. These procedures that teach the clients how to communicate better, solve problems, and work on agreed-upon goals are described in some detail by Sisson and Azrin (1989).

CASE APPLICATION

Debbie was a 26-year-old mother of two who had been married to Dick for 5 years. When they were dating each other, they would both drink, and go to country and western bars and dance. Dick was currently working at a local factory that depressed him. Within the previous 2 years, Dick had begun to drink more heavily, stopping off almost every night at a local tavern before coming home. During the previous 6 months he had been drinking very heavily, not coming home until very late. His personality had changed and he had become very quick-tempered. He had recently come home very late, drunk, and an argument had begun; he had struck Debbie, blackening her eye. The next morning he said he did not remember it but assured her it wouldn't happen again. He said he was not going to stop drinking. Debbie had heard of our services from a friend whose husband had a similar problem.

When Debbie came in for the first session, her eye was blackened and she was very upset. The CRT program was described to her and she said she was willing to give it a try.

Debbie picked up the procedures quickly because she was very motivated. She used the positive communication techniques and asked Dick not to drink. When he didn't drink, she was very nice to him and made him his favorite meals. She scheduled family outings and picnics with the children. They went out together to dinner with friends who did not drink. During the first month, Dick drank very little. They spent more time together and things appeared to be getting better.

Dick then began to bring a six-pack of beer home about every other evening for a week. Debbie continued to do the procedures. Then Dick didn't come home one night until very late and had been drinking very heavily. Although Debbie was upset, she did her best to ignore him. After about another week of not drinking, Dick drank very heavily during an entire weekend. They got into several arguments despite Debbie trying to avoid him. Late Sunday night, after going to a bar and driving the car into a ditch, Dick came home. They had another argument and while Debbie was getting ready to leave, Dick struck her again. Debbie went to her mother's home with her kids.

Early the next morning Dick went to her mother's home to talk to Debbie. He apologized for the way he had behaved and said that he would stop drinking. She told him that she loved him, but would not return home unless he went to counseling for his alcohol problem. He agreed. She called her counselor at home and they came into the clinic at 9:00 A.M. Dick agreed to take Antabuse and Debbie monitored it. They learned the communication procedures and made agreements on their social activities, financial management, and how to raise their children. Dick got a more rewarding job using the job club procedures and has been sober for about a year.

RESEARCH SUMMARY

Several studies have evaluated the effectiveness of the CRA when the drinker is in treatment (Hunt & Azrin, 1973; Azrin, 1976; Azrin et al., 1982). These studies have found the CRA to be a successful approach to help inpatient or outpatient alcoholics remain sober, employed, and out of institutions. The Azrin et al. (1982) study evaluated the relative contribution of different components of the CRA and found that the "Antabuse assurance" procedures alone resulted in almost total sobriety for married or cohabiting clients.

Sisson and Azrin (1986) evaluated the effectiveness of the procedures described in this chapter for getting drinkers to stop drinking and enter treatment. Twelve family members were given either community-reinforcement counseling or a traditional (Al-Anon) type of counseling. To ensure that clients assigned to traditional counseling went to Al-Anon, they were introduced in the session to an Al-Anon member who took them to their meetings. The results of the study showed that the drinkers in the traditional and CRT groups were comparable in the terms of their frequency of drinking and intoxication prior to treatment. The reinforcement training of the nonalcoholic family members alone was found to result in a reduction of drinking in the alcoholic before he was counseled directly, and the extent of this reduction was about 50%. Additionally, the reinforcement training of the family members resulted in the initiation of treatment for six of the seven alcoholics in that group. In contrast, none of the alcoholics whose wives received the traditional Al-Anon method entered treatment. Once the drinker entered the CRA counseling, drinking by the alcoholic was further reduced. Finally, time spent abstinent was significantly greater for the alcoholics whose wives received the reinforcement training than for their counterparts whose wives went to Al-Anon.

CONCLUSIONS

Although there has been only this one study, the results suggest that having family members attempt to intervene directly with a problem drinker can be effective. As it is estimated that only 15% of the people with alcohol problems ever reach treatment and the use of illegal drugs, such as cocaine and heroine, has recently been increasing, much more research is needed to develop techniques to get people into treatment programs. In order to do this, the traditional concepts of alcoholism with its related ideas of family codependency and recovery must be reevaluated. Family and friends of individuals with alcohol and drug problems do not need to idly watch as their loved ones destroy themselves. Behavioral psychology offers an alternative perspective and a method for developing and evaluating treatment techniques.

REFERENCES

Azrin, N. H. (1976). Improvements in the community reinforcement approach to alcoholism. *Behaviour Research and Therapy, 14,* 339–348.

Azrin, N. H., Sisson, R. W., Meyers, R., & Godley, M. (1982). Alcoholism treatment by disulfiram and community reinforcement therapy. *Journal of Behavior Therapy and Experimental Psychiatry, 13,* 105–112.

Hunt, G. M., & Azrin, N. H. (1973). A community reinforcement approach to alcoholism. *Behaviour Research and Therapy, 11,* 91–104.

Sisson, R. W., & Azrin, N. H. (1986). Family-member involvement to initiate and promote treatment of problem drinkers. *Journal of Behavior Therapy and Experimental Psychiatry, 17,* 15–21.

Sisson, R. W., & Azrin, N. H. (1989). The community reinforcement approach. In R. Hester & W. R. Miller (Eds.), *Handbook of alcoholism treatment approaches* (pp. 242–258). New York: Pergamon Press.

Chapter 3

Using Family Influence to Motivate Alcoholics to Enter Treatment
The Johnson Institute Intervention Approach

Michael R. Liepman

OVERVIEW

This chapter describes an approach for motivating persons who suffer from alcohol problems but are reluctant to enter treatment and begin recovery. First described as "Intervention" by the Johnson Institute in Center City, Minnesota (Johnson, 1973), this popular technique has been used widely by the alcoholism treatment field. With the benevolent assistance of family members, it has been used to motivate such celebrities as former First Lady Betty Ford and thousands of other recalcitrant clients to enter a variety of recovery programs. This powerful, brief family-systems approach begins with building an Intervention team of family and significant others. It then assesses the situation and empowers the team to perform a constructive confrontation of the target drinker at the end of the process.

Chronic alcoholism is known for its resistance to recovery. The alcoholic's defensive denial may prevent entry into treatment. However, family processes also may interfere (Koppel, Stimmler, & Perone, 1980; Liepman, 1984; Liepman, Silvia, & Nirenberg, 1989; Silvia & Liepman, 1991; Steinglass, Bennett, Wolin, & Reiss, 1987). Abstinence required for recovery entails giving up drinking and drinking-related (drinker and family) behavior, often an essential component of the family behavioral repertoire that contributes to family homeostasis. Once treatment has begun, many families discover that relapses occur periodically

despite desires to have the drinking stop. Families that are able to support abstinence in the alcoholic drinker often suffer other consequences
of family pathology that were not apparent or expected when the
drinker was chronically drinking (Liepman, 1984; Smilkstein, 1980).

Using family influence to motivate the alcoholic to begin recovery
is important in two ways. First, the family, as a significant and meaningful component of the social network, can have substantial influence that
seems to enhance the likelihood that the alcoholic will initiate and stick
with recovery. Such up-front involvement of the family and significant
others assures greater social support for sobriety during and after treatment. Second, the involvement of the family in this initiation phase
can provide an opportunity for the therapist to hook family members
into the recovery process so that family recovery occurs in tandem with
the individual recovery of the alcoholic.

The pre-Intervention training actually is a form of family therapy
that helps family members individually to progress through stages of
change (i.e., precontemplator $\rightarrow$ contemplator $\rightarrow$ prepared for action)
in reference to behaviors that previously, overtly or covertly, supported
or enabled the alcoholic's drinking (Prochaska & DiClemente, 1986).
The novel behavior the family presents to the alcoholic at the Intervention confrontation reflects awareness about alcoholism, teamwork (and
a united front), assertiveness, improved communication skills, and a
refusal to resume enabling.

This clinical approach seems to enhance both the family outcome
and the individual outcome of the alcoholic (Liepman et al., 1989). In
particular, Intervention seems to accelerate entry of the alcoholic and
the family into treatment. It may also be used to improve outcome for
someone who already has begun to half-heartedly address chronic
relapsing alcoholism but is not making satisfactory progress.

SPECIAL CONSIDERATIONS

Alcoholics Likely to Benefit from Intervention

Many persons with denial can be convinced to try treatment or recovery simply by discussing with them the consequences of their drinking. Individually oriented motivational counseling techniques have been
developed to facilitate this process (Miller & Rollnick, 1991). Coercive
approaches have been used with some success by criminal justice and
child protection agencies, by employers, by licensing agencies (e.g.,
drivers, pilots, doctors, pharmacists), and by parents of adolescents, to
motivate individuals under their authority to enter treatment and/or

begin recovery (Collins & Allison, 1983; Freedberg & Johnston, 1980; Salmon & Salmon, 1983; Smart, 1974; Tucker, 1974; Williams & Moffatt, 1975). One advantage of coercive approaches is that those with some sort of leverage over the alcoholic have the capacity to influence the alcoholic to seek help now rather than waiting until he or she naturally becomes ready to take action. This may initiate recovery far sooner, hence preventing many of the later consequences that probably would have occurred had recovery onset been delayed. Like early surgical intervention for a small, growing cancer, Intervention can prevent substantial suffering and even loss of the capacity to achieve and enjoy recovery.

The Intervention procedure is best utilized for those who quite stubbornly resist entering treatment or beginning recovery but who may not have any single individual or institution with sufficient authority over them who can or wants to coerce them into treatment. Persons who already are or have been involved in prior treatment also may benefit if it seems that satisfactory progress is not being made. If there appears to be a need to initiate treatment or alter the type or quantity of help the alcoholic is obtaining, or if there is a need to convince the alcoholic to use treatment to address additional issues that so far have been neglected, Intervention may be an ideal way to do this if other simpler approaches have failed to make an impact.

Persons to Include in the Intervention

This approach is dependent upon the influence of trusted family members and other meaningful persons in the alcoholic's social support network. Usually family members participate. Sometimes close friends and work associates also participate. Occasionally clergy and health-care professionals may be willing to become involved.

The choice of who participates can be very important. Some members of the social network may be potent enablers of the drinking, and their participation could be disruptive; on the other hand, their lack of participation could position them to undermine the efforts of those who did participate. For example, if the alcoholic typically drinks with his brother, an Intervention that excluded this brother could easily be undermined by the brother's innocent and self-serving support for continuing to drink together. Although it may be necessary to exclude certain individuals from the process, the relative proportion of family members and other significant social network members who participate should be as large as possible.

Those alcoholics who have very little social involvement or those whose social network is limited to quite superficial relationships (e.g., drinking associates at a bar) are not as likely to benefit from an Intervention, nor is it likely that an Intervention could be constructed from this sort of network. For example, an elderly widow living an isolated life in an elderly housing unit is nearly unapproachable as regards her drinking unless family with leverage can convince her to change her behavior.

Ethical Concerns

Several ethical criticisms have been levelled at Intervention. The process of conspiring behind the back of the target alcoholic raises questions of confidentiality and undue influence. Typically the source of all information about the target alcoholic is from the participants. Discussion centers around the concerns of these participants. Secrets about private interactions participants have had with the alcoholic are revealed and discussed by the participants under the guidance of the interventionist.

The Intervention process does resemble a conspiracy. Although the purpose of the conspiracy is intended to benefit the target alcoholic, the goal is to influence the alcoholic to alter choices, hence impacting on personal freedom. D. Berenson (personal communication, 1980) has suggested phoning the target alcoholic to inform him or her that the therapist is conspiring with family to find a way to resolve the drinking problem and inviting the alcoholic to participate. This may succeed in bringing the alcoholic into the process; on the other hand, if this is tried before the team has coalesced and agreed on goals and strategies, further meetings of the team and further progress in the meetings may be jeopardized if the alcoholic finds out and tries to interfere. This approach is generally not followed by most who do Interventions; they usually keep the conspiracy a secret until the confrontation is ready.

A second concern is that the Intervention may lead to harmful consequences such as paranoia, suicide attempts, or family violence. If done skillfully, this seems not to be a common consequence of Intervention. The constructive tone of the messages and the option of recovery and family support mitigates against such a negative outcome. However, only one study has been published on the long-term outcome of a small series of Interventions (Liepman, Nirenberg, & Begin, 1989); more such studies should be done. The alternative of continued unrestrained progression of the alcoholism poses substantial risks that should be compared to risks of Intervention.

A third concern is that Intervention may be used by "for profit" treatment facilities to recruit (perhaps unnecessary) admissions to costly inpatient detox/rehab programs when less costly outpatient approaches might be equally effective (Miller & Hester, 1986). Some facilities do Interventions as a service to the families of their prospective clients, and it is common for the interventionist to recommend admission to the host program. However, neither case reports nor data have been published documenting abusive practices such as using undue influence of the interventionist to skew treatment recommendations towards the host facility when other treatment might have been more appropriate.

DESCRIPTION OF THE TREATMENT METHOD

First Contact by Family Emissary

The first step in Intervention is taken by a family member who is sufficiently concerned about the alcoholic to seek help. This person who makes initial contact has been called the help-seeking emissary from the family to the treatment system (Liepman, Wolper, & Vazquez, 1982; Smilkstein, 1980). Typically this family member contacts a treatment program or professional with questions about what can be done for someone who refuses help or who doesn't think he or she needs help. Frustrated by having "tried everything" to no avail, this family member usually is quite skeptical that any further efforts will succeed in motivating the alcoholic to enter treatment or quit drinking, but any ray of hope may be welcomed nonetheless. Table 3.1 outlines the steps and content of the Intervention approach.

Assessment

Once the family emissary and the interventionist meet, an assessment begins. The interventionist needs to determine the structure of the family and social support network, focusing on who the players are and what their roles are in relation to the drinking and consequences. A genogram may help determine who in the family tree has symptomatic substance-abuse problems. In addition, an ecomap, which presents the alcoholic's social network in visual form, is helpful in identifying positive and negative supports for drinking as well as showing how invested the target alcoholic is in each support (Hartman & Laird, 1983; Liepman, Wolper, & Vazquez, 1982). The use of the genogram and ecomap as tools in the assessment process will be described more fully in the case application later in this chapter.

TABLE 3.1. Steps in the Intervention Approach

First contact by emissary

Assessment
    Description of presenting problem
    Determination of structure of family and social network
    Selection of Intervention team members

Training
    Introductions of team members
    Explanation of process
    Education about alcoholism and recovery
    List of concerns and feelings
    Negotiation of desired outcomes
    Identification of contingencies ("what if" clauses)
    Rehearsal with feedback on presentation

Confrontation
    Explanation of process
    List of concerns and feelings
    Identification of contingencies ("what if" clauses)
    Negotiation of desired outcomes
    Referral to selected treatment

Postconfrontation session
    Celebration if alcoholic accepts treatment
    Reflection on family progress and commitment to continued assertion
    Reaction to confrontation and evaluation of components
    Consideration of options for continuing recovery of family
    Decisions about changes in family interaction

Selection of Team Members

Once the social network has been identified, decisions are made by the emissary and interventionist as to who should be invited to participate in the Intervention team training sessions. Often the significant members include some who are geographically distant; nonetheless they may be invited, and marathon sessions may be set up for their convenience. Interpersonal conflicts between team members are not uncommon. Selection may involve considering how these conflicts will be addressed early in the process to prevent interference. Relatives and former friends who have become alienated from the target alcoholic may be included because their alienation often is due to the continued drinking or consequential behaviors.

Team Training

The assembled team members are introduced to the interventionist (and to each other when necessary). The purpose of the team meetings is stated: to prepare the team to express to the target alcoholic their concerns about continued drinking and their desire for cessation of drinking and acceptance of treatment. An explanation about alcoholism is often necessary for at least some of the team members who may not be aware of what constitutes alcoholism. Some participants may doubt that the target alcoholic has alcoholism, perhaps because of their own denial. Others may be unaware of the extent to which the target alcoholic has become alcohol impaired.

A movie (*I'll Quit Tomorrow!* [Johnson Institute, 1975]) or pair of videotapes (*The Enabler* and *The Intervention* [Johnson Institute, 1978a, 1978b]), may be shown to demonstrate the processes of Intervention and Intervention training. An outline of the steps of preparation is reviewed with a schedule worked out for subsequent meetings and the final meeting at which the alcoholic will be confronted (see Table 3.1).

List of Concerns

Each participant is asked to make a private list of incidents that made him or her worry about the target alcoholic. The list should be specific rather than general. Some items from the list will be described during the confrontation, hence all items must be clear and specific enough to withstand challenge by the alcoholic. Each item is listed with the author's associated feelings. The list-making process generally convinces most doubtful team members that the Intervention is necessary and will be worth the effort.

Negotiation of Desired Outcomes

The desired outcomes are identified by each team member. Differences in outcome are negotiated with the help of the interventionist. Some team members may need to be educated about the natural history of alcoholism or alcohol problems so that they can make realistic decisions about what would be an acceptable outcome of the Intervention process. Knowledge of prior treatment and recovery attempts is useful in treatment planning. Identification of special problems (e.g., concurrent handicaps or comorbidities) that could complicate recovery should help avoid unrealistic treatment plans.

Improvement of Delivery Style

Lists of consequences are reviewed in the group setting. Items are presented to the group first to select for appropriateness and to refine the presentation. Communications skills techniques are taught to team members to assure that the presentations are likely to be heard without eliciting inordinate defensiveness. Comments must be specific rather than vague. They are placed within the context of expressions of love and concern and are not stated in a hostile manner. Blaming, name calling, and judging are prohibited. The description of the incident is followed by an explanation of how it made the speaker feel. Each team member ends with a request that the target alcoholic enter treatment.

Identification Contingencies: "What if" Clauses

Each team member is asked to consider any decisions he or she would make if the target alcoholic still refused to accept treatment and continue to drink after the confrontation. The team helps him or her to present this in such a way that the alcoholic will be able to hear what is being said. These statements are called "what if" clauses because they specify *what* each family member is prepared to do *if* the alcoholic refuses to recover. To maintain credibility, it is very important that these not be empty threats; rather they must be seriously contemplated, realistic decisions about how one will proceed with life if the alcoholic continues to drink (e.g., "I refuse to ride with you anymore when you drink and drive"). Expressions of mutual support by other team members at this juncture may facilitate decisions to alter one's behavior in relation to the alcoholic (e.g., "If you ever need a ride, just call me").

Rehearsal

Rehearsal via role-play techniques permits the interventionist and other team members to see exactly how each presentation would be delivered and received. The team provides feedback, and opportunities to repeat the role-play performance are used to improve poor presentations.

Site Selection

The site for the Intervention is carefully selected considering the need for adequate space, time, and privacy, as well as ease or difficulty getting the alcoholic to be there, preferably in a sober condition. The group assigns one or more team members the task of inviting (or better yet, escorting) the alcoholic to this location at the selected time to prevent aborted confrontations. Sometimes the group invites itself to the alcoholic's home, however, there is risk that the team will be refused entry or be asked to leave. Occasionally the team resorts to petty trickery (as one might do for a surprise party) to assure the alcoholic's attendance. The comfort (and safety) of all the team members, including the interventionist, must be considered in site selection, preferably at a neutral location.

The Confrontation

The target alcoholic is invited or brought to the specified meeting place where all the participants have assembled. The target alcoholic is introduced to the interventionist who explains that the group has assembled in order to communicate concerns; he or she is asked to listen quietly until everyone has finished presenting concerns. Team members present their statements in the prearranged order. When done, they ask the target alcoholic to agree to enter treatment, as decided in the training. If the alcoholic remains resistant, they present their "what if" statements and again ask for treatment acceptance. If the alcoholic becomes defensive, argues, or expresses hostility, the interventionist (and/or some of the team members) may express their love and good intentions and request that the alcoholic listen rather than speak as initially promised. However, if the alcoholic acquiesces to recovery, a referral is made and a team member is identified who will monitor the successful completion of treatment. The team commits itself to a follow-up meeting to process the Intervention and plan future confrontations or make other changes that might facilitate family recovery.

CASE APPLICATION

First Contact by Emissary

Joan presented to a family counseling agency with concerns about her younger sister. Her story was one of years of worry about Cheryl, a bright and talented 35-year-old legal aid attorney whose life was in disarray. Joan lived in the same city as Cheryl, and though they were fairly close geographically, their emotional distance had become substantial. Joan had tried many times to convince Cheryl to settle down and stop using alcohol and other drugs (tranquilizers, cocaine) to no avail. But it was the intoxicated behavior in clubs and picking up strange men that worried Joan the most—the risk of contracting HIV was frightening.

The family counselor referred Joan to an interventionist whose office practice was located nearby. Joan explained her concerns once again, this time to Melinda, a social worker with 15 years experience. They agreed on a fee that Joan paid out of pocket.

Initial Assessment

Melinda's inquiry about Joan's attendance at Al-Anon was met with puzzlement, nor had Cheryl availed herself of prior treatment. Despite alcoholism in both parents during childhood, no one in the family ever had received any form of treatment or support. Joan's father had become abstinent in response to a medical crisis, but her mother continued to drink and take tranquilizers prescribed by her doctor. Joan did not wish to target her mother at this time, but was encouraged to consider that as an alternative or eventuality.

It has been suggested (Black, 1982; Wegscheider, 1976) that children raised in alcoholic homes often take on stereotyped roles. In one popular formulation, the eldest child enacts the role of "Family Hero" (Wegscheider, 1976) or "Placater" (Black, 1982) in which he or she becomes parentified, accepting responsibilities ordinarily belonging to parents because the parents are preoccupied with drinking or controlling the drinker and the consequences of the drinking. As the oldest sibling in an alcoholic family, Joan had become a caretaker for her sisters. She was the logical one to initiate this process of Intervention. Joan's concerns about her sister were substantial. Although some therapists might have focused on helping Joan to let go of this internally imposed sense of responsibility, since Joan was not impaired or symtomatic, Melinda simply suggested Al-Anon and proceeded to work with Joan's goal of helping her sister achieve sobriety.

Assessment of the Target Alcoholic and Social Support Network

Cheryl worked various jobs with little stability. She had worked in several law firms doing briefs. She also had worked with a public interest firm, an environmental group, and a political campaign. But she never had passed the Bar exam so she could not practice law. Her financial status was uncertain at times — she occasionally came to Joan for help with her utility bills and rent.

The therapist constructed a genogram (see Figure 3.1) for Cheryl as part of the assessment. The family of origin consisted of Mom and Dad, Joan (the oldest sibling), Donna (the next oldest), then Susan, and lastly Cheryl. Only Joan had married; she had two sons. Dad, a retired

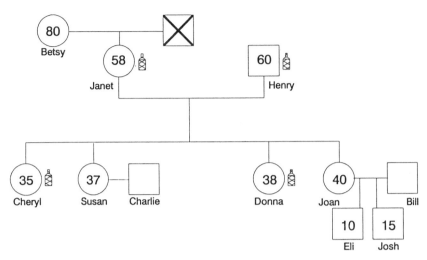

FIGURE 3.1. Cheryl's Genogram as generated by Melinda during assessment phase of intervention.

plumber, quit drinking on advice from his doctor after having suffered a mild stroke in addition to having ulcers and liver problems. Mom, a housewife, had decreased her drinking since Dad had begun to abstain, but she still took prescribed tranquilizers along with her wine. They lived in a suburban area near a midsize city.

Donna was a sales representative for a large manufacturing firm who traveled a lot on the job. Joan had concerns about Donna's drinking, but compared to Cheryl's, both volume and frequency were lower. Donna did not use drugs and was concerned about Cheryl's drug use.

Susan and her live-in boyfriend, Charlie, lived on and worked a small farm. Susan also did crafts that she sold at craft fairs to supplement their meager farming income. Charlie drank occasionally, but no one thought he had a drinking problem.

Grandma Betsy lived nearby in a retirement home. She visited frequently, usually joining the family of origin for ritual Sunday dinners and other holiday and family celebrations.

Cheryl had dated Malcolm on and off over 10 years. Although they had considered marriage at one time, this seemed not to be an active concern now. Both went out with others as well.

Barbara had been the secretary at the environmental organization; subsequently, she and Cherly continued to see each other socially. Barbara, also single, frequented bars and clubs, often joining Cheryl as they "picked up" men.

Father Casey was the parish priest and had known the family since before the girls were born. He knew the family well and was a trusted confidant.

George, a schoolmate and friend from law school, practiced law in the city. He was married and had three small children. Nevertheless, he had retained his friendship with Cheryl. As a person in recovery (sober 7 years), involved as he was in the 12-step programs, he had hovered around the periphery of this family hoping that someday they might be interested in recovery. He had offered to accompany them to AA meetings and had spent time discussing with Joan the treatment needs of Cheryl and her parents.

Figure 3.2 presents the ecomap completed by the therapist Melinda as part of the assessment process. It displays Cheryl's social support network and was used to select team members for the intervention.

Selection of Team Members

Having completed the initial assessment, Melinda proceeded to discuss with Joan the steps of the Intervention process. She asked Joan to help her assemble an Intervention team from among the persons mentioned above. They decided that both parents would be included, despite Mom's "active" status as a chemically dependent person and Dad's "dry without recovery" status. It was recognized that much education would be needed to deal with the attitudes of Joan's parents, but their concern for their daughter would undoubtedly outweigh the ignorance factor. There

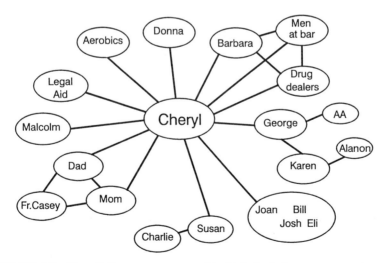

FIGURE 3.2. Cheryl's Ecomap as generated by Melinda during assessment phase of intervention.

had been tension between Cheryl and her parents, largely centered around her apparent loose sexual values and her resistance to settling down. Nonetheless, it was decided that this could be overcome with focusing efforts.

Joan's husband, Bill, and her two sons, Josh (age 15) and Eli (age 10), would be invited. They shared Joan's concerns; the boys had strong antidrug attitudes and Josh worked as a peer counselor at his school's Students Against Drunk Driving (SADD) chapter.

Donna would come; they would have to work around her travel schedule. Her prodrinking attitudes might weaken her resolve to help Cheryl, but her antidrug values would be helpful. There was the risk of overidentification between these sisters, both single professional women in the male work-world.

Susan and Charlie would come as long as it was not done during the harvest season. Their wholesome attitudes had been hard for Cheryl to accept, but they both cared about her.

Grandma Betsy would be invited and would come if provided transportation. She was respected by Cheryl, even though perceived as "old fashioned." Betsy had been through a marriage marred by her husband's alcoholism and had an alcoholic father as well.

They decided to include George because of his concern for the family and his background in recovery. Father Casey also would be invited and probably would attend. Barbara would be excluded because she seemed to be as impaired as Cheryl with an equal degree of substance involvement. But Malcolm would be invited and was likely to come.

Pre-Intervention Training

The first pre-Intervention training session was to be scheduled by telephone once Joan had spoken to the potential participants and determined the best time for a meeting. Melinda gave her several open times that could be offered to save Joan from extra delays. A group room at Melinda's office could be used for the meeting as a videotape would be shown and a large-screen TV was available.

Joan made the calls. Her parents were reluctant to attend. Despite their substantial concerns, Mom seemed to minimize the role of the tranquilizers and alcohol, focusing on the loose sexual mores and the cocaine. Dad was less clear as to his concerns, but he too focused on the sexual and cocaine issues. But ultimately they both agreed to participate. They would provide transportation for Grandma Betsy who also agreed to attend. Father Casey was delighted to attend, as long as no emergencies arose that would interfere.

George was pleased to attend, but asked to bring his wife Karen;

having learned what was happening, Karen wanted to participate. Karen had drunk with Cheryl and George during the law school days; she too had gone into recovery and was now 6 years sober.

George also inquired about whether to invite Cheryl's boss, Henry, the head of the local legal aid agency. Without revealing his knowledge that Henry was active in Al-Anon, George hinted that he felt Henry would be helpful in the process. Joan feared that his involvement would be going a step beyond her level of comfort. Although she really wanted this process to work, she was afraid to risk her sister being fired from her job. Ultimately, George and Joan decided to ask the opinion of the rest of the team at the first meeting. George decided to ask Henry's permission to disclose his Al-Anon connection at the first meeting.

The First Pre-Intervention Training Meeting

Education about Alcoholism and the Intervention Process

The team met as planned with everyone in attendance. They picked a Saturday morning when work interference would be minimal and they could work through lunch into the afternoon if needed. After everyone was introduced, and the day's activities were summarized, they viewed the videos *The Enabler* and *The Intervention* (Johnson Institute, 1978a, 1978b). The former showed a family struggling in vain to control the alcoholism of the wife and mother in the family. The latter showed how an Intervention was done and used to convince her to enter treatment. During the discussion that ensued, questions arose about what constitutes chemical dependency and what kind of treatment Cheryl should be encouraged to seek. The interventionist reviewed the treatment facilities in the area and explored what the family knew about Cheryl's insurance status to see what options she might have. She explained that many people need an intense initial training experience in recovery that often is provided either in an inpatient rehabilitation setting or in an intensive outpatient (day or evening) program. This usually is followed by low-intensity outpatient treatment accompanied by involvement in a 12-step self-help recovery program. Melinda explained the chronic nature of chemical dependency and the need for continuing attention to recovery. This was reinforced by George and Karen, who disclosed details about their recoveries and their continuing relationships with AA and Al-Anon. Melinda added that she would not be fully able to assess Cheryl's needs until she met her, but that from the sounds of it, Cheryl had strong denial about the severity of her addiction problem that could interfere with sobriety maintenance. Given Cheryl's apparent lack of previous treatment, it was difficult to be cer-

tain how intense a treatment she would need, but Melinda indicated
she would be willing to help assess this.

Melinda explained that the team would try to help Cheryl overcome her denial by loving confrontation about how her alcohol and
drug problem was affecting her life and her relationships with them.
Each team member would have the opportunity to say something about
this. Melinda said it would be best to structure their comments as follows: "Describe an incident familiar to both you and Cheryl that caused
you concern, making clear the connection to her substance abuse. Explain how you felt about the incident. Request that Cheryl recover from
her addiction through professional help and 12-step support." Following this instruction, each member in turn was given an opportunity
to provide one example.

List of Alcohol-Related Incidents by Family
and Other Team Members

Figure 3.3 presents Joan's List of Concerns Form about her sister Cheryl's
drinking. Joan began by disclosing that last month Cheryl had come
to her seeking money ($4,000) to pay bills that she had neglected and
now were overdue. This was the third loan this year, and Joan was doubtful that she would ever get the money back. Joan felt angry and sad over
this. She wanted to tell Cheryl that she was "being a jerk" to not pay
her own bills before spending money on drinking and drugs. Melinda
stopped Joan by saying, "Name calling is dangerous in Intervention — it
can cause Cheryl to shut out what you have to communicate. Cheryl
needs to hear that we care about her and have confidence in her ability to change." Joan restated her complaint saying that she wished Cheryl
would become responsible again — that her alcohol and drug problem
had led to irresponsible choices. The team applauded, realizing that
the tone of this confrontation had to be positive to be effective.

Mom volunteered next, remarking that her interactions with Cheryl
had not been positive lately. She felt guilty that perhaps her approach
had pushed Cheryl away. Melinda reminded the team that the key to
Intervention is to do a better job this time than we have done in the
past. Mom looked relieved as she presented her incident. Cheryl had
come to her upset about a romantic rejection by a man who had been
dating her. Cheryl thought he seemed to be upset about the drinking
and cocaine use and had terminated the relationship. Mom had told
Cheryl she shouldn't be drinking heavily and using cocaine. Cheryl had
stormed out of the house yelling that Mom had "a lot of nerve" criticizing her for alcohol and drug use. Mom cried, saying that she felt she
had been a poor example for Cheryl, sometimes taking too many tran-

My Name: ____JOAN_____   Date: _6/15/92_

My concerns are about: ___CHERYL_____

MY CONCERNS	MY FEELINGS
THAT YOU'LL GET HIV	FEAR
LOOSE SEXUAL VALUES	ANGER, DISGUST, SADNESS
DRUNK DRIVING ARREST	FEAR, ANGER
FINANCIAL PROBLEMS —	ANGER, FEAR, SADNESS
LIVING OUTSIDE MEANS	
NEVER PASSED BAR EXAM	SADNESS, FEAR
UNSTABLE WORK PATTERN	SADNESS, FEAR
THAT YOU'LL END UP	FEAR
LIKE MOM + DAD	
NEED TO SETTLE DOWN	ANGER
AT 35	

FIGURE 3.3. Example of List of Concerns Form filled out by Joan in reference to her sister Cheryl.

quilizers when she was overwhelmed with her emotional problems. Melinda responded again reminding Mom that this was not a time to dwell on the past, but rather to focus on the message that Cheryl needed to hear. She continued pointing out that Mom had lived her life in a particular way, doing the best she could do in her circumstances. Cheryl needed advice that would set her on a new course that the family believed would be healthier than the one she had been following. Melinda indicated that if Mom wanted her own help with her current pattern of alcohol and drug use, a referral for counseling could be made.

George asked to go next. His concern was seeing Cheryl function poorly in court, coming to hearings or trials ill-prepared. This was not the Cheryl he studied with in law school — always prepared, knowing the law on the topic being litigated. Her reputation was poor among his colleagues, and he knew she was capable of much more than she had been doing. Karen added that her experiences with Cheryl were similar. She also had seen Cheryl settle for men who had much less to offer than she would ever have tolerated during her law school days.

Dad went next, pointing out that he had refused to give Cheryl money last month. "Let some of the men she sleeps with pay her bills!" he barked at Joan, referring to her recent loan of $4,000. "She has to learn to pay her own bills!" Joan snapped at him saying that Cheryl was at risk of losing her car, apartment, phone, and heat. Melinda observed the tension building between Joan and Dad and responded, "The chemically dependent person becomes manipulative as the disorder progresses. Her addiction will get its way, even at the cost of pitting one relative against another. We will be far stronger if we approach her united than if we approach her divided. Each of you has had to make hard decisions in relation to Cheryl and her disorder. You each love and care about Cheryl, the person, but you are frightened of her illness and what it can do to her. Now we have gathered together to help Cheryl to fight her own disorder — to separate herself from its effect on her life. We need each other to tackle this problem. We can't risk alienating Cheryl or each other."

Others had their turns as well, each getting feedback from Melinda and from the team. They took a lunch break, and each worked individually on making a list of concerns while waiting for the pizzas to arrive.

After lunch, George raised his suggestion that they include another person, Cheryl's boss Henry, in the Intervention. There was controversy about the risk of Cheryl losing her job if Henry heard what was going on with Cheryl. "She could be arrested and lose her eligibility for a law license if her cocaine use became public knowledge." George remarked that Cheryl's drinking and drug use was no secret, but admitted that Henry might find himself in an uncomfortable position with respect to the law and the Bar Association if he formally knew his employee was buying and using illicit drugs. In fact, George admitted that he probably should have reported Cheryl to the impaired lawyers committee long ago. They could coercively put conditions on her license including random or regular urine and breathalyzer monitoring. "Perhaps I can save that as a strategy in the event that Cheryl resists all of the supportive feedback from the Intervention team." Melinda suggested that he save this for the "what if" portion of the Intervention. Considering how far the team had come today, it would seem unwieldy to add another person (Henry) to the team at this point. In fact, Susan suggested that it might be worth trying to do the Intervention later today. Melinda was willing as long as she was out of the office by 6:00 pm. Susan thought Cheryl was planning to drop by her house at 3:00, so perhaps the team could move to the farm. They agreed to do so after some more rehearsals of the presentations.

Rehearsal of the Intervention Confrontation

Melinda pretended to be Cheryl in a role-play of the Intervention. She became defensive whenever she sensed a judgmental attitude, and there were frequent interruptions to give feedback and instant replay of what just had been said. Charlie became a good assistant coach, taking on Melinda's role while Melinda played Cheryl. Effective communication, they learned, involved being specific rather than general, focusing on only one issue or event at a time, surrounding criticisms with compliments and positive affirmations to make it easier to listen, and distinguishing the behavior from the person. Donna mentioned a time when Cheryl came over so drunk that she could barely walk: "I shudder whenever I think about that day. You were driving past the elementary school only two minutes before you arrived at my apartment!" Cheryl had passed out on the sofa and slept until the next morning. Charlie complimented Donna for being so detailed and specific. He also reminded Donna to use compliments and positive statements like: "I was shocked that a responsible lawyer like you would risk driving while intoxicated, but I was very glad you agreed to sleep it off at my apartment rather than driving home in that condition." Melinda complimented Charlie for giving such good feedback.

The Intervention

They assembled at Susan and Charlie's farm, hiding the extra cars behind the barn to retain the element of surprise. Fortunately, Cheryl was 30 minutes late, but sober. Melinda had warned that doing the Intervention while Cheryl was intoxicated would be pointless. Melinda explained to Cheryl that the purpose of the meeting was to give her family and friends an opportunity to tell her how they felt about her alcohol and other drug problems and that her job was to listen carefully until everyone had a chance to speak. Cheryl started to walk out on the meeting, complaining that she had been ambushed, but Karen and Father Casey managed to talk her into staying to hear what they had to say.

The team did a fine job of presenting their concerns in a nonjudgmental way. Cheryl became defensive on several occasions, attacking her father for his former alcoholic indiscretions, her mother for being drugged up throughout her childhood, and Joan for bossing her and her sisters around all the time. Each time, Melinda or one of the other team members stepped in to redirect the process towards Cheryl doing the listening and the team doing the speaking. Melinda pointed out that this was not a perfect family, as no such families exist, but it was a caring family that wanted to make things as right as possible today.

Josh told his aunt Cheryl that he looked up to her as a lawyer—that maybe someday he'd like to go into law too—but he was worried that she would be arrested and lose her license to drive and her right to practice law. Dad, Joan, and George told Cheryl that they wanted her to sign herself into the local rehabilitation program. George and Karen offered to take Cheryl to AA or NA meetings and introduce her to some of their friends after she was discharged.

Hearing from most of the team, Cheryl composed herself and responded that she appreciated their concerns for her, but that it was her life to live and "if you don't like it, well that's too bad!" She got up to leave but Father Casey touched her arm and reminded Cheryl that he had baptized all four sisters and he had watched them grow to maturity. He knew Cheryl as a choir girl and had written a letter of character reference for her to get into law school. He had been listening earlier today to her family and friends talk with genuine concern about what was happening to Cheryl's values and relationships. He knew that somewhere inside there must be a small voice, a conscience, saying that it was time to make a change in her life. He said, "Please, I beg of you, reconsider our request that you seek treatment for your alcohol and drug problem and our offer of support while you concentrate on your recovery."

George studied her face for an indication of her response. A few tears welled up in her eyes as she looked down, then around the room, then down again. George decided to take the soft approach, saying, "We really care a lot about you, Cheryl, otherwise we would not have taken the risk of losing our friendship with you by speaking to you so honestly. We want you to get well from your addiction sickness, just as Karen and I and millions of others have before. We want to help and support you. We can't stand by watching you run yourself into the ground. Please give treatment a chance. See how it is to live sober. Don't reject this opportunity." Karen went over and gave Cheryl a hug. Joan joined in. Cheryl agreed to go to treatment. Everyone was relieved. Melinda called the treatment center to verify the admission.

RESEARCH SUMMARY

Given the popularity and rather widespread use of the Intervention in clinical practice in the United States, there has been surprisingly little research on the efficacy of Intervention. Logan (1983) reported a 90% rate of treatment entry motivated by Intervention on a series of 60 confronted alcoholics. Of those, at 6-month follow-up, 83% completed treatment, and 58–70% became sober, active members in AA.

Another outcome study reported on a series of 24 cases in which an emissary presented to an outpatient agency that offered Intervention (Liepman, Nirenberg, & Begin, 1989). The family emissary was the spouse of the target alcoholic in 15 (62.5%) of the cases. The remainder of emissaries were children, siblings, employers, or other relatives of the target alcoholic. Three-quarters of the target alcoholics were male, and age ranged from 25–76 years with a mean of 44.2 years. Only a third of the alcoholics had sought prior treatment for their alcohol problem and a similar percentage of the emissaries also had sought prior help. The social network assessments identified an average of six additional persons who might become involved in Intervention. An average of four (including the emissary) actually did take part in the pre-Intervention counseling and/or the confrontation (excluding the emissaries, 50% of additional participants were offspring of the alcoholic, 10% were siblings, 10% were friends, 6% were spouses, 18% were other relatives, and the rest were employers or professionals).

The study used a quasiexperimental design for ethical reasons; all appropriate family emissaries presenting to the agency were offered Intervention. Outcomes were compared between the 7 alcoholics who participated in a confrontation session with their family members and the 17 alcoholics who did not participate in a confrontation session despite the preparation and planning sessions with the family.

Outcomes were examined for the 2 years after the family contacted the treatment agency for assistance. Results showed that alcoholics who were confronted in at least one counseling session by their social network were significantly more likely to enter an alcohol detox or rehab program (85.7%) than were nonconfronted alcoholics (16.7%; $\chi^2(1)$ = 10.43, p < .001). Confronted alcoholics also were significantly more likely to both attend AA and enter an alcohol detox or rehab program (57%) than nonconfronted alcoholics (11%; $\chi^2(1)$ = 7.36, p < .01). Moreover, confronted alcoholics remained continuously abstinent significantly longer (M = 11.0 months, SD = 6.2) than nonconfronted alcoholics (M = 2.8 months, SD = 5.7; $t(1)$ = 3.03, p < .01).

Only a disappointing 7 (29%) of social networks actually performed a confrontation! Among families who did perform the confrontation, alcoholics showed good success rates with respect to entry into detox or rehab and subsequent months of continued abstinence, contradicting the old adage often heard from AA members that you must wait until people "hit rock bottom" before they can be helped. The nonconfronting families did not meet with such positive outcomes, suggesting that the formal confrontation, rather than the preparatory family counseling alone, is a necessary component. At least in those families and social networks that were willing and able to confront their alcoholic, readiness for treatment and recovery were enhanced. Unfortunately, because only 29% of networks achieved the confrontation, its dramatic 86% efficacy with that group is diluted to 25% when the entire population of cases is considered.

A series of analyses were conducted to examine differences between families who did and did not complete a confrontation. There were no significant differences between confronted and nonconfronted groups on gender of the alcoholic, the number of members in the social networks that were involved in the counseling, or the number of prior treatments sought by network members or the alcoholic. Neither were there differences in the time span over which the treatment protocol occurred nor the total number of hours of staff–network contact.

Interestingly, the families with an older target alcoholic were less likely to perform the confrontation than those whose target alcoholic was younger. Why the target alcoholics in the nonconfronted group were older is presently unknown. Perhaps the older alcoholics had progressed to a more serious and handicapping stage of their addiction, which made them less likely to permit themselves to be confronted. Perhaps their social network had become so discouraged by their chronicity that they were reticent to spend energy confronting them (though both groups spent comparable time in the motivational counseling program). Perhaps their advanced age intimidated their younger relatives from confronting them out of "respect" or fear. Perhaps the disruptive effect of alcoholism on families of procreation (e.g., children and wives) made the social networks of older alcoholics less likely to carry out this complex and demanding process than the social networks of younger alcoholics which primarily consisted of families of origin (e.g., parents and siblings). It would be important in future studies of this technique to study the process in depth to determine why so many of the families did not follow through to the confrontation and to attempt to obtain a greater yield of confronting families. Only future studies can provide more definitive explanations.

The studies in the literature that measure efficacy of Intervention are insufficient. The only two published studies, described above, were both preliminary. Neither had precise criteria for clinical outcomes, used a randomized clinical trial design, nor had rigorous standards for the process of the pre-Intervention counseling or Intervention. The Logan (1983) report, in its brevity, gave very little detail on the alcoholics and their social networks. Our study had a small number of subjects and a high rate of families who failed to perform the confrontation of the alcoholic. It used a control group that was self-selecting, and raters of outcome were not blind to the treatment condition. Only six (25%) female target alcoholics were studied. Future work should address these shortcomings. In addition, the components of the process should be studied to determine how important each is to the success of the Intervention. Despite the substantial flaws of the two published studies, they are quite consistent in their outcomes. Both studies reported substantial rates of treatment entry by resistant alcoholics when the family was able to complete a confrontation meeting with the alcoholic. Recovery indicators showed substantial improvements in the alcoholics' drinking subsequent to the Interventions. Given the population, this seems remarkable and deserves further study. Family resistance and other factors (e.g., therapist skill and cooperation by the alcoholic) related to completing the Intervention process require further study. Indicators of family recovery outcomes also should be further elaborated. Given the finding that coerced alcoholics seem to do as well as self-motivated alcoholics after similar rehabilitation (Freedberg & Johnston, 1980), there seems little reason to ignore this approach for getting them to enter treatment. Use of Prochaska's stages of change applied to family participants and to the alcoholic would enhance our understanding of this procedure (Prochaska & DiClemente, 1986).

CONCLUSIONS

The Intervention is a promising technique for motivating alcoholics to enter treatment through the efforts of family members and significant others directed by a skilled interventionist. Given the high human and economic costs of untreated alcoholism, this approach provides hope for concerned families when the alcoholic seems mired in denial and refuses to seek treatment. The complexity of the process and the intensity of the involvement required of the family are substantial, but with interest and proper guidance, Intervention can be accomplished. Essential ingredients for a successful Intervention are a well-trained interventionist, a family that is highly motivated to stop living with the alcoholic's drinking, and an alcoholic who attends the Intervention meeting.

REFERENCES

Black, C. (1982). *It will never happen to me*. Denver: MAC Printing and Publication Division.

Collins, J. J., & Allison, M. (1983). Legal coercion and retention in drug abuse treatment. *Hospital and Community Psychiatry, 34*, 1145–1149.

Freedberg, E. J., & Johnston, M. A. (1980). Outcome with alcoholics seeking treatment voluntarily or after confrontation by their employer. *Journal of Occupational Medicine, 22*, 83–86.

Hartman, A., & Laird, J. (1983). *Family-centered social work practice*. New York: Free Press.

Johnson Institute (1975). *I'll quit tomorrow!* Center City, MN: author.

Johnson Institute (1978a). *The enabler*. Center City, MN: author.

Johnson Institute (1978b). *The intervention*. Center City, MN: author.

Johnson, V. (1973). *I'll quit tomorrow*. New York: Harper & Row.

Koppel, F., Stimmler, L., & Perone, F. (1980). The enabler: A motivational tool in treating the alcoholic. *Social Casework: Journal of Contemporary Social Work, 61*, 577–583.

Liepman, M. R. (1984). Alcohol and drug abuse in the family. In J. Christie-Seely (Ed.), *Working with the family in primary care: A systems approach to health and illness* (pp. 422–448). New York: Praeger.

Liepman, M. R., Nirenberg, T. D., & Begin, A. M. (1989). Evaluation of a program designed to help family and significant others to motivate resistant alcoholics into recovery. *American Journal of Drug and Alcohol Abuse, 15*, 209–221.

Liepman, M. R., Silvia, L. Y., & Nirenberg, T. D. (1989). The use of Family Behavior Loop Mapping for substance abuse. *Family Relations, 38*, 282–287.

Liepman, M. R., Wolper, B., & Vazquez, J. (1982). An ecological approach for motivating women to accept treatment for drug dependency. In B. G. Reed, G. M. Beschner, & J. Mondanaro (Eds.), *Treatment services for drug dependent women* (Vol. 2, pp. 1–61; DHHS Publication No. ADM 82-1219). Washington, DC: US Government Printing Office.

Logan, D. G. (1983). Getting alcoholics to treatment by social network intervention. *Hospital and Community Psychiatry, 34*, 360–361.

Miller, W. R., & Hester, R. K. (1986). Inpatient alcoholism treatment: Who benefits? *American Psychologist, 41*, 794–805.

Miller, W. R., & Rollnick, S. (1991). *Motivational interviewing: Preparing people to change addictive behavior*. New York: Guilford Press.

Prochaska, J. O., & DiClemente, C. C. (1986). Toward a comprehensive model of change. In W. R. Miller & N. Heather (Eds.), *Treating addictive behaviors: Processes of change* (pp. 3–27). New York: Plenum.

Salmon, R. W., & Salmon, R. J. (1983). The role of coercion in rehabilitation of drug abusers. *International Journal of the Addictions, 18*, 9–21.

Silvia, L. Y., & Liepman, M. R. (1991). Family Behavior Loop Mapping enhances treatment of alcoholism. *Family and Community Health, 13*, 72–83.

Smart, R. G. (1974). Employed alcoholics treated voluntarily and under constructive coercion: A follow-up study. *Quarterly Journal of Studies on Alcohol, 35*, 196–209.

Smilkstein, G. (1980). The cycle of family function: A conceptual model for family medicine. *Journal of Family Practice, 11,* 223–232.

Steinglass, P., Bennett, L. A., Wolin, S. J., & Reiss, D. (1987). *The alcoholic family.* New York: Basic Books.

Tucker, J. R. (1974). A worker-oriented alcoholism and "troubled employee" program: A union approach. *Industrial Gerontology, 1,* 20–24.

Wegscheider, S. (1976). *The family trap: No one escapes from a chemically dependent family.* Minneapolis, MN: Johnson Institute.

Williams, R. L., & Moffat, G. H. (Eds.). (1975). *Occupational alcoholism programs.* Springfield, IL: Charles C. Thomas.

Chapter 4

A Group Program for Wives of Treatment-Resistant Alcoholics

Joan E. Dittrich

OVERVIEW

For women who live with alcoholics, life can be a stressful merry-go-round of promises broken and hopes unrealized. Some women can live for years with an alcoholic husband unaware that the problems within the marriage are connected to the husbands' drinking or to her own "codependent" or "enabling" responses. The progression of alcoholism is frequently so insidious that wives often do not identify alcoholism as a serious problem until it is in the middle or late stage. By then, of course, the husband's denial may be so firmly embedded and the wife's enabling patterns so entrenched that it becomes virtually impossible for her to convince her husband that he needs treatment. Under such circumstances a woman may seek help for herself.

In recent years, anyone who is living with an alcoholic and is seeking help is sure to encounter an array of self-help books, self-help groups, and professional treatment programs that deal with "codependency." There is such a range in the definitions of codependency (Cermak, 1986; Schaef, 1986; Whitfield, 1984) that it has become a rather generic term. Thus, although much of the advice contained in the codependency literature is sage, it is often very generalized and not always directly applicable to wives of alcoholics. Fortunately, there are a number of self-help books that deal specifically with the problems of those living with non-recovering alcoholics (Al-Anon, 1989; Drews, 1983, 1986; Maxwell, 1976; Wallace, 1990; Woititz, 1979.) Al-Anon was developed with the specific objective of helping those who live with alcoholics to break through their own denial and find self-acceptance (Al-Anon, 1979). Although the professional literature is replete with discussions of the characteristics of wives of alcoholics (Edwards, Harvey, & Whitehead, 1973; Jacob, Favorini, Meisel, & Anderson, 1978; Kogan & Jackson, 1965; Orford, 1976) there are only a few examples in the literature of professional treatment programs designed specifically for wives of nonrecovering alcoholics. Most of these describe individual treatment approaches and do not report any related empirical findings (Bailey, 1963; Estes, 1981; Howard & Howard, 1978; Schutt, 1985). The treatment program described in this chapter targets codependence, or more specifically "co-alcoholism" (Whitfield, 1984) as it applies specifically to wives of alcoholics. It is a systematic program of treatment that was developed so that outcomes can be empirically measured as well as rationally perceived.

The program is a time-limited group treatment for women living with nonrecovering alcoholics. There are eight 1½-hour sessions organized into a three-phase format, similar to Estes' (1981) approach to individual counseling of wives of alcoholics. The first phase (weeks 1–3) is primarily educational; the second phase (weeks 4–6) is experiential; the third phase (weeks 7–8) emphasizes goal setting and planning. The objectives are for the women to (1) increase understanding of alcoholism and family interactions, (2) identify and decrease enabling behaviors, (3) increase self-esteem, (4) decrease depression, and (5) decrease anxiety. The group members' progress can be evaluated pre- and post-treatment via standardized measurements and self-report. A new assessment tool, the Enabling Behaviors Inventory (EBI) (Dittrich & Trapold, 1984) was developed to measure enabling behaviors.

SPECIAL CONSIDERATIONS

This program is intended for women married to nonrecovering alcoholics. The treatment objectives are to help the women decrease their co-alcoholic behaviors, develop positive coping strategies, and make positive plans for their lives. Some programs focus on helping wives modify their husband's behavior (Sisson & Azrin, 1986; Thomas & Santa, 1982). This program is primarily focused on helping wives with their own dysfunctional behaviors such that any modifications of husbands' behavior that occur are considered incidental to the wives attending to their own needs.

Characteristics of Clients

Although there need be no specific requirements regarding the duration or severity of husbands' alcoholism, most of the women who sought out this treatment did so only after years of unsuccessful attempts at other treatments. It was not at all unusual for the alcoholic husbands to have made several attempts at sobriety over the course of the marriage, including having attended AA meetings or gone through professional treatment programs. Many of the women had also sought help in the past through either Al-Anon, individual counseling, family work conjunctive to their husbands' professional treatment, or marital counseling. Women who were in individual therapy or attending Al-Anon at the time of treatment were encouraged to continue doing so.

Upon occasion, women who were either recently separated or divorced from their husbands were included in the program. Most of these women had continuing contact with their estranged partners, often because of child-rearing or financial matters, and so still needed to deal with the alcoholic on a fairly regular basis. Having one or two of these women in a group added perspective, providing group members who still lived with their alcoholic spouses with models for managing their lives if they were to elect separation.

The groups were restricted to female spouses of male alcoholics for several reasons. First, most of the research on characteristics and problems of spouses of alcoholics has been conducted on women (Edwards, Harvey, & Whitehead, 1973). Second, it was assumed that women are likely to perceive themselves as having more experiences in common with other wives of alcoholics than with husbands of alcoholics, thus increasing the chances of group bonding, trust, and support. Indeed, the literature supports the notion that the experiences and behaviors of male and female spouses of alcoholics differ in several ways (Estes & Baker, 1981). Third, there was a clinical concern that if both male and female spouses of alcoholics were included in these groups, the women group members might tend to "care-take" the men group members, adding a codependent dynamic to the group that would be difficult to identify and manage.

Screening

Screening of group members is important and is best conducted in pregroup individual interviews. Family drinking, psychological, and marital histories should be taken. The Michigan Alcoholism Screening Test (MAST) (Selzer, 1971) has been adapted to screen for alcoholism in both the husband and the wife (Dittrich & Trapold, 1984). If it becomes evident that the wife may have a drinking problem herself, this needs to be addressed before membership in the group is acceptable. Group members also need to be able to tolerate the structure of the group and its educational format. Women who are in acute crisis (e.g., threatening or threatened with severe violence or suicide) obviously need more immediate intervention. Similarly, women who are so agitated, depressed, or psychotic that they cannot tolerate the group format or cognitively process the information given, will be better served by a different treatment modality.

Treatment Setting and Format

All groups have been conducted in outpatient settings, in either private practice or mental health clinics. Although it is conceivable that similar groups could be conducted by alcoholism treatment centers on an outpatient basis, it should be emphasized that this is a primary treatment modality for women living with active alcoholics, and is intended neither as an adjunct to the alcoholics' treatment nor as an intervention to convince the alcoholic to seek help.

The group format was chosen because wives of alcoholics tend to believe that they should be able to solve their own and their husbands' problems by themselves. Alcoholic husbands frequently blame the wives for their drinking and for family problems and reinforce the notion that it is up to the wives to solve these problems. Wives typically have few confidants, and sometimes they find that the people they do confide in collude with the alcoholic and hold the wife responsible. Thus, wives learn to hide their problems and to isolate themselves. Group support and identification can be effective for the development of self-esteem and as an antidote to isolation. Gentle confrontations by group members can also help spouses break down denial and recognize their enabling and other dysfunctional behaviors. A group size of five to eight members seems to be ideal for promoting positive interactions among group members. Sessions are typically scheduled for 1½–2 hours, depending on group size.

Therapist Characteristics

Because loss of trust is a crucial issue in the alcoholic marriage, it is essential for group members to trust the therapists. To this end, it was assumed that wives of alcoholics would feel more comfortable with female therapists who were familiar with their issues. The therapists must be professionally trained and experienced in group dynamics and psychotherapy and be knowledgeable in the areas of substance abuse, codependency, and family dynamics. Although it is not necessary for therapists to be "recovering" people, it is essential that they have a working familiarity with 12-step recovery programs. A therapist who has "been there before" often earns group members' trust and positive regard more quickly. If the professional therapist is not personally involved in recovery work, it is advisable to have a cotherapist who is in a 12-step program.

DESCRIPTION OF THE TREATMENT METHOD

This group treatment program for wives of nonrecovering alcoholics is divided into an educational phase (Sessions 1–3), an experiential phase (Sessions 4–6), and a goal-setting phase (Sessions 7–8). Table 4.1 provides a general outline of the group treatment plan.

Educational Phase (Sessions 1–3)

The first three group sessions have a primarily educational focus. The therapist spends much of the group time giving informal lectures about alcoholism and family dynamics. Group members are introduced to a variety of books and articles about alcoholism and family relationships. Although group members are given the opportunity to discuss the information provided and to process it in terms of their own situations, they are not required to disclose in-depth information about themselves

TABLE 4.1. Overview of Treatment Program for Wives of Alcoholics

A. Screening
    1. Pre-group individual interviews
    2. Use of tests to screen for spouse's alcoholism

B. Educational Phase (Sessions 1–3)
    1. Definition of alcoholism
    2. Education on the alcoholic husband
    3. Family dynamics
    4. Co-alcoholism and enabling behaviors of wives
    5. Sexuality in the alcoholic marriage
    6. Treatment and recovery
    7. Guided imagery and homework

C. Experiential Phase (Sessions 4–6)
    1. Identification and management of feelings
    2. Assertive responding
    3. Role-plays of interactions with alcoholics
    4. Introduction to lifestyle options
    5. Homework and In Vivo practice

D. Goal-Setting Phase (Sessions 7–8)
    1. Discussion of lifestyle options
    2. Development of contingency plans
    3. Access to support groups and treatment options

during this phase. Thus trust is allowed to develop gradually as group members become more familiar with each other and the therapist.

Session 1

Introductions

The first order of business is for the therapist to introduce herself, including her experience and credentials. Next, the therapist needs to describe confidentiality, both in terms of the obligations and exceptions involved in the therapist's privilege and in terms of the expectation that group members will maintain confidence in regard to each other. The therapist states that she will attempt to model effective communication by addressing group members in a direct yet supportive and caring manner and asks group members also to attempt to communicate with one another in this way. The ideal group climate is described as a supportive, trusting environment that allows individuals to feel comfortable making changes and trying new behaviors. The therapist also informs the group that the material is presented in a sequential, building-block format, and so asks for consistent attendance and participation. The group members are then asked to introduce themselves by name and they are invited to make a brief comment, if they wish.

Group Objectives

Objectives are described to the group members in the following manner. First, the focus is to remain on the group members and what can help them, in contrast to focusing on the alcoholic husbands and what group members can do to help them. Second, they will learn about alcoholism and how it affects family members, especially spouses and children. Third, they will learn to identify and stop negative coping strategies and adopt and practice positive coping strategies. Fourth, they will learn to make rational and assertive decisions about their current lifestyle and future goals. Finally, they will find support in the group and learn about other support systems to participate in after this program is completed.

Alcoholism Described

In this first lecture, the therapist describes alcoholism as a disease process (King, Bissel, & Holding, 1978). Alcoholism is defined based on three sources: the revised third edition of the *Diagnostic and Statistical Manual of Mental Disorders* of the American Psychiatric Association

(DSM-III-R; APA, 1987), the National Council on Alcoholism (1972), and Step One of AA—"We admitted that we were powerless over alcohol. . ." (Alcoholics Anonymous, 1976). Alcoholism is further described as an illness with a progressive and insidious course. The wives are informed that from 10–15% of the American drinking population will have a drinking problem at some point in their lives and many of these will become full-fledged alcoholics (Cahalan, 1970). Early-, middle-, and late-stage alcoholism are described, as well as Johnson's (1980) model of the addictive process. Group members learn that most alcoholics start drinking because it makes them feel euphoric, but as the alcoholism progresses, they feel bad much of the time and need to drink just to approximate feeling normal. They also learn that alcohol becomes the priority in the alcoholic's life, in spite of his protests to the contrary. Physical complications related to alcohol are described in some detail and group members are referred to books and articles that also discuss the physical effects of alcohol (Estes & Heineman, 1981; Gibbons, 1992; Wallace, 1985). The familial nature of alcoholism is also discussed. Genetic inheritability is presented as a definite phenomenon, citing Goodwin's (1976) twin studies. Environmental and psycho-social factors are also emphasized, noting the observations that children of alcoholics tend to marry and even remarry alcoholics, in spite of stated intentions not to repeat the mistakes of their parents in adulthood (Black, 1981). Group members are also informed that multiple addictions are not unusual, and that many alcoholics engage in compulsive behaviors related to sex, food, work, gambling, or drug use.

Psychology of Alcoholism

In this second lecture, the phenomenology of the alcoholic is described (cf. Wallace, 1981). This is done to help the wives realize that many of their husbands' unpleasant behaviors are defensive manifestations of the alcoholic disorder and not necessarily deliberate attempts to hurt, humiliate, or confuse the spouse.

Denial is described as the hallmark psychological sign of alcoholism and as a pervasive defense mechanism that develops to protect the alcoholic from facing the reality of his drinking and its consequences. The alcoholic's denial also serves the function of keeping others off-track, so that they too may be kept from acknowledging the full impact of the alcoholic's drinking. It is proposed that most alcoholics do not start drinking with the intention of becoming alcoholic and even as their drinking becomes increasingly problematic, they are unlikely to adopt "alcoholic" as a role they ascribe to themselves. Alcoholics cannot accept the guilt they feel over putting their addiction in front of their other priorities. If they acknowledged their guilt, they might have to acknowledge their alcoholism and its impact on the family, so instead their guilt is projected on to others in the form of blame. Wives of alcoholics need to understand the processes of denial and projection in order to see why they are frequently accused of overreacting and why they are often blamed for things that are not at base their fault.

Depression and alcoholism are also discussed. The correspondence between alcoholism and suicide is noted (Schuckit, 1979). Group members learn that some alcoholics are depressed prior to drinking, and that some become depressed by virtue of the physiologic effects of alcohol on the central nervous system. The energy required to maintain denial and to keep functioning despite a progressing addiction is believed to deplete the person's inner resources and contribute to depression. Depression in alcoholism is often atypical as it may be masked by drinking "highs." The wife of an alcoholic may not observe typical depressive symptoms such as expressed hopelessness or dsyphoria, either because the alcoholic is hiding these symptoms from her as part of the denial process, or because his depression is expressed primarily through withdrawal from family activities, irritability, or even occasional rages. The high correspondence between alcoholism and family violence is also noted (Roy, 1977). This lecture is often a somber one for wives to hear, so a bit of hope may be given by talking about the potential benefits of treatment and recovery. However, the group members are again reminded that the purpose of the group is to help them make choices about their own lives, and that this is not a class on how to get their spouses into treatment.

Homework

During the following week, group members are encouraged to consider the characteristics of alcoholism that apply to their own situation. They are also asked to think about the development and progression of their husbands' alcoholism and any emerging physical complications. Telephone numbers are exchanged and group members are encouraged to make contact with one another between sessions. The EBI is distributed and they are asked to complete it for the following week.

Session 2

The lecture topics for this session, "alcoholism as a family disease" and the concepts of "enabling" and "co-alcoholism," are introduced. Before the lectures, group members are encouraged to share their impressions from last week's session and to share an incident during the week that they perceived differently in light of what they have learned. They are also asked if any of them reached out with phone calls to the others, and they are encouraged to make calls again this week.

Family Disease

Alcoholism is described as a disease or disorder that affects the entire family. Denial is perceived to serve a similar function for the family as it does for the alcoholic individual, that is, denial in the family protects the whole family from acknowledging the full negative impact of the drinking behaviors. Denial also maintains homeostasis because if the negative consequences of drinking are not realized, there will be no perceived need for radical changes in family structure, such as full recovery or removal of the alcoholic from the home. Homeostasis is also maintained via what Jackson (1954, 1956) called the "family crisis and adjustment cycle." In this cycle, any new stress experienced by the family as a result of the alcoholic's drinking is responded to with some sort of behavioral adjustment by one or more family members. Each adjustment is typically characterized by family members, particularly the spouse, assuming a greater burden of responsibility for family matters. Thus with each adjustment, less is expected from the alcoholic. He may become increasingly psychologically and/or physically withdrawn from the family, which actually provides him more time to engage in drinking behaviors. The wife, on the other hand, is assuming more and more responsibility to compensate for her husband's withdrawal and she eventually becomes overwhelmed and resentful in regard to her increased share of family responsibilities.

Enabling Behaviors and Co-alcoholism

In this lecture, enabling behaviors are described as emotional, behavioral, or cognitive reactions to the alcoholism that are counterproductive to the wife's self-esteem and also inadvertently reinforce the husband's continued drinking. Examples of typical enabling behaviors are listed in the EBI. Group members are directed to review their EBI responses and analyze how these behaviors are enabling. To illustrate, the therapist uses the EBI response "drove with the alcoholic while he was intoxicated." Most group members admit to having engaged in this behavior despite their knowledge that an intoxicated driver is dangerous to himself, his passengers, and other motorists. They often explain that they made the decision to ride with the alcoholic in order to reduce tension. For example, if a wife offers to drive or attempts to keep the car keys from her drunk husband, he may become threatening or rageful and "make a scene." Thus, in order to avoid public humiliation, the wife will ride with him. The alcoholic may also minimize his intoxication, deny that his judgment and reaction time are dulled, or even assert that his intoxicated driving is still better than her sober driving, thus intimidating the wife into submission. The alcoholic's grandiosity and denial interacts with the wife's denial, need for privacy, and low self-esteem to create a situation in which the wife consents to a behavior that she knows is not in her own best interest. Furthermore, her compliance with his wishes reinforces the alcoholic's behavior and bolsters his psychological defense system. Once this example has been analyzed, group members are asked to think of other behaviors in which they typically engage that might be enabling.

Co-alcoholism is then defined as a general tendency to react and adjust to the alcoholic's behaviors in order to reduce conflict and preserve the family unit, without addressing the co-alcoholic's own needs or the stress that accumulates within the family as a result of tolerating the alcoholic's inappropriate behavior. Co-alcoholism is considered a general syndrome, with enabling behaviors as the specific symptoms. Group members are encouraged to become aware of both the overall tendency to act in ways that are co-alcoholic and to identify and change specific enabling behaviors.

Guided Imagery Exercise

The Al-Anon (1989) concepts of "detachment" and "responding versus reacting" are introduced to help group members learn how to change enabling behaviors. Detachment is defined as the ability to notice one's emotional and cognitive reactions to a given situation, without making an immediate or automatic reaction. Responding is defined as positive behaviors that are deliberately executed and not enabling. The example of riding with an intoxicated spouse is again used to illustrate. Group members are instructed to close their eyes and focus on their breathing in order to relax. They are then guided to imagine themselves in a situation in which their husband is drunk and insistent on driving. They imagine this scene as if it were occurring in the present moment and simply notice their emotional and cognitive reactions. They imagine themselves reacting as they would if they were to express their automatic or immediate reactions. Then they are guided into a deeper state of relaxation in which they are experiencing a strong sense of integrity and self-worth. In this state, they are asked to imagine making positive responses in which their needs are clearly asserted and in which they are not attempting to protect the alcoholic from the consequences of his own behavior. The goal of this exercise is to help group members experience detachment and proactive responding as an alternative to reactive enabling behaviors.

Homework

During the following week each group member is told to note five incidents of reactive behaviors and to analyze how these behaviors were enabling. They are also to note five incidents in which they detached from a situation and were able to change the process from a reactive to a responsive one. Group members are again encouraged to phone one another and share some of their experiences at attempting to stop enabling. They are also asked to read Wegsheider's (1981) description of family enabling roles, and the chapter on sex in *The Dilemma of the Alcoholic Marriage* (Al-Anon, 1989).

Session 3

The third session begins with a review of the group members' week, their attempts to phone one another, and a discussion of their experience of the homework assignment on enabling behaviors. The lecture topics for this session, "roles of family members" and "sexuality in the alcoholic marriage," are introduced.

Family Roles

In this lecture, the development of roles within the family is described as a process whereby family members defend against core feelings and deny or circumvent the problems of alcoholism and co-alcoholism. In many alcoholic families, there is such a large degree of denial and minimization around what the real problems are, that family members begin to doubt their own perceptions. Children may witness their father drink to the point of passing out only to be told, "Daddy's just tired, sweetheart." They may be discouraged from talking about Dad's drinking amongst themselves as well as to people outside the family. As Black (1981) observed, the family code becomes, "Don't feel, don't think, don't talk." In order to defend themselves against their inner feelings and perceptions that are disallowed in the family, each member develops characteristic defense mechanisms and behavioral roles. These roles provide family members with a predictable pattern of interaction and diminish the likelihood that any one family member will step outside his or her assigned role and force the family to address core issues, such as alcoholism, that are at the root of the family's dysfunction. Wegsheider's (1981) alcoholic family roles are described in detail and group members are encouraged to identify themselves and their family members in the various roles of the "Dependent," the "Chief Enabler," the "Family Hero," the "Lost Child," the "Mascot," and the "Scapegoat." Whereas wives of alcoholics tend to assume the Chief Enabler role, it is explained that roles may be interchangeable among family members, especially the children, and that not all roles are always assumed in a given family.

Group members are encouraged to think about their family of origin and to consider the roles they may have assumed as children. They are asked to recall their own attitudes and feelings toward both the Dependent and the Chief Enabler, especially if they came from alcoholic or dysfunctional families. They are then asked to consider how their own children might view them in their present role of Chief Enabler. This discussion invites the group members to acknowledge any resentment their children might have toward them for their co-alcoholism and enabling behaviors. This discussion needs to be handled delicately, as wives of alcoholics are acutely sensitive in regard to their child-rearing practices. They may resist exploring how their own behavior could be hurtful to their children and instead may prefer to focus on the negative impact of the alcoholics' behavior.

Sexuality

Group members are often anxious to hear this lecture, as sexuality is something they typically do not discuss. They are directed to the books in their bibliography that address sexual issues (Al-Anon, 1989; Drews, 1983, 1986; Woititz, 1979). Both the psychological and physiological dynamics of sex in the alcoholic marriage are presented.

There is a variety of sexual dynamics that occur in an alcoholic marriage. First, there is the situation in which the wife loses interest in sex. Her loss of interest or desire can be the result of several factors. As the husband's alcoholism progresses, his self-care habits may deteriorate, and she may find him physically less appealing. When drunk he may demand sex or be insensitive to his wife's needs and desires. The alcoholic may also begin to experience impotence, or his arousal threshold may change. In order to achieve arousal or orgasm, he may begin to experiment with sexual behaviors that his wife finds unpleasant or even repulsive. An alcoholic will sometimes engage in affairs in attempts to "cure" sexual dysfunctions. His wife will then refuse to be sexual with him out of hurt and anger, or in some cases due to relief that he is getting his needs met elsewhere and not bothering her anymore.

The majority of wives of alcoholics who withdraw from sex seem to do so as the alcoholism progresses and the wife assumes the greater share of family responsibilities and control. She may lose respect for the alcoholic and cease to enjoy his company in everyday situations. Because she no longer feels like there is an intimate, sharing partnership between them, she may have no desire for physical intimacy. Group members are advised that loss of sexual interest is a natural response to a withdrawn, nonparticipatory, or rageful spouse. However, the women are reminded that sexuality is an integral and potentially rewarding part of married life, and that their loss of desire may represent a loss to themselves as well as to their husbands.

Another dynamic common to the alcoholic marriage occurs when the wife continues to have sex not so much for the fulfillment it can provide but as a means of appeasement or conflict avoidance. For example, some wives will have sex to make things right after a fight, to assure the alcoholic's fidelity, or as a reinforcer to control the alcoholic's drinking or other abusive behaviors. The concept of sexual addiction is introduced and group members are informed that some alcoholics may have sexual compulsions that are separate from alcoholism (Schneider, 1988; SLAA, 1989). Finally, it is also affirmed that in some alcoholic marriages, the sexual relationship remains intact and mutually satisfying, even if other aspects of the marriage are dysfunctional. A satisfying sexual relationship can provide the foundation for rebuilding a relationship if recovery occurs.

Treatment and Recovery

The various types of alcoholism treatment are reviewed (inpatient, outpatient, AA, behavior therapy, family and marital therapy). The relative merits of each treatment modality are discussed. The wives are encouraged to participate in conjoint treatment as much as possible and to also find a group or individual therapist for themselves, if and when their husbands do enter treatment. The wives are also informed that during the early stages of recovery the alcoholic is often very self-involved and that spouses often feel left out (Drews, 1983). Furthermore, wives are informed that there is a great deal more to the recovery process than simple abstention from alcohol and that the marital relationship is often as much "at-risk" during early recovery as during active drinking.

Homework

Group members are asked to think about and discuss how their own sexuality and sexual interest has correlated with the progression of their husband's alcoholism. They are to write a brief summary of all the ways they have changed as their husband's alcoholism has progressed (e.g., what roles have they taken on? what enabling behaviors do they engage in now that they would not have found acceptable at one time? how has their sexuality changed?) Finally they are to imagine new ways of behaving that are more in line with how they would genuinely like to be.

Experiential Phase (Sessions 4–6)

The next three group sessions are more interactive and process orient- ed than the initial educationally oriented sessions. Group members should by now have a working understanding of alcoholism and co- alcoholism and should have enough trust in the therapist and other group members to begin more in-depth processing of their own ex- perience and behaviors. Although the therapist still imparts informa- tion, her style gradually becomes less didactic and more facilitative. Group members are encouraged to share their own experiences as well as provide supportive and gently confrontative feedback to other group members. The experiential phase focuses on the identification and management of feelings and the practice of communicating with as- sertive, nonenabling responses.

Session 4

Identification of Feelings

The session begins with a brief lecture on the recognition of feeling states. Five basic feelings states are identified; scared, hurt, mad, sad, and glad. These are presented in hierarchical format, with "scared" (abandonment fear, separation anxiety) considered the most basic nega- tive emotion and often the most difficult to acknowledge or tolerate, whereas "glad" is considered the most acceptable and easy to tolerate. The intervening feeling states, "hurt" (rejection, humiliation, shame); "sad" (depression, sadness); and "mad" (anger, irritation, frustration) are considered to be respectively higher-level defensive reactions to the more basic "scared" feelings, and as such are often more acceptable to the individual and more readily expressed. This hierarchical classification of feeling states is presented to group members as a heuristic device to help them identify their own affective reactions and to realize that they may frequently experience feeling states at a level outside of their immediate awareness. For example, the wife who reacts with rage when her husband arrives late, may only be aware of her anger and not recog- nize deeper feelings of rejection or abandonment.

Exercise in feelings identification and management

Each group member shares a situation that occurred during the previ- ous week and to which she had an emotional reaction. She is then asked to identify as many of the five basic feeling states as she can recall experiencing in the situation. Other group members are encouraged to respond supportively to the woman sharing her experience, and to identify the feeling states they might have experienced in a similar situation. Ideally, a variety of feeling states are identified as different levels of affective responses to a single situation. The group members are then asked to apply what they learned in Session 2 about detachment and responding and to develop hypothetical responses to the presented situation, taking into consideration a fuller awareness of their feeling reactions. In other words, once a group member has accurately identified and acknowledged her affective reactions to a situation, she is better able to formulate a behavioral response that is consistent with her feeling state. The therapist actively models this process of recognizing feeling states and developing appropriate responses. All group members are encouraged to share and process situations in this manner. If they are unable to recall situations from their own lives, the therapist provides hypothetical situations.

Homework

Group members are encouraged simply to notice their feeling reactions to situations that occur in the upcoming week. They are asked to make a daily list of situations, their feeling reactions, and their behavioral responses.

Session 5

Assertive Responding

The focus of the next session is on assertive responding. The group members are briefly introduced to the concepts of assertive, passive, and aggressive responses. They are asked to apply their newly acquired feelings-identification skills in assertive "I-statements." They are given the sentence formula, "When you . . . *(offending behavior),* then I feel . . . *(feeling state),* and my request/preference is for you to . . . *(assertive request).* Group members are taught not to get distracted by the person they are responding to and to make bottom-line requests. For wives of alcoholics, the bottom-line request is frequently related to asking the alcoholic to stop drinking or get treatment. The group members are encouraged to make these requests occasionally and always in a rational, assertive, and nonemotionally charged manner. However, they are also encouraged to make behavior change requests that are relevant to the specific offending behavior, not just to drinking. For example, a wife might make the following assertive statement: "When you drink, you ignore the children's requests for time with you, and I am saddened and concerned for their self-esteem. . . . " Instead of simply requesting that the husband stop drinking, the request might be " . . . and I would like you to give the children your attention more consistently." Group members are shown that learning to communicate assertively helps them to directly state the problem as they see it. Thus, they will not be colluding with or enabling the alcoholism. They are reminded that although effective communication combats their co-alcoholism, it offers no guarantee that the alcoholic will respond in the ways that they have requested.

Exercise

Group members use the situations listed in their homework assignments to practice identifying feelings and formulating assertive, nonenabling responses. The therapist facilitates discussion and role-play around these situations.

Homework

The members' assignment for the next week is to make a daily list of situations, their feeling states, and their behavioral responses. They are to practice making assertive responses in these real-life situations.

Session 6

Practice

This session is dedicated to more practice of identifying feeling states and assertive responding. At this point in the group's development, group members are typically quite comfortable with one another and the interactions are lively and supportive. Group members review the real-life situations described in their homework and provide one another with feedback and suggestions, so they are problem solving with one another. Ideally, the therapist is able to take a much less active role in this session, although she still facilitates role-play and discussion and keeps the group focused and on task.

Homework

Toward the end of Session 6, group members are presented with five lifestyle options. These options are presented in preparation for the last phase of treatment, which focuses on goal setting and lifestyle planning. The five lifestyle options are: (1) maintain status quo; (2) improve coping strategies—stop enabling and be more assertive; (3) intervention—make preparations for separation contingent upon whether the alcoholic takes steps to stop drinking or get into recovery within a specified time frame; (4) separation from alcoholic—consider reunification if recovery occurs after separation; (5) divorce. These options are described in detail in Table 4.2. For homework, they are asked to write scenarios for each one of these lifestyle options. They are asked to consider what might occur in their lives to prompt them to choose each of the options, and what might need to happen in order for each scenario to become a positive choice.

Goal-Setting Phase (Sessions 7–8)

The final two sessions are used to help group members set goals for themselves and apply the knowledge and skills they have acquired to problems they may encounter in the future.

Session 7

Lifestyle Options and Goal Setting

At the beginning of this session, each group member reads her homework assignment on her five lifestyle options, and the feasibility of these options now and in the future is discussed. Each woman is then encouraged to identify the option she feels most comfortable with for the present. She is asked to set goals for herself in terms of practicing skills and behaviors that will bring her more gratification in her present lifestyle. She is also instructed to establish criteria that would signal the time to move into a different lifestyle option. For example, a woman might feel that with the self-confidence she has gained from the treatment program, she is able to set the goal of enrolling in college. Whereas she may be willing to tolerate her husband's criticism of her return to school, his refusal to provide financial support for the endeavor might be the criterion behavior that signals her to choose a new lifestyle for herself, such as separation or divorce.

As the wife's co-alcoholism diminishes, so may her toleration for the alcoholic's inappropriate behavior. Thus, some of the lifestyle options considered by the wife are associated with a choice to separate from the alcoholic unless he stops drinking or gets into treatment. The therapist may review information presented in Session 1 about alcoholism treatment and recovery. Methods of encouraging a resistant alcoholic to pursue treatment are discussed. Guided Intervention (see

TABLE 4.2. Five Livestyle Options

Option	Behavior	Degree of change
1. Maintain status quo	Continue enabling	No lifestyle change
2. Improve coping strategies	Stop enabling Become aware of feelings Make assertive responses	Minimal lifestyle change
3. Intervention	Ask alcoholic to enter treatment and/or abstain within specific time frame Prepare to separate from alcoholic if above conditions not met Prepare for conjoint treatment and/or relapse management if alcoholic does enter treatment	Considerable *potential* lifestyle change (dependent on alcoholic's response)
4. Separation from alcoholic	Having decided current living conditions are intolerable, physically separate from the alcoholic Stipulate conditions for reunification (e.g., alcoholic enters treatment, abstains from alcohol and/or verbal abuse, marital counseling) Consider divorce if above conditions not met in certain time frame	Extreme lifestyle change in terms of living arrangements, property division, finances, child custody and visitation
5. Divorce	Having considered or attempted any of options 1–4, and finding those options unworkable or unsuccessful, separate and file for divorce Take positive steps in creating a new life and avoid dysfunctional relationships	Radical lifestyle change in terms of legal implications, fear of the unknown, psychological sense of finality and loss

Chapter 3, this volume) is presented as a future option for wives who have ample support systems. Each group member assesses the feasibility of this method for her situation, given the support systems available to her.

Homework

The final homework assignment is to write about "the most important thing I learned in the treatment program" and "my present and future plans." The latter is to include an accounting of immediate goals and a plan to reassess those goals and to recognize when goals or lifestyle options should be changed.

Session 8

Finalization of Goals and Plans

For the final session, progress is reviewed, individual problem-solving strategies are discussed, and goals and plans as outlined in the home-work assignment are finalized. Evaluation forms are completed and post-tests are administered. Group members make commitments to further meetings or treatment. They are encouraged to stay in contact with one another and to attend Al-Anon. Individual follow-up sessions with the therapist are offered. Some groups make plans to meet again in 6 months to follow up their progress on goals, some decide to continue to meet together regularly, whereas others make plans to attend Al-Anon together. During this session, the therapist also talks about the joys and struggles of alcoholism recovery (Johnson, 1980; Larsen, 1987; O'Far-rell & Cowles, 1989). In order not to provide false hope, group members learn that many marriages do not survive the early stages of recovery. They are advised that both for the alcoholic and for the fami-ly, recovery can be lifelong work, with lifelong struggles and rewards. Marital or family therapy designed specifically for couples in recovery is recommended. The treatment program is usually concluded with a closing exercise such as the one below.

Closing Exercise

Each member thinks of one tangible, material gift that she would like to give to the person on her right. In round-robin fashion, each person offers her right-hand neighbor the imagined material gift. Then each member thinks of an intangible gift or wish for her left-hand neighbor, and in turn these immaterial wishes are given out.

CASE APPLICATION

The group selected for case study was chosen because group members showed progress both in terms of dependent measures and self-report. Additionally, events that occurred in some of the individual members' lives had significant influence on group behavior and interaction, providing extra challenge for the therapists. This group was conducted by a professional therapist, and a cotherapist who was married to a recovering alcoholic and who had been in Al-Anon for five years.

There were six group members, who ranged in age from 31 to 68, with a median age of 42. Table 4.3 presents identifying information for each group member. All of the women were in their first marriage, and

TABLE 4.3. Characteristics of Case Example Group Members

Name[a]	Age	Years Married	Main treatment issues	Status at follow-up
Alice	68	45	Resigned to caring for her ailing husband, she sought companionship and support from the group; husband died of alcohol-complicated heart disease during the treatment program	Widowed
Elaine	53	26	Depressed, complaining; two alcoholic children; resistant to change at first, eventually separated from husband who then entered treatment	Separated and reunited
Colette	39	14	Husband had multiple affairs and was alcoholic; she learned to identify and express her feelings of anger and betrayal and to trust husband's commitment to change	Married
Sylvia	45	16	Pursued graduate degree to obtain financial independence; avoided husband at children's expense; reinvolved herself in children's lives	Divorced
Beverly	31	9	Staged a guided intervention without sufficient support; eventually left husband because marriage was no longer fulfilling to her	Separated, divorce in process
Mary	38	17	She physically abused her unemployed husband; learned to recognize her anger, practiced assertiveness, and stopped aggressiveness	Married

[a]Names and exact ages of group members have been altered to protect confidentiality

had been married an average of 18 years. Their husbands had been drinking problematically an average of 16 years. All but one of the women had attended Al-Anon at one time or another. All of their husbands had attempted to quit drinking on their own, but only three of them had actually sought professional or AA assistance. None of the husbands were abstinent at the time of the group. Scores on the MAST confirmed that all the husbands were indeed alcoholic and suggested that at least two of the wives had engaged in problem drinking at one time. Interviews confirmed that none of the group members had drinking problems at the time of treatment. Occasional spousal violence had occurred among three of the six couples, and in one case it was the wife who frequently hit her alcoholic husband. Four of the six wives reported that they were convinced or suspected that their husbands had been sexually unfaithful to them.

During initial screening interviews, it became apparent that many of the women had high expectations of what the group might do for them. Although several of them might be classified as "long-suffering" codependents, they also presented as sick and tired of the way things were. They had exhausted their own coping skills repertoires and were looking for new strategies to effect changes in their lives. They were, in effect, anticipating a "way out" of their long-suffering status. In contrast to this overall mood for change was Alice, who was 68 years old and the group's senior member. Her husband of 45 years was ill from several alcohol-related diseases and still drinking. Alice was resigning herself to a bleak future of caring for her sick and "ornery" husband and hoping only for support and companionship from the group members.

Educational Phase

As previously described, this treatment is primarily didactic and highly structured by the therapists. Most of the group members seemed comfortable enough with this format, although it was apparent that several of them would have liked to jump into problem solving immediately. Elaine, age 53, who eventually separated from her husband of 26 years, and who had attended Al-Anon for years, especially seemed to want to monopolize group time. The structure of the treatment program actually provided the therapists with a means for gently redirecting Elaine back to the group agenda. Thus, during this early part of treatment when trust and relationships were first developing, the therapists were able to rely on structure rather than confrontation to keep the group focused and prevent one member from dominating the floor.

The group members were encouraged to make phone contact with one another throughout the 8-week period. During the educational phase, they were reminded each week to call the person on their right for a brief supportive "check-in." There were few calls the first week. The women were not used to reaching out, and they hesitated to make a call for fear they might be seen as intrusive. The next week, the cotherapist made a couple of "prompting" phone calls. After that, group members began to stay in touch regularly and reported looking forward to their midweek phone calls.

Session 1

The lectures for this session are about alcoholism as a disease and the psychology of the alcoholic. Most group members seemed reassured by the disease concept. By presenting alcoholism as a disease with multiple etiologic factors, the co-alcoholic is relieved of assuming responsibility for the husband's drinking (King, Bissell, & Holding, 1978). The group members were interested in learning about how alcoholism progresses and eager to classify their husbands in early-, middle-, or late-stage alcoholism. Elaine and Alice both thought their husbands were in the late stage, whereas most of the others thought their husbands might still be in the middle stages. Only one member, Colette, age 39, wondered if her husband was still in the early stage. They all listened intently to the physical complications of alcoholism, and Sylvia, who was a 45-year-old nurse, described the devastating effects of alcohol on some of her hospital patients. It was at this point that Alice disclosed that her husband had heart problems and liver disease and Beverly, age 31, and Elaine both disclosed that their husbands had high blood pressure. Other group members identified in their husbands several other physical complications of alcohol abuse, such as gastritis, obesity, and blackouts.

Group members also identified with the psychological complications of alcoholism. Mary, age 38, whose husband was unemployed and passively allowed her to hit him, recognized that he had been depressed for a long time. Elaine also believed that her husband was depressed and worried that if she were to leave him he might commit suicide. Furthermore, she recognized that he was a compulsive overeater and spender. Colette, who was the only one who thought her husband might be in early-stage alcoholism, had recently discovered that he had multiple affairs and was afraid that he might be sexually addicted.

These discussions of the physical and psychological complications of alcoholism and the group members' disclosures of their husbands' symptoms and behaviors were to a large extent disquieting to the women. However, these discussions definitely softened the women's denial and minimization of their husbands' alcoholism and its effects and helped to strengthen their resolve to make responsible changes in their own lives.

Session 2

The second session began with a brief review of the women's reflections from the intervening week. The therapists noted that a shift seemed to have taken place in terms of how the group members viewed their husbands' alcoholism. Instead of seeing the alcoholism as a major irritation perpetuated by their husbands to inconvenience their family life, they recognized it as a disorder with potentially devastating consequences for the husbands' health and their families' well-being. Sylvia and Colette both brought in articles on alcoholism that they had read and wanted to share with the group. This suggested to the therapists that a group identification was already forming and that the women were ready to take a good hard look at the impact of alcoholism on their lives.

The first lecture in Session 2 is on alcoholism as a family disease. The women strongly identified with Jackson's (1954, 1956) family crisis and adjustment cycle. Beverly gave the following example. After several instances of her husband not showing to pick up her children at ball practice, she had accommodated by changing her work schedule so that she could do the pick-up and no longer rely on her husband. However, she realized that this "adjustment" actually protected her husband from taking responsibility for his behavior and created more inconvenience for herself while also serving to further isolate her husband from his family. She decided she would talk to her husband and ask him to resume the responsibility of picking up the children. But, she pondered, what if her husband was drinking when he came to pick the children up? Should he drive them home?

This was a perfect lead-in to the lecture on enabling and to discussion and role-play around the behavior of riding in a car with the alcoholic who has been drinking. With the exception of Sylvia, all the women acknowledged sometimes riding with their drunken husbands and feeling bad about themselves for doing so. Through guided imagery, each women imagined herself assertively refusing to ride with her husband, in spite of humiliating protests. Mary then demonstrated how she had, in actuality, patently told her husband she would never get in a car with him if she had any reason to suspect that he was drinking. Beverly and Mary role-played a scenario in which Beverly told her husband that she expected him to arrive on time and sober to pick the children up. She also informed him that she had instructed the kids that if they smelled alcohol or noticed him acting strange, they were to leave the practice, go to an appointed phone booth, call their mother, and wait for her. Although Beverly did not like the idea of the children assuming so much responsibility, she felt that they were resourceful enough to carry out this plan, and that otherwise they were being put in a position of deny-ing the problem or making excuses for their father's behavior.

Through the guided imagery and role-plays, group members learned to recognize their enabling behaviors and develop alternative responses to the alcoholic's behavior that neither compromised them-selves nor protected the alcoholic from the natural consequences of his behavior.

Session 3

For the lecture on family roles, Wegsheider's (1981) designations were described. All the women identified themselves as the Chief Enabler, although Mary and Beverly felt that their husbands' mothers might also fit that role. The women expressed deep concern and sorrow for their children, both those grown and gone and the little ones still at home. They were referred to literature on Children of Alcoholics and to Alateen, Alatot, and ACA groups. They were encouraged to speak openly, honestly, and without judgment to their children about their father's drinking and its impact on them. They were gently encouraged to think about the roles the children had taken on and how the children might perceive them in the Chief Enabler role. Elaine said that her two adult children were now substance abusers themselves, and that they resent-ed her for always "blaming everything" on their father's drinking. Sylvia said that her school-age children resented that she was seldom home because of commitments at work, 12-step meetings, and college. Sylvia was getting an advanced degree in order to gain financial independence in the event she were to leave her husband, but she also admitted to being so uncomfortable around the house that she stayed away whenever she could find legitimate opportunities. She realized that this left her children to cope with their father on their own and expressed deep re-morse over this. It was quite painful for Sylvia and the others to acknowl-edge how their co-alcoholic behaviors were hurtful to their children.

The lecture and discussion on sexuality had a strong impact on several of the group members. Although most of the women dressed carefully and attractively, several stated they felt unattractive and sexu-ally unappealing. Sylvia, who dressed fashionably and somewhat seduc-tively, reported that she had lost all interest in sex with her husband, but was not interested in looking around either. Beverly began to cry at that moment. She complained that she has gained 20 pounds and had stopped having sex with her husband months ago because she was convinced that her husband had affairs and she was angry and distrust-ful. She realized that she was also cutting herself off from a part of her marriage that she had once cherished, and this left her with a hopeless feeling. She was encouraged to see whether she could find a way to ex-press her sexuality without compromising her values or her marriage. She decided that she would experiment with reintroducing sex into the marriage without compromising her stand that many of her husband's behaviors were unacceptable to her. Colette disclosed that prior to com-ing to the group, she had found credit card bills suggesting that her husband was going to bars and taking women to motel rooms. She was devastated by this, and although her husband had asked for another chance, he was still refusing treatment. She wanted to continue the mar-riage but also wanted guarantees that the deceptions had ceased. She was referred to a book on surviving affairs (Schneider, 1990) that she found very helpful. The group members were very supportive of one another, and all seemed relieved to have the opportunity to talk about their sexuality and sexual problems.

Experiential Phase

Although the initial educational phase of the treatment is primarily didactic, it should be obvious from the foregoing that group members began to interact and experience new behaviors during the initial phase. The experiential phase (Sessions 4–6) provides more time for group members to share and analyze their experience and to practice new skills of feelings identification and assertive communicating.

Session 4

After a review of their homework, the group members were introduced to the five basic feelings of glad, mad, sad, hurt, and scared. They were asked to share an upsetting situation that had occurred during the week and to try to identify the feelings they had experienced. Mary mentioned that her unemployed husband had spent a day fishing and drinking with her son-in-law and that she had been mad. This had led to another fight where she hit her husband. The therapist asked her if she had had any other feelings about the incident, but she could only identify anger and exasperation. Some of the other group members spoke of how they imagined they might feel in such a situation, and Mary began to acknowledge that she actually felt sad that she worked so much and thus missed out on the few fun times her husband had. She also real-ized that when her husband did fun things, he was always drinking and she felt abandoned. She feared that her husband didn't like her anymore because she was always serious and "nagging," and admitted that she was actually ambivalent about his unemployment: On the one hand, it forced her to work too hard and resent him; on the other hand, he remained dependent on her, which made her feel secure that he wouldn't leave. She also realized that she was quite sad that he was so depressed and passive that he "allowed" her to hit him. His passivity scared her because she saw this as his way of isolating from her and leaving her lonely. She began to realize that she really missed her "old husband" (the way he was before alcoholism) and that she was willing to risk changing some of her behaviors to let him know she wanted him to get sober and become more alive again.

Alice described an incident in which her husband kept delaying her from leaving for her bridge group by asking her to do petty things for him that she could just as well have done later. She ended up missing the bridge group and burned his supper. Like Mary, the only feeling Alice could identify at first was anger that she had missed time with her friends. With some prompting and group support, she realized that her husband had been telling her that he was sick and needed her at home with him. She was then able to identify that she felt sad that her husband was unable to make a simple direct request of her, and she felt scared that he was so sick that he didn't feel comfortable being left alone. She realized that burning the dinner was a way of "acting out" her frustration, and that it would have been preferable to have recognized that her husband was having a difficult time and either volunteered to stay or, having provided him with a contingency plan and some reassurance, gone ahead to her bridge group.

As each group member shared her feelings, it became clear that anger and resentment were generally the easiest feelings for them to identify because they were the easiest to tolerate. When they experienced anger, they were able to project blame on the alcoholic and thus didn't have to take action to change themselves or their situations. By facing their hurts and fears, they began to realize that they were losing their joy, their self-esteem, and their family and social relationships, and it was up to them, not the alcoholic, to salvage their own lives. They were asked to practice identifying their feelings during the next week.

Session 5

During this session, group members learn to assertively state their feelings and learn to recognize what they want and how to ask for it. This is important work because at this point group members are finally recognizing how they feel and are beginning to formulate what they need.

Elaine was tired of being criticized by her husband and adult children and wanted them to do their own recovery work. She realized that she'd been trying to do it for them for years and was being labeled as a "nag" as a result of her efforts. She recognized that for a time she might need to live separately from her husband to gain clarity and regain lost self-esteem. With help from the group, she practiced making assertive, non-nagging requests. Sylvia was recognizing that by avoiding her husband she was also avoiding her children and she began practicing making assertive and caring statements to her kids. Mary practiced letting her husband know that she really wanted a full partner in their marriage, but that she felt that he would have to stop drinking and become employed in order to be a full partner. She determined to substitute assertive statements for aggressive behavior. Colette recognized that she had withdrawn from her husband in many ways and she was willing to engage again but needed his fidelity and sobriety. Beverly determined to regain her attractiveness and sexuality, but realized she did not trust her husband enough to do this within the marriage unless he were willing to get into recovery. And Alice decided she was willing to take care of her sick husband, but that she was determined also to have a life of her own.

As the group members practiced and role-played assertive statements, they seemed to gain a sense of integrity and confidence in their new behaviors. They were encouraged to practice assertive responding at home during the week.

The therapist received a phone call between Session 5 and 6 that had a profound impact on the remainder of the treatment program. Alice's husband had died of a heart attack and she would not be returning as she lived quite a distance away and naturally had many things to attend to. The therapists gave her some referrals for grief counseling in her area that she declined, but she did invite the group members to stay in touch with her.

Session 6

This session is typically dedicated to practicing feelings identification and assertive responding and to introducing the five lifestyle options. In this instance, however, quite a bit of time was spent by group members processing their reactions to the news about Alice's husband. All of the group members were surprised and sad for Alice. Although everyone had known that her husband was ill, no one (including Alice) had expected such a sudden end. The event seemed to stir up panic among the group members and polarized them into two camps. Colette and Mary suddenly were hesitant to "rock the boat" in their marriages.

Whereas both of them had been progressing nicely in their practice of nonenabling and assertive behaviors, they suddenly lost their motivation to make changes for themselves and were instead motivated to maintain the status quo at all cost. Elaine, Sylvia, and Beverly felt pressure to take some action immediately in order to avoid ending up like Alice. Elaine and Sylvia had already considered leaving their husbands, and this seemed to push them more in that direction. Beverly, who really wanted to stay with her husband, talked about doing a "Guided Intervention" to convince her husband to get help.

Although Guided Intervention is usually not discussed until Session 7, it seemed best to discuss this option now in response to Beverly's anxiety and eagerness to take action. Her support systems were evaluated. As it turned out, many of her husband's family members were alcoholics, including both parents and three of his five siblings, as well as his boss and several coworkers. Beverly could identify only a few of her relatives, one of his relatives, and one good friend who would possibly support her in a Guided Intervention. Given this paucity of support, the therapists advised Beverly against Guided Intervention and recommended that she consider a less risky option at this time. Colette and Mary also encouraged her to be conservative whereas Elaine and Sylvia suggested that she might go ahead and try a limited Intervention anyway. There was a kind of argumentative tension between the two camps.

It was apparent to the therapists that the group's anxiety over Alice's predicament had allowed their original reactivity to resurface and their newly won detachment to fade into the background. The therapists recommended that they all take some time for their reactions to Alice's news to sink in before taking any action. In the meantime, they were encouraged to put a great deal of thought into the written homework assignment of visualizing and describing themselves acting in each of the five lifestyle options.

Goal-Setting Phase

Session 7

During this phase group members formulate an action plan and make plans to carry it out. Ideally, the previous week's homework has given them a chance to carefully evaluate their behavioral options and they are aware of their preferences. For example, some women may choose to stop enabling and make assertive requests for their husbands to get treatment, whereas others might choose to do the above and make plans for separating if their quality of life has not improved within a certain time period. Group members are cautioned against presenting their choices as ultimatums. They are encouraged to explain to their husbands that any time limits they set represent their own limits of toleration, not an intended demand on the husband.

In this case, Beverly did not follow the advice of the therapists. Instead, during the week she solicited the support of several friends and family members and attempted to stage her own Intervention. By her report, the Intervention failed because she did not get professional assistance and because she had set it up as an ultimatum, telling her husband that he must either get treatment right away or she would leave. She was temporarily living with her children at her mother's when she came to Session 7. When she described the failed Intervention to the group, she was met with sympathy and a lack of any judgmental reaction. She realized that she had acted peremptorily and was grateful for the group's acceptance. She also decided that she would return home with her children and stay there until she could earn enough money to find a nice place for herself and the kids. As her panic subsided, she seemed to make a clear decision that she would not live for 45 years with a husband who was an alcoholic and unfaithful, as Alice had done. She decided she would make realistic plans to move out when she was financially able, if her husband did not get help and make some serious changes in his behavior toward herself and the children.

Once Beverly had settled down and made her plan, the other group members' anxiety seemed to decrease and they seemed more comfortable interacting with one another and discussing their options. Each woman read her homework out loud, so that she had the opportunity to verbally "try out" each option. Colette and Mary were back to practicing assertive responding and even considering separation in the future if things did not improve. Sylvia seemed to feel a little less pressure to leave her husband right away. She developed a plan for increasing her involvement at home and practicing positive coping strategies while also securing enough money for a down-payment on a new home. If this plan did not provide her with the personal satisfaction she required within 6 to 12 months, she would move out with the children and file for divorce. Elaine opted for a temporary separation, with the intent of reuniting if her husband were to enter treatment.

Session 8

During the final session the therapist spoke briefly on alcoholism treatment and the stages of recovery. This reminded the women that recovery from alcoholism and co-alcoholism can be a long-term process that doesn't stop when the drinking or enabling behaviors cease. This was a sober message for the final session because group members needed to hear once again that getting their spouses into treatment does not guarantee a happy ending. What is more likely to constitute a happy ending is for the individual women to feel that their own lives are more manageable and that they are behaving with integrity rather than reacting out of a need to control someone else's behavior.

As the group members read their final homework assignments on what they had gained from the treatment program, it was clear that most of the group members felt they had made significant progress and they felt bonded with one another. They had spoken with each other frequently over the phone, especially since Alice's husband had died. They had stayed in touch with Alice, too. It is not unusual for groups to make plans to meet socially or to ask for "booster" sessions at a later date. Such plans are encouraged by the therapists and group members are also directed toward Al-Anon. However, this group had a particular interest in remaining intact and not dispersing into various Al-Anon groups. They decided to meet weekly on their own for a while. The therapists hypothesized that Alice's trauma had instigated a shock from which the group had not yet fully recovered, which caused them to feel somewhat "unfinished" and dependent on one another. The therapists decided it was advisable for a facilitator to continue to meet with the group for a while so the cotherapist agreed to meet with them for 6 weeks.

Group members' closing comments suggested that they had learned much from the program and one another. In the final exercise, the "gifts" that were passed around were those qualities that mark women who are struggling to be healthy and strong; passion, integrity, forthrightness, confidence in their own perceptions and feelings, and the ability to recognize their shortcomings.

Follow-Up

All group members continued to meet with the cotherapist for 6 weeks. Alice returned to meet with them occasionally during this time. Colette and Sylvia attended irregularly. Elaine, Alice, Beverly, and Sylvia continued to meet together at least once a month for 1 year after the treatment. During that year, Sylvia divorced her husband, bought a house, and began a new relationship. Elaine separated from her husband; he went into treatment, and they were re-united. Colette's husband began attending AA and claimed to have no more affairs. Colette was in a codependency therapy group and reported being much happier. Mary reported that although her husband was still drinking, he had found a job, the hitting had stopped, and their home was more peaceful. Beverly, who had moved back with her husband after the failed intervention, separated from him again after becoming more financially stable, and she was in the process of divorce. She was ambivalent about her decision, because she still loved her husband. But she felt that she had little choice because his alcoholism had progressed, she had found evidence of new affairs, and she was again making excuses to her children for their father's neglect. Alice had moved on with her life and had an active schedule of grandchildren, volunteer groups, and women friends. She wished that she had sought help years earlier, not because she believed her husband would have changed, but so that she could have been more understanding, coped more effectively, and gotten more enjoyment out of those years. Alice said that because of her religious upbringing and financial dependence she would never have divorced her husband, but she felt Beverly was doing the right thing. All of the group attended Al-Anon, some more consistently than others.

Dependent measures were administered after the session to all group members but Alice. They all showed gains in self-concept scores. Depression and anxiety had decreased to within normal ranges. Enabling scores had decreased dramatically. Perhaps the most important gain for group members, however, is that each of them found the "way out" of an intolerable situation, which is what they had been seeking when they came to treatment. For some, the solution was in learning to detach and respond in nonenabling ways; for others, the solution was in a more radical lifestyle change. For all of them, these were self-affirming steps that they had not had the understanding or courage to take before. For all of them, the support of the group helped them to find the strength to make changes. As Sylvia wrote in her final homework assignment, "We came together as strangers, and we leave here as sisters."

RESEARCH SUMMARY

The treatment program outlined in this chapter is unique for two reasons. First, it describes a model of group treatment developed specifically for the wives of alcoholics who are not in recovery. Second, the program was developed as a research study so that its effectiveness could be empirically and statistically evaluated. Details of the study can be found in Dittrich and Trapold (1984).

Subjects for the study were women ($n = 23$) married to nonrecovering alcoholics. The women were of middle to upper-middle socioeconomic level, had a mean age of 45, and had been in their present marriage an average of 22 years. Husbands had been drinking at problematic levels, according to their wives, for an average of 17 years. All husbands were currently drinking and were classified alcoholic by the MAST.

Subjects were randomly assigned to an experimental group ($n = 10$) or to a wait-list control group ($n = 13$). They all participated in individual intake interviews in which histories were taken and the dependent measures were administered. The MAST was administered in a modified format so that the subjects answered it twice — once for themselves and once for their husbands. In this way, alcoholism could be confirmed in the husbands' cases or screened out in the wives' cases. The dependent measures were (1) the Tennessee Self-Concept Scale, total positive score (Fitts, 1965), (2) the Beck Depression Inventory, short form (Beck & Beck, 1972), (3) the Taylor Manifest Anxiety Scale (Taylor, 1953), and (4) the EBI (Dittrich & Trapold, 1984). The dependent measures evaluated subjects' self-esteem, depression, anxiety, and enabling behaviors, respectively. The EBI was developed specifically for this study and was found to have good test–retest reliability and criterion validity (Dittrich & Trapold, 1984).

The EBI is a checklist of 90 potentially enabling behaviors. Subjects are instructed to indicate which of these behaviors they have engaged in during the past month. (Sample items include: drove with the alcoholic when he or she was intoxicated; helped conceal your spouse's drinking or drug use from business associates; made threats you later did not carry out; tried to hide your spouse's drinking from the children and/or relatives; kissed the alcoholic to check his or her breath.)

The experimental group was divided into two treatment groups that both received the 8-week program, whereas the control group remained untreated but on a waiting list. Prior to treatment, the experimental and control groups scored comparably on the dependent measures. Specifically, all subjects had low self-concepts, were mildly to moderately depressed, were moderately anxious, and engaged in numerous enabling behaviors ($M = 30$). After the experimental group had received treatment, their scores reflected statistically higher self-concepts, less depression, less anxiety, and fewer enabling behaviors ($M = 13$). During this time the scores for the wait-list controls remained virtually unchanged. Once the control subjects had been divided into two treatment groups and received the 8-week treatment, their scores also changed significantly, so that they too showed elevations in self-concept and decreases in depression, anxiety, and enabling behaviors. Dependent measures were repeated for both experimental and control subjects at 8 to 16 weeks posttreatment, and all treatment effects held for these follow-ups.

A posttreatment self-report questionnaire was also administered, and subjects reported gaining overwhelming improvement in the areas of knowledge about alcoholism, ability to express feelings, assertiveness, awareness of options, and self-confidence. The one area in which subjects did not seem to feel they had made significant gains was their sexual self-image, suggesting that it is indeed very difficult for one partner to heal a dysfunctional sexual relationship when the other partner is actively alcoholic.

Telephone follow-ups were done at 12 months. It was striking to learn that 50% of the subjects were still meeting informally with members of their groups. They were either meeting informally for supportive social contact, going to Al-Anon meetings together, or both. Of the 23 subjects, 9 (39%) were divorced or separated from their husbands. Eleven husbands (48%) had entered treatment (either professional treatment or AA). Four of the husbands who entered treatment did so after separation and of those, two couples were considering reunification.

The high incidence of divorce and separation found in this study is noteworthy. Although alcoholic marriages typically do have a high incidence of divorce, marital dissolution was not an objective of the treatment program. However, it was an objective of the program to help women be aware of the full range of their options and to provide them the knowledge, skills, and confidence to choose and carry out their own best option. Separation appeared to be the preferred option for almost 40% of the subjects in the study, probably for reasons similar to those mentioned in the case application. Upon closer scrutiny, it was found that the husbands of the women who separated had the highest MAST scores and were most likely the more severe and late-stage alcoholics.

The results of this study clearly demonstrate that the group treatment program was effective in helping wives of alcoholics improve their self-esteem, become less depressed and anxious, and engage in fewer enabling behaviors. Additionally, the wives reported that they became more aware of their feelings and better able to assert themselves. They had assessed and exercised their options, so that within 12 months of treatment, major changes had occurred for most of the women. A surprising 48% of husbands had gone into treatment. Although exact figures on husbands' abstinence were not available, all of these women reported an improved quality of life. Of those women who were separated, some found it quite a struggle emotionally and financially, but for the most part they were relieved and felt they had made the best choice for themselves and their families. Of the seven women who were still at home with their actively alcoholic husbands, the majority felt that the group had been extremely helpful and supportive in teaching them to stop enabling behaviors and maintain their own sense of personal integrity in spite of the various stresses of living with an alcoholic.

CONCLUSIONS

This chapter has described a brief group treatment for women married to nonrecovering alcoholics. Typically these are women who have been in a marriage that has been unsatisfying for many years. They have repeatedly experienced their husbands' drunkenness, behavioral unpredicability, and mood swings. They may also have managed raising children, their own careers, and being victims of verbal or physical abuse. They may have tried many times without success to encourage their husbands to change or get help. It is not surprising that many of these women have low self-esteem, are depressed and anxious, and believe they have run out of options.

The group treatment program educates these women about alcoholism and family dynamics. They are trained in positive communication and coping skills. They are presented with options for dealing with the alcoholic in their life. In a group format, which allows them to share and compare their experiences, these women can find the tools and courage to make significant changes in their lives. For some women, change means learning to recognize their feeling reactions and to respond in an authentic and assertive manner. For other women, change means being willing to radically change their own lifestyles if their husbands will not abstain or get help. For still others, it means tolerating the situation as it is, but knowing their limits of toleration and developing contingency plans if the situation worsens.

The research study for which this program was developed statistically demonstrated that wives of alcoholics decreased enabling behaviors, decreased symptoms of depression and anxiety, and increased self-esteem in response to this program. It was also found that almost half of the women were separated or divorced from their husbands within 1 year of treatment. Such findings suggest that treatment gave many women the impetus to change after years of feeling stuck.

These trends were true for the case example group as well. As Elaine, married 26 years to an alcoholic and with two alcoholic children, wrote "This group gave me a chance to change. . . . Our group is a tiny part of those who cope with an alcoholic husband. Here we are, different ages and at different levels, but still sisters." By helping these women out of isolation into a supportive environment where they can develop positive coping strategies and gain new perspectives on their lives, this treatment may help them to make healthy, often difficult, choices for themselves and their families.

REFERENCES

Al-Anon Family Groups. (1979). *Al-Anon faces alcoholism.* New York: Author.

Al-Anon Family Groups. (1989). *The dilemma of the alcoholic marriage.* New York: Author.

Alcoholics Anonymous World Services. (1976). *Alcoholics Anonymous.* New York: Author.

American Psychiatric Association. (1987). *Diagnostic and statistical manual of mental disorders* (3rd rev. ed.). Washington, DC: Author.

Bailey, M. B. (1963). The family agency's role in treating the wife of an alcoholic. *Social Casework, 44,* 273–279.

Black, C. (1981). *It will never happen to me.* Denver: M. A. C. Printing and Publications Division.

Beck, A. T., & Beck, R. W. (1972, December). Screening depressed patients in family practice: A rapid technic. *Postgraduate Medicine,* 81–85.

Cahalan, D. (1970). *Problem drinkers.* San Francisco: Josey-Bass, Inc.

Cermak, T. L. (1986). *Diagnosing and treating co-dependence.* Minneapolis: Johnson Institute Books.

Dittrich, J. E., & Trapold, M. A. (1984). A treatment program for wives of alcoholics: An evaluation. *Bulletin of the Society of Psychologists in Addictive Behaviors, 3*(4), 91–102.

Drews, T. R. (1983). *Getting them sober* (Vol. 2). South Plainfield, NJ: Bridge.

Drews, T. R. (1986). *Getting them sober* (Vol. 3). South Plainfield, NJ: Bridge.

Edwards, P., Harvey, C., & Whitehead, P. (1973). Wives of alcoholics: A critical review and analysis. *Quarterly Journal of Studies on Alcohol, 34,* 112–132.

Estes, N. J. (1981). Counseling the wives of an alcoholic spouse. In N. J. Estes & M. E. Heinemann (Eds.), *Alcoholism: Development, consequences, and interventions* (pp. 259–265). St. Louis, MO: C. V. Mosby.

Estes, N. J., & Heinemann, M. E. (Eds.). (1981). *Alcoholism: Development, consequences, and interventions.* St. Louis, MO: C. V. Mosby.

Fitts, W. H. (1965). *Tennessee self concept scale manual.* Nashville, TN: Counselor Recordings and Tests.

Gibbons, B. (1992). Alcohol: The legal drug. *National Geographic, 181*(2), 2–35.

Goodwin, D. (1976). *Is alcoholism hereditary?* Oxford: Oxford University Press.

Howard, D. P., & Howard, N. T. (1978). Treatment of the significant other. In S. Zimberg, J. Wallace, & S. B. Blume (Eds.), *Practical approaches to alcoholism psychotherapy* (pp. 137–162). New York: Plenum Press.

Jackson, J. K. (1954). The adjustment of the family to the crisis of alcoholism. *Quarterly Journal of Studies on Alcohol, 15,* 562–586.

Jackson, J. K. (1956). The adjustment of the family to alcoholism. *Marriage and Family, 18,* 361–369.

Jacob, T., Favorini, A., Meisel, S., & Anderson, C. M. (1978). The alcoholic's spouse, children, and family interactions: Substantive findings and methodological issues. *Journal of Studies on Alcohol, 39,* 1231–1251.

Johnson, V. (1980). *I'll quit tomorrow.* New York: Harper & Row.

King, B., Bissell, L., & Holding, E. (1978). The usefulness of the disease concept of alcoholism in working with wives of alcoholics. *Social Work in Health Care, 3*(4), 443–455.

Kogan, K. L., & Jackson, J. K. (1965). Stress, personality, and emotional disturbance in wives of alcoholics. *Quarterly Journal of Studies on Alcohol, 26,* 487–495.

Larsen, E. (1987). *Stage II relationships: Love beyond addiction.* San Francisco: Perennia Library.

Maxwell, R. (1976). *The booze battle.* New York: Ballantine Books.

National Council on Alcoholism. (1972). Criteria for the diagnosis of alcoholism. *American Journal of Psychiatry, 129*(2), 122–135.

O'Farrell, T. J., & Cowles, K. S. (1989). Marital and family therapy. In R. K. Hester & W. R. Miller (Eds.), *Handbook of alcoholism treatment approaches* (pp. 183–205). New York: Pergamon Press.

Orford, J. (1976). A study of the personalities of excessive drinkers and their wives, using the approaches of Leary and Eysenck. *Journal of Consulting and Clinical Psychology, 44,* 534–545.

Roy, M. (Ed.). (1977). *Battered women: A psychosociological study of domestic violence.* New York: Van Nostrand Reinhold.

Schaef, A. W. (1986). *Co-dependence: Misunderstood–mistreated.* Minneapolis, MN: Winston Press.

Schneider, J. P. (1990). *Back from betrayal: Recovering from his affairs.* New York: Ballantine Books.

Schuckit, M. A. (1979). Inpatient and residential approaches to the treatment of alcoholism. In J. H. Mendelson & N. K. Mello (Eds.), *The diagnosis and treatment of alcoholism* (pp. 257–282). New York: McGraw Hill.

Schutt, M. (1985). *Wives of alcoholics: From co-dependency to recovery.* Pompano Beach, FL: Health Communications.

Selzer, M. L. (1971). The Michigan Alcoholism Screening Test: The quest for a new diagnostic instrument. *American Journal of Psychiatry, 127,* 1653–1658.

Sex and Love Addicts Anonymous (SLAA). (1989). *Sex and love addicts anonymous.* Boston: SLAA Fellowship-Wide Services.

Sisson, R. W., & Azrin, N. H. (1986). Family-member involvement to initiate and promote treatment of problem drinkers. *Journal of Behavior Therapy and Experimental Psychiatry, 17,* 15–21.

Taylor, J. A. (1953). A personality scale of manifest anxiety. *Journal of Abnormal and Social Psychology, 43,* 285–290.

Thomas, E. J., & Santa, C. A. (1982). Unilateral family therapy for alcohol abuse: A working conception. *American Journal of Family Therapy, 10,* 49–60.

Wallace, A. (1990). *Loving tough, loving smart, loving you: You and the alcoholic.* Solvang, CA: Challenger Press.

Wallace, J. (1981). Alcoholism from the inside out: A phenomenological analysis. In N. J. Estes & M. E. Heinemann (Eds.), *Alcoholism: Development, consequences, and interventions* (pp. 3–14). St. Louis, MO: C. V. Mosby.

Wallace, J. (1985). *Alcoholism: New light on the disease.* Newport, RI: Edgehill.

Wegsheider, S. (1981). *Another chance: Hope and health for the alcoholic family.* Palo Alto, CA: Science and Behavior Books.

Whitfield, C. (1984, Summer). Co-alcoholism: Recognizing a treatable disease. *Family and Community Health, 7,* 16–25.

Woititz, J. G. (1979). *Marriage on the rocks: Learning to live with yourself and an alcoholic.* Pompano Beach, FL: Health Communications.

Part II

STABILIZING SOBRIETY AND RELATIONSHIPS WHEN THE ALCOHOLIC SEEKS HELP

Chapter 5

Family Treatment in Short-Term Detoxification

Richard Bale

OVERVIEW

In recent years the inclusion of family members in alcoholism treatment has achieved widespread acceptance and increasingly is viewed as crucial for the recovery of the alcoholic, as well as the family members themselves (O'Farrell, 1989). Treatment strategies for families have evolved in their sophistication and elegance, bolstered by new studies of alcoholic relationships (Jacob & Leonard, 1988; Jacob & Seilhamer, 1989; Steinglass, Bennett, Wolin, & Reiss, 1987) as well as the characteristics of codependence (Cermak, 1989). Treatment paradigms, however, rely on the successful engagement of families early in the recovery process. Overcoming the fears, distrust, anger, hopelessness, and resistance of family members at the outset of treatment represents a central challenge to addiction therapists.

We describe a four-part strategy that has successfully engaged family members during a brief 2-week hospitalization for detoxification and referral. Its essential features include:

Preadmission contact with the families to explain the program's view of the alcoholic as competent and to demonstrate limit setting for the codependents.

Orientation meeting to join with the families by acknowledging their catalog of feelings and concerns, while taking over caretaking responsibilities. This frees families to begin considering their own needs; basic concepts of codependence are introduced only subtly.

Discharge planning meeting at the end of the hospitalization to clarify the primary goal of abstinence, outline recommendations for further treatment, and negotiate contingency contracts between the alcoholic and his family.

Continued connection with the family to provide assistance with the family crises that accompany sobriety, as well as the decisions involved in relapse.

SPECIAL CONSIDERATIONS

Setting

The Substance Abuse Evaluation and Referral Program is a 20-bed, 2-week inpatient ward program offering medically supervised withdrawal from addictive drugs including alcohol and providing careful assessment and individualized referral to longer-term treatment. The program is part of one of the largest substance abuse units in the Department of Veterans Affairs (VA) system. Located on the Menlo Park campus of the VA Medical Center at Palo Alto, California, the Drug and Alcohol Rehabilitation Unit includes four additional inpatient programs ranging in length from 45 days to 4 months and a large outpatient clinic offering methadone maintenance, Antabuse, naltrexone, and evening support groups. The unit programs' structure and results of controlled studies have been described elsewhere (Bale et al., 1984).

The withdrawal program has the fewest entry requirements of all the programs. Telephone applications are screened only for mental illness and serious medical conditions; abstinence is required only for the few hours preceding admission. Consequently, the program attracts a large number of veterans who, at least initially, are unable or unwilling to meet the substantially greater requirements of time and commitment characteristic of the longer-term programs. About one-third of the patients continue in residential treatment after the withdrawal period, another third enroll in outpatient therapy, often with prescribed Antabuse, and the remaining third reject all further treatment.

Patients

The treatment population are veterans, predominantly male, with a mean age of about 37 years, and at admission about half live with a wife, girlfriend, or parents. Approximately one-half are primarily addicted to alcohol, one-quarter to heroin and other opioids, and one-quarter to cocaine and amphetamines. Roughly 50% are white, about 35% are black, and 15% are Hispanic. More than half have spent time in jail or prison, and one quarter are currently on probation or parole. In part because of recent stringent VA eligibility requirements, only 20% are currently employed at admission.

Identification of Family Members

In addition to other system members (court officers, employers, other treatment providers) the program absolutely requires for admission signed confidentiality releases allowing the staff to establish contact with important family and friends, as defined by the following criteria: (1) any person with whom the veteran is currently living; (2) any person who has provided money, food, overnight lodging, valuable goods, or services in the past year; and (3) a wife, whether or not she and the patient are currently living together, and an ex-wife if there are shared children or regular contact.

Our familial contact has characteristically involved the wives of alcoholics rather than the parents of addicts (Marotta, Lehr, Moltzen, Pohlman, & Bale, 1986), which is similar to other programs' experiences (Zeigler-Driscoll, 1979) and longitudinal research results (Vaillant, 1966). Although most of our family work involves general principles, differences with respect to nuclear versus family of origin will be noted where appropriate, as well as the importance of ethnicity and culture (Bennett, 1989).

DESCRIPTION OF THE TREATMENT METHOD

Preadmission Contact

Treatment begins with the first phone call (see Table 5.1). More often than not, the inquiry is from a wife or parents. The rules and parameters for the rest of therapy are set in this initial contact and will be difficult to undo later. Although we will briefly describe our program, we require the veteran seeking treatment to handle all other negotiations, including admission requirements, coordination of ancillary medical and legal documentation, proof of veteran status, and so forth. Family members hoping we can "fix" their loved one (where they have "failed") are quickly introduced to quite a different notion of recovery—holding the substance abuser responsible for initiating and maintaining treatment. Sometimes, in fact, it may be months after our contact with the family before the abuser is ready to schedule an admission. In these cases we have found it extraordinarily useful to begin working with the family in these intervening weeks. Turning their attention to their own needs and the community resources available to them is often easier without the presence of the abuser.

Entry into residential treatment and the abrupt separation involved is the first major trauma faced by the family. Often wives and mothers

TABLE 5.1. Overview of the Treatment Method

1. Preadmission Contact
   a. First phone call with patient
   b. Admission to treatment
   c. Initial interview of family and invitation to meetings

2. The Family Orientation Meeting
   a. Invitation
   b. Staff
   c. Basic rules
   d. Rapport
   e. Resources for families
   f. Money
   g. Role-plays
   h. Homework

3. The Discharge Planning Meeting
   a. Restraint-from-change directive
   b. Abstinence as the requirement
   c. One-Year Plan for continued treatment
   d. Contingency contracts
   e. Antabuse

4. Continued Connection
   a. Normalizing crises
   b. Negotiating readmissions

are seen trudging up the steps to our admission office, several feet ahead of the veteran, sometimes carrying heavy luggage, looking relieved that help is near but apprehensive about a myriad of concerns. Their efforts to manage and control the admission process (answering questions directed to the veteran, stuffing money into his pockets, even evaluating the withdrawal medication) are politely but firmly constrained.

Within minutes they are asked to say a brief goodbye and escorted to a separate room for an informal chat with a friendly, mature staff member. The very limited goals of this initial encounter are to (1) separate the family from the patient, (2) establish a feeling of warmth and acceptance, (3) answer any burning questions, and (4) issue an invitation to an "orientation" meeting a few days hence, while (5) relieving the family member from further responsibility for the veteran's recovery. We also clarify our separation policy of no phone calls (letters are OK) and no face-to-face contact outside the formal family events. We have found it imperative to mandate this separation to avoid the frequent if unintentional sabotage of treatment by families, as well as the frequent regression (and sometimes impulsive elopement) of patients after unstructured contact. Family members are assured that they may check on the veteran's status by calling the staff at any time.

Finally, we begin some basic assessment of the family, and attempt to set in motion some new concepts, by posing two questions: (1) What will the family do if the veteran leaves treatment early? and (2) To whom do the individual family members turn for support? Family members are often confused by these questions. The more codependent the family member, the greater the confusion.

Family Orientation Meeting

Invitation

We write and telephone all friends and family members who qualify by our criteria, including those we may have met on the day of admission. As stated above, these include persons with whom the patient has been living, those who have provided economic support in the past year, and the wife or ex-wife if there are shared children or regular contact. They are invited to a 2-hour "orientation" meeting, held a few days after the patient's admission, in which they may learn more about the nature of the program and additional resources. We have found that most families are initially fearful and resistant to any family "group" or "session" that connotes therapy or self-disclosure, so instead we describe this first formal contact as a one-way experience in which they can receive, and not give, information. The choice to share about themselves is always presented and supported as one only they can make.

Often families are extremely reluctant to attend anyway, often citing work or transportation difficulties. We politely but firmly insist on their attendance, sometimes pointing out that they could probably overcome these hindrances if the veteran were suddenly hospitalized for a serious medical problem. (This is a serious medical problem!) Sometimes it is important to clarify that attendance does not in itself imply commitment to the relationship and to suggest that those considering a divorce or other formal separation can be helped to do so more effectively with the resources discussed at this first meeting. Sometimes the patient will elope before this first meeting in order to ensure continuation of the codependent relationship. Codependents will typically see no further reason to attend, but we tell them that now, more than ever, it is essential for them to come. Rather than challenge their enabling behavior, we focus on planning for the inevitable subsequent admission. With particularly emeshed families we may even make a subsequent admission contingent upon attendance.

The invitation of children is a complex issue involving available program resources. We generally ask a wife to bring those older than 10, but we will try to offer childcare for younger children when we can, rather than lose the wife for lack of this resource. Mothers are often puzzled by our request to bring their children (" . . . they're not affected by this, they can't help . . . "). We address the effect of addiction on children in this first meeting, as well as suggest selected readings (see "homework"). We exclude younger children not because they are unaffected or naive — they are probably the least naive of all family members — but because they have a difficult time in the controlled group setting and can be subtly manipulated by families to disrupt the meeting.

Staff

In addition to two trained staff members familiar with the current residents, we have found it extremely helpful to include a current resident who has no family present to describe the program and demonstrate to the family the degree of responsibility assumed by the residents in their recovery. Also helpful are family members of former residents that serve as peer counselors to the attendees, answering their concerns and questions from a position of recent and successful participation. Because many wives and girlfriends feel excluded from the treatment process by therapists who have "usurped" their role, we have found it especially important to include nonthreatening, warm, and often older therapists in this initial meeting.

Basic Rules

The meeting begins with a statement of our four essential rules:

1. No one may attend the meeting under the influence of alcohol or a nonprescribed drug. Chemically dependent family members are generally not invited; they are instead referred to treatment resources. Sometimes "resistance" in this meeting turns out to be denial of a family member, often a sibling, of his or her own substance abuse problem.

2. The meeting is to describe the workings of the program and not to answer questions about individual patients. By drawing a boundary around the issues of the patient we gently redirect the focus to the family members, while beginning to model some separation from responsibility for the loved one's recovery (Kaufman, 1984).

3. Sharing of personal information by family members is always optional, and some families may choose only to obtain information in this meeting. It is counterproductive to force or confront family members at this stage. In actuality family members can rarely resist identifying with the disclosure of others in the meeting, and our reassurances that they do not have to share often has the paradoxical effect of inducing more material.

4. All information shared in the meeting is confidential to the attendees and the treatment staff, with the exception of reported behavior involving the safety of others (suicidality, homicidality, child abuse).

Significantly, the delineation of this basic contract respecting the rights and privileges of the group members is often the family's first experience with such boundaries in relationships. It lays a foundation for the contingency contracting that is at the heart of the next session (see "discharge planning meeting" described below).

Rapport

As many systems therapists have suggested (Minuchin, 1974), the therapists must first achieve rapport or "join" with family members. This is best accomplished by facilitating and normalizing the immediate feelings of the attendees by having them hear from other patients' families. The group setting is not only cost effective but gives families and friends an opportunity to hear others' "stories," a gentle introduction to the Al-Anon process (Thomas, Weaver, Knight, & Bale, 1986).

A variety of feelings may be expressed. These feelings normally will include guilt about having failed to "fix" the loved one, hopelessness about the possibility of recovery, and embarrassment about disclosing family secrets to strangers. Anger and resentment at the damage done to the family by the abuser and feelings of exhaustion from the effort involved (which may include the additional stress posed by the meeting itself) are common. Finally, fear about a number of issues (Will he stay in treatment? What is the future of our relationship?) may be expressed.

Fear will be the last expressed and the most difficult to share (Ketcham & Gustafson, 1989), especially if the attendee is fearful of the patient. It is not unusual for our patients to advise family members by letter that their attendance is "not required" or to keep quiet about "personal matters." Sometimes there is a history of physical violence (Sisson & Azrin, 1986; Thomas, Santa, Bronson, & Oyserman, 1980), sexual abuse (Elkin, 1984), or threats of suicide by the patient, and families are understandably frightened. We consistently underestimate the intimidation faced by family members who have been the target of a variety of explicit and implicit threats: to harm them, use substances, commit suicide, or just disappear. A sullen, silent, unresponsive family is often one living with such extortion. Joining with such a family is impossible without acknowledgment of these fears. Often a realistic discussion is needed concerning protection (e.g., court restraining orders), the manipulative aspects of suicide threats, and child-abuse reporting.

A very particular and common fear worth special attention is the belief that the entire relationship with the abuser is built upon the addiction, and that sobriety will end it. Simply stated, the unstated fear is, "If my loved one becomes sober, he won't want me anymore!" These are extremely unsettling feelings and especially difficult to share with others, because they involve such core issues of self-esteem. It is very important that these fears be normalized and understood as common. Sometimes we will show families a videotape of a couple early in treatment who are discussing the pragmatics of his treatment plans: the mortgage, the caretaking of young children, other financial worries, and so forth. After a few minutes we stop the tape and ask the families to guess what the man and his wife are *not* saying to each other. Then the second part is played, in which the husband and wife, as individuals, address the camera and talk about fears of changing or losing the relationship. Families are most struck by the symmetry—the abuser and this wife have the same unexpressed fears! This is both a powerful and sensitive intervention, because the discussion may be kept at the level of "those people" on the videotape, or brought closer to home at the willingness and choice of the family members.

Resources for Families

The discussion of resources available (e.g., Al-Anon, Alateen) is the first concrete step to shift the focus to the welfare of the families (Wright & Scott, 1978). We agree with Treadway (1989) that it is insulting to tell family members that "they should go to Al-Anon because they need it or have a disease, too." Instead, we suggest it is the best and most immediate way for them to participate in their loved one's recovery. We point out that the abuser now has 24-hour support, while the family must carry on all the continuing responsibilities of living—with virtually no support! Our question, ("Who takes care of *you*?") previously asked at admission, is the key to this part of the meeting. After a period of stunned silence, families often become tearful as they begin to feel— and hear from other families—their isolation and neediness. As others have pointed out (Cermak, 1989), the parallel process of abusers and their families is striking, but there is no example more dramatic than the families' beliefs that willpower is the central requisite and that "they can do this alone."

Money

To paraphrase the old adage, money is at the root of much addiction. We find it imperative to introduce the notion of subsidized addiction in this first meeting. It is not at all unusual to have a patient in his late 30s living at home with his parents, with three square meals a day, his laundry done regularly, his bills paid with "loans," and regular use of the family car while he "looks for work." Role-plays with attending patients or recovering staff members are often needed to clarify to such a family how their resources are actually going toward the purchase of alcohol or other drugs. The myth of substance abuse as an independent, rebellious act of individuation is one of the great fallacies of addiction. In our experience most addiction depends on subsidies from families, welfare agencies, benefit programs, and, yes, even treatment programs.

The notion that the family actually provides resources for addiction is a tough one to accept for most families, in part because the financial abandonment—which we will recommend in the next meeting—seems unconscionable. Fortunately, we are in a position to assure the family that the treatment programs available at our hospital provide free shelter, food, clothing, and vocational rehabilitation for up to a year. There is, in fact, no reason for any patient to leave the hospital without a place to stay in the community, a job, and a support system—the basics of an independent life. Of course these resources are only available to those who are willing to abide by a variety of social contracts requiring respectful behavior towards others and, most of all, abstinence from alcohol and other drugs. Over time the family engaged in treatment is able to adopt this model for themselves.

For a family in entrenched denial about these issues of subsidization, we sometimes resort to what we have called "real-time" contracting (Moltzen, Tucker, & Bale, 1986). In this exercise we gently extract and record the parameters of the kind of deal that actually exists in the kind of family described above. Then we ask the family to sign a written contract agreeing to continue that (heretofore unconscious) arrangement for one month. The family's usual response is, "What kind of a fool would sign a contract like this?"

Because the topic of support is so loaded for families, we do not attempt to help families achieve insight as to their enabling. The potential for additional guilt or just frank resistance outweighs any possible benefits of these new concepts. Furthermore, at this stage of treatment insight isn't necessary, only the cessation of unconditional support. We simply share with the family what we know empirically from 20 years of work with abusers: that addicts with available subsidization for their addiction leave treatment prematurely and do not recover. This is not hard to understand. The process of recovery in our treatment programs is very hard work. If patients have another option, a better deal, they will take it. Our families understand the notion of hard work.

Two typical cases are worthy of special mention. First, the nonworking wife with children often faces an overwhelming financial burden in considering separation from her husband, a reality to be kept in mind during the negotiations about contracts in the next meeting (see discharge planning meeting). A consulting anthropologist once expressed amazement at our staff's notions about codependence. In his experience with native, relatively "uncivilized" peoples, a dysfunctional male would be exiled, and the community would organize to provide the female with food, repairs to her roof, childcare, and company. She would be expected to neither "confront" her husband's behavior nor make up for his abandoned responsibilities!

Second, there may be strong financial reasons for an older wife to stay "enmeshed" in what appears to be a frightfully abusive relationship. Jointly owned business or managed property, for example, can make separation very costly and difficult. Some years ago we were disabused of our facile interpretation of masochistic behavior by a gentle lady in her mid-60s who had vowed to stay with her husband no matter what the cost to her. What we learned later was that her husband's impending death from severe end-stage alcoholism would result in an insurance payoff of over $200,000, a sum she would forfeit if she divorced him. On some reflection it was difficult for us to fault this lady's desire for some compensation for the years of abuse she had weathered from this recalcitrant man. Moreover, we had to realize that should our therapy "work" and this man's abstinence were to purchase an additional year or two of life, she faced even more caretaking.

Role-Plays

For some families, the discussions and examples utilized in introducing the many new concepts simply don't register. Often they can better experience new ideas through acting out various roles in structured role-plays guided by the staff. Typical of these would be (1) several group members physically leaning on a young mother, (2) having family members hold up a person who continues to try to fall over, or (3) have a wife verbally resist another's entreaties to assume his responsibilities. A previously quiet or inhibited group will often burst into spontaneous discussion of helplessness, powerlessness, or resentment after such a demonstration.

Homework

Because so much of the content of this first formal meeting is new and emotionally provocative, we rely on several take-home assignments to continue and deepen the family's consideration of key issues:

1. What will they do if the patient elopes from the program, or fails to abide by staff recommendations for further treatment? Each family member is provided a blank copy of our overprint Plan for Continued Treatment that lists many potential recommendations for recovery activities. A week later the Plan will be individualized, with key appropriate elements checked off for the patient (see Figure 5.1).

2. What Al-Anon or other support groups are available in their neighborhood? We strongly recommend that they attend at least two support meetings, and that they "shop around" for a meeting that "feels right for them." Family members from previous weeks in attendance are especially helpful at these moments, often sharing how they traveled from meeting to meeting before finding one that "clicked" for them. If not so forewarned, families often abandon the idea of support groups after attending one meeting they did not like, assuming other meetings will be similar. In fact, 12-step meetings are remarkably variable in many ways, (e.g., size, mood, level of organization, membership, quality of surroundings), any of which may affect their attractiveness to different family members (Edwards, 1990).

3. Those with children may consider the roles of "Hero," "Scapegoat," "Lost Child," and "Mascot" as described by Wegscheider-Cruse (1989). Which role best describes each child in their family? Following the style of the "illusion of alternatives" (Watzlawick, Weakland, & Fisch, 1974), we do not ask whether the children have been affected, but how. Children, in fact, are profoundly affected by parental substance dependence. Questions implying they may not be invite naivete and denial.

The Discharge Planning Meeting

Held conjointly with families and patients, typically a week after the "family orientation meeting" and just prior to the patient's discharge, this 2-hour meeting lays the foundation for recovery. Its methods and structure all derive from the concept of newly established sobriety as a toxic, stressful state for families (Elkin, 1984; Treadway, 1989; Cermak, 1989) that profoundly disrupts an otherwise homeostatic, albeit painful, condition (Haley, 1963; Jackson, 1957; Watzlawick, Bavelas, & Jackson, 1967). To be effective, treatment staff (again, two trained staff members familiar with the residents) must appreciate the inertia involved in alcoholic family systems. They must understand the potential for treatment to be used as respite, in order that everyone can return to the old arrangements (Usher, Jay, & Glass, 1982).

Restraint-from-Change Directive

Graduation day is a difficult, awkward time for everybody. The families are supposed to feel happy, proud, and congratulatory, but they don't.

Drug Dependence Evaluation and Referral Program 103B4, VA Medical Center
795 Willow Road, Menlo Park, CA 94025 (415) 493-5000 x 2305

PLAN FOR CONTINUING TREATMENT

ONE YEAR Treatment Recommendations for ___*JERRY*___ Admission Date:
SUBSTANCE ABUSE DIAGNOSES:

___*ALCOHOL DEPENDENCE, COCAINE DEPENDENCE*___

Your addiction is harmful to your well-being and endangers your life. It also harms and endangers your family, friends, and others in your community. To begin your recovery from addiction and its consequences, you need to stop using alcohol and/or other drugs. After reviewing your history of addiction and treatment efforts, the 103B4 professional staff STRONGLY RECOMMENDS that, starting immediately, you take each of the steps checked below for a period of ONE YEAR to enable you to recover from addiction. All the services recommended may be obtained at or through the Menlo Park VA.

[✔] Do not live with substance abusers. Remember that any association with substance abusers may jeopardize your recovery.

[✔] Do not have any contact with your family while you are abusing alcohol or other drugs.

[✔] Do not accept financial help, free shelter, food, transportation or other goods or services from your family or friends for one year. If you need *housing*, you may wish to continue inpatient treatment at a long term substance abuse program, live in a halfway house, or a self-supporting working community such as Delancey Street in San Francisco.

[ ] Further inpatient residential treatment is not likely to help you recover from substance abuse and addiction at this time.

[✔] Complete a long-term residential treatment program for substance abusers following your treatment at 103B4.

[✔] Take Antabuse daily for one year, supervised at least three times per week.*
[ ] Take Naltrexone daily for one year, supervised at least three times per week.*
[ ] Provide supervised clean urines at least two times per week for one year.
   **If you are not allowed to use Antabuse or Naltrexone while in another residential treatment program, make arrangements to begin or resume taking such medications upon discharge from that program.*

[✔] Attend an AA/NA/CA or other support meeting at least _3_ times per week.
[ ] Attend an Adult Children of Alcoholics meeting at least once per week for four weeks, starting in six months.

[ ] Consult an outpatient psychotherapy group therapist and follow his/her treatment recommendations.

[ ] Consult an individual psychotherapist and follow his/her treatment recommendations.

[✔] Encourage your adult family members to attend the 103B4 Family Meeting on Tuesdays from 1:00 to 3:00 or 7:00 to 8:30 pm. *These meetings are free of charge. Arrangements to attend may be made by calling (415) 493-5000 x2305 or (415) 617-2766.* Encourage those living at a distance to attend Al-Anon, Nar-Anon or Adult Children of Alcoholics (ACA) meetings in their area.

[ ] Encourage your children over 12 to attend Al-Ateen meetings, and your children under 13 to seek professional counseling to deal with issues raised in having an addicted parent.

[✔] Call 103B4 at (415) 617-2766 if you need support or a referral for support. A telephone message machine will allow you to leave a message, and a staff member will get back to you. Please leave us a message if you change your address or phone number.   *over...*

FIGURE 5.1. Treatment recommendations for Jerry.

Additional Treatment Recommendations:

PARENTS MUST SIGN AGREEMENT TERMINATING

FINANCIAL SUPPORT FOR ONE YEAR

INFORMING YOUR SUPPORT NETWORK

As part of your continuing treatment plan, copies of these recommendations will be sent to the members of your support network named below:

Name	Relationship
MARTHA	MOTHER
PETE	DAD

The treatment services recommended can all be obtained at or through the Menlo Park VA. The 103B4 staff can help you locate other agencies to obtain them if you live at a distance. If you intend to follow these recommendations and sign that you agree below, we will make every effort to help you and your family through this next difficult and challenging year.

_____   1990
Richard Bale, Ph.D.   Date
103B4 Program Director

****

I have carefully read the treatment recommendations above and *agree to follow each of them* for one year.

_____   _____
Name   Date

I have carefully read the treatment recommendations above but *do not agree to follow them.* I understand that these recommendations will be kept in a confidential file at 103B4 and I will be required to agree to them before receiving any future treatment from 103B4.

_____   _____
Name   Date

FIGURE 5.1. (cont.)

Instead, they are full of apprehension and dread, which shows through the thin veneer of smiles and "best behavior" that characterizes the beginning of this meeting. Wives who have successfully managed children, households, and life outside the hospital are wary of sharing control with husbands who have promised so much and delivered so little. Years of contained anger and resentment, as well as acquired competencies, are to be set aside. We used to view the wife's "resistance" at this stage, obviously seeking power and control, as the "disturbed personality" described by many theorists of previous decades (Whalen, 1953). Helpful to us was clinical experience with the wives of Vietnam POW's, who earnestly prayed for their husbands' return, but were apprehensive about the upheaval such a reintegration might bring. They were right, and many reunited families were soon split again by divorce.

Patients have a similarly unrealistic set of expectancies. Racked by guilt and shame for having abandoned their responsibilities, especially to their families, and bolstered by newly found pride and personal health (the "pink cloud" as described by Edwards, 1990), they want to make up for past years in the first few weeks of recovery. They won't be able to do it.

Addressing all of these concerns, the staff issues the following strongly worded directives:

1. "You can't make up for the past, so don't try. Live your life in the present and for the future, as best you can."

2. "For the immediate future, don't change the organization of the household responsibilities or the lines of authority in parental discipline. Let the wife continue in her role; let the husband become the family expert in recovery." (Treadway, 1989)

3. "Trust takes two years to recover, and efforts to hurry that schedule will backfire. Don't promise anything to each other—you have too little credibility, and each of you will pay more attention to what the other does than what they say." As Treadway (1989) points out in his description of couples work at this stage, "unlike traditional therapy, clients are taught how to live with difficult feelings rather than attempt to resolve them." One of the most confusing experiences in recovery occurs when the addict has done everything "right" for several months and suffers a verbal barrage of old hurts and resentments from his spouse. Rarely is he able to see that his respectful, responsible behavior has led his wife to feel safe enough to express these long buried feelings. We recommend that such "museum tours" (Bach, 1974) be conducted under therapeutic supervision.

4. "Focus on abstinence."

Abstinence as the Requirement

Drug-dependent patients are at least ambivalent about abstinence, especially alcoholics who often consider a return to controlled, or "social" drinking. Families, too, are typically unsure and confused. They also remember the times before alcohol "got out of hand," wonder if abstinence is necessary, and worry that too high or unreasonable a goal will backfire, leading to complete relapse back into full dependence. Drug users with no reported history of alcohol abuse also will see little to justify abstinence from alcohol, and families may actually encourage this shift to the "less dangerous" drug.

We sidestep all these issues. For us the first year of recovery is like pregnancy—a very special time in which something new and extremely vulnerable is growing. Like pregnancy, this is a time-limited period (we judge it to be 1 year) for abstention from all alcohol and other drugs, as well as other diversions (e.g., sexual promiscuity or compulsive overwork). Decisions about limited drinking or the use of alcohol by former drug addicts are best considered after a year of abstinence. Families intuitively understand the metaphor of pregnancy and are generally pleased to set aside loaded questions until later. One year later, in fact, it is rare to find a sober alcoholic and his family interested in "controlled" drinking.

The One-Year Plan for Continued Treatment

Families are handed the staff's written recommendations for the "minimal conditions necessary for the patient's recovery in the next year." Normally these include continuation of residential or outpatient treatment; regular, frequent attendance of 12-step or other support meetings; the use of Antabuse (for alcoholics) or naltrexone (for narcotic addicts); and the cessation of further financial support by the family. The rationale for this last requirement, stated at the previous meeting, is reiterated, as is the reassurance of hospital resources. In making this recommendation, staff must be sensitive to ethnic and cultural differences around issues of individuation and dependency (Bennett, 1989). For a relatively unacculturated Hispanic family, for example, it might be not at all uncommon to have an extended family including siblings in their 40s living together. Negotiations would more helpfully focus on defining the obligations of a dutiful son, rather than establishing a separate residence.

Contingency Contracts

The family is now ready for the most difficult, and probably most important, part of the meeting. The patient has usually signed off that he agrees to follow the recommendations for continued treatment. Now the families must face the question: What will I do if my loved one doesn't recover, if he relapses?

First, we define relapse. If "relapse" is defined as drinking or using drugs again, it is often too late for anything less than a major intervention, or rehospitalization. By that time everyone's judgment is impaired as the family is thrown into crisis. Instead, we encourage patients and families to define relapse as noncompliance with the written treatment recommendations. Because they are presented as the minimal conditions necessary for recovery, relapse is only a matter of time after their abrogation. It is easier for a wife or parent to consider noncompliance as relapse when we speak of "raising the bottom" (Elkin, 1984) and frame it as protecting the family from the truly dangerous, precipitous situations involved in readdiction.

Second, the family is asked to state, sometimes in writing, what they will do if and when this "relapse" occurs. Most initial statements are courageous and vague, and the work of the therapist is to help the families make them both realistic and concrete. Most statements initially involve changes in the addict's behavior ("I'll insist that he reenter treatment") over which the family has no control, and the therapist must redirect. Will they move to a separate bedroom? Change the locks? Move out? Do nothing? Each plan is examined in pragmatic terms: Is this financially, legally, or emotionally possible? The most important aspect of this negotiation is that the family create a plan they can uphold. In another striking example of parallel process, the family has often lied (about what they will do if he uses drugs again) as frequently as the addict (about how he will quit) and neither side has any credibility. Occasionally, a wife or mother will even say "If I've told him once, I've told him a thousand times . . . " which precipitates an immediate smile from the addict and, after a few moments, laughter from the group.

To achieve credibility, we strongly encourage a realistic plan, even if it means a plan to do nothing! That is, families that would like to set limits but feel unable or not yet ready to do so, are encouraged to say exactly that to their loved one. In the long run, it is the credibility that will be crucial to the recovery of the relationship. Moreover, we warn families who have made empty threats in the past to expect that their loved one will repeatedly test any new resolutions. That is the legacy of unfulfilled promises. Addicts are extremely uncomfortable with stated or written plans to "do nothing" and it is a rare, clarifying moment in therapy when their externalization of responsibility is most evident.

A variety of contingency contracts have been described by others (Boudin, 1977; Caddy & Block, 1983; Moltzen et al., 1986; Ossip-Klein, Van Landingham, Prue, & Rychtarik, 1984; Page & Badgett, 1984). Such contracts can be very useful in a range of behaviors, including the distribution of household responsibilities, financial arrangements (e.g., payment of room and board by those living with parents), and a variety of other relationship parameters.

Antabuse

Although research has yielded conflicting results (Azrin, Sisson, Meyers, & Godley, 1982; Keane, Foy, Nunn, & Rychtarik, 1984) we have found monitored (observed by another) Antabuse to be extremely useful in early recovery. This medication is more than an aid to dissuade impulsive relapse; it is in fact a prosthesis for trust.

Because it takes so long for trust to recover, families must anxiously tread a line between acceptance and vigilance. The problem here is that it is difficult to play two roles — for example, cop and lover. Antabuse can remove the "cop" role by independently verifying sobriety. For some families, the monitoring is best accomplished by the wife or parent; for others, this is a disaster. If the monitoring itself feels regressive (the cop role again) it can be assigned instead to friends, employers (often employee assistance program workers), pastors, treatment programs, or anyone who has regular contact with the alcoholic and is trusted by the family. The agreement must be that a failure to take the Antabuse is immediately reported to the family. Only under this arrangement can the family let go of its vigilance and begin to assume other, more truly supportive roles.

In our experience there is only one real reason to discontinue Antabuse in the first year of recovery: the alcoholic has made a decision to resume drinking. Protestations of psychological health, achieved sobriety, religious conversion, wanting to "test the recovery," and even desire for a "drug free" life notwithstanding, there is no credible reason to discontinue. Framing the use of Antabuse around issues of vigilance and trust helps the families sidestep the protestations.

Continued Connection

In the final moments of the discharge planning meeting, our staff makes a clear declaration of availability for future contact: in person or by telephoning the program at any hour or day of the week. In making this dramatic statement we want to make it clear to all that the hard work is just beginning, that their greatest challenges are yet to be faced, and that we will be there to help. Although our own program offers a long-term group for codependents, we know that, because of travel time and distance, relatively few will avail themselves of this option. Our attempt is to normalize the inevitability of crisis in recovery, encourage the use of support systems like Al-Anon, and set up an open line for continued communication.

Families, in fact, do call as the crises unfold. Typically, a wife or mother calls when the alcoholic has discontinued Antabuse and she finds herself unwilling to abide by her own contract as well. At these times, if a family member is sincerely trying to uphold his or her commitment, (e.g., to move out of the house), we will make an unusual, extra effort to offer immediate treatment to the patient, even though he may try to sabotage his readmission by lying, being uncooperative, or simply not showing up. By being more willing to work with resistant behavior at this crucial time, we are able to support the family, relieve them of their sense of obligation, and place responsibility squarely back in the hands of the alcoholic.

Alternatively, families call to plead for readmission but are unwilling to consider their own broken contract. In these times we strongly encourage the family to reread the Plan for Continued Treatment and to ask themselves whether the loved one is following it. The best plan may not be readmission (although it may certainly offer respite to the family, which is what this is all about), but adherence to the recommendations, (e.g., attending support meetings, taking his Antabuse). Even very emeshed families sometimes can understand with a simple analogy: You go to a doctor with a bad cough and he prescribes two medications — treatment recommendations. Months pass and your cough persists, but you don't take the medications. What is the first question your doctor will ask you? Families intuitively understand that a reappointment is unlikely before the recommended treatment is tried.

For especially codependent families with a history of hospitalizations and unfulfilled promises of limit setting, we will often require attendance at our own family meetings, proof of Al-Anon attendance, and/or documentation that they have abided by certain agreements (e.g., to move out, if realistically possible), before readmitting the alcoholic. Even in a family searching for only respite, this can create powerful leverage for the resumption of treatment. We are more than willing to play the bad guy in this instance. This may enable a wife or parent—including one who is frightened and intimidated by possible retaliation—to disclaim responsibility. "Look, honey, they made me do this and said they wouldn't see you again if I didn't. . . . I did it for you!"

Staff unwilling to take tough stances of this kind during the recovery process, to do what is necessary to make things happen, are often ignorant of the tremendous physical, emotional, and financial costs of alcoholism (Elkin, 1984).

CASE APPLICATIONS

Case #1: Jerry, His Parents, and the Gourmet Meal

When we first saw Jerry he was in his late 20s, and had been abusing alcohol for several years. He came to the hospital when his first few uses of cocaine had produced frightening, paranoid episodes. He hadn't seen his parents in some time, and he prided himself somewhat on his independence. He compared himself favorably to his older brother Chuck, who was unemployed and "living off the parents" at home. Jerry was not through with partying, knew it, and saw treatment as a way of controlling a dangerous turn in his use of drugs. He left the program prematurely. We didn't see him again for 6 years.

When we saw Jerry again he looked extremely depressed and hopeless. Gone was his youthful, even charming, optimism about himself and other people. The partying was clearly over. He was now heavily dependent on alcohol and would occasionally binge on cocaine when some of his old friends got "lucky." They would "score" some dope and show up at his parents' house, where Jerry was now living. Jerry came alone to admission, but we quickly invited his parents to join us at the family orientation meeting the following week.

His mother, Martha, was a pleasant but anxious woman in her late 50s. She reported that her husband was unable to make the meeting due to a demanding work schedule. That was just as well, she said, because she and her husband Pete often fought over how to treat their younger son. She felt it would be important not to bring that additional burden into an already difficult situation.

Slowly and tearfully, Martha revealed how pleased she and Pete had been when Jerry had broken up with his drug-using girlfriend and moved back into their home "temporarily" 2 years before. She recited a litany of attempts to help him get back on his feet, while helplessly watching him sink deeper into his alcohol addiction. Once, a few weeks after Jerry was finally able to land a job, he was arrested for drunk driving. By bailing him out of jail and hiring a good lawyer, she made it possible for him to return to work immediately, but he lost the job soon after. She had given up on her husband, whose anger towards Jerry only made things worse and even seemed to make Jerry drink more.

Martha was stunned when a "graduate" family member (attending the meeting as a volunteer) suggested to her that the time might be approaching when she would have to choose between her husband and her son. She was further surprised to hear the patient representative describe a home situation much like her own, in which he had achieved almost total control of his entire family. She was shocked to hear him describe the anger he felt towards his family's patronizing tolerance.

We strongly suggested that Martha encourage Pete to attend the discharge planning meeting the following week. We said that we would be inviting him by phone ourselves, as well. When Pete showed up for the meeting, we were pleased.

Pete was a husky man in his early 60s. He had worked his way up the ladder of a small manufacturing plant and was looking forward to his impending retirement and release from many responsibilities. Pete had been relieved when his eldest son Chuck had finally gotten his act together and moved out and very disappointed and resentful when Jerry moved in a few months later. Yet Pete felt his wife had been right, that given a little encouragement and support, Jerry would land on his feet too.

In the discharge planning meeting, when Jerry announced to his parents that he had decided to remain in the hospital for further residential treatment (as recommended in the Plan for Continued Treatment in Figure 5.1), his father was distressed. What Jerry needed, he felt, was an honest job and not to be further indulged as a hospital patient. He seemed somewhat mollified when a staff member described the 6-day-a-week, 18-hour workdays of the inpatient programs.

Because of their severe enmeshment, we immediately struck a deal with Martha and Pete. If they would sign an agreement to discontinue supporting Jerry financially for the next year (see Figure 5.1), we would keep the hospital door open for him. With Jerry headed to a 6-month program, financial or other support issues seemed to be in the remote future, and they signed.

Two days later Jerry showed up at 3:00 A.M. in the morning on his parents' back porch; he was drunk and pleading for "a bed for the night." In the morning he revealed to them how a staff member in the new program "had it in for him" and "threw him out on the street," just as he was getting used to the new routines. What Jerry didn't tell his parents was that the residents of the new program had confronted him on his helpless irresponsibility, and that he had left the program voluntarily. He had sneaked out the back door in the middle of the night.

Jerry's parents were angry and resentful of this betrayal of their newly established trust by the hospital staff and were at first skeptical when we told them the real story of Jerry's departure. We reminded them of the fact that our patients who had achieved an unconditional "good deal" at home were likely to leave at the first confrontation in treatment. As an offer of good faith, we offered to readmit Jerry the following morning, if they would agree to honor their agreement to cease financial support. They were surprised when Jerry was not especially pleased with our offer.

Over the next several months Jerry left treatment twice more. Once he returned from pass intoxicated, and he was banned from readmission for 30 days. His parents came in twice to the evening long-term family meeting for support during this month, but they didn't budge from their commitment to deny him shelter and other resources, repeatedly deflecting Jerry's pleas by reminding him of their promises to the hospital staff.

Finally, as Jerry came to believe that his parents were no longer available to shield him from what life had to teach him, he committed himself to the treatment program. He heard some difficult feedback from both staff and fellow residents and dished some out himself. He began to feel a growing pride in himself and a new sense of self-respect. When he graduated from the program he moved with two other graduates into a local, inexpensive apartment, modest, even grungy by his parents' standards. With a little money left over from his new job as a clerk trainee, he took cooking classes. His greatest sense of pride in his first year of recovery came when he invited his parents over to enjoy a gourmet meal he had prepared himself.

Case #2: Harry, June, and "Cycletherapy"

Harry was probably the nastiest alcoholic we had admitted in some time. It took us a week to realize that his abrasiveness was an effective cover for a number of cognitive impairments. In his late 60s, Harry was becoming senile, perhaps because of his drinking. As a municipal bus driver he had overlearned his route and could probably have driven it in his sleep. But when a new, young supervisor reorganized the schedules, Harry was given a new route, and he fell apart. His inability to sort out maps, his failed memory, and his inability to ask for help added up to a suspension and recommendation for immediate retirement.

Harry's pride was shattered, and he was scared that he was losing his mind. He resented the youthful energy of the treatment program and its crazy business of "cycletherapy" (Harry's term for psychotherapy). He actually never did participate in the treatment activities and was irascible for the entire 2 weeks of detoxification. Withdrawal, in fact, took almost a year, and his cognition returned very slowly.

June had married Harry shortly after their graduation from high school. She talked in the family orientation meeting about looking forward to their 50th "golden" wedding anniversary the following year. She was a well-organized woman of considerable warmth who had retreated from her husband's drinking into her garden and housekeeping. She was worried about Harry and was a little surprised that, after a few days of initial relief, she felt lonely without him. And so she was pleased in the discharge planning meeting the following week when Harry announced that he had absolutely no plans to continue in residential "cycletherapy" and that he was returning home on Antabuse (one recommendation in the Plan for Continued Treatment in Figure 5.2).

A month later they returned to our long-term family meeting. June looked miserable, much worse than we had seen her before, and we assumed that Harry had resumed his drinking. To the contrary, Harry had

Drug Dependence Evaluation and Referral Program 103B4, VA Medical Center
795 Willow Road, Menlo Park, CA 94025 (415) 493-5000 x 2305

PLAN FOR CONTINUING TREATMENT

ONE YEAR Treatment Recommendations for ___*HARRY*___   Admission Date:

SUBSTANCE ABUSE DIAGNOSES:

___*ALCOHOL DEPENDENCE*___

Your addiction is harmful to your well-being and endangers your life. It also harms and endangers your family, friends, and others in your community. To begin your recovery from addiction and its consequences, you need to stop using alcohol and/or other drugs. After reviewing your history of addiction and treatment efforts, the 103B4 professional staff STRONGLY RECOMMENDS that, starting immediately, you take each of the steps checked below for a period of ONE YEAR to enable you to recover from addiction. All the services recommended may be obtained at or through the Menlo Park VA.

[ ] Do not live with substance abusers. Remember that any association with substance abusers may jeopardize your recovery.

[ ] Do not have any contact with your family while you are abusing alcohol or other drugs.

[ ] Do not accept financial help, free shelter, food, transportation or other goods or services from your family or friends for one year. If you need *housing,* you may wish to continue inpatient treatment at a long term substance abuse program, live in a halfway house, or a self-supporting working community such as Delancey Street in San Francisco.

[✓] Further inpatient residential treatment is not likely to help you recover from substance abuse and addiction at this time.

[ ] Complete a long-term residential treatment program for substance abusers following your treatment at 103B4.

[✓] Take Antabuse daily for one year, supervised at least three times per week.*
[ ] Take Naltrexone daily for one year, supervised at least three times per week.*
[ ] Provide supervised clean urines at least two times per week for one year.
     **If you are not allowed to use Antabuse or Naltrexone while in another residential treatment program, make arrangements to begin or resume taking such medications upon discharge from that program.*

[✓] Attend an AA/NA/CA or other support meeting at least _4_ times per week.
[ ] Attend an Adult Children of Alcoholics meeting at least once per week for four weeks, starting in six months.

[ ] Consult an outpatient psychotherapy group therapist and follow his/her treatment recommendations.

[ ] Consult an individual psychotherapist and follow his/her treatment recommendations.

[✓] Encourage your adult family members to attend the 103B4 Family Meeting on Tuesdays from 1:00 to 3:00 or 7:00 to 8:30 pm. *These meetings are free of charge. Arrangements to attend may be made by calling (415) 493-5000 x2305 or (415) 617-2766.* Encourage those living at a distance to attend Al-Anon, Nar-Anon or Adult Children of Alcoholics (ACA) meetings in their area.

[ ] Encourage your children over 12 to attend Al-Ateen meetings, and your children under 13 to seek professional counseling to deal with issues raised in having an addicted parent.

[✓] Call 103B4 at (415) 617-2766 if you need support or a referral for support. A telephone message machine will allow you to leave a message, and a staff member will get back to you. Please leave us a message if you change your address or phone number.   *over...*

FIGURE 5.2. Treatment recommendations for Harry.

Additional Treatment Recommendations:

FOLLOW "DIVISION OF HOUSEHOLD DUTIES" CONTRACT

INFORMING YOUR SUPPORT NETWORK

As part of your continuing treatment plan, copies of these recommendations will be sent to the members of your support network named below:

Name	Relationship
JUNE	_WIFE_

The treatment services recommended can all be obtained at or through the Menlo Park VA. The 103B4 staff can help you locate other agencies to obtain them if you live at a distance. If you intend to follow these recommendations and sign that you agree below, we will make every effort to help you and your family through this next difficult and challenging year.

_1991_
Richard Bale, Ph.D.   Date
103B4 Program Director

****

I have carefully read the treatment recommendations above and *agree to follow each of them* for one year.

_____   _____
Name   Date

I have carefully read the treatment recommendations above but *do not agree to follow them.* I understand that these recommendations will be kept in a confidential file at 103B4 and I will be required to agree to them before receiving any future treatment from 103B4.

_____   _____
Name   Date

FIGURE 5.2. (cont.)

not touched a drop of alcohol, and in fact had introduced two old friends to the VA treatment programs and the benefits of this wonder drug, Antabuse. He had also become an absolute menace around the house, disrupting June's carefully organized cleaning schedules and storage layouts.

Over the next several weeks we helped Harry and June draw up a series of carefully worded contracts that would reintegrate Harry into his home and give him a role and purpose in his forced retirement, while protecting June's autonomy and accomplishments. We helped them assign chores, relegate areas of responsibilities, and even divide up territories of the house. When Harry's ambition for additional responsibility exceeded that offered by the house, we introduced him to a network of 12-step meetings that needed organizing.

Harry became a constant visitor to our outpatient clinic where he picked up his Antabuse regularly. He was often on his way to 12-step meetings or his volunteer job with the county mental health organization as their liaison to self-help groups. Occasionally he would bump into some of the old detox staff, for whom he now felt some fondness, but he would often remark how strange it was that "such nice young people would get so mixed up with that cycletherapy business."

RESEARCH SUMMARY

The treatment techniques described have been developed over the last 8 years of our program (1984–1992), during which time family attendance has been mandatory. For the preceding 8 years (1975–1983), we struggled with a variety of techniques to induce families to attend conjoint therapy sessions, with minimal success. With fewer than 10% of families attending, we became increasingly worried that any gains in treatment could be reversed easily within a few days back home. We became aware of the extensive family subsidization of addiction, and like others (Hahn & King, 1983) our own research showed that our patients living with wives, girlfriends, or parents were much less likely to continue in treatment (Marotta & Bale, 1986). In the late spring of 1984, we conducted an all-day staff "retreat" solely to analyze the substantial resistance of families to treatment. What we found that day was a great surprise to us all.

It seemed true that the feelings of fear, remorse, embarrassment, guilt, anger, and hopelessness in both patients and their families worked strongly against the development of a family program. However, there existed a deeper and more entrenched resistance to family contact *among the staff.* On a superficial level, the staff was apprehensive about the potential for increased work load, some thorny issues of confidentiality, and a fear that requiring family attendance would severely decrease our attractability to new clients. More importantly, the staff was resentful about the swift and profound regressions during family visits that undermined much therapeutic progress, which had sometimes resulted in premature termination. And many staff felt unprepared and untrained to deal with family dynamics.

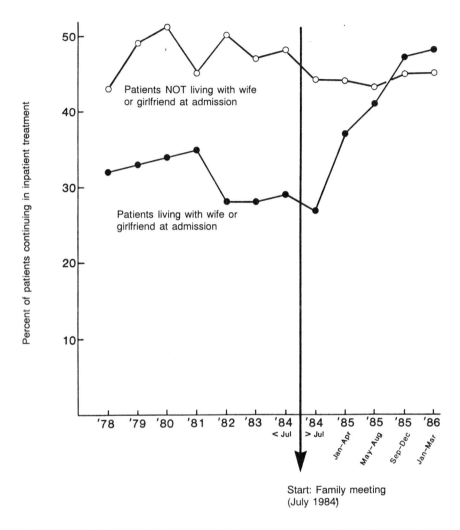

FIGURE 5.3. Percent of patients continuing inpatient treatment before and after starting Family Meeting program in short-term detoxificaiton unit.

Nevertheless, we came to view our avoidance of family work as a shared denial of the importance of the outside world on our clients, and we resolved to make family attendance mandatory. Once we had resolved our own ambivalence, the patients and families quickly followed. Family attendance increased from 9% in 1983 to 42% in 1984, and rose to 65% by 1986, where it has since remained fairly steady. The effect of the family contact on treatment retention was powerful: patients with wives or girlfriends (the first focus of our treatment efforts) were almost twice as likely to continue in inpatient treatment as those in earlier years (see Figure 5.3).

We hope to further refine our family work with results from our current research on family support compliance, monitoring strategies for antabuse, and conflict resolution techniques in early recovery.

CONCLUSIONS

We have described a four-point strategy for engaging the families of substance abusers in the first stages of treatment. Essential to this approach is the notion that most addiction is subsidized and that families often play an unwitting but powerful role in maintaining the substance dependence. With continued financial support during the addiction—in the form of money, goods, shelter, or transportation—the addict is unlikely to "hit bottom" and make the sacrifices necessary to fully participate in treatment.

Establishing an initial rapport with families is best accomplished in meetings that have an informational, rather than therapeutic, emphasis. Usually notions of enabling or codependence are premature at this point. Instead, trained staff assist the families in finding resources for their own support.

As the substance abuser progresses through this initial period of inpatient assessment and evaluation, an individualized 1-year Plan for Continued Treatment is developed. In a second family meeting this plan is discussed, and relapse is defined as noncompliance with the treatment recommendations—rather than as a resumption of substance use. The use of monitored Antabuse is stressed, and special contingency contracts are developed as concepts of limit setting and sanctions evolve.

Finally, we establish a continued connection with the families and make ourselves available on-call for further advice and support. In the event of relapses, we often relax our readmission criteria to support a family that shows a willingness to set limits with the substance abuser.

REFERENCES

Azrin, N., Sisson, R., Meyers, R., & Godley, M. (1982). Alcoholism treatment by disulfiram and community reinforcement therapy. *Journal of Behavior Therapy and Experimental Psychiatry, 13,* 105–112.
Bach, G. (1974). *Creative aggression.* New York: Doubleday.
Bale, R., Van Stone, W., Engelsing, T., Kuldau, J., Elashoff, R., & Zarcone, V. (1984).

Process and outcome in three therapeutic communities. *Archives of General Psychiatry, 41,* 185–191.

Bennett, L. (1989). Family, alcohol, and culture. In M. Galanter (Ed.), *Recent developments in alcoholism* (Vol. 7, pp. 111–127). New York: Plenum Press.

Boudin, H. (1977). Contingency contracting with drug abusers in the natural environment. *International Journal of the Addictions, 12,* 1–16.

Caddy, G., & Block, T. (1983). Behavioral treatment methods for alcoholics. In D. Goodwin (Ed.), *Recent developments in alcoholism* (Vol. 3, pp. 139–165). New York: Plenum Press.

Cermak, T. (1989). Al-Anon and recovery. In M. Galanter (Ed.), *Recent developments in alcoholism* (Vol. 7, pp. 91–104). New York: Plenum Press.

Edwards, J. (1990). *Treating chemically dependent families.* Minneapolis, MN: Johnson Institute.

Elkin, M. (1984). *Families under the influence.* New York: W. W. Norton.

Hahn, J., & King, K. (1983). Client and environmental correlates of patient attrition from an inpatient alcoholism center. *Journal of Drug Education, 12,* 75–86.

Haley, J. (1963). *Strategies of psychotherapy.* New York: Grune & Stratton.

Jackson, D. (1957). The question of family homeostasis. *Psychiatric Quarterly, 31* (Suppl.), 79–90.

Jacob, T., & Leonard, K. (1988). Alcoholic–spouse interaction as a function of alcoholism subtype and alcohol consumption interaction. *Journal of Abnormal Psychology, 97,* 231–237.

Jacob, T., & Seilhamer, R. (1989). Alcoholism and family interaction. In M. Galanter (Ed.), *Recent developments in alcoholism* (Vol. 7, pp. 129–145). New York: Plenum Press.

Kaufman, E. (1984). The family that wouldn't give up: Structural–dynamic family therapy in a dry system. In E. Kaufman (Ed.), *Power to change: Family case studies in the treatment of alcoholism* (pp. 293–312). New York: Gardner Press.

Keane, T., Foy, D., Nunn, B., & Rychtarik, R. (1984). Spouse contracting to increase Antabuse compliance in alcoholic veterans. *Journal of Clinical Psychology, 40,* 340–344.

Ketcham, K., & Gustafson, G. (1989). *Living on the edge: A guide to intervention for families with drug and alcohol problems.* New York: Bantam Books.

Lawson, G., Peterson, J., & Lawson, A. (1983). *Alcoholism and the family.* Rockville, MD: Aspen Systems.

Marotta, J., & Bale, R. (1986, April). *Marital variables and treatment completion.* Paper presented at the National Council on Alcoholism Forum, San Francisco.

Marotta, J., Lehr, B., Moltzen, R., Pohlman, F., & Bale, R. (1986, April). *Differential effects of marital status on treatment completion: Addicts vs. alcoholics.* Paper presented at the National Council on Alcoholism Forum, San Francisco.

Minuchin, S. (1974). *Families and family therapy.* Cambridge, MA: Harvard University Press.

Moltzen, R., Tucker, W., & Bale, R. (1986, April). *Let's make a deal: Pre-treatment contracting and the support network.* Paper presented at the National Council on Alcoholism Forum, San Francisco, CA.

O'Farrell, T. (1989). Marital and family therapy in alcoholism treatment. *Journal of Substance Abuse Treatment, 6,* 23–29.

Ossip-Klein, D., Van Landingham, W., Prue, D., & Rychtarik, R. (1984). Increasing attendance at alcohol aftercare using calendar prompts and home based contracting. *Addictive Behaviors, 9,* 85–89.

Page, R., & Badgett, S. (1984). Alcoholism treatment with environmental support contracting. *American Journal of Drug and Alcohol Abuse, 10,* 589–605.

Sisson, R., & Azrin, N. (1986). Family-member involvement to initiate and promote treatment of problem drinkers. *Journal of Behavior Therapy and Experimental Psychiatry, 17,* 15–21.

Steinglass, P., Bennett, L., Wolin, S., & Reiss, D. (1987). *The alcoholic family.* New York: Basic Books.

Thomas, E., Santa, C., Bronson, D., & Oyserman, D. (1987). Unilateral family therapy with spouses of alcoholics. *Journal of Social Service Research, 10,* 145–163.

Thomas, A., Weaver, J., Knight, L., & Bale, R. (1986). *Family treatment in short-term detoxification.* Paper presented at the National Council on Alcoholism Forum, San Francisco.

Treadway, D. (1989). *Before it's too late: Working with substance abuse in the family.* New York: W. W. Norton.

Usher, M., Jay, J., & Glass, D. (1982). Family therapy as a treatment modality for alcoholism. *Journal of Studies on Alcohol, 43,* 927–938.

Vaillant, G. (1966). A twelve year follow-up of New York narcotic addicts: The relation of treatment to outcome. *American Journal of Psychiatry, 127,* 1646–1651.

Watzlawick, P., Bavelas, J., & Jackson, D. (1967). *Pragmatics of human communication.* New York: W. W. Norton.

Watzlawick, P., Weakland, J., & Fisch, R. (1974). *Change: Principles of problem formation and problem resolution.* New York: W. W. Norton.

Wegscheider-Cruse, S. (1989). *Another chance: Hope and health for the alcoholic family.* Palo Alto, CA: Science and Behavior Books.

Whalen, T. (1953). Wives of alcoholics: Four types observed in a family service agency. *Quarterly Journal of Studies on Alcohol, 14,* 632–641.

Wright, K., & Scott, J. (1978). The relationship of wives' treatment to the drinking status of alcoholics. *Journal of Studies on Alcohol, 39,* 1577–1581.

Zeigler-Driscoll, G. (1979). The similarities in families of drug dependents and alcoholics. In E. Kaufman (Ed.), *Power to change: Family case studies in the treatment of alcoholism* (pp. 19–39). New York: Gardner Press.

Chapter 6

The Hazelden Residential Family Program
A Combined Systems and Disease Model Approach

J. Clark Laundergan
Terence Williams

OVERVIEW

Hazelden, located in Center City, Minnesota, is well known in the alcohol and drug treatment field for its inpatient rehabilitation of chemically dependent men and women, as well as for its educational services that publish and distribute addiction-related literature. Other programs available at Hazelden are a Renewal Center, Continuing Education Workshops, Counselor Training, and the Family Program.

The Hazelden Family Program began in 1972 as a 3-day residential program for the family members and significant others of chemically dependent persons. By 1975, a staff of three provided family treatment for 764 participants and, in 1977, a new facility was constructed for the family program. In 1979, the family program expanded its treatment from 3 to 5 days and served 922 participants (Williams, Schroeder, Spicer, Laundergan, & Jones, 1981). A 1986 facility expansion from 9 to 12 double occupancy rooms and an increase in group meeting space permitted the annual number of participants to reach 1,600.

The family program emphasis is on the participating family member and the family system rather than on the chemically dependent person. Recovery within the context of the 12-step Al-Anon program is stressed with the treatment experience serving as a catalyst for bringing about the beginnings of change. The procedures used in the family program include lectures, videotape presentations, small group activities, a personal inventory, and the development of a personal plan of change with the guidance of a counselor. Informal interactions between participants are a central part of the family program experience.

Program expectations are for improved self-awareness, recognition of the disease concept of chemical dependency, knowledge of how chemical dependency affects the family, and improved awareness of the change options that are available. Many participants arrive at the program experiencing diminished self-worth and are stuck in their thought and behavior patterns. These feelings and patterns are not fully associated in their thinking with the adaptations that have been made to the chemically dependent behavior that has affected their lives. They are told that alcohol and drug abuse constitute chemical dependency that may be understood as a chronic disease. Chemical dependency is associated with family relationship patterns that are assumed to be appropriate, but need to be recognized as nonproductive for the family system and family members. Family members are encouraged to improve their understanding of chemical dependency and of how they are capable of changing relationship dynamics and their feelings of self-worth.

SPECIAL CONSIDERATIONS

It is felt that family members can learn from alcoholics and drug addicts with whom they are not emotionally tied, and that alcoholics can similarly gain insight from family members other than their own who have the experience of living with a chemically dependent person. The Hazelden Family Program is *not* a conjoint experience participated in by the chemically dependent person and his or her family. A unique characteristic of the program is that the participant family members have an opportunity to interact with chemically dependent persons from the rehabilitation program who were previously strangers to them. Family program participants remain in the family program for 5 days and patients from the rehabilitation units are referred by counselors to be rehabilitation participants in the family program for 3 days.

What occurs is a sharing between family and rehabilitation participants about feelings, perceptions, and resentments. The family program promotes interaction and information exchange that, in turn, develops the awareness that what takes place in chemical dependency family relationships is not unique to one's own family unit. The alcoholic and drug addict behavior is depersonalized from the chemically dependent family member when similar thoughts and actions are described by another, recently met, chemically dependent person. Similarly, the family reaction to the chemical dependency that is expressed to rehabilitation patients by family program participants fosters a new appreciation for rehabilitation patients of what has been occurring in their families.

The capacity of the family program is 24 family/significant other participants. Additional rooms are available in the neighboring CORK Center (a building funded by the Kroc Foundation), so this capacity may be temporarily increased. The 5-day program has a 7-day lecture schedule and participants may enter and leave at any point during the week. Because of turnover, the census is not always at capacity. No more than three rehabilitation patients enter the family program per day. This means that no more than 9 rehabilitation patients are included in the family program at any time, with 15 rehabilitation patients having been a part of the family program during a family/significant other's 5-day stay in the program. Other potential participants may come from aftercare, the clergy-trainee program, the counselor-trainee program, and professionals in residence. The highest number of persons in the family program at one time has been 62, but most often the census is in the 30–35 range.

The program is optional for family members and significant others in that it is a separate program from primary rehabilitation and only some of the family/significant others of rehabilitation patients elect or can afford to participate. Some family participants do not have a family member currently in primary rehabilitation. The chemically dependent person in their lives may either have received treatment earlier at Hazelden or elsewhere or may still be an active alcoholic/drug addict.

Similarly, only a portion of the 1,700 patients admitted to primary rehabilitation are referred by their counselors to spend 3 days in the family program. Rehabilitation patients continue to reside on their primary treatment units during their involvement in the family program, although they spend their days and early evenings in the Family Center. Confidentiality is expected of all who participate in the family program: "What is said in the Family Center is not to be shared outside." This confidentiality is considered a cornerstone of all Hazelden programs: "Who you see here, what you hear here, when you leave here, let it stay here."

DESCRIPTION OF THE TREATMENT METHOD

Table 6.1 provides an overview of the objectives and key elements of the Hazelden Residential Family Program that will be described in detail in this section. Each of the program elements will be described next. Finally, methods used to foster program acceptance and to deal with resistance will be discussed.

TABLE 6.1. Overview of Hazelden Residential Family Program

A. Program Objectives
 1. Become more knowledgable about chemical dependency and the process of recovery.
 2. Recognize how chemical dependency involves family and friends.
 3. Develop new strategies for coping with family relationships and lowering anxiety.
 4. Share thoughts and feelings with others, learn to trust.
 5. Accept Al-Anon and the 12-step program.

B. Key Program Elements
 1. Personal inventory and plan.
 2. Daily schedule of program activities.
 3. Information to achieve program objectives.
 4. Social and physical environment conducive to growth.

Personal Plan

The Family Center Personal Plan form (see Figure 6.1) is given to each guest by the counselor during the initial meeting with the explanation that guests formulate their personal plan during their stay in the program. The personal plan should be ready to hand in to the counselor and present in a group meeting on the last day of residence. Counselors are available to help guests with their personal plan if they have questions or need feedback. Guests are expected to formulate realistic and specific plans in three areas: (1) a commitment to oneself for continuing help and support from others (e.g., I will ask for help from family and friends when I need it; I will attend Al-Anon once each week); (2) changes in daily routine to reduce stress (e.g., I will take a half-hour walk three times each week); (3) increase enjoyment of life (e.g., I will take a self-improvement class that will help me take time for myself and reflect on the positive events of the day).

Typical Schedule of Program Activities

Table 6.2 summarizes the daily schedule of activities experienced by program participants. An opportunity for activities of one's choice is available from 6:30 to 7:45 in the morning. Participants may choose to meditate, get some light refreshment from the refrigerator in the kitchenette off the lounge (coffee is usually on and tea water is always hot), take a walk on nature trails, or use the exercise room or pool in the CORK Center. At about 8:00 A.M., participants gather in the lounge and walk either by way of an enclosed concourse system or outdoors to the dining facility. A cafeteria-style arrangement permits guests to select their food, which they carry on a tray to a dining room reserved at that

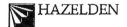 HAZELDEN

FAMILY CENTER PERSONAL PLAN

When you leave the Family Center, how will you use what you have learned here? Please take some time to write down a specific, realistic, and creative plan that will help guide you through the days ahead.

BE SPECIFIC: "I'm going to get more exercise" might be a good general goal, but a more specific goal is to decide that "I will walk for a half-hour at 7:30 a.m. on Mondays, Wednesdays and Fridays."

BE REALISTIC: To say "I'm going to quit worrying about X's drinking" is a big order; however, deciding that "I will leave the porch light on and go to bed instead of waiting up for X is possible.

BE CREATIVE: Think of something you could do that would be especially enjoyable or important to you. Maybe you want to learn how to drive a car and get your license. Or you may want to learn karate, or meditation. Or do some traveling you've always hoped to do. Create a plan that will help you enjoy life more thoroughly.

1. I make the following commitment to myself for continuing help and support from others:

_____

_____

_____

(Al-Anon contact number) _____

2. To reduce stress, I will make the following specific change in my daily routine:

_____

_____

_____

3. In order to enjoy life more thoroughly, I commit myself to the following plan:

_____

_____

_____

HAND IN LAST DAY

FAM-0126
Rev. 3/89

Name: _____

Date: _____

White: Participant file
Yellow: Participant's copy

FIGURE 6.1. Hazelden Family Center Personal Plan.

time for the family program. All participants are expected to go to breakfast even if they choose not to eat. Conversation at breakfast often picks up on topics of the previous day, although it may consist of pleasantries such as commenting on the weather.

A community meeting begins at 9:00 A.M. back at the Family Center. This is a time to introduce new participants, announce appointments

TABLE 6.2. Typical Daily Schedule of Hazelden Family Program

Time	Experience
6:30–7:45 A.M.	Opportunity for morning meditation, light refreshment, walking nature trails, and/or use of the gymnasium and pool
8:00–8:15	Announcements, introduction and orientation of new residents, and discharge information for residents leaving
8:15–9:00	Breakfast
9:00–10:15	Community meeting and lecture with related worksheets provided
10:15–10:30	Worksheet preparation
10:30–12:15	Group discussion, 6–8 participants per group
12:30–1:15 P.M.	Lunch
1:15–1:30	Afternoon roll call and announcements
1:30–2:30	Stress management techniques and practice
2:45–3:30	Small group discussion of the AA/Al-Anon Twelve Steps
3:30–4:00	Participants leaving the program present their personal plan and receive their medallion
4:00–6:15	Film, optional activity, free time
6:15–6:45	Dinner
7:00–7:30	Evening lecture or film
7:30 until retiring	Informal interaction, reading, thought, personal plan formulation

with counselors, and take care of program housekeeping details. A morning lecture follows the community meeting. The lecture, given by a staff person, lasts about 45 minutes with 15 minutes of question, answer, and discussion. A sheet summarizing the lecture and asking some questions for further discussion is distributed to the participants. Those in attendance are then subdivided into groups of six to eight people. Approximately 15 minutes is available for preparation of the questions and then the group discussion begins. Each person in the discussion group has 10 minutes to share responses to the prepared questions, raise related issues, and engage in discussion with group members. The discussion groups break before 12:30 P.M. lunch.

Afternoon begins at 1:15 P.M., with afternoon roll call and announcements, followed at 1:30 with stress management techniques and practice. This session may consist of a video and mini-lecture on a topic such as humor as a stress reducer or the participants may go to the

CORK Center relaxation room for instruction and practice in relaxation therapy. Consideration of one of the AA/Al-Anon Twelve Steps begins at 2:45 P.M. with a mini-lecture, worksheet, and small group discussion. At 3:30, persons leaving the family program are presented with a medallion after they have presented their personal plan to the assembled participants. Rehabilitation patients who have completed their 3-day stay in the family program receive a medallion, as do 5-day family program participants. Good-byes are difficult because in many instances people feel close to those they have met in their family program stay because of the intimate sharing and exchange of insight that has taken place.

From 4:00 P.M. until dinner starting at 6:15 there is free time. During this free time, family program participants with a family member in primary rehabilitation may visit with that patient. Others may walk, visit, read, or view an optional video. The evening lecture is in the lecture hall from 7:00 to 7:30 P.M. where the primary rehabilitation patients assemble three times each day for lecture. The evening lecture is usually given by someone from AA/Al-Anon describing their own experience and recovery. Following the lecture, participants gather back in the Family Center for informal conversation, reading, thinking or working on formulating their personal plan until retiring.

Use of Information as the Program Focus

Psychoeducation

The Hazelden Family Program may be understood within the emerging approach of working with families termed "psychoeducation." Although the family program *has not* contributed directly to the developments that have led to psychoeducation work with families, which has been done largely with families of persons with ongoing mental disorders, both approaches have much in common in their orientation and practice. Ryglewicz (1989a) describes psychoeducation work with families as a new approach in which, instead of the family being viewed as dysfunctional, the family is seen as being capable of contributing to its own problem resolution. This is accomplished through workshops that educate about the disorder affecting the family and instruct family members on ways to reduce anxiety within the family system.

Psychoeducation is, "A deliberate and planned effort to *teach* individuals or groups understandings, skills or competencies in the area of human relations" (Ivey, 1977, p. 23). Five essentials of psychoeducation have been identified by Ryglewicz (1989b) as follows: (1) a body of information; (2) an assumption that the disorder(s), transition(s), behavior(s), and/or skill deficits(s) being addressed are at least in part an independent entity; (3) guidelines derived from this knowledge; (4) an educational framework and redefined roles; and (5) use of individual and/or group situations for processing of information conveyed in a supportive manner. Each of these five essentials will be discussed in relation to the Hazelden Family Program to show its commonality in approach to psychoeducation.

Body of Information

What is the body of information that the Hazelden Family Program wishes to transmit to the participants? First the participants need to better understand chemical dependency, chemical dependency treat-ment, and the process of recovery. Participants will be informed about the "no fault" approach to chemical dependency. The chemically de-pendent person did not chose to be alcoholic or drug-addicted. The alcoholism or drug addiction may be understood as a disease that in-volves a loss of control over the drinking or drug taking, a pathological dependence upon the mood-altering substance, and an adaptive im-poverishment including physical, psychological, social, and spiritual problems (Anderson, 1981).

Chemical dependency is a source of anxiety within families and the high anxiety within the family serves to stimulate the chemical de-pendency. Family members are informed on how they are caught up in the problem, on how their efforts to contain or resolve the problem of chemical dependency have paradoxically maintained and promot-ed the condition. It is inaccurate for the family members to blame them-selves for the chemical dependency, but they need to see that the normal things any anxious caring person would do to be helpful can sometimes exacerbate the very problem they are trying to address.

Rational Emotive Therapy

Staff teach some basic principles of Rational Emotive Therapy (RET) (Ellis, 1973) so that program participants begin to alter their thinking and adopt more realistic views of themselves and their social environ-ment. Participants learn how their ideas and actions support negative self-fulfilling prophesies when they believe that they can help the chem-ically dependent persons in their lives and that those persons cannot help themselves. Through lectures and worksheets, program participants begin to identify actual problems, as opposed to imagined ones, and to discriminate between serious problems and less serious problems.

With the emergence of more realistic views of themselves and their surroundings, participants are ready to learn new strategies for coping with family problems. Instead of focusing on the identified problem person, clients learn to focus on their ability to make personal changes that will impact family interactions. Participants learn to view the whole family as a system, to recognize patterns and processes in the family system, and to place the chemical dependency within that framework.

Reduction of Controlling Behavior and Anxiety

An early influence in the conceptualization of the Hazelden Family Program was the work of Murray Bowen (Bowen, 1978; Kerr & Bowen, 1988). Lectures communicate two principle variables of Bowen's theory. The first is differentiation of self—understanding that, although you care deeply about another person, the other person is separate, not under your control, and responsible for their own action, and that you are not dependent on their approval for your actions. The second concerns chronic anxiety—maintaining an ongoing state of personal anxiety that provokes situational anxiety among group members that in turn feeds the ongoing state of personal anxiety.

The emphasis is on the power the individual has to influence the functioning of the family system by minimizing controlling reactive behavior and reducing anxiety. These lectures, worksheets, and discussions are not abstract but presented in layman's terms to promote the examination of participants' own roles in family patterns and processes. Stress management techniques and information on how to monitor distress and anxiety are also presented. Small achievable behavioral goals are assigned during participants' individual interviews with staff. These goals may involve activity scheduling (setting times for relaxation), a behavioral rehearsal (being appropriately assertive in expressing ideas), or homework (obtaining and completing reading assignments). Behavioral goals are intended to address issues related to "differentiation of self" and "chronic anxiety."

Al-Anon

The final step in communicating the body of knowledge is for family program participants to learn about Al-Anon and similar mutual help groups and to experience some of the benefits that they can provide. It is explained that Al-Anon provides a program of living that parallels the 12-step program of Alcoholics Anonymous, but with the focus on the family member or concerned other person rather than on the alcoholic or drug addict. Lectures about the Al-Anon Twelve Steps (see Table 6.3) along with worksheets and discussions serve to inform, apply the

TABLE 6.3. Al-Anon Twelve Steps

These steps can be a way of life for the families of alcoholics:

1. We admitted we were powerless over alcohol — that our lives had become unmanageable.
2. Came to believe that a Power greater than ourselves could restore us to sanity.
3. Made a decision to turn our will and our lives over to the care of God *as we understood Him.*
4. Made a searching and fearless moral inventory of ourselves.
5. Admitted to God, to ourselves, and to another human being the exact nature of our wrongs.
6. Were entirely ready to have God remove all these defects of character.
7. Humbly asked Him to remove our shortcomings.
8. Made a list of all persons we had harmed, and became willing to make amends to them all.
9. Made direct amends to such people wherever possible, except when to do so would injure them or others.
10. Continued to take personal inventory and when we were wrong promptly admitted it.
11. Sought through prayer and meditation to improve our conscious contact with God *as we understood Him,* praying only for knowledge of His will for us and the power to carry that out.
12. Having had a spiritual awakening as the result of these Steps, we tried to carry this message to others, and to practice these principles in all our affairs.

step to participant's circumstances, and demonstrate the power of sharing with other people who have similar life experiences. Two Al-Anon pamphlets are included in the folder given to every participant in the family program: "This is Al-Anon" (Al-Anon, 1981) and "The Twelve Steps and Traditions" (Al-Anon, 1965). The following quote from the "This is Al-Anon" pamphlet illustrates the congruence between the family program emphasis and the Al-Anon approach.

> From the very outset we learn that we are powerless to control the alcoholic's drinking. This is a fact that must be accepted before the newcomer can progress with the program. Until we stop trying to control, we will continue to live with the frustration that made us turn to Al-Anon. Once we learn to let go of the problem, however, the loving concern and help of the other members will provide strong support to help us understand what the Al-Anon program can do for us. (p. 3)

Because the family program has a brief, 5-days' duration for family participants, the importance of attending Al-Anon and working the Twelve Steps is strongly emphasized. The experience in the family program demonstrates to participants how nonjudgmental sharing with others can relieve anxiety and how a safe environment for sharing thoughts and exploring alternatives can provide insight into ways of changing. The spiritual basis of Al-Anon is communicated both in the means provided in Steps Two and Three for accomplishing changes as summarized in the motto "Let go and let God," and in the family program's practice of ending group meetings with the Serenity Prayer.

> God grant me the serenity
> to accept the things I cannot change,
> the courage to change the things I can,
> and the wisdom to know the difference.
> — REINHOLD NIEBUHR

Family Entity Assumption

The second essential of psychoeducation asserts that the " . . . disorder[s] . . . being addressed are at least in part an independent entity" (Ryglewicz, 1989a). Returning to Bowen's family systems theory provides a framework for conceptualizing partial independence in working with the chemically dependent family. Bowen sees the unit to be worked with as being the family rather that the alcoholic patient. The part of the family having the most capability for change should then be encouraged to recognize the ability to change and to begin to consider alternative family roles and responses. Where the family is bogged down in anxiety and emotional interdependence, the family member(s) capable of change need information and encouragement to begin to deal with anxiety and to disengage from the emotional captivity that comes with extreme interdependence (Bowen, 1982).

Guidelines

The third essential of psychoeducation calls for guidelines to be derived from the knowledge base. These guidelines are summarized as follows: (1) Become more knowledgeable about chemical dependency and the process of recovery; (2) Recognize how chemical dependency involves family members and friends; (3) Develop new strategies for coping with family relationships and lowering anxiety; (4) Share thoughts and feelings with others, learn to trust; and (5) Accept Al-Anon and similar mutual help groups as providing a safe place for sharing and the 12-step program as a powerful program for changing and promoting realistic awareness about self and family. Like the Twelve Steps, these guidelines need to be continually revisited so as to prevent backsliding to familiar but nonproductive ways of thinking and acting.

Education and Role Redefinition

The educational framework referred to in the fourth essential of psychoeducation may be described by way of the family program lecture series with accompanying worksheets and discussion. "Active learning" is the term that is used to describe the educational process of introducing information, utilizing the information, and then sharing the results with others (Johnson & Johnson, 1983). Because the family program is focused on the family in relation to chemical dependency and the participants are interacting almost exclusively with each other, the opportunity for active learning to play out over time is one of the strengths of a program that may be described as more "laid back" than intensive.

Information Conveying and Processing

The fifth essential of psychoeducation is the use of individual and/or group situations for processing of information conveyed in a supportive manner. "What is Chemical Dependency?" is a lecture describing the characteristics associated with alcoholism and drug addiction. The worksheet then asks participants to individually respond to questions such as describing an experience related to any of the symptoms presented in lecture. Individual preparation time is provided for responding to three or four questions following every lecture. Then participants meet in small groups to share their thinking and feelings identified in response to the lecture and questions.

Other lectures use the same presentation format with topics and sample questions summarized in Table 6.4. This presentation format of lecture, followed by worksheet preparation, then discussion, meets the fifth essential of psychoeducation in that participants' situations are shared with the group in a supportive, nonjudgmental setting of six to eight people. Rehabilitation patients spending 3 days in the family program are talking about their worksheet responses with family program participants and vice versa. This interchange creates a new awareness for each category of participants.

Program Environment

The family program provides a safe, nonjudgmental setting. Staff and guests are respectful and caring. The normative structure of the program is openness, "We help one another by sharing our strength, wisdom, and hope—and our feelings of helplessness and vulnerability as well." An ongoing dynamic results where guests of several days feel safe in talking about their thoughts, feelings, and personal situations, thereby

TABLE 6.4. Hazelden Family Program Lecture Topics and Sample Work Questions

Topic	Sample Question
What is chemical dependency?	Describe an experience that relates to any of the symptoms discussed in lecture.
Anxiety and the first three steps.	Describe a situation/relationship about which I have anxiety today.
Detaching with love.	My most serious problem right now is:
Acceptance in family of origin.	Examine my behavior as part of this family.
Hope for relationships.	Identify my part in adapting.
Intimate relationships.	What are some of the ways I may have missed opportunities for intimacy?
Letting go of resentments.	Have I been hurt? By whom?
Creative grieving.	Describe how you have experienced a loss.

encouraging newcomers to interact similarly. Both the *social* and the *physical* environment of the program are designed to be conducive to personal growth. These two aspects of program environment are discussed next.

Social Environment of the Program

Using the subscale categories (italicized in this section) of the Ward Atmosphere Scale (WAS) as descriptors (Moos, 1974), it is possible to characterize the social atmosphere of the Family Center. *Involvement* is expected of every one, not only in scheduled activities, but also in informal exchanges. There is a large lounge area where furniture is arranged to permit a number of small group conversations at a time. Guests are expected to use this space for informal discussion rather than "hiding out" in their rooms. Most guests want to gain something from the family program and they understand that they will take from the program in proportion to what they put into the program.

Support is enhanced by the acknowledgment of "consciousness of kind"; here are people who understand because their life experiences with chemical dependency and the family functioning are similar. The program is nonconfrontational and therefore not threatening, with the result that sharing thoughts never previously expressed to another person occurs and is responded to in a caring manner. This element of *spontaneity* is enhanced by the nondirective role played by staff. Daily events are scheduled, but ample time is provided for guests to relate to one another. The scheduled events, such as lectures, are intended to set the stage for individuals to explore their own issues and communicate their developing awareness about their lives with others. The interpersonal discussions that follow are sometimes routine information exchanges, but more often they become times of developing insight nurtured by spontaneous connecting with the thoughts and feelings of others.

Guests are not programmed in their thoughts and actions and are able to exercise a fair degree of *autonomy*. There are times to be with the group and times to take a walk, read a book, or engage in reflection. The *practical orientation* of the program allows for individual difference, not all guests are at the same place in their lives, so uniqueness of situations is acknowledged as well as commonality. The *personal problem orientation* is a strong focus of the family program with the 12-step program approach (AA/Al-Anon) presented as a program of change for addressing personal problems.

Anger and aggression are not exhibited in the Family Center but are acceptable topics of discussion when exploring feelings and behavior. Staff don't have to monitor guests regarding angry outbursts or aggressive behavior because, for the most part, the normative controls discourage such actions in favor of a calm, safe environment. The *order and organization* of the family program is provided in part by the daily schedule, but it is clear that the organization is not so much imposed as it is accepted and perpetuated by the guests. *Program clarity* is high to the extent that activities are scheduled, but within the schedule there is flexibility to explore one's own agenda within reasonable limits. It is always possible to personalize a conversation by introducing a feeling or thought and seeing how others relate to what has been shared.

Staff control is extremely low by intent. Counselors meet with guests on their first day in the program after a "family information questionnaire" has been completed. Staff also give lectures and facilitate some groups, but their group facilitation is nondirective and provides more of a norm clarification and modeling function than a therapeutic function. In fact, the family program is not seen as a therapeutic setting; rather it is a mutual help environment structured to promote sharing and self-discovery.

Physical Environment of the Program

The Family Center consists of a two-story building, with the second-story bedroom area arranged hotel fashion with double-occupancy rooms.

Each room has its own bath and some of the rooms have sliding door access to small balconies overlooking South Center Lake. There is no smoking in the Family Center except in one designated room off the lounge. The lower level has direct access to the outside where patio furniture is located. In addition to the large lounge and the smoking room there are staff offices, a large meeting room, and several small meeting rooms on this level. Most of the activity of the program takes place in the Family Center except for meals, the evening lecture, and use of the recreational facilities in the neighboring CORK Center.

Program Acceptance and Dealing with Resistance

Commonality of family program participants' life concerns creates a bond that leads to program acceptance. Some newly arrived participants are astounded to find that others have not only had experiences similar to their own but are willing to talk openly about them. The daily schedule is arranged so that there are ample opportunities, both structured and unstructured, to talk with particular family participants with whom there is identification and commonality. It is not unusual for a dinnertime conversation to prompt an impromptu meeting between two or three participants to discuss their family situations and ways that needed changes might occur.

The living–learning environment of the family program is responsive to the needs of participants through mutual help rather than dependence on staff. Staff, however, work hard to create the conditions for mutual help to operate, both through the information provided in the instruction that takes place and through the organization, which expects participants to care for themselves through sharing thoughts and feelings with others. When new participants arrive, they are greeted and oriented by a participant who has been in the program for 3 or 4 days; staff are available, but are not the center of the initial family program experience. Participants learn to trust and encourage each other, but because of the constant turnover, relationships of dependence are not given an opportunity to develop.

Occasionally, new participants fail to integrate into the family program environment. Some may return to their sleeping rooms at every opportunity, others may be physically present but not engaged in what is going on around them, and others may engage only in superficial conversation. Both staff and other participants will draw the noninvolved participant out of this withdrawal mode. To varying degrees this integration of participants into the family program is successful, with some making slow beginnings and others embracing the new experience of dealing with thoughts and feelings that have been long suppressed.

Of those entering the family program, 95% remain to complete the program.

Resistance to the program may revolve around an unwillingness to deal with personal issues. One of the principle rationalizations given by reluctant participants is, "The other participants have real problems and my problems aren't that great." This response could either be a result of long-time minimizing of one's personal situation or as a strategy for avoiding having to deal with painful circumstances and feelings. Because the program is nonconfrontational and utilizes a "no fault" approach to understanding family dynamics, resistance of this type is usually transitory, although occasionally it will persist. It is difficult for participants to maintain a stance of avoiding their own circumstances when others are openly sharing their life situations in an environment where norms preclude judging or confronting others.

Some family members and significant others (5%) make reservations for the family program but cancel or fail to register in the program. Others are encouraged by rehabilitation staff and their family member, who is in primary chemical dependency treatment, to enroll in the family program but refuse. Common reasons given for refusal are: family problems making it impossible to leave home, lack of time because of other, more important commitments, and lack of money to pay for transportation and the cost of the family program. A few family members will reconsider and attend the family program after the treated chemically dependent family member has returned home.

One of the common misconceptions about the family program is that it will provide the tools for the family member to fix the alcoholic or drug addict. To the contrary, participants learn that they cannot fix the chemically dependent person, but they can do some positive things for themselves and their family systems. Some participants may be disappointed to learn that trying to manipulate the chemically dependent family member is nonproductive and may therefore resist making the shift in emphasis to themselves. Most are relieved to "accept the things they cannot change" and begin to work on changes that are possible for them. However, some participants are reluctant to focus on themselves rather than on the chemically dependent person.

CASE APPLICATIONS

The following composite case studies are an effort to describe some typical Hazelden Family Center clients and experiences. They are not the histories of particular clients and families but are based on recollections of different clients and their families.

The Case of Susan

Background and Events Leading to Program Participation

Susan had firmly believed that if she came to the Family Center she could help her husband Jack to sober up. Susan was an exceptionally able and accomplished young woman. She had always been the kind of person who got things done successfully. But Jack's drinking was something that had defeated her. No matter what she said or did, she could not seem to help him. Still she kept on trying.

Susan and Jack lived in a new suburban housing development in Des Moines with their children, Dan (8) and Lisa (10). Susan had put her career as a lawyer on hold until the children were old enough for private day-school. She said that she still was enjoying being a mother, after 2 years of combining the law and motherhood, and that the children were doing very well too. On top of all this, she was soon to be made a full partner in her firm. She had managed to accomplish all this while at the same time trying to keep Jack from wrecking his career—or killing himself.

Jack was an architect who until 2 years previously had been on a fast career track with a construction company. When admitted for treatment, Jack was facing a third DWI indictment and probably would lose his job. When Jack's counselor called her, Susan took a leave of absence from her law firm and drove up to Minnesota without hesitation.

During her first day at the Family Center, Susan was unhappy to realize that she wouldn't be with Jack during daily program activities, that he would continue to be involved in his own separate program. At her intake interview, she told the counselor that her goal was to help her husband make a commitment to AA and to stay sober after he left treatment.

Susan had been concerned about Jack's drinking when they were in college, long before they married. She had always thought he would settle down after they were married, that the drinking problem was something they could work out together. For a long time she couldn't let herself believe he might really be an alcoholic. It was true that he drank too much, once in a while. There had been some embarrassing social scenes and some bad arguments. But Jack was very successful in his work, her own career had begun to flourish, and they had a great life together with their children. Everything was fine. But was it?

Even as Jack was making his way up the corporate ladder, winning the perks and promotions of success in business, he would now and then drink recklessly, taking big chances, risking everything. During a period of several years, Susan found herself worrying constantly and increasingly about Jack. Susan regularly got after him about drinking too much, too often, but she always accepted his skillful explanations. She never accused him of deception, even when she had doubts. She continued to hope that eventually he would snap out of it. Jack's drinking, Susan's recriminations, his explanations, and her tearful and worried acceptance of his excuses became a pattern of interaction that was eroding the quality of their family life. Finally, two of Jack's colleagues from work who were also her friends called and asked her to meet them for lunch and a talk—about Jack. They urged her to persuade him to go to a treatment center. This unusual meeting shocked Susan out of any doubts she may have had.

When she confronted Jack that evening, his response to her pleading left her in despair. Just as he had every other time she brought up this subject, he said he didn't have any serious problems and he could take care of himself if he did. And then Jack was arrested once again for driving while intoxicated.

Program Participation

At the Family Center, Susan stayed up late into the night talking with others, long after the staff had gone home. They talked about the lecture they heard that morning on giving the alcoholic responsibility for his own recovery. This made no sense to her. She wanted more action, specific directions from the Family Center staff, or direct encounters with Jack in therapy sessions.

Others in the group, those who had earlier experience in therapy or in Al-Anon, or who had just been in the Family Center a day or two longer, counseled her to be patient. They reminded her of the AA and AL-Anon slogans, "Easy Does It," and "Let Go and Let God." She hated these damn slogans. In the end, Susan went to bed troubled and restless, slogans ringing in her ears.

Susan awoke early with the sun, after a restless night. She found herself again thinking about the resentment that Jack seemed to register whenever she told him how concerned she was about him. She thought again about the lecture of the day before. And she thought about the discussion they had had last night and the slogans. Her thoughts were mixed. Could she be trying too hard to make everything all right for Jack? Was she trying too hard to be a perfect wife?

She sat at lunch that day next to a woman patient who was participating in the family program. Susan talked about her anxiety about her husband, about her efforts to help him. Then the patient told Susan about her own history of repeated treatment programs and repeated failures. She said that she had a new outlook now on her responsibility for herself. Her family finally said that they loved her but that they couldn't take care of her any longer. Right then Susan began to get the point.

During afternoon community meetings, participants take time to discuss briefly how they're doing and what they're learning. When it came around to Susan's turn to speak, she found herself saying something she really hadn't planned to say. Without thinking, she explained that she had come to the Family Center in order to help her husband, but that she came to realize that she was there to help herself.

In her discharge questionnaire, Susan said that she had learned several things at the Family Center. First, she had not caused Jack's drinking problem. Second, she couldn't cure him. And third, that the best thing she could do for Jack was to love him enough to let him find his own way. It was hard to accept this new way of looking at the problem, she said, but she was going to try.

She would begin by making a point not to ask Jack every day, or several times a day, how he was doing. This was a very small thing, but it could be a frequent reminder of her new resolve. She said she felt encouraged by the idea that there were other changes that she could make to improve things. She decided to focus on her own role in the problem and see how she herself could contribute to resolving their family problems.

The Case of Mike

Background and Events Leading to Program Participation

Mike was a 30-year-old construction worker from a northern suburb of Chicago. For a year he had been married to Cathy, a college student who also worked part-time as a bartender. Cathy had been a patient in Hazelden's rehabilitation program for almost a month. Mike had signed up for the family program at the same time Cathy had made her reservation for rehab, and he said that he had several good reasons for doing this.

First, he had wanted Cathy to know that he supported her, so he had told her he would drive up to be with her. Second, he had sobered up in AA, without a treatment program, and he was curious to know what treatment was all about. Finally, he was worried about the future of their marriage. At AA meetings, he had heard a lot of stories about the failures that occur when two newly recovering alcoholics try to build a relationship together. He wanted to learn what kinds of problems he needed to avoid in order to save their marriage.

After Mike sobered up, their relationship had become strained. He wanted to spend his evenings with Cathy, but he was no longer interested in hanging out with their old friends in the bar. He didn't know how to go about making a new social life for himself, let alone how to interest Cathy in new friends and new things to do. He was torn by a desire to please her, and by an understanding that he wanted to stay sober. At AA, his pals said, "If you want to avoid having a slip, just stay out of slippery places." That made a lot of sense to Mike, but it didn't do anything for Cathy. They were both pretty unhappy. And then, late one night about 6 months after Mike sobered up, Cathy had a bad car accident driving home after closing the bar for the night. She was seriously hurt. The police filed a DWI report at the hospital. With Mike's encouragement, the doctor's recommendation, and some pressure from their lawyer, Cathy went directly from her hospital stay into Hazelden's rehabilitation program.

Three weeks later he drove up to the Family Center. They met in the visitors' lounge late in the afternoon, shortly after Mike checked in. They talked enthusiastically about her treatment program and what she was learning. Mike tried to compare notes with her about his own experiences in AA. They talked about what he might expect in the family program, because Cathy had also been through this program. He didn't understand what she tried to say about Al-Anon and about "letting go."

Program Participation

This was the question that he brought to the Family Center counselor during his interview the next morning. The counselor asked Mike to identify with people in the Family Center who were not alcoholics themselves but were overly concerned and overly reactive to their friends and loved ones. He wanted Mike to realize that it would be a good idea for Cathy to have an AA sponsor of her own, that it would be very difficult for Mike to try to guide her in her early recovery. Just because Mike was sober didn't mean that he could be an expert on how to keep Cathy sober.

The best thing Mike could do to ensure that he and Cathy had a good future together was to concentrate on his own program for sobriety. His anxiety about her program for recovery could only lead to more difficulties — resentments and recriminations — for the two of them. Finally, the counselor urged Mike to practice being thoughtful, compassionate, considerate, and optimistic. Al-Anon calls it "Act As If" behavior, the counselor explained. As old timers like to say, "Fake it 'til you make it." Mike tried to put these rules to work right there and then, in the family program.

Would he and Cathy be able to work things out with one another in the long run? Would she be willing to give up her job at the bar and concentrate on school for a change? Would she go to AA meetings? Would she get a sponsor? Could they beat the odds and make a good marriage when both of them were in recovery programs? Mike realized suddenly that those questions weren't the important questions. They were several jumps out in front of the important ones. The situation was both simpler and harder than he had thought. The point wasn't how to control the future. It was not about asking for iron-clad guarantees. The point was to enjoy every day and make the best of it, one day at a time. The point was to learn how to live gracefully with all the uncertainty of life.

RESEARCH SUMMARY

Research on the family program began in the middle of the 1970s. At the time of the initial research evaluation, the family program lasted 3 instead of 5 days. The program had recently moved to the Family Center, but had only about half the space available in the current Family Center. Participants entering the family program during January through March of 1977 were given a 20-item inventory of cognitive goals and responded to the same inventory when they left the program. A total of 207 family program participants, not including rehabilitation patients, responded to the before-and-after program inventory (Laundergan, 1970). The study reported that with the exception of some items that had limited change potential because of the high initial agreement, the Hazelden family program seemed to be realizing its cognitive change objectives.

The next study of the family program covered the period of the last 6 months of 1978 and the first 6 months of 1979. During this time period, the family program had increased from the previous 3 days to 5 days for family participants, although rehabilitation patients continued to participate 3 days as is presently the case. Family program participants responded to a revised Hazelden Family Program Inventory at three time periods: (1) when they entered the family program, (2) when they left the family program, and (3) 6 months after they left the family program. In addition to the revised Hazelden Family Program Inventory, the 6-month follow-up included questions having to do with social functioning and Al-Anon attendance. A total of 381 participants were in the study and 366 (96%) responded to the 6-month questionnaire (Laundergan et al., 1980).

Table 6.5 reports the revised Family Program Inventory results at the three measurement periods. This table indicates that the attitude changes that occured during the family program were, for the most part, sustained 6 months later. Additional statistically significant findings from this study using χ^2 test of significance include: (1) Although half the former participants were not attending Al-Anon 6 months after leaving the family program, females had more frequent postprogram Al-Anon attendance than males; (2) Postprogram Al-Anon attendance was associated with positive ranking of two family program activities— "informal patient conversations" and "full group meetings"; (3) Postprogram Al-Anon attendance was associated with improved psychosocial functioning in three areas— "relationship with other relatives," "relationship with Higher Power," and "job performance."

A third study of the family program used the same methodology as Laundergan et al.'s 1980 study. During 1979, 1,159 persons participated in the family program. Of that number, 20% were rehabilitation patients, with the remaining 922 consisting of family members and significant others. The 922 were followed up 6 months after their participation in the family program with a resulting 76% ($n = 702$) response rate (Williams et al., 1981). The attitude change patterns reported (Table 6.5) were, not surprisingly, very close to those reported for the 1980 study, in part because a portion of the respondents were the same as in the earlier study. In both the 1980 and 1981 studies, "small group meetings," "the living environment," and "informal conversations with participants" were ranked the highest in being helpful and "time alone for thought" the least helpful.

Data were gathered from family program participants during four months—January, April, July, and October—of 1989 (Hazelden, 1989). Among the 229 former family program participants responding, "small group discussions" and "informal conversations with other participants" were ranked as the most helpful program activities. A further revision of the Hazelden Family Program Inventory was used resulting in an 85% or better follow-up appropriate response rate for all items except to the statement, "I don't need to know the cause of alcoholism or other forms of chemical dependency in order to learn how to cope effectively with it." Variations of this statement in 1979, 1980, and 1981 show a consistent unwillingness of respondents to alter the notion that knowledge of the cause of chemical dependency is important in resolving associated problems. For some, this preoccupation with "cause" can be a barrier to taking actions that could positively affect their quality of life. On balance, the family program evaluation research has shown consistent changes in the direction of the family program cognitive goals. Post-participation Al-Anon attendance is reported for about half of the former family program participants. Informal conversations with other

TABLE 6.5. Attitude Change of Family Program Participants from Intake to Discharge and at the Last 6-Month Follow-Up: 1978–79 and 1979

(Desired response for all items is "No")	Last six mo. 1978, First 6 mo. 1979 (n = 366)			Calendar year 1979 (n = 702-922[a])		
	% correct at intake	% correct at discharge	% correct at 6 mo. follow-up	% correct at intake	% correct at discharge	% correct at 6 mo. follow-up
I believe that people with addictions are people who lack willpower and determination.	89	96	94	88	96	94
I believe that unhappy childhood experiences cause people to become addicted.	73	91	86	70	87	85
I can't feel good unless my concerned person is feeling good.	71	94	90	66	91	88
I believe that stressful working conditions and/or particular kinds of family pressure cause people to become chemically dependent (alcoholic).	46	83	85	59	84	78
I have to learn to behave so that I won't upset the others in my family.	55	77	79	56	76	78
I should devote my energies to helping loved ones solve their problems as part of my recovery.	53	85	72	52	83	75
I cannot quit worrying until my concerned person starts taking better care of him/herself.	46	83	85	49	84	86
I think that it is important for family members to know what they have been doing to make the addictive member drink and/or use drugs.	40	63	71	36	59	67
I should do as much as I can to find out what causes alcoholism or other forms of chemical dependency.	14	30	30	14	29	30

[a]The number of responses varies by question; data was available on 922 clients at admission and discharge and 702 clients at 6 months after discharge.
Note. Laundergan (1980) and Williams (1981).

participants are seen as very helpful, but that response must be understood in the context of the program where much of the processing of information and small group sharing is done in informal conversations. It would be incorrect to interpret this high helpfulness ranking as informal conversations alone being sufficient to bring about the changes that have been reported. Generally high rating of all family program services, with the exception of "movies and videotapes," suggests it is the whole and not any identifiable part that makes the family program effective.

CONCLUSIONS

The structure and process of the Hazelden Family Program has developed pragmatically, with the result that the programming fits well with the approach known as psychoeducation. Influences such as Bowen theory (Bowen, 1978) and Al-Anon have guided program content. With the emphasis on active learning and mutual support, participants learn to view the family system and their own behavior as capable of change through their own actions. They also come to appreciate that they cannot make the recovery happen for the chemically dependent person in their life.

Improved self-awareness, recognition of the disease concept of chemical dependency, knowledge of how chemical dependency affects the family, and realization of available change options are the program expectations for the participants. A personal plan developed by participants during their stay in the program provides specifics that will guide changes in actions and understandings after returning home. New skills for reducing anxiety and detaching with love that have been practiced in the supportive environment of the family program are to be tested in the family and community setting. Al-Anon is recommended as a support group and resource for continuing the growth of understanding and changed behaviors begun in the family program.

Case studies illustrate circumstances that present themselves at the Family Center. New ways of considering these circumstances and of dealing with feelings are explored during the 5-day stay in the family program. Research indicates that the cognitive changes that begin during the family program are sustained 6 months after leaving the program. Although only about half of the family program participants attend Al-Anon after they leave the family program, the exposure to Al-Anon thinking and other related understandings appear to have an influence on how family members behave and respond to the chemically dependent person in their life.

REFERENCES

Al-Anon Family Groups. (1965). *The twelve steps and traditions.* New York: Author.

Al-Anon Family Groups. (1981). *This is Al-Anon.* New York: Author.

Anderson, D. J. (1981). *Perspectives on treatment: The Minnesota experience.* Center City, MN: Hazelden Foundation.

Bowen, M. (1978). *Family therapy in clinical practice.* New York: Jason Aronson.

Ellis, A. (1973). *Humanistic psychotherapy: The rational–emotive approach.* New York: Julian Press.

Hazelden. (1989). *Family program 2-month follow-up results* (internal report). Center City, MN: Hazelden Foundation.

Johnson, D. W., & Johnson, R. T. (1983). The socialization and achievement crises: Are cooperative learning experiences the solution? In L. Beckman (Ed.), *Applied Social Psychology Annual* (Vol. 4, pp. 119–164). Beverly Hills, CA: Sage.

Ivey, A. E. (1977). Cultural expertise: If the counselor is to become a teacher, toward what should that teaching be directed. *Canadian Counselor, 12,* 23–29.

Kerr, M. E., & Bowen, M. (1988). *Family evaluation: An approach based on Bowen theory.* New York: W. W. Norton.

Laundergan, J. C., Schroeder, M. R., & Barnett, B. S. (1980, May). *Family program client changes.* Paper presented at the meeting of the National Alcoholism Forum in Seattle, WA.

Laundergan, J. C., & Williams, T. (1979, Summer). Hazelden: Evaluation at a residential family program. *Alcohol Health and Research World,* 13–15.

Moos, R. H. (1974). *Evaluating treatment environments: A social ecological approach.* New York: Wiley.

Ryglewicz, H. (1989a). Psychoeducational work with families: Theme and variations. *Tie Lines, 6*(3), 1–3.

Ryglewicz, H. (1989b). Psychoeducation: A wave of the present. *Tie Lines, 6*(2), 1–2.

Williams, T., Schroeder, M. R., Spicer, J., Laundergan, J. C., & Jones, D. R. (1981). *Families in crises: A study of the Hazelden family program.* Center City, MN: Hazelden Foundation.

Chapter 7

A Behavioral Marital Therapy Couples Group Program for Alcoholics and Their Spouses

Timothy J. O'Farrell

OVERVIEW

Steinglass (1976) traced the development of marital and family treatment approaches to alcoholism. He indicated that the field started with the treatment of each spouse separately in either individual or group therapy, developed into the conjoint treatment of both spouses together, and later progressed to multiple-couples group therapy. Couples group therapy has been considered the treatment of choice for married alcoholics by some (Gallant, Rich, Bey, & Terranova, 1970). A variety of formats for couples groups with alcoholics have been described in the literature (e.g., Cadogan, 1973; McCrady, Paolino, Longabaugh, & Rossi, 1979). A very promising current approach is a behavioral marital therapy (BMT) couples group program that combines pregroup couple sessions—to establish a therapeutic relationship, negotiate an Antabuse Contract, and conduct a careful assessment—with couples group sessions in which homework assignments and behavioral rehearsal are used to promote sobriety, increase positive couple and family activities, and teach communication and negotiation skills (O'Farrell, Cutter, & Floyd, 1985; O'Farrell, Cutter, Choquette, Floyd, & Bayog, 1992).

The purpose of the present chapter is to describe an outpatient BMT couples group program that the author developed and has been running since 1978 at the Brockton–West Roxbury (Massachusetts) Veterans Affairs Medical Center, a Harvard-affiliated hospital in the greater Boston area. This BMT group program has been called the Counseling for Alcoholics' Marriages (CALM) Project. The Project CALM BMT couples group program described in this chapter is for alcoholics who have made at least an initial commitment to change their drinking. They recognize that a problem exists and have made a decision, often with strong encouragement from the spouse or other outside influences, to do something about their drinking problem. A major purpose of the BMT group program is to stabilize and maintain the process of change in the drinking problem and the marriage that has already started when the alcoholic and spouse come to their first Project CALM appointment.

SPECIAL CONSIDERATIONS

Clients Most Likely to Benefit

Guidelines Based on Clinical Experience

Approximately two-thirds of our patients begin Project CALM treatment immediately after hospitalization at the VA Medical center for a 28-day inpatient alcoholism rehabilitation program or for a 7-day detoxification period. The other third come from the community in response to our outreach efforts. To be candidates for the Project CALM BMT group program, the couple has to be currently living together and legally married for at least a year or in a stable common-law relationship for at least 2 years. Couples who are separated at intake often are seen for a series of sessions to help them decide whether they wish to reconcile at least for the duration of the BMT program to give their marriage "one last try." In addition, the alcoholic presenting for treatment has to accept abstinence as a goal at least through the end of the BMT group, the other spouse can not also be an alcoholic unless he or she has been abstinent 6 months or more, and neither partner can suffer from a current problem with drug abuse[1] or a current major psychiatric disorder.

Couples who do not meet these criteria are judged unlikely to benefit from and likely to be disruptive to a short-term structured BMT couples group. Such couples are seen in single couple conjoint BMT sessions instead. The conjoint sessions, as compared to the BMT group, allow the therapist to proceed at a slower pace, to individualize the treatment to a greater degree and to deal with the more varied and more frequent obstacles and resistances presented by such cases. Strategies for dealing with some of the more difficult cases have been presented elsewhere (O'Farrell, 1986).

Compliance with the initial month of outpatient treatment is a process measure that seems to predict likely benefit on a clinical basis. This includes maintaining abstinence, keeping scheduled appointments, and completing any required assignments.

Guidelines Based on Research Findings

Unfortunately, studies examining predictors of response to BMT and other types of marital and family therapy with alcoholics are not yet available. However, studies of factors that predict alcoholics' acceptance and completion of BMT and other marital and family therapy (Noel, McCrady, Stout, & Nelson, 1987; O'Farrell, Kleinke, & Cutter, 1986; Zweben, Pearlman, & Li, 1983) provide some information on clients most likely to benefit from such treatment, because the clients must accept and stay in therapy to benefit. Clients most likely to accept and complete BMT have the following characteristics: (1) a high school education or better; (2) employed full-time if able and desirous of working; (3) older; (4) have more serious alcohol problems of longer duration; (5) enter therapy after a crisis, especially one that threatens the stability of the marriage; (6) alcoholic, spouse, and other family members without serious psychopathology or drug abuse; and (7) absence of family violence that has caused serious injury or is potentially life-threatening. Further, evidence that the alcoholic is motivated to change and to take an active role in a psychologically oriented treatment approach also suggests potential for benefitting from BMT. Such evidence includes contact with the treatment program personally initiated by the alcoholic and a history of successful participation in other outpatient counseling or self-help programs (as opposed to only detoxification for relief of physical distress due to heavy drinking, without further active ongoing treatment participation).

Necessary Therapist Attributes and Behaviors

Our clinical experience suggests that certain therapist attributes and behaviors are important for successful BMT with alcoholics. From the outset, the therapist must structure treatment so that control of the alcohol abuse is the first priority, before attempting to help the couple with other problems. Many of our clients have had previous unsuccessful experiences with therapists who saw the couple in marital therapy without dealing with the alcohol abuse. The hope that reduction in marital distress will lead to improvement in the drinking problem is rarely fulfilled. More typically, recurrent alcohol-related incidents undermine whatever gains have been made in marital and family relationships.

Therapists must be able to tolerate and deal effectively with strong anger in early sessions and at later times of crisis. The therapist can use empathic listening to help each spouse feel they have been heard and insist that only one person speaks at a time. Helping the couple defuse their intense anger is very important, because failure to do so often leads to a poor outcome (Gurman & Kniskern, 1987).

Therapists need to structure and take control of treatment sessions, especially during the early assessment and therapy phase and at later times of crisis (e.g., episodes of drinking or intense marital conflict). Many therapists' errors involve difficulty establishing and maintaining control of the sessions and responding to the myriad forms of resistance and noncompliance presented by couples. Therapists must steer a middle course between lack of structure and being overly controlling and punitive in response to noncompliance. He or she must clearly establish and enforce the rules of treatment, while acknowledging the couple's approximation to desired behavior changes despite significant shortcomings.

Finally therapists need to take a long-term view of the course of change. Both the alcoholism problem and associated marital distress may be helped substantially only by repeated efforts, including some failed attempts. Such a long-term view may help the therapist encounter relapse without becoming overly discouraged or engaging in blaming and recriminations with the alcoholic and spouse. The therapist also should maintain contact with the couple long after the problems have stabilized.

DESCRIPTION OF THE TREATMENT METHOD

Table 7.1 provides an outline of the Project CALM BMT couples group program that will be described in detail below. It is important to describe the entire program including pregroup sessions, the BMT couples group, and follow-up sessions. Earlier papers describing this BMT group program (e.g., O'Farrell et al., 1985) have described the groups in detail but have not included other aspects, especially the pregroup sessions. The pregroup sessions have evolved over time and we now believe they are essential to the clinical success of the BMT couples group program.

Pregroup Sessions

Six to eight weekly conjoint couple sessions precede and prepare couples for participation in the BMT couples group. Careful execution of the pregroup sessions is very important to ensure a good outcome for the BMT group sessions that follow. We have traced many of our failures and difficulties with BMT groups to problems with therapist implementation and/or client noncompliance during these pregroup sessions. We now tell prospective clients that the extent of compliance with the initial phase of outpatient treatment, including abstinence, keeping scheduled appointments, and completing any required assignments, generally

TABLE 7.1. Overview of the Counseling for Alcoholics' Marriages (CALM) Project—
An Outpatient Behavioral Marital Therapy (BMT) Couples Group Program

---

A. Pregroup sessions (6–8 weekly conjoint meetings)
   1. Initial interviews
   2. Antabuse Contract
   3. Formal assessment
   4. Feedback
   5. Group preparation

B. BMT Couples Group (10 weekly group meetings)
   1. Alcohol and Alcohol-related interactions
      a. Review Antabuse Contract
      b. Monitor urges to drink
      c. Crisis intervention for drinking episodes
      d. Discussion about preventing relapse
   2. Increase positive couple and family activities
      a. "Catch your spouse doing something nice"
      b. Caring days
      c. Shared rewarding activities
   3. Communication skills training
      a. Listening skills
      b. Direct expression of feelings
      c. Communication sessions
   4. Negotiation of behavior change agreements
      a. Positive specific requests
      b. Negotiation and compromise
      c. Couple agreements

C. Plan for maintenance of change
   1. BMT program behaviors to continue
   2. Periodic follow-up contacts

---

predicts who will be likely to benefit from the BMT groups and the rest of the program. Couples who have serious difficulty during pregroup sessions can be seen conjointly until they have stabilized sufficiently to join a couples group.

Initial Interviews

In the initial interview with prospective BMT program clients, the therapist needs to: (1) determine what stage the alcoholic has reached in the process of changing his or her alcohol abuse, (2) evaluate whether there is a need for crisis intervention prior to a careful assessment, and (3) orient the couple to the assessment and to the Antabuse procedures. Usually a second session will be scheduled at which time the clients must decide whether or not they wish to enroll in the program.

In the initial session, the therapist's clinical interview gathers information about a series of issues. First, the therapist inquires about *the alcoholic's drinking* (especially recent quantity and frequency of drinking), whether the extent of physical dependence on alcohol requires detoxification to obtain abstinence during the assessment, what led to seeking help at this time and prior help-seeking efforts, and whether the alcoholic's and spouse's goal is to reduce the drinking or to abstain either temporarily or permanently. Second, the *stability of the marriage* is examined in terms of current planned or actual separation as well as any past separations. Third, *recent violence* and any fears of recurrence are discussed. Finally, the therapist determines whether there are any *alcohol-related or other crises* that require immediate attention. Allowing 75–90 minutes for the initial session and including 5–10 minutes separately with each spouse alone provides sufficient time to gather the needed information and to learn of important material (e.g., plans for separation, fears of violence) that either spouse may be reluctant to share during the conjoint portion of the interview. More detailed information about the marital relationship and the drinking can be obtained in subsequent sessions.

Session 2 when the clients commit themselves to the Project CALM program involves three important steps. First, verbal commitments are obtained from the husband and the wife: (1) to live together for at least the course of the group therapy, and not to threaten divorce or separation during this period, (2) to do their best to focus on the future and the present (but not the past), and (3) to do weekly homework assignments agreed to as part of the BMT sessions. The extent to which each spouse has kept these commitments is reviewed at the start of each pregroup session. Second, work on the "Antabuse Contract" is begun. Third, the formal assessment procedures are scheduled.

The Antabuse Contract

Antabuse (disulfiram), a drug that produces extreme nausea and sickness when the person taking it ingests alcohol, is widely used in alcoholism treatment as a deterrent to drinking. Unfortunately, Antabuse often is not effective because the alcoholic discontinues the drug prematurely. In preparation for the BMT group we use an Antabuse Contract to maintain Antabuse ingestion and abstinence from alcohol and to decrease alcohol-related arguments and interactions between the alcoholic and spouse. Before negotiating such a contract, the therapist should be sure that the alcoholic is willing and medically cleared to take Antabuse and that both alcoholic and spouse have been fully informed and educated about the effects of the drug. In the Antabuse Contract the alcoholic agrees to take Antabuse each day while the spouse observes and to thank the spouse for witnessing the Antabuse inges-tion. The spouse, in turn, agrees to thank the alcoholic for taking Anta-buse, to record the observation on a calendar provided by the therapist, and not to mention past drinking or any fears about future drinking. In addition, both spouses agree to contact the therapist if the taking of Antabuse is not observed for two consecutive days. Finally, the cou-ple agrees to maintain the contract to the end of the BMT group at which time the therapist discusses with the couple the possibility of renewing the contract for another period of time. It is extremely im-portant that each spouse view the agreement as a cooperative method for rebuilding lost trust, and not as a coercive checking-up operation. More details on the Antabuse Contract are available elsewhere (Azrin, 1976; O'Farrell & Bayog, 1986).

Assessment Targets and Procedures

A series of assessment issues or targets are investigated in progressive-ly greater depth as the assessment progresses after the initial interview sessions. Table 7.2 describes these targets and the instruments we use in our research clinic for investigating each area in depth. The formal instruments are not essential but gaining detailed information about each of the assessment target areas is important.

Assessment of the Alcoholic's Drinking

We use a structured interview (Sobell, 1979) with each spouse separate-ly that covers alcohol-related medical and physical symptoms includ-ing withdrawal symptoms, prior treatment contacts, legal consequences, employment history, adverse consequences from drinking, and marital separations and other negative consequences of the alcoholism. The Time-Line Follow-Back (TLFB) Drinking Interview (Sobell, Sobell, Maisto, & Cooper, 1985) is one part of the structured interview and uses a calendar and specialized interviewing methods to reconstruct the al-coholic's drinking behavior during the year prior to the interview. Each spouse also completes the Michigan Alcoholism Screening Test (MAST) (Selzer, 1971) about themselves and about their spouse to determine the extent to which their drinking habits and consequences resemble those of alcoholics. Discrepancies between the alcoholic's and spouse's reports about aspects of the alcoholic's drinking history and behavior, as well as internal inconsistencies on the part of either respondent, are noted and pursued in further joint and individual interviews. Such fur-ther inquiry often leads to increased accuracy of information and decreased "denial" on the part of the alcoholic. The alcoholic also com-

TABLE 7.2. Targets and Procedures in Assessing Alcoholic Couples

Assessment Target Area	Instrument/Procedure[a]
1. The alcoholic's drinking	
a. Drinking history	
Frequency and quantity of drinking	Time-Line Follow-Back Drinking Interview (Sobell et al., 1985)
Drinking situations	Inventory of Drinking Situations (Annis, 1985)
Antecedents to drinking	Situational Confidence Questionnaire (Annis, 1982)
b. Dependence syndrome	Alcohol Dependence Scale (Skinner & Allen, 1982)
Impaired control over drinking	
Increased tolerance	
Relief of withdrawal symptoms through drinking	
c. Problems related to drinking	Michigan Alcoholism Screening Test (Selzer, 1971)
Biomedical (e.g., traumatic injury, liver disease, pancreatitis)	Lab test results (O'Farrell & Maisto, 1987)
Psychosocial (e.g., work, family, legal problems)	Structured interview (Sobell, 1979)
d. Goal for drinking—reduction or abstinence (temporary/permanent)	Clinical interview
2. Marital stability	Marital Status Inventory (Weiss & Cerreto, 1980)
3. Marital violence	Conflict Tactics Scale (Straus, 1979)
4. Alcohol-related crises	Clinical interview
5. Marital relationship	
a. Overall adjustment	Marital Adustment Test (Locke & Wallace, 1959)
b. Changes desired	Areas of Change Questionnaire (Margolin et al., 1983)
c. Sexual adjustment	Sexual Adjustment Questionnaire (O'Farrell, 1990)
d. Communication skills	Videotaped sample of communication (Floyd et al., 1987)

[a]References cited provide more information about each instrument. A clinical interview can also be used alone or in conjunction with these intruments to assess each area.

pletes the Alcohol Dependence Scale (Skinner & Allen, 1982) to measure the extent of physical and psychological dependence on alcohol.
Finally, the Inventory of Drinking Situations (Annis, 1985) and the Situational Confidence Questionnaire (Annis, 1982) determine, respectively,
types of situations associated with abusive drinking in the past year and
how confident the alcoholic is that he or she could encounter such situations now without drinking.

Assessment of the Marriage Relationship

Each spouse completes separately a series of questionnaires about the
marriage. The Marital Status Inventory (MSI) (Weiss & Cerreto, 1980)
evaluates steps toward separation and divorce. The Conflict Tactics Scale
(CTS) (Straus, 1979) assesses the extent of verbal and physical abuse experienced. The MSI and CTS, which supplement the initial interview
questions about marital stability and violence, respectively often provide additional information on these important topics because some
people find it easier to reveal such sensitive information on a questionnaire than in an interview. Other aspects of the marital relationship
are assessed using the Marital Adjustment Test (Locke & Wallace, 1959)
to determine overall relationship satisfaction and areas of disagreement,
the Areas of Change Questionnaire (Margolin, Talovic, & Weinstein,
1983) to establish relationship changes desired, a Sexual Adjustment
Questionnaire (O'Farrell, 1990), and a videotaped sample of communication (Floyd, O'Farrell, & Goldberg, 1987).

Separate Interviews with Each Spouse

Next, each spouse is interviewed separately to review their questionnaire responses and provide an opportunity to clarify anything that
is ambiguous. These individual interviews review any discrepancies between spouses or inconsistencies in responses to the drinking history
questions, the MSI, CTS (especially any indications of serious violence),
and Sexual Adjustment Questionnaire. Finally, the other assessment
materials are reviewed and additional inquiry is completed in order
to formulate answers to these two questions: (1) What changes are needed in marital and family life as well as other day-to-day activities in order
to achieve and maintain the goal for the alcoholic's drinking? and (2)
What marital changes are desired to increase marital satisfaction if one
assumes that the drinking goal will be achieved?

Feedback of Assessment Results and Preparation for BMT Group

After the assessment information has been gathered, the couple and
therapist meet for a feedback session in which the therapist shares im-

pressions of the nature and severity of the drinking and marital problems and invites the couple to respond to these impressions. The first goal of the feedback is to increase motivation for treatment by reviewing in a nonjudgmental, matter-of-fact manner the quantity, frequency, and negative consequences of the excessive drinking. One part of each feedback session is review of a drinking "score card" based on the TLFB Interview about the previous year's drinking. Table 7.3 presents a sample score card for an alcoholic who considered himself "only a beer drinker" and questioned his need to abstain even though he had agreed to an Antabuse Contract through the end of the BMT group. The score card impressed the alcoholic with the extent of his drinking. In particular, conversion of quantities of beer to equivalent amounts of whiskey made an impact on the alcoholic who indicated he had not realized the full extent of his drinking.

A second goal of the feedback session is to prepare the couple to begin a short-term BMT group. Toward this end, the therapist emphasizes the value of couples groups in achieving sobriety and a more satisfying marriage and tries to promote favorable therapeutic expectations. The therapist also has the couple renew their commitments made at the start of the program to refrain from threats of separation, focus

TABLE 7.3. Sample Time-Line Drinking Score Card

Behavior	No. of Days in past year	% of past year
Abstinent (no alcohol)	20	5.5%
Light drinking (6 standard drinks or less[a])	0	0.0%
Heavy drinking (7 standard drinks or more[a])	339	92.6%
Hospitalized for alcohol treatment	7	1.9%

Daily drinking quantities

Lighter than usual:
    5 beers[b] = 5–7 oz whiskey = almost a ½ pint
Usual quantity:
    12 beers = 12–16 oz whiskey = ¾ to a full pint
Heavier than usual[c]:
    24 beers plus 2 to 4 shots whiskey = 26–36 oz whiskey = a quart or more of whiskey

[a]One standard drink contains the same amount of alcohol regardless of the type of beverage. One standard drink = one ounce of 80–100 proof spirits = 12 oz beer = 4 oz wine.
[b]Patient drank 12 oz cans of beer some of the time and 16 oz beers at other times so a range of equivalent amounts of whiskey are given.
[c]During periods of heavier drinking such as the months immediately preceding treatment, the patient drank both beer and whiskey.

on the present and future, and do homework assignments. Finally, the therapist gives an overview of the course of the group and tells the couple in more detail about the content of the first few sessions.

Obstacles Frequently Encountered During Pregroup Sessions

Alcohol-Related Crises

Despite their seeming suitability for marital therapy, many alcoholics and their spouses will present the therapist with substantial obstacles. Common problems encountered during assessment are pressing alcohol-related crises (e.g., actual, impending, or threatened loss of job or home; major legal or financial problems) that preclude a serious and sustained marital therapy focus. The therapist can help the couple devise plans to deal with the crisis or refer them elsewhere for such help after establishing a behavioral contract about drinking and alcohol-related interactions (e.g., Antabuse Contract). Other preparations for the BMT group can be started when the crisis has been resolved.

Potential for Violence

Many alcoholic couples whose negative interactions escalate quickly have difficulty containing conflict between sessions and pose a potential for violence in some instances. Responses to initial interviews with the couple and with the spouses separately, the CTS, and the videotaped communication sample help identify many such couples during the pretherapy assessment. Once identified, these couples have conflict containment as an explicit goal of their therapy from the outset. For couples with a history of violence, it is important to determine whether the violence was limited to occasions when the alcoholic had been drinking. If so, then methods to deal with the alcohol abuse may relieve much of the couple's concern about violence. In cases where violence still seems likely, an additional procedure described by Shapiro (1984) can be very useful. This involves a written agreement that spouses are not to hit or threaten to hit each other, and that if they do, one of the spouses (named in the agreement) will leave the home and go to a designated place for 48–72 hours. A "time-out" agreement is another useful procedure for containing conflict. In this procedure if either party gets uncomfortable that a discussion may be escalating, he or she says, "I'm getting uncomfortable. I want a 5-minute time-out." Spouses go to separate rooms, where each relaxes (deep breathes) and tries to stop thinking about the argument. Afterward, the couple may restart the discussion if both desire it. If a second time-out is requested, then the couple definitely must stop the discussion.

The Blaming Spouse

Interpreting the nonalcoholic spouse's frequent conversations about past or possible future drinking as an attempt to punish the alcoholic or sabotage the alcoholic's recovery, or in other ways overtly disapproving of the spouse's behavior, usually is not helpful. The therapist can empathize with the spouse by sympathetically reframing the spouse's behavior as trying to protect the couple from further problems due to alcohol. From this perspective, the spouse's talk about drinking is intended to be sure the alcoholic (1) knows fully the negative impact of the past drinking (and this is plausible because often the drinker does not remember much of what happened); (2) is aware of the full extent of the problem so his or her motivation toward sobriety will be fortified; and (3) is prepared for situations that may lead to a relapse or lapse in motivation. Once the spouse feels understood, he or she becomes more receptive to the therapist's suggestion that the spouse has been "doing the wrong thing for the right reasons" and to suggestions about more constructive methods to achieve the same goal.

BMT Couples Group Interventions

Overall Structure of Groups

Table 7.1 above lists the four major areas targeted in the BMT group, each of which is described in detail below, roughly in order of their coverage in the group sessions. Division of the BMT group into the four content areas does not indicate a rigid sequence of nonoverlapping interventions; in fact, there is considerable overlap across the different areas from one session to the next. The BMT couples groups consist of four to five couples with an alcoholic spouse in early recovery, a male and female cotherapist team (at least one member of which conducted each couple's pregroup sessions), and an observer who takes process notes during each session. Interns and therapists serve as observers as part of their training to conduct future groups. Group leaders use a detailed treatment manual with a preplanned outline for each session and spend at least 30 minutes planning each session. Each couples group meets for 10 weekly 2-hour sessions with a 10-minute midsession refreshment break. Couples take turns providing refreshments, and the meeting room is open 30 minutes before and after the session, both of which allow for informal interaction among group members and help build group cohesion. Group sessions tend to be highly structured, with the therapists setting the agenda at the outset of each meeting. Each session (after the first, which starts with introductions) begins with an inquiry about compliance with the Antabuse Contract and about any drinking or urges to drink that have occurred since the last session. Next the homework assignments from the previous session are reviewed. The rest of the meeting covers new material, such as instruction in and rehearsal of skills to be practiced at home during the week, and ends with the assignment of homework and answering questions. Generally, the first few BMT group sessions focus on increasing positive exchanges in order to decrease tension and build goodwill. This prepares couples for dealing with marital problems and desired relationship changes in later group sessions using communication and problem-solving skills training and behavior change agreements. Finally, the group observer phones each couple midweek to prompt homework completion, monitor progress, and confirm attendance at the next session.

Alcohol-Focused Interventions

Although the majority of time in the BMT groups is spent on relationship skills building, each session has some time spent on drinking to maintain sobriety, intervene quickly to prevent or minimize drinking, and prepare couples for preventing relapse after the BMT group. Maintenance of abstinence is facilitated by *reviewing each couple's compliance with the Antabuse Contract* at the beginning of each group session. In addition, the early warning system of the contract (by which spouses agree to call the therapists if Antabuse is not taken and observed for 2 days in a row), midweek phone calls to prompt homework completion, and *monitoring the alcoholic's daily record of urges to drink,* which therapists review at each session, all serve to inform the therapists of lapses in the Antabuse agreement and other precursors of a drinking episode. We have experienced relatively few drinking episodes during the course of BMT groups and none that got very far along without the therapist's knowledge. Once it was known that the alcoholic had taken a drink, therapists' goals were *crisis intervention to get the drinking stopped* and the couple to the clinic for a conjoint conference to use the relapse as a learning experience. At the clinic session therapists are extremely active in assisting the couple to restart the Antabuse Contract, identify what couple conflict (or other antecedent) may have led to the drinking, and generate solutions other than drinking for similar future situations. The success of this approach, which minimizes drinking during the BMT groups, seems to be due to two factors. First, all the alcoholics had been abstinent on the Antabuse Contract prior to starting the group and this prevented drinking in the majority of cases. Second, the midweek phone calls and the tracking of urges to drink allowed intervention very soon after drinking started, when needed. *Discussions about preventing relapse* occur just prior to the end of the group. Husbands and wives complete a worksheet, adapted from Marlatt's (1976) Drinking Profile, to help specify high-risk situations for relapse. Group discussions focus on possible coping strategies the alcoholics and spouses can use to prevent or minimize relapse when confronted with these or similar situations.

Increasing Positive Couple and Family Activities

Pleasing Behaviors

The goal of this part of the BMT group is to increase a couple's awareness of benefits from the relationship and the frequency with which spouses notice, acknowledge, and initiate pleasing or caring behaviors on a daily basis. Caring behaviors are defined to couples as "behaviors showing that you care for the other person," and illustrated by a variety of examples.

Noticing daily caring behaviors starts in Session 1 of the group with homework called "Catch Your Spouse Doing Something Nice." This requires each spouse to record one caring behavior performed by the partner each day on sheets provided by the therapist. This procedure is designed to compete with the spouses' tendency to ignore positive and focus on negative behavior. In Session 2, spouses read the caring behaviors recorded during the previous week.

Acknowledging caring behaviors is introduced next as a way spouses can reinforce what they want more of and start opening their hearts to each other. Group leaders model acknowledging caring behaviors ("I liked it when you. . . . It made me feel . . . "), noting the importance of eye contact; a smile; a sincere, pleasant tone of voice; and mention of only positive feelings. Each spouse then practices acknowledging caring behaviors from his or her daily list for the previous week. After the couple practices the new behavior in the therapy session, the therapist assigns for homework a 2- to 5-minute daily communication session in which each partner acknowledges one pleasing behavior noticed that day.

Initiating more caring behaviors comes after couples begin to notice and acknowledge daily caring behaviors. Often the weekly reports of daily caring behaviors show that one or both spouses are fulfilling requests for desired change voiced before the therapy. In addition, many couples report that the 2- to 5-minute communication sessions serve to initiate conversation about everyday events. A final assignment is that each partner give the other a "caring day" during the coming week by performing special acts to show caring for the spouse. Couples who engage wholeheartedly in this assignment often influence the more negative group members to begin acting more positively toward each other. The therapist also encourages reluctant partners to take risks and to act lovingly toward the spouse rather than wait for the other to make the first move. Finally, spouses are reminded that at the start of therapy they agreed to act differently (e.g., more lovingly) and then assess changes in feelings, rather than wait to feel more positively toward their partner before instituting changes in their behavior.

Shared Recreational and Leisure Activities

Many alcoholics' families have discontinued or decreased shared leisure activities because in the past the alcoholic has frequently sought enjoyment only in situations involving alcohol and embarrassed the family by drinking too much. Reversing this trend is important because participation by the couple and family in social and recreational activities is associated with positive alcoholism treatment outcome (Moos, Bromet, Tsu, & Moos, 1979). Work on planning and engaging in shared rewarding activities (SRAs) is started in the BMT group by having each spouse make a separate list of possible activities for homework after Session 2. Each activity must involve both spouses, either by themselves or with their children or other adults, and can be at or away from home. When couples report their SRA lists in Session 3, therapists often will find and can point out that a number of activities appear on both partner's lists even when a couple has serious conflicts about SRAs. Planning and doing an SRA is the next assignment. Before giving the couple a homework assignment of planning an SRA, the group leaders model an SRA planning session illustrating solutions to common pitfalls (e.g., waiting until the last minute so that necessary preparations cannot be made, getting sidetracked on trivial practical arrangements). Therapists also instruct the couple to refrain from discussing problems or conflicts during their planned SRAs. Similar SRA assignments are given weekly thereafter with one spouse responsible for planning an activity and the other spouse having one veto in order to show that taking turns is one simple way to resolve conflicts.

Communication and Negotiation Skills Training

Communication Skills Training

Inadequate communication is a major problem for alcoholic couples (O'Farrell & Birchler, 1987), and the inability to resolve conflicts and problems can cause abusive drinking and severe marital and family tensions to recur. Training in communication skills begins with group leaders defining effective communication as "message intended (by speaker) equals message received (by listener)." The chart presented in Figure 7.1 helps explain this definition further, including factors (e.g., "filters") in each person that can impede communication and the need to learn both "listening" and "speaking" skills. Therapists use instructions, modeling, prompting, behavioral rehearsal, and feedback to teach couples how to communicate more effectively. Learning communication skills of listening and speaking and how to use planned communication sessions are essential prerequisites for negotiating desired behavior changes. The training starts with positive or neutral topics and moves to problem areas and charged issues only after each skill has been practiced on less problematic topics.

Communication Sessions are planned, structured discussions in which spouses talk privately, face-to-face, without distractions, and with each spouse taking turns expressing his or her point of view without interruptions. Starting with group Session 2, Communication Sessions are introduced as homework for 2–5 minutes daily when couples first practice acknowledging caring behaviors. In later group sessions, 10- to 15-minute Communication Sessions three to four times a week are assigned for the couples to practice various communication and negotiation skills. The therapists discuss with the couples the time and place that they plan to have their assigned communication practice sessions. The success of this plan is assessed at the next session, and any needed changes are suggested. Establishing a Communication Session as a

FIGURE 7.1. Illustration of communication used at start of training in communication skills. From Gottman, Notarius, Gonso, and Markman (1976, p. 1). Copyright 1976 by Research Press. Adapted by permission.

method for discussing feelings, events, and problems can be very help-ful for many couples. Couples are encouraged to ask each other for a Communication Session to discuss an issue or problem and to follow the ground rules of behavior that characterize such a session.

Listening skills help each spouse to feel understood and supported and slow down couple interactions to prevent quick escalation of nega-tive exchanges. Spouses are instructed to use a listening response ("What I heard you say was . . . . Is that right?") to repeat both the words and the feeling of the speaker's message and to check to see if the message they received was the message intended by their partner. When the listener has understood the speaker's message, roles change, and the first listener then speaks. Teaching a partner in an alcoholic marriage to sum-marize the spouse's message and check the accuracy of the received mes-sage before stating his or her own position is often a major accomplishment that has to be achieved gradually. A partner's failure to separate understanding of the spouse's position from agreement with it is often an obstacle that must be overcome.

Both how the couples *do* the listening skill and how they *view* it are important. In terms of doing the skill, couples are instructed to keep each message to a reasonable length that the listener can digest and to use the exact words of the listening response until they have mastered the skill. Couples generally need repeated practice with feedback stress-ing both verbal and nonverbal (eye contact, voice tone, facial expres-sion, posture) components. Spouses are taught specifically how to respond when the listener does not receive the message intended by the speaker. The speaker first has to indicate what part of the message was correctly repeated by the listener and then state what additional information he was trying to convey; the interchange is complete when the speaker's intended message has been understood by the listener. Some couples will view this exercise in terms of credit and blame; so when a message sent is not received accurately, one partner is to blame—either one spouse is a bad listener or the other is an inade-quate speaker who has not made his or her message clear. Group lead-ers should teach couples that the listening exercise is a cooperative, task-oriented effort, that it is equally likely over the long run that un-clear reception of messages will arise from unclear speaking as from inaccurate listening, and that the technique is most useful when initial communication is somewhat unclear.

Speaking skills to express both positive and negative feelings direct-ly are taught in the BMT group as an alternative to the blaming, hostile, and indirect responsibility-avoiding communication behaviors that characterize many alcoholics' marriages (O'Farrell & Birchler, 1987). Group leaders instruct that when the speaker expresses feelings directly, there is a greater chance that he or she will be heard because the speaker says these are his or her feelings, his or her point of view, and not some objective fact about the other person. The speaker takes responsibility for his or her own feelings and does not blame the other person for how he or she feels, thus reducing listener defensiveness and making it easier for the listener to receive the intended message. Differences between direct expressions of feelings and indirect and ineffective or hurtful expressions are presented along with examples. Statements beginning with "I" rather than "you" are emphasized. After rationale and instructions have been presented, the group leaders model correct and incorrect ways of expressing feelings and elicit the group members' reactions to these modeled scenes. Then couples take turns role-playing a communication session in which spouses take turns being speaker and listener, with the speaker expressing feelings directly and the listener using the listening response. During this role-playing, the therapists actively coach the couple as they practice reflecting the direct expressions of feelings. Similar communication sessions, 10–15 minutes each three to four times weekly are assigned for homework. Subsequent group sessions involve more practice with role-playing during the sessions and as homework, and the topics on which the couples practice increase in difficulty each week.

Starting with Session 5, the second half of each group meeting consists of supervised practice of communication sessions about couple problems and conflicts. For this practice, the group is split into two subgroups, each consisting of the husbands and wives of half the couples in the group, and each therapist works with one of the subgroups to find a specific resolution to a problem or conflict that the couple will then try to negotiate in the coming week. Negotiation of behavior change agreements are important parts of this intensive phase of the BMT group.

Behavior Change Agreements

Many alcoholics and their spouses need to learn positive methods to change their partner's behavior to replace the coercive strategies used previously. Many changes that spouses desire from their partners can be achieved through the aforementioned caring behaviors, SRAs, and communication skills. However, the deeper, emotion-laden conflicts that have caused considerable hostility and coercive interaction for years are more resistant to change. Learning to make positive specific requests (PSRs) and to negotiate and compromise are prerequisites for making sound behavior-change agreements to resolve such issues.

PSRs replace couples' all-too-frequent practice of complaining in vague and unclear terms and trying to coerce, browbeat, and force the other partner to change. Therapists indicate that "each partner has to learn to state his or her desires in the form of: (1) positive—what you want, not what you don't want; (2) specific—what, where, and when; (3) requests—not demands that use force and threats, but rather requests that show possibility for negotiation and compromise." Therapists give sample requests and couples indicate the requests that meet the PSR criteria and rewrite those that do not. For homework each partner lists at least five PSRs.

Negotiation and compromise comes next. Spouses share their lists of requests, starting with the most specific and positive items, and the therapists and group members give feedback on the requests presented and help rewrite items as needed. Then therapists explain that negotiating and compromising can help couples reach an agreement in which each partner will do one thing requested by the other. To help couples compromise on a stated request, they are instructed to translate each request onto a continuum of possible activities in terms of frequency, duration, intensity, or situation, rather than present the request in all-or-none terms. For example, if a husband stated his desire for more independence and time to work on his hobbies, this general, vague goal might be translated into explicit dimensions of activity such as when, how often, how long, and where. Perhaps he and his wife could agree to his spending an hour three times weekly after supper in the basement or garage.

After giving instructions and examples, the group leaders coach one of the couples in the group while they have a communication session in which requests are made in a positive specific form, heard by each partner, and translated into a mutually satisfactory, realistic agreement for the upcoming week. Therapists need to be sure that the couple uses all the communications skills taught previously to help them reach a reasonable compromise. Agreed-upon requests must be realistic, reasonable, and commensurate with previously demonstrated skill levels of the spouses because fanciful and overly optimistic promises generally make for a weak agreement with little chance of success. Finally, the agreement is recorded on a homework sheet that the couple knows will be reviewed during the next session. After this demonstration, each therapist works with half of the couples in the group to help each couple negotiate an agreement that each partner will fulfill one request in the next week.

Agreements are a major focus of a number of BMT group sessions in which written behavior-change agreements are negotiated for the forthcoming week, often with very good effects on the couple's relationships. During the sessions, unkept agreements are reviewed briefly, and the group leaders and members provide feedback as to what went wrong and suggest changes needed in the coming week. After completing agreements under supervision in the group each couple is asked to have a communication session at home to negotiate an agreement on their own and to bring it to the following session for review. A series of such assignments can provide a couple with the opportunity to develop skills in behavior change that they can use after the therapy ends. We encourage good-faith agreements (Weiss, Birchler, & Vincent, 1974) in which each partner agrees to make his or her change independent of whether or not the spouse keeps the agreement and without monetary or other rewards or punishments. To increase the perception that each spouse freely chooses to do his or her part of the agreement, each spouse chooses which request he or she desires to fulfill from the partner's PSR list. Thus each spouse volunteers to make changes needed to improve the marital relationship.

Resistance and Noncompliance in the BMT Couples Groups

Resistance to Rationale and Structure of the Groups

Frequently, spouses will want the other to change first, loving feelings to precede loving action, and to solve their most difficult problems first before committing themselves further to therapy or the relationship. Often these attitudes and feelings are understandable given the couple's history. In such cases, therapists need to stress that the couple has neither the skill nor the goodwill and positive feeling needed for the negotiation and compromise that could help them resolve their major problems and differences. Therapists can point out that the couple's approach has not been working and that they must use a different method if they really want to see if their relationship can improve. Group leaders should acknowledge that really giving their relationship a good chance to improve by changing how they act with each other requires risk and vulnerability, but that there is no other way. Presentation and repetition of this rationale often helps spouses decide initially to engage fully in the therapy and later to recommit themselves to the effort after backsliding.

Couple and Therapist Resistance to Role-Playing

Couples' initial resistance to engaging in behavioral rehearsal usually is overcome fairly easily if the therapists (1) give clear instructions and rationale for the role-playing so group members know what they are supposed to do and why it is important and (2) model the desired behavior to give couples a picture of how to perform the specific behaviors. The first role-playing in the BMT group starts with practice in acknowledging caring behaviors in which spouses read from their record sheets, and therapists can prompt a spouse's response by providing the first words if necessary. To encourage further practice, group leaders and members give positive feedback first, followed by suggestions for improvement. Once one couple has role-played, the others are less reluctant. Although reluctance to role-play generally decreases in later sessions, some resistance often remains and requires skillful effort of the type just described to overcome it.

Therapists also can be reluctant to engage in behavioral rehearsal. We have observed especially among therapists who are new to this approach that, although therapists and couples talk a lot about the new skills and about the small amount of role-playing that is being done, often very little time is actually being devoted to behavioral rehearsal. To deal with this problem the group observer can record the amount of time spent role-playing and give feedback to the therapists at mid-session break and at the end of the session. This generally increases time spent on rehearsal during the sessions.

Compliance with Homework Assignments

Weekly homework assignments, which are designed to transfer new behaviors learned in the group to the couple's day-to-day life at home, require specific procedures to gain compliance. In the pregroup orientation session, therapists must explain the reasons for and the types of weekly assignments and that therapists and other group members will take a verbal commitment to do the homework as a serious pledge. The midweek phone calls between sessions to prompt and reinforce performance of the assignments also are explained and therapists determine the best time to call the couple. How the homework is assigned in the group is also very important. We use a detailed homework assignment sheet, discuss each part at the end of the group session, and ask each couple to make a verbal commitment to complete the assignments.

Group leaders start each session by asking for a couple who completed the previous week's assignment and got something positive out of it. Couples who complete homework assignments have approximately 10–15 minutes to report on their progress and any problems; those not completing an assignment have only 5 minutes. Throughout the group sessions, the leaders refrain from giving negative attention to noncomplying couples, but rather use the 5-minute contingency and a matter-of-fact request for better effort in the future. The greater success of other couples frequently serves as a model for the more resistant couples through vicarious learning. Although therapists sometimes feel reluctant to exert such strong control over the couples' reporting at the beginning of each session, we have become impressed with the importance of doing this. Often noncomplying spouses are angry with each other when the session starts and each wants to present "their side of the story" first to gain group support for their position and to coerce the partner into changing. If allowed to go unchecked, this frequently can lead other couples, including those who are making positive progress, to present the negative side of their situation. The session can take on a depressing, hopeless air and most of the couples will leave feeling worse than when they came and less committed to behavior change at home in the coming week—an unfortunate occurrence in a short-term group.

Planning Maintenance of Change at End of BMT Group

BMT Program Behaviors to Continue

For homework after group Session 9, couples are asked to discuss what interventions or behavior changes accomplished during the group they would like to continue after the group ends. In session ten, each couple discusses what they wish to continue. The Antabuse Contract, regular SRAs, and Communication Sessions are frequently mentioned maintenance goals. Specific behavior change agreements that were negotiated in the group also often are mentioned. Agreements pertaining to the couple's handling of their finances and their children are among those most frequently chosen as goals for maintenance after the group. Group discussion focuses on how each couple can ensure that they will be likely to engage in the desired behavior after the group when needed. Group leaders and members can discuss and rehearse how to cope with situations likely to interfere with the new behavior. It is also suggested that couples reread handouts from the group periodically and agree to periodic monitoring of their maintenance goals at follow-up contacts (see below).

Another method used in planning maintenance is to anticipate what high-risk situations for relapse to abusive drinking may be likely to occur after treatment (see above under Alcohol-Focused Interventions). Group discussions then focus on how to prevent relapse when faced with such situations.

Periodic Follow-Up Contacts

Project CALM has always included periodic follow-up contacts after the BMT group. These started as data collection contacts to collect questionnaire and interview data about drinking and marital adjustment in our research studies. We became impressed with the important continuing care and maintenance functions served by these follow-up contacts. Currently all Project CALM patients have inclinic or at-home quarterly follow-up visits for 2 years after the BMT group ends. This ongoing contact with the couple is a very useful method to monitor progress, to assess compliance with planned maintenance procedures, and to evaluate the need for additional preventive sessions. The therapist takes responsibility for scheduling and reminding the couple of these follow-up sessions because this is necessary if continued contact is to be maintained successfully. The following rationale is given to couples for the continued contact: Alcoholism is a chronic health problem that requires active, aggressive, ongoing monitoring by the therapist and couple to prevent or to quickly treat relapses for an extended period after an initial stable pattern of recovery has been established.

CASE APPLICATION

Background and Presenting Problem

Steve and Mary Donahue were referred to the Project CALM BMT Program while Steve was an inpatient in an alcoholism rehabilitation program. The referring counselor felt the CALM program might help the couple, who had been separated for the majority of the year before Steve entered the rehab program, to decide whether Steve should return to live with his wife after leaving the rehab. Steve and Mary were both in their late 40s. They had been married 24 years and had three children, a 23-year-old son living on his own and two teenage daughters at home. Steve was an unemployed salesman and Mary worked full-time as a supervisor at the telephone company. Steve's alcohol problem had started over 20 years earlier with excessive drinking at parties and during business activities associated with his work as a salesman of building materials.

About 15 months prior to the initial contact with the CALM BMT program, the Donahues had separated at Mary's insistence when Steve was fired from his job for drinking and arrested for the second time for drunken driving. Steve refused to get treatment and continued to drink very heavily on a daily basis after the initial separation. About 5 months after the separation, Steve fell and hit his head while intoxicated after which he was hospitalized and in a coma for almost 4 weeks. After regaining consciousness and beginning speech therapy for the mild aphasia caused by the head injury, Steve was transferred to an alcohol rehab program. On discharge from this rehab, Steve returned home to live with Mary but only stayed at home for 2 weeks before resuming drinking and being asked by Mary to leave again. After another 2 months of daily heavy drinking, Steve entered another rehab program that he left after 10 days and returned to drinking and living alone.

Two weeks later, feeling sick from drinking up to two quarts of vodka a day but afraid to stop for fear he would suffer a withdrawal seizure, Steve contacted Mary saying he wanted to come home and to stop drinking for good. Mary agreed that Steve could return home for no longer than a week while arranging to enter a treatment program. Mary also told Steve she would consider giving their marriage "one last try" if he completed the rehab program, established an aftercare plan that seemed reasonable, and remained abstinent. Steve entered an initial 7-day detoxification period, followed by a 28-day rehab program during which he was referred for an evaluation for the BMT program.

Pregroup Sessions

Initial Sessions

Meeting #1

Both Steve and Mary felt that they had had a reasonable marriage before the negative effects of Steve's alcoholism had brought them to the brink of divorce. Although Steve wanted very much to return home, Mary was frightened and distrustful that Steve would return to drinking. She wanted to think about the BMT program and hear what else Steve had planned for aftercare before she made a decision about the program. Mary also revealed that the couple's oldest son, who also had a serious active alcoholism problem, had returned home while his father was in the rehab program. Serious conflicts had occurred in the past between father and son, especially when one or both had been drinking. The therapist explained the BMT program and questioned whether Steve would be medically cleared for taking Antabuse and whether the aftereffects from Steve's head injury might interfere with his ability to participate in the BMT program. Steve's speech was somewhat slowed. The therapist also wondered whether the head injury might have caused problems with memory and acquisition of new learning that could interfere with the BMT program and pose risks of Steve drinking on Antabuse.

Given the many factors that needed to be considered prior to Steve's return home and the couple's entry to the BMT program, a second couple meeting was set. It was agreed that prior to this second meeting: (1) The therapist would request and Steve would complete a medical evaluation to determine suitability of Antabuse and a neuropsychological evaluation to determine suitability for the BMT program; (2) Steve would formulate his aftercare plans with his rehab program counselor and discuss these plans with Mary; (3) Mary would discuss her ambivalence about Steve's return home with her Al-Anon group and decide under what conditions she would agree to this; and (4) Steve and Mary would discuss what should be done about their son and his drinking.

Meeting #2

At the second couple meeting, Steve indicated that the physician in the rehab program had prescribed Antabuse after a careful review of Steve's medical history and current liver function tests. Steve had already started taking Antabuse and told Mary he would be willing to stay on Antabuse as long as either of them felt it was necessary. The neuropsychological testing results indicated that Steve's post-head-injury problems did not involve memory or learning problems and were limited to mild to moderate severity word-finding difficulties that were not judged a barrier to BMT program participation. In addition, these difficulties might continue to improve with the speech therapy Steve was receiving. Steve presented his aftercare plan, which involved four to five AA meetings and an individual alcoholism aftercare counseling session each week. Mary's Al-Anon group had advised her to stand firm that she would not tolerate Steve drinking while living at home and had also supported Mary following her heart and giving their marriage "one last try." Given these developments, Steve and Mary decided to start the BMT program the following week after Steve's discharge from the rehab program.

Their son's problems had taken a turn for the worse. He had left their home in an intoxicated state and had not been heard from. Mary had been extremely upset and worried about her son. After discussions with Steve and her Al-Anon group, Mary concluded there was nothing she could do but wait to hear from the son. She and Steve decided that the son could not live at home while actively drinking. They would consider letting him return home after he had entered a treatment program and had remained abstinent for 6 months.

Meeting #3

This meeting occurred 2 days after Steve's discharge from the rehab program. The police from a nearby state had called to say their son was in jail for creating a disturbance while intoxicated. Steve and Mary had decided not to post bail. Although this was difficult, especially for Mary, the couple and therapist agreed it was the best course of action. They decided further not to pay any fines or court costs that might be imposed on their son for his intoxicated behavior, and to stick with their requirement of 6 month's abstinence before the son was allowed to return home.

After discussing the son, the therapist introduced the Antabuse Contract. The couple was asked to try doing the behaviors of the Antabuse Contract in the coming week and the Antabuse observation procedure was rehearsed in the session (Steve had brought his Antabuse to the session as requested). The couple felt awkward thanking each other during this rehearsal and the therapist had them repeat the rehearsal until they became more comfortable with this aspect. Mary also said she was still very resentful about Steve's past drinking and did not think it made sense for her to forget about all the problems caused by Steve's drinking. The therapist clarified that the contract required the couple not to discuss past drinking at home because this generally led to arguments and emotional upset and sometimes to relapse. The contract was one way to begin to remove Steve's drinking from being the central focus in their relationship. It was clarified further that the therapist expected Mary to continue to have thoughts and feelings about the past drinking and that the past drinking would be discussed in the couple sessions but not at home. With these clarifications, Mary agreed to try the contract for a week. Steve and Mary signed an Antabuse Contract at the following session after successfully completing the contract for 1 week.

The final part of the third couple meeting consisted of Steve and Mary each agreeing to keep three "Project CALM promises" for the coming week: (1) not to threaten separation or divorce or talk about whether they would stay together after the end of the BMT couples group (the trial period established when they agreed that Steve would return home after the rehab program); (2) to do their best to focus on the present and the future and to refrain from negative discussions of past events; and (3) to keep their agreement to do the Antabuse Contract faithfully. Steve and Mary each agreed to these promises after some discussion about the challenges they would face in doing so. Mary reported that in the few days since Steve had come home she had experienced frequent thoughts about divorce. She feared that this trial reconciliation would only trap her in the marriage and lead to short-term improvement but subsequent disappointment when Steve relapsed again as he had done in the past. She agreed not to voice these feelings to Steve at home for the coming week after the therapist empathized with Mary's feelings and indicated he would assist the couple with the process of separation and divorce and help Steve find an alcohol-free living environment if the reconciliation did not prove successful. Steve was concerned he would have difficulty not bringing up past incidents in anger but agreed that he would try this for a week because he could see how this could help reduce tension at home.

Assessment and Other Pregroup Sessions

The Donahues had a total of 10 pregroup sessions including the two initial meetings while Steve was still in the rehab program. In the fourth meeting, the Antabuse Contract was signed and the couple agreed to continue the three CALM promises until the start of the BMT couples group. With a few minor exceptions, the couple was compliant with these two aspects of the BMT pregroup sessions. The therapist continued to inquire about the couple's son during these sessions. After some anxiety over whether they had been too harsh in setting limits on the son, the couple gradually became less upset as they learned about the progress the son was making in his own recovery program. The son had entered a half-way house and gotten a job to pay the fine imposed by a judge who had give him a choice between further time in jail or a fine with probation. The remaining pregroup sessions involvled a detailed assessment of Steve's drinking problem and the couple's marital relationship, feedback about the assessment results, and orientation to the BMT couples group.

Assessment of Steve's Drinking Problem

The TLFB Drinking Interview showed that Steve had been abstinent while living in the community for only 10 days (3%) of the previous year with the remainder spent drinking heavily (63%) or hospitalized (34%) for alcohol-related injuries or for detox or rehab. He had drunk a pint to a quart of vodka daily to prevent withdrawal symptoms (shakes and seizures), which he had experienced previously, and to forget his problems. In addition, much of his drinking had been done with friends and acquaintances at the veterans club post to which he had belonged for many years. Steve's history and the Alcohol Dependence Scale (score = 26) indicated a significant degree of physical dependence on alcohol. Serious negative consequences from his drinking included a head injury that had produced residual speech problems, an enlarged liver, five job losses, two arrests for drunken driving with subsequent probation, six hospitalizations for detox or rehab, two extended marital separations, and the loss of his children's respect. Steve's very elevated score of 46 on the MAST was consistent with these negative consequences.

Steve indicated that his goal was to give up drinking even though he was not sure this was possible.

Assessment of the Marital Relationship

Steve's drinking had seriously threatened the stability of the couple's marriage and had led to two extended separations. Mary's score of 9 on the MSI indicated she had taken a number of steps toward divorce, including establishing an independent bank account and contacting a lawyer to make preliminary plans for divorce. Steve's MSI score was 0 indicating no desire to end the marriage. The CTS about the year prior to starting BMT revealed elevated levels of verbal aggression in the top 10% for U.S. couples for both Steve and Mary because of their frequent, heated arguments. Mary had slapped Steve and pushed and shoved him during an intense argument. Steve had not been violent. The Marital Adjustment Test indicated a moderate level of marital problems (score of 87 for Steve and 91 for Mary). On the Areas of Change Questionnaire, Steve requested minimal change (score of 1) wanting Mary to argue less. Mary requested a number of specific desired changes (score of 36) including improved communication, more time together in social and other activities, and greater participation by Steve in dealing with the couple's financial problems.

Feedback of Assessment Results and Preparation for the BMT Groups

Two weeks before the BMT group started, Steve and Mary met with the male therapist they had been seeing and with the female therapist who would be coleading their couples group. After the female therapist was introduced, their progress to date and the results of the assessment were reviewed with the couple. It was pointed out that Steve had been abstinent for over 3 months (1 month in the rehab program and 2 months at home while attending weekly pregroup sessions). This was the longest period he had been abstinent since he started drinking in high school. It was the first time he had taken Antabuse or attended AA regularly. This was the longest time the couple had lived together over the past 2 years. Their son had started a recovery program of his own. The therapist congratulated Steve and Mary on their commitment to a better life and acknowledged that they had made a good beginning.

The review of the assessment results provided few surprises to the couple, but they were interested by the very high MAST score and impressed with the number of serious negative consequences that had been caused by the drinking. The need for continued abstinence was stressed. It also was suggested that if any drinking occurred they should contact the therapists with the goal of ending the drinking episode as quickly as possible. The therapist pointed out that the Donahues had a strong marriage that had been tested severely by Steve's alcoholism. Mary's courage and willingness to work on the relationship were acknowledged. Steve in a touching moment told Mary how grateful he was that she had stood by him.

Mary's desires for more joint activities and their mutual desire for improved communication were described as goals that would be addressed by the BMT group emphases on SRAs and communication skills training. Mary's concerns about finances and Steve's unemployment were targeted as issues for negotiation and compromise in the later BMT group sessions. The other components of the BMT group were also described. Finally, the Donahues recommitted themselves to the promises made at the start of the program that they would refrain from threats of separation, focus on the present and future, and do homework assignments faithfully once they had agreed to do so. Steve and Mary said they were looking forward to starting the group.

BMT Couples Group Sessions

The Donahues attended 10 weekly 2-hour BMT couples group therapy sessions. Four other couples, all with newly sober alcoholic husbands, also participated in the couples group. The male and female cotherapist team who led all group sessions consisted of the male therapist the couple had seen since the start of the program and the female therapist who had participated in the feedback and group preparation meeting. The therapists used extensive behavioral rehearsal of new communication skills, specific weekly homework assignments, written behavior change agreements, and other BMT techniques described above to help couples change specific behaviors during the group sessions and at home. The general goals of the BMT group were to promote sobriety for the alcoholic and recovery of the marriage through increased positive activities and better communication.

Methods for Promoting Sobriety

Reviewing the Antabuse Contract, monitoring urges to drink, and planning to prevent relapse (described later under maintenance planning) were the methods used to promote sobriety. Compliance with the Antabuse Contract was reviewed at the start of each BMT group meeting. The Donahues missed doing the Antabuse Contract on two occasions only during the 10 weeks of the group, both when Mary had to work very late and Steve had already gone to bed before she returned home.

Steve also shared with the group that his regular attendance at AA meetings helped him cope with the frustration of trying to find work and to stay sober in spite of this frustration.

At the start of each group meeting, Steve and the other alcoholics in the group completed a form on which they recorded any urges or thoughts of drinking they had experienced during the previous week. They recorded the day, time, and circumstances surrounding the urge to drink and how strong the urge had been on a 1 ("weak") to 10 ("very strong") scale. Figure 7.2 presents a graph of urges to drink reported by Steve at each of the 10 BMT group sessions. Through many of the early group meetings, Steve reported thoughts of drinking that were of moderate to high intensity. Two types of situations accompanied Steve's thoughts of drinking: (1) incidents in which Mary commented about his being unemployed and their serious financial problems, and (2) times when he was alone and his mood became dysphoric after thinking about some of the unresolved problems in his life. He seemed to benefit from discussing these thoughts of drinking in the group. Learning that others had similar experiences and the therapists' pointing out that he had successfully coped with the urges were helpful. The therapists' suggestions that he try actively to distract himself with other thoughts and activities when confronted by the thought of drinking proved particularly appealing to Steve who liked the prospect of actively controlling his urges to drink. As indicated in Figure 7.2, Steve reported no further urges to drink after the sixth group session.

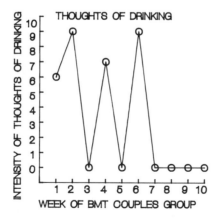

FIGURE 7.2. Thoughts of drinking for each week of 10-week BMT couples group (intensity ratings: 0 = no thought of drinking; 1 = weak thought of drinking; 10 = very strong thought of drinking).

Increasing Positive Couple and Family Activities

Steve and Mary had stopped doing fun activities together because in the past Steve had so frequently sought enjoyment only in alcohol-involved situations and embarrassed his wife when he drank too much. Further, as their marital relationship deteriorated over the years, Steve and Mary had spent less and less time doing any activities together. The first SRA they planned in the group, having pizza together at a local pizza parlor, was not as enjoyable as it might have been because Mary started to discuss their financial problems when they were out together. Steve, who felt guilty about the money problems, became angry at Mary for wanting to discuss the problem. He walked out of the pizza parlor and waited in the car while Mary finished eating. Needless to say, this initial SRA was not very successful. The therapists and other group members suggested that problem discussions and fun together should not be combined. As they progressed during the group, the Donahues agreed not to focus on problems when out together and they gradually tried longer and more meaningful activities together. They went out to dinner to a nice restaurant, entertained another couple at home, and spent a weekend away together by the end of the group sessions. Finally at the last group meeting they announced that they had made reservations for a week's vacation together alone in the near future.

Steve had difficulty with the "Catch Your Spouse Doing Something Nice" procedure initially because he overlooked small, daily behaviors (e.g., his wife preparing meals), instead trying to find special, out-of-the-ordinary behaviors. After considerable discussion about the dangers of taking your partner for granted and observing other group members doing the assignment completely, Steve began to notice a variety of pleasing behaviors performed by his wife. Although somewhat difficult for the Donahues, repeated role-playing with extensive prompting, coaching, and modeling (especially by other group members) succeeded in getting them to acknowledge genuinely in the group the behaviors they had appreciated from the prior week. A 2- to 5-minute daily communication session was assigned for further practice of acknowledging pleasing behaviors at home.

"Caring days" involved planning ahead to do something special for the partner to show caring. For example, Steve brought Mary flowers on one occasion and on another cleaned the house, did the laundry, and had dinner waiting when Mary returned home from work. Mary gave Steve a card acknowledging his efforts in his recovery program and made his favorite meal to celebrate when he reached 6 months sobriety.

Both spouses indicated that Catch Your Spouse Doing Something Nice (especially the daily acknowledging of pleasing behaviors at home) and caring days contributed a great deal to a more positive relationship. Mary noted that this helped decrease her resentments about Steve's past transgressions by helping her see the positive things he was doing now. The weekly ratings of overall happiness taken from Azrin, Naster, and Jones' (1973) Marital Happiness Scale, graphed over the 10 weeks of the BMT group and presented as part of Figure 7.3 show a gradual increase in the couple's happiness with their relationship. Figure 7.3 also shows increased happiness with social activities together, especially on Mary's part, as a result of the SRA planning.

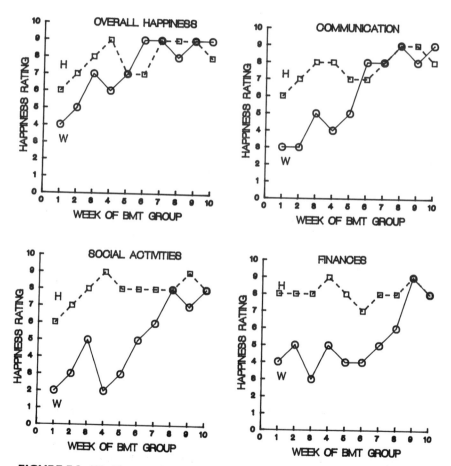

FIGURE 7.3. Weekly marital happiness ratings for husband and wife during 10-week BMT couples group for overall happiness with relationship, communication, social activities, and finances. Using Marital Scale administered weekly: 1 = completely unhappy; 10 = completely happy; H = husband; W = wife.

Communication and Negotiation Skills Training

The benefits of the training in communication can be seen in the gradual increase over time in satisfaction with communication reported by the Donahues and represented by Figure 7.3 in graphic form. Once better communication and renewed goodwill in the relationship had begun, training in negotiation skills was undertaken to help the couple obtain agreements for specific changes each wanted from the other. Steve and Mary spent considerable time in the group and at home discussing and negotiating about Mary's unhappiness with the fact that Steve was not working and the consequent financial problems. Steve disliked Mary's angry outbursts when she was feeling the financial pressures (e.g., when a creditor called). He also objected to her frequent questions about whether he had been looking for a job and what his prospects were of getting a job. A series of agreements concerning these issues were negotiated and successfully carried out. The first agreement was that they would have a weekly discussion in which Mary would inform Steve about the current bills and Steve would review his job-hunting activities of the prior week and his plans for the coming week. Both agreed to use the communication skills they had been learning during this weekly discussion. Mary further agreed to refrain from angry outbursts or other discussions about the money and unemployment problems; and Steve agreed to have a brief communication session about these issues during the week if Mary requested it. At their weekly discussions at home and in the group, further progress was made. They wrote a joint letter to their creditors explaining their situation and arranged extended payment plans in most cases. After considerable discussion, Steve agreed to broaden his job search to include a much wider variety of positions. He also took a part-time job delivering pizza to provide some income while he continued his job search. Figure 7.3 displays the increased satisfaction regarding finances that occurred as a result of these agreements.

Plan for Maintenance of Change

During the last two group sessions, some time was spent discussing factors that might precipitate renewed drinking and what plans they could make to prevent relapse. Steve and Mary decided to continue the Antabuse Contract for an additional year after the end of the BMT group. They had both been pleased with the beneficial effects that the Antabuse Contract had produced in terms of both Steve's sobriety and Mary's willingness to reinvest in the marriage. Continuing the contract was something both of them decided to do to prevent relapse. Steve also decided to continue AA meetings at least three times a week and to see his aftercare alcoholism counselor monthly. Mary planned to continue her weekly Al-Anon meeting. The Donahues and other couples in their group also specified the behaviors initiated during the BMT group that they wished to continue. Steve and Mary decided to continue planning regular, fun activities together. They also wanted to continue their weekly discussions about finances.

Outcome and Follow-Up Information

At the end of the BMT couples group, regular treatment sessions were terminated. Quarterly check-ups to monitor progress were scheduled for the next 2 ½ years (the extended follow-up was part of the research project in which they participated). When the Donahues ended formal treatment, it had been nearly 7 months since Steve's last drink prior to his hospital admission. Information obtained during the follow-up contacts showed continued positive outcomes. Steve had been abstinent 3 years at the time of the final follow-up. He continued Antabuse, AA, and periodic outpatient individual alcoholism counseling throughout this period. The factors he deemed important in helping him maintain sobriety changed over time, with external factors (e.g., Antabuse, AA attendance) most important at the outset and internal factors (e.g., recalling benefits of sobriety and problems caused by drinking, keeping sobriety as his top priority) becoming increasingly important toward the end of the follow-up period. He had finally regained full-time employment 2 years after the end of the BMT group. The couple's financial problems had slowly been resolved. The couple's marital relationship also had stabilized. There had been no further separations. Scores on the Marital Adjustment Test had risen to 120 at the end of the BMT group and fluctuated between 105–120 at the various follow-up contacts with all scores in the range for nondistressed couples. Mary's elevated pretreatment score on the Areas of Change Questionnaire had dropped to the range for nondistressed couples after BMT and during the follow-up period. The verbal aggression score for the CTS, which had been above the 90th percentile before treatment, dropped to much lower levels indicating a substantial decrease in marital arguments. Finally, the oldest son had made considerable progress in his own recovery. Although he had experienced one serious relapse and two minor ones, he had been abstinent most of the time. At the time of the Donahue's last follow-up, the son had been abstinent for the past 15 months and continued to work and live independently from his family.

RESEARCH SUMMARY

Early case reports, uncontrolled studies, and more recent controlled research (reviewed in O'Farrell, 1992) indicate favorable results for various forms of BMT. The BMT couples group program described in this chapter[2] was evaluated in a study that sought to determine whether adding BMT to individual alcoholism counseling led to better marital and drinking outcomes and whether BMT was a more effective addition than interactional couples group therapy, an alternative type of couples group that had been frequently used with alcoholics (Gallant et al., 1970; McCrady et al., 1979). In this study married male alcoholics, who had recently begun individual outpatient alcoholism counseling, were randomly assigned to a no-marital-treatment control group or to 10 weekly sessions of either a BMT or an interactional couples therapy group. The results of this research have been described for the time from before to after treatment and for the 2 years after treatment.

Results from Before to After BMT
Couples Group Treatment

Couples who received BMT improved significantly from before to after treatment on a variety of measures of the marriage relationship (O'Farrell et al., 1985), including overall marital adjustment, extent of desired relationship change, marital stability, and positiveness of communication when discussing a current marital problem. Interactionally treated couples improved on extent of desired relationship change. The control couples did not improve on any of the marital relationship variables. BMT produced better results than no marital therapy on marital adjustment and stability and on positive communication behaviors for those couples who displayed at least moderate levels of positive communication at the outset. BMT did better than interactional therapy on overall marital adjustment and differed significantly at the multivariate level (when all marital functioning measures were considered together) from the interactional group. In addition, there was no measure on which interactionally treated couples were significantly better than BMT or the controls. Finally, although alcoholics in all three treatments showed very substantial short-term improvements in their drinking, alcoholics in the BMT group spent fewer alcohol-involved days during treatment than their interactional group counterparts and did better than both interactional and control groups on an index of overall drinking outcomes. This last result led us to speculate that the interactional group focus on relationship issues without providing specific skills to resolve problems may have led to increased conflict and drinking, whereas the Antabuse Contract may have protected the BMT group couples as they learned new skills to confront their marital problems without alcohol.

The findings indicate that adding BMT to outpatient alcoholism treatment produced statistically and clinically significant improvements in the marriage relationships of male alcoholics, and BMT was superior to having no marital treatment and equal or superior to a frequently used alternative marital treatment. Given these favorable short-term outcomes, results after treatment were of considerable interest.

Results in the 2 Years After BMT Couples Group Treatment

In the 2 years after treatment, alcoholics and their wives who received BMT couples group in addition to the husbands' individual alcoholism counseling showed significant improvements in both drinking and marital adjustment and better marital outcomes than couples in which the husband received individual alcoholism counseling only (O'Farrell et al., 1992). Although BMT remained superior to individual counseling alone on wives' marital adjustment and days separated throughout much of the 2-year follow-up, the strength and the consistency of marital relationship findings favoring BMT diminished as time after treatment increased.

In terms of drinking outcomes, the advantage for BMT over the control and interactional groups noted during treatment was no longer apparent for the 2-years after treatment, when the addition of BMT no longer produced better results than individual treatment alone. Although BMT and interactional couples group did not differ on drinking or marital adjustment, both types of marital therapy had fewer days separated during most of the 2 years after treatment, suggesting that the common effect of both types of marital therapy was to promote marital stability during the long and arduous period of recovery from alcoholism. Finally, alcoholics with the most severe marital and drinking problems prior to treatment had the worst outcomes in the 2 years after treatment.

Taken together, these results suggested that future studies of BMT couples groups in alcoholism treatment should give more attention to maintaining gains produced by BMT with a special focus on preventing relapses and strengthening sobriety, especially among cases with more severe problems. Chapter 12 describes our latest work in which couples relapse prevention sessions were used after a BMT couples group for this purpose.

CONCLUSIONS

This chapter describes a BMT couples group program for alcoholics who have made at least an initial commitment to change and sought help for their drinking problem. A major purpose of the BMT group program is to stabilize and maintain the process of change in the drinking problem and the marriage that led the alcoholic to seek help. This BMT couples group program consists of six to eight weekly pregroup sessions conducted conjointly with each couple and 10 weekly BMT couples group sessions.

The pregroup sessions consist of (1) an initial interview; (2) crisis intervention for drinking or marital crises that must be resolved prior to further work; (3) negotiation of an Antabuse Contract in which the alcoholic takes Antabuse each day while the spouse observes and verbally reinforces the alcoholic for taking Antabuse, and the couple agrees not to argue about drinking; (4) development of a therapeutic relationship; (5) assessment of the drinking and marital problems and feedback to the couple of the assessment results to increase motivation for continued treatment; and (6) preparation for participation in the couples group.

The BMT couples group sessions consist of 10 weekly meetings of four to five couples in which weekly homework assignments and behavioral rehearsal are used to help couples: (1) maintain abstinence and decrease alcohol-related arguments by monitoring compliance with the Antabuse Contract, reviewing urges to drink, and providing crisis intervention for drinking episodes; (2) notice, acknowledge, and initiate daily caring behaviors; (3) plan SRAs; (4) learn the communication skills of listening, expressing feelings directly, and the use of planned communication sessions; and (5) negotiate desired changes using PSRs, compromise, and written agreements. The final part of the program involves planning for maintenance of therapeutic gains at the end of the BMT group and quarterly follow-up contacts for 2 years after the group.

Methods are described for overcoming frequently encountered problems including resistance and noncompliance. A case description of the successful application of the BMT program is provided. Finally, research is summarized that shows that the addition of BMT to individual alcoholism counseling produced better marital and drinking outcomes during and immediately after treatment than individual counseling alone or the addition of a nonbehavioral, interactional couples group. In the 2 years after treatment the added BMT still produced better marital outcomes, especially fewer and shorter separations, than individual counseling alone but no longer produced better drinking outcomes.

The addition of relapse prevention to improve long-term drinking outcomes after BMT is described in Chapter 12.

This chapter provides relevant, practical information about the conduct of BMT couples groups with alcoholics. Hopefully, making this behavioral format for a couples group available to alcoholism practitioners will encourage the use of these promising BMT methods in other alcohol treatment programs, many of which now use nonbehavioral couples groups.

ACKNOWLEDGMENTS

Preparation of this chapter was supported by grant R01 AA08637 to the author from the National Institute on Alcohol Abuse and Alcoholism and by a grant from the Smithers Foundation. The research and treatment program described in this chapter was supported by the Office of Research and Development, Medical Research Service, of the Department of Veterans Affairs.

NOTES

1. Although our published research studies have excluded alcoholics with current drug abuse problems, we no longer exclude such cases from our BMT clinical program. Additional procedures (e.g., weekly urine drug screens) that are beyond the scope of the present chapter are required for such cases.

2. The BMT program evaluated in the study described here was an earlier version of the program that had fewer and less well-developed pregroup sessions than the program described in this chapter. It also was used as an adjunct to individual counseling, whereas the current BMT pregroup plus group program frequently is the only counseling received by the alcoholic.

REFERENCES

Annis, H. M. (1985). *Inventory of Drinking Situations*. Toronto: Addiction Research Foundation.

Annis, H. M. (1982). *Situational Confidence Questionnaire*. Toronto: Addiction Research Foundation.

Azrin, N. H. (1976). Improvements in the community-reinforcement approach to alcoholism. *Behaviour Research and Therapy, 14,* 339–348.

Azrin, N. H., Naster, B. J., & Jones, R. (1973). Reciprocity counseling: A rapid learning based procedure for marital counseling. *Behaviour Research and Therapy, 11,* 365–382.

Cadogan, D. (1973). Marital group therapy in the treatment of alcoholism. *Quarterly Journal of Studies on Alcohol, 34,* 1187–1194.

Floyd, F. J., O'Farrell, T. J., & Goldberg, M. (1987). A comparison of marital observational measures: The Marital Interaction Coding System and the Communication Skills Test. *Journal of Consulting and Clinical Psychology, 55,* 423–429.

Gallant, D. M., Rich, A., Bey, E., & Terranova, L. (1970). Group psychotherapy with married couples: A successful technique in New Orleans Alcoholism Clinic patients. *Journal of the Louisiana Medical Society, 122,* 41–44.

Gottman, J., Notarius, C., Gonso, J., & Markman, H. (1976). *A couples guide to communication.* Champaign, IL: Research Press.

Gurman, A. S., & Kniskern, D. P. (1978). Deterioration in marital and family therapy: Empirical, clinical and conceptual issues. *Family Process, 17,* 3–20.

Locke, H. J., & Wallace, K. M. (1959). Short marital-adjustment and prediction tests: Their reliability and validity. *Journal of Marriage and Family Living, 21,* 251–255.

Margolin, G., Talovic, S., & Weinstein, C. D. (1983). Areas of Change Questionnaire: A practical approach to marital assessment. *Journal of Consulting and Clinical Psychology, 51,* 920–931.

Marlatt, G. A. (1976). The Drinking Profile: A questionnaire for the behavioral assessment of alcoholism. In E. J. Mash & L. G. Terdal (Eds.), *Behavior therapy assessment: Diagnosis and evaluation* (pp. 121–137). New York: Springer.

McCrady, B. S., Paolino, T. J., Longabaugh, R., & Rossi, J. (1979). Effects of joint hospital admission and couples treatment for hospitalized alcoholics: A pilot study. *Addictive Behaviors, 4,* 155–165.

Moos, R. H., Bromet, E., Tsu, V., & Moos, B. (1979). Family characteristics and the outcome of treatment for alcoholism. *Journal of Studies on Alcohol, 40,* 78–88.

Noel, N. E., McCrady, B. S., Stout, R. L., & Nelson, H. F. (1987). Predictors of attrition from an outpatient alcoholism treatment program for alcoholic couples. *Journal of Studies on Alcohol, 48,* 229–235.

O'Farrell, T. J. (1986). Marital therapy in the treatment of alcoholism. In N. S. Jacobson & A. S. Gurman (Eds.), *Clinical handbook of marital therapy* (pp. 513–535). New York: Guilford Press.

O'Farrell, T. J. (1990). Sexual functioning of male alcoholics. In R. L. Collins, K. E. Leonard, B. A. Miller, & J. S. Searles (Eds.), *Alcohol and the family: Research and clinical perspectives* (pp. 244–272). New York: Guilford Press.

O'Farrell, T. J. (1992). Families and alcohol problems: An overview of treatment research. *Journal of Family Psychology, 5,* 339–359.

O'Farrell, T. J., & Bayog, R. D. (1986). Antabuse contracts for married alcoholics and their spouses: A method to insure Antabuse taking and decrease conflict about alcohol. *Journal of Substance Abuse Treatment, 3,* 1–8.

O'Farrell, T. J., & Birchler, G. R. (1987). Marital relationships of alcoholic, conflicted, and nonconflicted couples. *Journal of Marital and Family Therapy, 13,* 259–274.

O'Farrell, T. J., Cutter, H. S. G., Choquette, K. A., Floyd, F. J., & Bayog, R. D. (1992). Behavioral marital therapy for male alcoholics: Marital and drinking adjustment during the two years after treatment. *Behavior Therapy, 23,* 529–549.

O'Farrell, T. J., Cutter, H. S. G., & Floyd, F. J. (1985). Evaluating behavioral marital therapy for male alcoholics: Effects on marital adjustment and communication from before to after therapy. *Behavior Therapy, 16,* 147–167.

O'Farrell, T. J., Kleinke, C., & Cutter, H. S. G. (1986). Differences between alcoholic couples accepting and rejecting an offer of outpatient marital therapy. *American Journal of Drug and Alcohol Abuse, 12,* 301–310.

O'Farrell, T. J. & Maisto, S. A. (1987). The utility of self-report and biological measures of alcohol consumption in alcoholism treatment outcome studies. *Advances in Behaviour Research and Therapy, 9,* 91–125.

Selzer, M. L. (1971). The Michigan Alcoholism Screening Test: The quest for a new diagnostic instrument. *American Journal of Psychiatry, 127,* 1653–1658.

Shapiro, R. J. (1984). Therapy with violent families. In S. Saunders, A. Anderson, C. Hart, & G. Rubenstein (Eds.), *Violent individuals and families: A handbook for practitioners* (pp. 112–136). Springfield, IL: Charles C. Thomas.

Skinner, H. A., & Allen, B. A. (1982). Alcohol dependence syndrome: Measurement and validation. *Journal of Abnormal Psychology, 91,* 199–209.

Sobell, L. C. (1979). *Alcohol and drug treatment outcome evaluation training manual.* Nashville, TN: Dede Wallace Center Alcohol Programs and Vanderbilt University.

Sobell, L. C., Sobell, M. B., Maisto, S. A., & Cooper, A. M. (1985). Time-Line Follow-Back Assessment Method. In D. J. Lettieri, M. A. Sayers, & J. E. Nelson (Eds.), *NIAAA Treatment Handbook Series (Vol. 2): Alcoholism treatment assessment research instruments* (DHHS Publication No. 85-1380, pp. 530–534). Washington, DC: National Institute on Alcohol Abuse and Alcoholism.

Steinglass, P. (1976). Experimenting with family treatment approaches to alcoholism, 1950–1975: A review. *Family Process, 15,* 97–123.

Straus, M. A. (1979). Measuring intrafamily conflict and violence: The Conflict Tactic (CT) Scales. *Journal of Marriage and the Family, 41,* 75–88.

Weiss, R. L., Birchler, G. R., & Vincent, J. P. (1974). Contractual models for negotiation training in marital dyads. *Journal of Marriage and the Family, 36,* 321–331.

Weiss, R. L., & Cerreto, M. C. (1980). The Marital Status Inventory: Development of a measure of dissolution potential. *American Journal of Family Therapy, 8,* 80–85.

Zweben, A., Pearlman, S., & Li, S. (1983). Reducing attrition from conjoint therapy with alcoholic couples. *Drug and Alcohol Dependence, 11,* 321–331.

Chapter 8

Alcohol-Focused Spouse Involvement with Behavioral Marital Therapy

Nora E. Noel
Barbara S. McCrady

OVERVIEW

In this chapter, we present an outpatient treatment protocol that includes both the alcoholic client and the nonalcoholic spouse as equal partners. The program incorporates three components: (1) a behavioral alcohol treatment program for the alcoholic, (2) interventions focusing on the spouse's behavior as it directly relates to the alcoholic's drinking, and (3) behavioral marital therapy.

In general, research has supported the hypothesis that including the spouse in the alcoholic's treatment leads to a slightly better treatment outcome (cf. Paolino & McCrady, 1977). The ideal level of spouse involvement, however, has been explored only relatively recently. Should the spouse's behavior, for example, also be a focus of therapy? The protocol described in this chapter was developed as part of a 4½-year study funded by the National Institute on Alcohol Abuse and Alcoholism (NIAAA) comparing three different modes of spouse involvement (McCrady, 1979) in an effort to answer that question. The results of this research, the Program for Alcoholic Couples Treatment (PACT) study, will be discussed briefly at the end of the chapter. The protocol described here is the one that appears to have produced the most successful drinking and marital outcomes (McCrady, Stout, Noel, Abrams, & Nelson, 1991).

SPECIAL CONSIDERATIONS

Before deciding to use this protocol, a therapist should consider several clinical guidelines. The PACT findings should not be generalized to all married alcoholics, at least not on the basis of this research alone. However, PACT study selection criteria could be used as guidelines for selecting couples who might be the ideal candidates.

First, all alcoholics included in the PACT study participated on a voluntary basis. If a potential client is not willing to participate, perhaps some initial motivational therapy (as presented in the previous chapters) would be appropriate instead. Second, spouses had to agree at the outset to participate fully in treatment. Cooperation is needed from both alcoholic and spouse because both are expected to make substantive changes in behavior. Third, neither the alcoholic nor the spouse could be a current abuser of other drugs, prescribed or not. Fourth, the spouse could not have a current drinking problem (although two spouses in the study were alcoholics who reported at least 2 years of abstinence). Finally, couples were excluded if the alcoholic showed evidence of a severe psychiatric or organic disorder. This protocol focuses on treating alcohol (not drug) abuse with non-psychotic alcoholics married to nonalcoholic spouses. A clinician would have to adapt the protocol for a specific couple if these conditions are not met.

On the other hand, potential clients were *not* excluded on the basis of drinking severity. All alcoholics in PACT had a drinking problem of more than 2 years with a minimum of four severe negative consequences (e.g., DUI arrest, job loss due to drinking) within the year prior to entering treatment. Thus, there is evidence that alcoholics with severe drinking problems can be successful using this protocol. In addition, female, as well as male alcoholics, were studied. Finally, the couples in the study did not necessarily have marital difficulties. The reasons for including marital therapy in the treatment protocol are discussed in the next section.

DESCRIPTION OF THE TREATMENT METHOD

Table 8.1 provides an outline of the treatment method including treatment goals, assessment tools, and format and content of treatment. These are described in detail in the next four sections.

Treatment Goals

As noted above, this treatment protocol appeared to be the most successful, in the long run, for the alcoholics who enrolled in PACT. Although it may appear to be a very structured program, it is actually quite flexible and adaptable if the following three major aims are maintained throughout.

TABLE 8.1. Overview of the Project for Alcoholic Couples' Treatment (PACT) Therapy Sessions

A. Initial treatment sessions (1–3 90-minute conjoint sessions)
   1. Initial clinical interview
      Description of rationale
      Goal setting
   2. Assessment
      Alcoholic's drinking (e.g., Time-Line Follow-Back Interview; Drinking Patterns Questionnaire; self-monitoring)
      Spouse's behavior related to alcoholic's drinking (e.g., Spouse Behavior Questionnaire)
      Marital relationship (e.g., Locke-Wallace Marital Adjustment Test; Areas of Change Questionnaire)
B. Treatment sessions (10–13 90-minute conjoint sessions)
   1. Interventions directed at alcoholic's drinking behavior
      Functional analysis of drinking behavior
      Stimulus control procedures
      Contingency rearrangement
      Cognitive restructuring
      Alternatives to drinking
   2. Interventions directed at spouse behavior
      Functional analysis of spouse's behavior related to alcoholic's drinking
      Stimulus control procedures
      Contingency rearrangement
      Cognitive restructuring
      Techniques to stop triggering and reinforcing drinking
   3. Couple (marital) interventions
      Plans for fun activities
      "Love days" (increasing the rewardingness of the marriage)
      Formal communication training
      Negotiation and problem solving
C. Termination and maintenance planning (1 90-minute conjoint session)
   1. Review of goals and treatment
   2. Description of "Abstinence Violation Effect"
   3. Plan for ongoing relapse prevention
D. Post treatment "booster" (Optional: Planned in last session)
   1. Review of changes in drinking behavior, spouse behavior and marital relationship (3–6 months posttherapy)
   2. Reinforcement of progress
   3. Assessment of need for further treatment

Alteration of the Alcoholic's Behavior that Triggers or Reinforces Drinking

The first aim is to decrease alcohol problems using a functional analytic approach to understand and to reduce or terminate the alcoholic's drinking. Functional analysis is the systematic assessment of a problem behavior: what exactly the behavior is, how it developed, and the environmental events that precede, accompany, and follow the behavior. Functional analysis of the drinking is accomplished through the use of self-monitoring by the alcoholic of drinking and drinking urges. The therapist uses these data as well as material from other assessments to teach both alcoholic and spouse basic facts about alcohol and specific methods that alcoholics can use to stop drinking or not respond to an urge.

Setting the drinking goal should be accomplished through negotiation and discussion among the alcoholic, the spouse, and the therapist. Assuming, without discussion, that all parties want the alcoholic to be abstinent may lead to misunderstandings and may even sabotage treatment. The therapist should consider that some alcoholics, and some spouses, come into treatment with the expectation that a reduction to low levels of drinking is sufficient to diminish drinking problems (Heather & Robertson, 1981). Indeed, this may be correct, especially if the alcoholic is committed to a goal of reduced drinking and has not yet developed physical or severe emotional problems as a result of drinking. However, if reduced drinking is the goal, care should be taken to specify exactly what the goal entails (i.e., specific acceptable levels of frequency and amount on any given occasion, any restrictions on setting or other circumstances, and, most importantly, indicators that the drinking is getting out of control or becoming a problem again and a plan to deal with the loss of control).

If both alcoholic and spouse agree on a goal of reduced drinking or if they are unsure about a goal of lifelong abstinence, we have found it helpful to request that they establish an initial period of abstinence (usually 6 months) in order to experience many life situations without alcohol. If, at the end of that period, the alcoholic wants to resume drinking, the therapist can help the couple develop a plan to learn appropriate drinking behavior (Noel, Sobell, Cellucci, Nirenberg, & Sobell, 1982). For convenience, in the description below abstinence is assumed to be the established goal of treatment.

Alteration of Spouse Behaviors that Trigger or Reinforce Drinking

The second aim of this treatment protocol is to understand and change the spouse's behavior as it directly relates to the alcoholic's drinking. Spouses do not cause drinking, but their behavior may make drinking consequences less aversive, or they may even, without intention, reward drinking. Spouses often protect drinkers from naturally occurring negative consequences of drinking. For example, if the alcoholic has a hangover, the spouse may call the alcoholic's employer to report that he or she has an illness. Thus, the second aim of the therapy protocol is to help spouses understand the role their behavior plays and to find alternatives that can have a more positive impact.

Again, this aim is accomplished through a functional analysis of the spouse's behavior specifically in regard to the alcoholic's drinking. Both alcoholic and spouse are provided with information about how spouse behavior can contribute to the development and maintenance of a drinking problem and how the spouse can modify this behavior. In addition, spouses are taught ways they can support alcoholics through the change process.

Enhancement of the Marital Relationship

The third aim is to enhance the quality and type of marital interactions and improve communication skills. This is important even when the marriage does not appear dysfunctional. The reasoning is that marital therapy can increase the positive value of the relationship. The increase in value can, in turn, increase the motivation of both parties to change their alcohol-related behavior in order to keep the marriage intact. The case example provided in this chapter illustrates the value of marital therapy even in a "good" relationship.

Session Format

In the PACT study, 15 conjoint outpatient sessions (90 minutes each) were scheduled, usually one per week. The number of sessions may be adapted based on the needs of the couple. However, we have found that at least 90 minutes per session is needed to cover the material. In addition, a reasonable amount of time between sessions allows for self-monitoring and homework completion.

If needed, the alcoholic should be detoxified before beginning this outpatient program. Both members of the couple are expected to be present for each outpatient session because they are considered equal partners in treatment. Each session begins with a breath test for the presence of alcohol. The therapist should explain that this is a routine procedure and not an "accusation" of drinking. However, any session will be postponed if either member shows up under the influence of alcohol or drugs. (Obviously, if this were to happen, the therapist should also assess for the need for detoxification.) The rationale is that because both members of the couple will be putting some effort into learning new behaviors, both must come to the session with cognitive abilities intact.

The next step in each session is going over the daily self-monitoring forms that each member of the couple is expected to complete. The alcoholic, for example, is asked to monitor daily drinking and urges to drink, if any. The alcoholic is encouraged to report drinking if it occurs. Drinking episodes are used to plan interventions and to assess progress. In addition, both the alcoholic and the spouse are asked to monitor daily marital satisfaction. Finally, homework is given at the end of each session and assignments from previous sessions are discussed.

After reviewing the self-monitoring and homework from the past week, the therapist presents the planned session content, using examples from the couples' self-monitoring sheets, homework, and other assessment data. Handouts reiterating the session content have proven useful. Many couples save their handouts and review them often.

Assessment

As noted, this protocol is flexible and can be tailored to specific couples. This flexibility is a result of thorough assessment and planning. To individualize the program for each couple, it is important for the therapist to consider several points. First, how appropriate is each intervention for the couple or for the person to whom it is directed? For example, a careful assessment may suggest that the alcoholic responds best to external changes and limit setting. In this case, the therapist might want to emphasize the use of stimulus control or environmental change techniques. In another case, the couple may communicate well, but what they are communicating is hostility and resentment. Perhaps, with this couple, negotiation, problem solving, and increased positive interactions should be emphasized.

A second issue is the timing of the interventions. Many of the interventions are skill-building techniques. The therapist should time the interventions based on the skills the person or couple already has. This requires an initial and ongoing assessment of the strengths of the alcoholic, spouse, and couple.

Thus, careful assessment is the key to planning and implementing effective and individually tailored treatment. In PACT, detailed assessments of drinking behavior and consequences, spouse involvement in drinking, and marital functioning were completed during two sessions prior to treatment and in the first few treatment sessions. Monitoring of drinking, drinking urges, and marital satisfaction was carried on throughout treatment. Detailed assessment followed treatment immediately and at 6-month intervals thereafter for 18 months. This level of assessment is much more than a therapist needs to implement the treatment protocol effectively. Nevertheless, some of the instruments used in the research were found to have a great deal of clinical relevance and may even constitute the initial phase of intervention. Therefore, some useful instruments are described below.

Time-Line Follow-Back Drinking Interview

Measurement of drinking behavior is quite important. Prior to the initiation of treatment, a daily drinking history can be obtained using the Time-Line Follow Back (TLFB) method (Sobell et al., 1980). For research purposes, we obtained a 365-day history from each alcoholic. More recent clinical work suggests that assessment of the 90 days prior to treatment is usually sufficient for clinical purposes.

In the TLFB procedure, the alcoholic, in this case with the help of the spouse, is asked to categorize drinking for each day as abstinent (no alcohol), light (1–2 drinks), moderate (3–6 drinks), or heavy (more than 6 drinks). To do this, the couple is given a blank calendar. The dates are filled in, and then the couple is asked to recall significant or special events such as birthdays, holidays, illnesses and vacations. Regular events, such as a weekly meeting or a biweekly payday are also noted (appointment books or social calendars can be helpful). Recalling these events helps the couple recall the daily drinking (e.g., "That was George's Cub Scout campout, so I tried not to drink that day," or "I drank a lot that night, because the next day my wife ended up helping me with my hangover instead of going to church services"). The process of completing the calendar is quite interactive among the alcoholic, the spouse, and the therapist. As an added benefit, by observing this process, the therapist can assess relationship behaviors (e.g., communication skills) of the couple.

The daily calendar produced can be quite useful to the therapist. For example, the relationship between particular events and drinking can be noted (e.g., the alcoholic was able to remain abstinent for George's campout). In addition, regular drinking patterns can be highlighted (the alcoholic drinks heavily every second Tuesday, which is payday). This kind of information is essential for developing specific interventions.

Daily Self-Monitoring

Two other assessments of drinking behavior can also be helpful. One is the daily self-monitoring card, introduced at the beginning of treatment. As noted above, the alcoholic records the exact time and situation for each drink consumed and the time, situation, and intensity (rated 1–7) of any urges to drink. These daily self-monitoring cards, collected at each session by the therapist, can be used to continue the calendar begun with the TLFB procedure. Regular patterns of continued strong urges or drinking can be spotted and addressed by the therapist. Together, the therapist and the couple can plan for high-risk situations (e.g., "You always have trouble with barbecues, and there's another one next Saturday").

Drinking Patterns Questionnaire

Another drinking assessment is the Drinking Patterns Questionnaire (DPQ) (Zitter & McCrady, 1979). The DPQ is a functional analysis questionnaire presenting over 200 situations, feelings, and thoughts often associated with drinking. The couple completes the inventory by endorsing all the items they believe are associated with the alcoholic's drinking and assigning a rank of importance to each set of items. The 10 major areas covered by the DPQ include environmental, work and financial factors, physiological states, interpersonal situations, marital problems, relationships with parents, problems with children, emotional factors, and recent major life stresses. In addition, major positive and negative consequences of drinking are checked, because both can reinforce drinking and lead to future drinking. The DPQ takes about 2 hours and can be assigned at the end of the first session as homework.

Spouse Behavior Questionnaire

Spouse behavior directly related to drinking can also be assessed using a functional analysis model. A useful instrument for accomplishing this goal is a modified version of the Spouse Behavior Questionnaire (SBQ) (Orford et al., 1975). The SBQ lists various behaviors spouses might use to control or cope with the drinking of the alcoholic (e.g., "Have you threatened to leave him or her because of his or her drinking?"). The SBQ consists of three subscales: (1) spouse-related drinking antecedents, (2) spouse's protection of alcoholic from negative consequences of drinking, and (3) spouse-produced negative consequences of drinking. For PACT, items were added describing spouse-produced positive consequences of sobriety (e.g., "Have you complimented him or her when he or she has been sober?"), because these are the specific behaviors we intended to teach as part of treatment. (The modified version of this questionnaire can be obtained from either author.)

Alcoholics and spouses are given separate forms of the SBQ and asked to rate the frequency in the last 12 months of each of the spouse behaviors. The SBQ can be completed in about an hour and also can be given to the couple as a homework assignment. Again, the responses to the SBQ help define the specific spouse behaviors that trigger or reinforce drinking so the therapist can target those behaviors for intervention.

Marital Relationship Assessment

A final area to be assessed in detail is the status of the marital relationship. Ongoing assessment can be accomplished through daily ratings of marital satisfaction by each member of the couple on a scale of 1 (very poor) to 7 (best ever). These ratings may be indirectly related to drinking or spouse behaviors affecting drinking, but often many other factors can play a role.The goal of the marital assessment is to identify the factors that the couple feels are the problems and strengths in their marriage and to target behaviors related to those factors. Hypothetically, as marital satisfaction increases, motivation for changing drinking-related behaviors indirectly increases.

There are several instruments available for assessing marital problems and strengths. The ones used in PACT included the Locke-Wallace Marital Adjustment Test (Locke & Wallace, 1959) and the Areas of Change Questionnaire (ACQ) (Birchler & Webb, 1977). With the Locke-Wallace test, the higher the score, the better the person feels about the marriage. The ACQ is helpful in (1) identifying behaviors that each member of the couple desires the other to change and (2) assessing each member's own awareness of the other's desires for change in them.

Session Content

Overview

Interventions during the sessions fall into three categories, corresponding to the three aims of treatment. The first category is interventions directed at modifying the client's drinking. These include didactic material about alcohol and its effects (e.g., physical, emotional) and methods to reduce or stop drinking. The second category, spouse-directed interventions, includes didactic material about spouses' effects on alcoholics' behavior and methods the spouse can learn to stop contributing to the development and maintenance of drinking problems. In the third category, of course, are couple interventions with the goal of enhancing communication, problem solving, and emotional support in the relationship.

Initial Session (Including Rationale)

When meeting for the first time with the couple, the therapist should give a treatment rationale to establish a positive expectancy and set the stage for functional analysis, self-awareness and change. The therapist may wish to paraphrase the following statement:

"I asked you to come to treatment as a *couple* because drinking affects many areas of life, including marriage. Spouses often have strong feelings and reactions to a partner's drinking: They may try repeatedly to help them stop, or they may give up and get angry or depressed. Sometimes the well-intentioned help that the spouses offer is not what's needed at the time, or it may even produce resentment and anger or depression and guilt on the part of the drinker. The purpose of therapy is to take a look at the drinking patterns of the client, the spouse's reactions, and the impact that the spouse's behavior may have on drinking. That way, I can help you both learn to deal more effectively with the drinking problem."

Usually, the couple will offer their own examples of interactions about drinking. A concern for the therapist at this point is to make sure that the spouse is not seen as a *cause* of drinking. The distinction between "triggers" (or cues) for drinking and causes of drinking is important throughout therapy. Again a paraphrase of the following statement to the client may help:

"There are many things that happen or have happened that make you want to have a drink. The important word here is 'want.' Your spouse's behavior may make you 'want' a drink, but no matter what another person does, you are always responsible for your own behavior. You choose whether to drink or not. Likewise, your spouse can choose to stop or continue the behavior you don't like. My job is to help you both recognize your choices and teach you ways to change your behavior. The choice to change is still, essentially, yours."

Explaining the rationale for marital therapy is also important:

"In many couples where one person has a drinking problem, there are also marital problems. For whatever reasons, couples no longer get positive rewards out of their marriage. Usually, communication between partners is poor or filled with negative emotions. Sometimes partners begin to spend time apart, even avoiding each other, and essential tasks, such as grocery shopping, getting the car fixed, taking care of the children, are neglected. At this point, couples may lose the ability to solve problems and make decisions together. Even if the drinking stops, the marital problems may remain. The goals of the marital therapy are to increase the positive interactions in your marriage, improve communication skills, and help you learn how to solve problems together."

The importance of self-monitoring and completing homework should also be stressed:

"Both of you will be working on breaking old habits in regard to drinking and your marriage. It is very hard to do this unless you practice your new skills between therapy sessions. For this therapy to work, it is essential that you do your homework and monitor any changes."

Of course, some couples will have difficulty learning to self-monitor and to complete homework assignments. The therapist should use behavioral principles to shape these skills. A combination of modelling by the therapist and a high level of positive reinforcement for successive approximations can be quite helpful.

After the rationale and daily self-monitoring are explained, the therapist can begin using specific techniques described below. Although the alcoholic, spouse, and couple interventions are presented sequentially, the therapist should not focus on only one at a time. For example, while teaching functional analysis of drinking, the therapist can also teach functional analysis of spouse behavior.

Interventions Directed at the Alcoholic's Drinking

This set of interventions includes (1) functional analysis of drinking, (2) stimulus control procedures, (3) contingency rearrangement, (4) cognitive restructuring, (5) alternatives to drinking. These interventions usually begin in the first session with an explanation to the couple of the functional analysis of drinking and assignment of the DPQ and self-monitoring for homework.

Functional Analysis of Drinking.

The *functional analysis* conceptualizes drinking as a behavior chain. The chain is broken down into different steps: (1) external antecedents of drinking ("triggers"), (2) internal events ("thoughts and feelings"), (3) the drinking behavior, (4) the short-term consequences (generally positive), and (5) the long-term consequences (generally negative). Individualized lists of triggers are developed from the DPQ and self-monitoring cards over the first few sessions. The alcoholic is helped to write out several personal examples of drinking behavior chains. This procedure can break up the perception that drinking behavior is "automatic." As alcoholics complete their own chains during sessions and for homework, the therapist can show how short-term positive consequences (e.g., relief from social anxiety) of a behavior such as drinking generally reinforce and maintain the behavior, even when the long-term consequences are negative. In addition, long-term negative consequences (e.g., a hangover) can sometimes serve as a trigger for another drinking episode.

The concept of spouse-related triggers can also be introduced here, so that the spouse's behavior can become a subject of discussion. Direct intervention with spouse behaviors is described below, but at this point, the couple might outline a few behavior chains in which an action by the spouse (e.g., having wine with a meal) might serve as a trigger. Again, the therapist should deemphasize spouse behavior as a cause of drinking. The spouse's behavior does not necessarily have to change. Instead, the alcoholic may learn to change his or her reaction.

As the alcoholic completes several written drinking chains, the couple should gain a basic understanding of the model. In addition, these behavior chains can serve as a blueprint for planning the rest of the drinking interventions.

Stimulus Control Procedures

Next, the therapist focuses on the external antecedents of drinking ("triggers") and teaches *stimulus control techniques*. With stimulus control (Miller, 1976) the alcoholic learns to alter triggers, either by avoiding or changing them, thus decreasing the likelihood of drinking. For example, if passing a certain bar on the way home from work was a strong trigger for drinking, the alcoholic may decide to minimize the risk by driving home on a different street. If a trigger is unavoidable, then rearranging the environment to minimize risk may help. For example, if cashing a paycheck is a trigger, the alcoholic may arrange for the check to be directly deposited into a bank. Stimulus control techniques do not prevent drinking. Rather, their purpose is to decrease triggers for drinking or to make drinking behavior feel less automatic — to interrupt the chain.

Stimulus control techniques require some planning to implement. Thus, couples are taught a problem-solving procedure called self-management planning. Several columns are drawn on a sheet of paper. The trigger (e.g., driving past the bar) is written in the left-hand column. Next, the couple brainstorms various ways to avoid or alter the trigger (e.g., take the bus home) and these are written in the next column. The negative and positive consequences of each solution are written in the next column, and finally, an evaluation of difficulty is done. Usually, at least one or two somewhat less than perfect solutions emerge from this exercise. Implementing one or two of these solutions is often a good homework assignment.

Contingency Rearrangement

The next set of interventions focuses on the reinforcement following drinking and involves contingency rearrangement. Drinking usually persists despite long-term negative consequences because the short-term consequences are rewarding. In contrast, sobriety is often not very rewarding in the short run. Three procedures are learned to help change the timing and nature of positive and negative consequences.

In the first procedure, alcoholics write a list of all the negative consequences of drinking that they have experienced. They can include potential negative consequences (e.g., health problems, break-up of marriage). On the other side of the paper, they list potential positive consequences of sobriety. Spouses are often quite helpful in adding to these lists. Both lists should be reviewed every day, so that when the alcoholic encounters a trigger, the reasons for staying sober can easily come to mind.

The second technique is self-contracting for achieving goals. In this case, it is essential that the contract be specific. For example, "If I do not stop at the bar on the way home, I will reward myself with one hour of my favorite video game when I get home." As with the self-management plans, the contracts should be preplanned and written. The spouse can often be involved in this process, perhaps even agreeing to supply the reward for the positive action (e.g., "If you review your list of consequences twice today, I agree to go out for ice cream this evening").

The third technique, covert reinforcement (Cautela, 1970), involves vivid rehearsal in imagination of a scene in which the alcoholic has a strong urge to drink, but refuses or does something else. The alcoholic then covertly administers a self-reward ("a pat on the back") for staying sober in the face of temptation. Frequent rehearsal of this scene and others can be assigned between sessions for homework.

Cognitive Restructuring

After mastering the two cognitive techniques, above, the couple should be ready to move on to modifying another part of the behavior chain, that is, the internal antecedents or triggers (thoughts and feelings). If a person's behavior in a social–emotional situation results in self-derogatory, retaliatory, or guilt-related thoughts, then these thoughts can become part of the chain leading to alcohol abuse. *Cognitive restructuring* teaches people to question the logic of these "irrational" thoughts and assumptions and replace them with more "rational" thoughts (Ellis & Harper, 1961). Alcoholics write out the circumstances of a situation that made them so depressed (angry, frustrated, anxious) that they "had" to have a drink. Below this, they write all the negative thoughts that led to the belief, "a drink would help me." Then they write constructive counterstatements. (Instead of "I'm an idiot!," they could write, "I made a mistake. I'm human. I'll try to fix what I can.") Reading each set of statements aloud can illustrate how much the statements affect emotions and the likelihood of drinking. For homework between sessions, alcoholics can be assigned to go through this exercise when they experience strong negative emotions.

Alternatives to Drinking

The next focus is on the actual drinking behavior and several techniques to provide alternatives to drinking. These alternatives include relaxation, assertion skills (including effective drink refusal), and problem-solving techniques.

A very common reason for drinking is to reduce anxiety, especially social anxiety. Relaxation training can be done through the tense-and-relax method (Jacobson, 1938) or the letting-go method. Either provides an alternative to drinking, but they must be practiced frequently in order to be effective. For some, this is a difficult requirement; for others, it is a skill readily learned. A therapist using this technique should assess the level of response and frequency of practice during each session.

Sometimes an alcoholic will react to a tense social situation with an aggressive or passive response. In either case, drinking is often part of the response. Learning to be assertive provides an alternative. To use this procedure, the alcoholic describes a situation in which an inappropriate passive or aggressive response was given. Using problem-solving techniques, similar to self-management techniques, the couple can brainstorm and evaluate more assertive responses to the situation. It is probably best to begin with a low-level situation (e.g., dealing with a store clerk) before moving into more emotionally charged areas (e.g., a disagreement with a relative or argument with the spouse). Role-playing in the session can be very helpful, and communication skills can be practiced by the couple.

Effective drink refusal is a specialized type of assertion. Often, alcoholics report a slip because of an unexpected offer of a drink in a social situation in which they could not think of what to say. We have found that role-playing (especially videotaped role-playing) can be quite effective in learning new ways to react. Alcoholics learn that the offer of a drink can be discouraged politely and firmly. "No," should be the first word, followed by a request for something else or a change of subject. For example, the alcoholic could say, "No thanks, I'm not drinking alcohol, but I would like some iced tea."

Spouses can also play an integral part in drinking refusal. Sometimes, especially with a persistent offer, the client may feel the need for support. Many couples have found it helpful to devise a "signal" meaning "I could use a little help here," to which the spouse responds with some prearranged action (e.g., "Hey, honey, would you take a look at this?"). Role-played rehearsal of drink refusal scenes can be assigned as homework.

Spouse Interventions

This set of interventions also includes (1) functional analysis, (2) stimulus control procedures, (3) contingency rearrangement, (4) cognitive restructuring, and (5) alternative behavior. However, the focus is on the spouse behaviors directly related to drinking. Because the techniques are similar, the therapist may want to teach them to both members of the couple in the same sessions. However, be aware that each may learn or incorporate these techniques at a different pace.

As described in the assessment section, spouse behavior falls into four categories: (1) spouse-related behavior that triggers drinking, (2) spouse's protection of the alcoholic from negative consequences of drinking, (3) spouse-produced negative consequences of drinking, and (4) spouse-produced positive consequences of sobriety. One way to show the connection between the drinker's and the spouse's behavior is to include the first three in the drinker's behavior chains as (1) antecedents or triggers, (2) positive consequences of drinking (protection can be seen as negative reinforcement), and (3) long-term negative consequences (and potential triggers).

Going beyond that, the spouse and therapist may do a functional analysis of specific types of spouse behavior. For example, the spouse may report fighting with the drinker to get him or her to stop. The trigger could be "the alcoholic drinks at a social event." Internal events may include the thought, "I must stop this! I'm really embarassed!" The fight then takes place; the drinker agrees to leave (short-term positive consequence—the spouse feels some control of the situation) and when they get home, the fight continues and becomes more intense (long-term negative consequence). Through functional analysis of the spouse behavior, the therapist can help the spouse to see how these dysfunctional patterns of interaction are maintained, and that the spouse's behavior is not really helpful to either one. Instead, the therapist can begin discussing alternatives with the spouse, including how the spouse might help by providing some positive consequences for sobriety and learning to ignore drinking by the alcoholic.

We have found that it is especially important to emphasize the issue of personal responsibility for one's behavior, because many spouses cling to the beliefs that they can (somehow, someday) gain control of the drinker's behavior and that they have no choice but to help or protect the drinker when he or she faces drinking's negative consequences. Cognitive restructuring techniques may be helpful early in therapy to help spouses combat these irrational beliefs with more rational ones.

In addition, therapists can provide spouses with alternatives early in therapy. Often, spouses agree to therapy because they want to help the drinker. Together, the couple can devise some ways that the spouse can effectively support the client. Some have been discussed above (e.g., rewarding the alcoholic for completing a homework assignment; helping the alcoholic brainstorm and evaluate alternatives while problem solving; supporting the alcoholic when asked in drink refusal situations). Others more directly address the spouse's behavior (e.g., teaching the spouse to relax, to be assertive with the alcoholic, and, through the use of covert rehearsal, to stop protecting the alcoholic). In general, the same techniques taught to alcoholics can also be used by spouses to change their behavior.

A question often arises: Spouses aren't the problem; why should they have to change their behavior? The simple answer is that they don't. However, the issue is really one of reciprocation: What will spouses (and alcoholics) gain by working so hard to change their behavior? What is the motivation? It is because of this issue that marital therapy assumes such an important role in this therapy protocol.

Couple Interventions

The marital interventions are intended to improve the couple's ability to communicate and to enrich the relationship. Some of the individually directed techniques described above (e.g., cognitive restructuring) are used with the couple, but others are also included: (1) plans for fun activities, (2) "love days" to make the marriage more rewarding, (3) communication training, and (4) negotiation and problem solving. Because the marital therapy is intended to provide fundamental motivation for the initiation and maintenance of drinking-related behavioral changes, these procedures should be instituted from the beginning of the protocol and carried on throughout all the sessions.

As an initial intervention, the therapist may draw a parallel between rewarding oneself and rewarding each other. Gottman, Notarius, Gonso, & Markman (1976, pg 152) suggest adding "more joy to your relationship" by "leaving the safety of day-to-day patterns." The couple is asked to plan a "fun activity" that both will enjoy. The fun activity is refined by asking each partner to describe three simple behaviors they would like to see from their partner during the activity. The behaviors should not be too burdensome or demanding (e.g., one may ask that the other hold hands for part of going out to a movie together). The fun activity is then assigned, along with the three behaviors from each, as a homework assignment.

Couples may have some initial objections to engaging in the fun activity together (e.g., "I'm really angry with her; why should we go out to dinner together?"). At this stage, it is often helpful for the therapist to encourage the couple to "just go ahead and try it." Often the couple will get some enjoyment from the activity and any problems that arise can be discussed in the next session.

After the couple has had some practice with the fun activity, the next step is the "love day." The purposes of the love day are (1) to help the couple generalize some of the specific behaviors they have been using in the fun activity and (2) to begin the transition to formal communication-skills training.

A good time to introduce the love day is during the process of teaching assertion skills. The therapist might point out that generally people are more polite and positive in their interactions with strangers than they are with their spouses. This erosion of positive communication often happens gradually in the course of a relationship, especially as daily irritations begin to increase. In order to reverse this trend, couples are asked to examine ways they can increase mutual positive interactions. For example, they could be more polite and considerate. They could stop and think before saying something negative and decide if it's really important. They could express more positive feelings and give compliments more often. They could express negative feelings in a constructive, rather than demeaning, manner. They could learn to listen and reflect on what the partner had to say and negotiate compromises. The love day is a way of beginning this process.

Because no one can be expected to change their behavior all at once, each partner is asked to pick one day in the next week as their love day. During that day, the partner makes a special effort to increase positive interaction with the other. A fun activity together could be part of the plan, but the idea is to generalize the positive interactions beyond the activity.

Next, the couple begins formal communication training. In PACT, we relied heavily on the Gottman et al. (1976) program, although a therapist could use any number of communication-skills training programs. The main intent was to teach a model of good communication that showed the difference between the intent of a statement (verbal and nonverbal) and its impact on the listener. Couples were taught to listen, reflect and attempt to clarify what they were hearing before making a reply. They were also encouraged to make their statements clear and understandable to the partner. For homework, couples are asked to identify particular instances in which they engaged in both poor and good communication with each other. These interactions can then be role-played in the session.

After the couple has gotten more familiar with good communication skills, problem solving and negotiation can begin. It is often helpful at this point to introduce the concept of a formalized family or couple meeting. These meetings can be scheduled for once or twice a week to talk about conflicts or problems that have come up and how to resolve them. The meeting has three stages: (1) "gripe time" (What are the problems?); (2) "agenda building" (What's the most important issue to resolve today?); and (3) problem solving (brainstorm, evaluate alternatives, decide on a course of action). Again, the formal family meeting can be role-played in the session and assigned for homework. The idea is to give couples the tools with which to make plans together and deal with conflicts in a constructive manner.

Maintenance Planning

In the last session or two, the therapist should help the couple consolidate all the material they have learned in the sessions. Reviewing handouts and homework is helpful. The goal is to give the couple positive expectations about the effect of their efforts to change their behavior. Positive changes over the course of therapy should be emphasized along with the expectation that these improvements will continue with sustained effort on the part of the couple.

The last session or two should also emphasize relapse prevention. Marlatt (1978) and others have suggested that the "Abstinence Violation Effect" is a powerful factor in drinking relapse (one "slip" means complete failure, so after one drink, the drinker gives up and goes into a full-blown relapse). Deemphasizing complete abstinence when setting the ideal goal can be some help in avoiding this effect. Another, probably more effective strategy, is to teach the couple what to do in case a slip occurs (e.g., Stop. Consider that a single slip is not all that unusual: you are not a failure. Look upon it as a learning experience: What do you still need to work on? If you feel you still need professional help, call your therapist.).

It can be helpful to make an analogy about the marital relationship as well. One "blow-up" does not mean that the marriage has failed.
After cooling off, the couple should review what led up to the problem
and use their coping skills to deal with the issue. Again, it may help
to call the therapist and perhaps even schedule a "booster" session a
few weeks or months after therapy ends. In some cases, we have found
it useful to plan a "booster" session 6 months later to review the couple's progress.

CASE APPLICATION

In order to illustrate the application of this treatment program, we will
present a short case history of one of the PACT couples. In some ways,
they represented the "ideal" couple because they had a good relationship before treatment and they were compliant with treatment.
Nevertheless, their case provides a good example of how enhancing the
relationship can enhance alcohol therapy. As with any specific couple,
some of the techniques were more important and pertinent than others
and these approaches were emphasized.

Presenting Problem

Charlotte B., age 41, a secretary, and her husband, Tom, age 42, a hospital orderly, called about treatment after reading a newspaper article
about PACT. Charlotte reported an alcohol problem of several years that
which had worsened in the last 6 months. Tom and Charlotte felt that
family and financial pressures had exacerbated her drinking. They had
five children, all teenagers, and Charlotte also helped out with her
mother and a chronically ill brother who lived nearby.

Assessment

Mrs. B.'s Drinking Behavior

A 366-day drinking history indicated that in the past year, Mrs. B. had
had only 60 abstinent days. Her calendar included 146 days of light
drinking, 154 of moderate drinking, and 6 of heavy drinking. However,
she pointed out that because she was only five feet tall, the moderate
level (3–6 drinks) was actually heavy for her.

The therapist noted several patterns in her drinking. Charlotte
drank more heavily just before her menstrual period and on nights
when she and Tom went out to dinner. In addition, until recently she

tended to drink less when Tom worked overnight because she was alone with the children and felt responsible for them. However, during the 2 months prior to therapy, when Tom had worked several nights to make more money, she had begun to drink more heavily while alone. This loss of control scared her and prompted her call to the alcohol program. Other negative consequences included blackouts and days missed at work because of hangovers.

The DPQ revealed more triggers, such as anxiety in social situations (feeling she was "too straight"), problems with coworkers who "hung around" her desk at work and distracted her (she "hated to be rude" to them), and resentment mixed with guilt when her mother made her take care of her brother. Financial problems and "too many bills" were also triggers, along with some resentment that Tom made all the financial decisions.

Mr. B.'s Behavior that Triggered or Reinforced Drinking

Spouse triggers from the DPQ and SBQ included Tom drinking at home, his ignoring her when she felt upset, disagreements over disciplining the children and his occasional bad moods. They described a pattern in which both would arrive home from work feeling drained, they would have a beer together, then she would continue drinking while he stopped after the first. He would try to stop her, they would argue, and she would criticize him until he let her alone. Similarly, when they went out to dinner together they would have a couple of drinks. Then after they arrived home, Charlotte would sit in the kitchen and continue to drink. Often, Tom would help her to bed, but she usually didn't remember this the next morning.

Marital Relationship

Despite the difficulties described above, the couple felt that in general they had a good relationship. Their Locke-Wallace Marital Adjustment Test scores were high (hers = 97; his = 136) and their ACQ score was low (6), suggesting strong liking for each other and good insight into the changes each wanted the other to make. They also reported a good sexual relationship, although both agreed that Tom had some difficulty with verbally expressing affection. The major areas of disagreement included disciplining the children, financial issues, and sharing the events of the day (mainly, they didn't spend enough time together to discuss these problems). They both felt that the children were not problems, just normal teenagers, and each cited the other's sense of humor as a strong support in getting through the day.

Course of Therapy

The couple attended all 15 scheduled sessions and their compliance rate was very high. Both kept the self-monitoring records of drinking and marital satisfaction throughout. Charlotte completed 87% of her homework assignments, Tom completed 76% of his.

Marital Enhancement

Tom and Charlotte were especially enthusiastic about the couple interventions. They completed all of the homework assigned to them as a couple (e.g., love days, communication skills training, planned family meetings). In addition, they were creative in completing these assignments. For example, they came back after the fun activity assignment to reveal that they had showered together, and they had a great time. Their therapy sessions were notable for the laughter and warm feelings they expressed. Both credited the marital interventions with adding a lot of enjoyment to their marriage.

Alteration of Mrs. B.'s Drinking

It is important to note, however, that marital therapy alone would not have been sufficient to help this client stop drinking. Indeed, she felt she had a strong, supportive relationship before entering therapy. As intended, the marital therapy helped supply the motivation and the positive expectation, but the client and spouse-related drinking interventions supplied the methods of coping. For example, one intervention that was especially helpful for Charlotte was cognitive restructuring. She learned that it was not "rude" to ask her coworkers to leave her alone. Once she had dealt with her irrational beliefs that they would not like her and that she "needed" to be liked, she was much more able to be assertive with them. She had similar beliefs regarding the disciplining of her children and the "obligation" to care for her brother. As she was better able to deal with these pressures, her resentment and guilt diminished.

In a similar manner, she learned to reward herself for sobriety with things that she enjoyed and were incompatible with drinking. For example, she liked church activities and over time became more involved with her church. In the process, she became reinvolved with some friends who supported her sobriety.

Another helpful technique for Charlotte was the stimulus control/self-management planning sheet. For example, one trigger was having people over and wanting to serve drinks, as Tom could not serve because he had barbecuing responsibilities. One plan she wrote was, "Serve something other than what I like." A positive consequence was "Keep the temptation down," but a negative was, "Someone may have the same taste as I do." Another plan was, "Have someone else mix and serve the drinks." She saw only a negative consequence of that plan, "Company should not have to work." The therapist urged her to think of more plans, so she added, "Give one of the men guests the honor of mixing the drinks. Have my son serve the drinks." Both the first and third plans were rated low in difficulty. Neither was "perfect", but both provided alternatives for her high-risk trigger.

Charlotte and Tom also saw the direct benefits of Charlotte's sobriety on their lives. Both often talked about how good it felt to not be spending so much money on alcohol. In addition, they said they both had more energy and were having more fun with their children and each other.

Alteration of Mr. B.'s Behavior Related to Mrs. B.'s Drinking

The changes in Tom's behavior were also important, both for her drinking and for his sense of well-being. Early in treatment, for example, he decided that if his drinking was a trigger for Charlotte, he would give it up. The therapist discussed this with him (e.g., would he feel resentment about giving up drinking), but he felt that drinking was never that important to him and he wanted to do something to help Charlotte.

In addition, Tom also worked to change his own feelings that he must protect Charlotte from the negative consequences of her drinking. In the past, when she would drink until late at night, he would have tried to stop her with "cold, hard logic" and, eventually, he would put her to bed. During therapy he agreed to a plan (and went through several covert rehearsals) in which he would check her occasionally to "make sure she was not in a dangerous state; but if she drinks again and she is downstairs on the floor, then that's where she'll stay." Both agreed that it was better to let her "face the music" by herself. In teaching covert rehearsal, the therapist emphasized that "it's important to imagine each situation [as you did here] in a really structured way; for you to sit down together and imagine the things you would do and kind of play it out together to be prepared." Both felt that imagining these situations helped to emphasize the negative effects of a resumption of drinking.

Therapy Termination and Evaluation

By the end of therapy, the B.'s had noted a number of improvements in their lives. Neither drank throughout the 16 weeks they were being seen by the therapist. During the first week of treatment, however, Charlotte noted at least four strong urges to drink, and even into the fourth week of treatment, she was still reporting five strong urges (rated 5 or 6 on a scale of 1–7), usually related to guilt or resentment of other's demands on her. She felt that Tom's increasing verbal support was helpful in resisting these urges (he was more likely to talk with her about her emotions and desire for a drink). In addition, she said it was especially important to her self-esteem that he began to compliment her appearance, especially since she stopped drinking. As therapy continued, the number of reported urges diminished to only once per week, with an intensity rating of 3. By the end of therapy, she felt reasonably sure that she could deal with her urges successfully.

Daily marital satisfaction ratings (1–7, with 7 being "extremely satisfied") were similar for both Charlotte and Tom. The ratings ranged around 4, 5 and sometimes 6 during the first 3 months of treatment. During the last month of therapy, the ratings went up to a solid 6 for both (with occasional 7s), evidence that they had seen improvement in the marriage.

The final session recapped all the improvements that had been made, both in drinking and the marriage. The therapist devoted particular attention to the Abstinence Violation Effect with this couple because there had been no slips; the couple had not had an instance during which to test some of their new behaviors. They wrote out a plan for both to have handy: "What To Do If A Slip Occurs."

Twelve-Month Follow-Up

A follow-up was done for research purposes 12 months after the end of therapy. The couple was still living together with all five children. Tom had changed jobs, so he wouldn't have to work at night so often. Both reported abstinence for the whole 12 months and both reported that they still had a good relationship (her Locke-Wallace score was 128, his was 127; not a significant change from pretreatment). Charlotte felt that her increased church attendance, Tom's job change, and Tom's compliments and other expressions of affection were a major positive influence on her continued sobriety.

RESEARCH SUMMARY

The PACT study from which this protocol was drawn was intended to assess the advantages and disadvantages of including the spouse at different levels in alcohol therapy. In this study, three modes of spouse involvement were compared: (1) Minimal Spouse Involvement (MSI) in which only drinking interventions were used and spouses were present as observers; (2) Alcohol-Focused Spouse Interventions (AFSI) including the drinking and the spouse-related interventions; and (3) Alcohol and Behavioral Marital Therapy (ABMT), described extensively in this chapter. Several papers detailing the research findings have been published to date (McCrady et al., 1986; McCrady et al., 1991; Noel, McCrady, Stout, & Nelson, 1987). In summary, several findings suggest that the ABMT treatment protocol can be effective for many married alcoholics.

First, there were several indications that involving the spouse was advantageous to process and outcome. For example, in all three conditions of spouse involvement, marked decreases in drinking were noted during and just after treatment. In addition, in all three conditions marital satisfaction and sexual activity increased from pre- to posttreatment, even when marital issues were deliberately not addressed. Finally, in all three conditions job stability increased pre- to posttreatment, possibly as a result of more stabilized drinking behavior and relationships.

Second, the ABMT condition showed superior outcomes when compared to the other two conditions. Drinking decreased faster during ABMT treatment than in AFSI; and these lower drinking rates endured longer. Marriages remained more stable (fewer posttreatment separations and divorces) and marital satisfaction was higher in ABMT than in MSI and AFSI. This second finding is especially interesting because the addition of marital therapy is the only difference between ABMT and the AFSI condition. Did AFSI couples get focused on relationship problems (spouse behavior), with no way to address them constructively? Finally, dropout from treatment was much lower in ABMT than MSI, suggesting that the additional spouse involvement and marital therapy provided motivation to continue treatment.

Most important overall is that the ABMT couples had more positive drinking outcomes in long-term (18 months posttreatment) follow-up than either of the other conditions. This was especially striking after 1 year of follow-up when it appeared that the ABMT couples had continued to improve even after active treatment was over. Why? We can only speculate, as above, that the marital therapy and the subsequent improvement in the relationship gave the couples the positive motivation they needed to continue working on their behavior changes.

In summary, then, the ABMT condition, described extensively here, appears to have the advantage when working with married alcoholics with nonabusing spouse. In fact, given the problems with the AFSI condition, we would suggest avoiding working on spouse behaviors *without* concurrent marital therapy. The combination of the three types of interventions appear to provide an effective alcohol treatment program for married alcoholics.

CONCLUSIONS

In this chapter, we have presented a detailed description of an outpatient behavioral therapy protocol that includes both the alcoholic client and the nonalcoholic spouse as equal partners in treatment. The protocol incorporates three components: (1) a program directed at changing the alcoholic's drinking behavior, (2) interventions directed at changing the spouse's behavior that triggers and reinforces the alcoholic's drinking, and (3) a program designed to enhance the marital relationship. Further, in order to illustrate how the protocol can be tailored to a specific couple, we have presented a case of an alcoholic woman and her spouse who completed this protocol successfully.

Taken together, our clinical experience, as well as the evidence from our research, suggests that that all three components of the protocol are equally important in producing change in the alcoholic's drinking that is long lasting. In future research, subdivision of the protocol may reveal which of the specific interventions are the most effective for which couples. Currently, however, we feel that a program that incorporates these three components will be an effective one for treating alcoholics and their nonalcoholic spouses.

REFERENCES

Birchler, G., & Webb, L. (1977). Discriminating interaction behaviors in happy and unhappy marriages. *Journal of Consulting and Clinical Psychology, 45,* 494–495.

Cautela, J. (1970). Covert reinforcement. *Behavior Therapy, 1,* 33–50.

Ellis, A., & Harper, R. (1961). *A guide to rational living.* Hollywood, CA: Wilshire.

Gottman, J., Notarius, C., Gonso, J., & Markman, H. (1976). *A couple's guide to communication.* Champaign, IL: Research Press.

Heather, N., & Robertson, I. (1981). *Controlled drinking.* London: Methuen.

Jacobson, E. (1938). *Progressive relaxation.* Chicago, IL: University of Chicago Press.

Locke, H., & Wallace, K. (1959). Short marital adjustment and prediction tests: Their reliability and validity. *Marriage and Family Living, 21,* 251–255.

Marlatt, G. A. (1978). Craving for alcohol, loss of control and relapse: A cognitive behavioral analysis. In P. E. Nathan, G. A. Marlatt, & T. Loberg (Eds.), *Alcoholism: New directions in behavioral research and treatment.* New York: Plenum.

McCrady, B. (1979). *Marital, spouse and self control therapy of alcoholics* (NIAAA RO1-AA-03984). Rockville, MD: National Institute of Alcohol Abuse and Alcoholism.

McCrady, B., Noel, N., Abrams, D., Stout, R., Nelson, H., & Hay, W. (1986). Comparative effectiveness of three types of spouse involvement in outpatient behavioral alcoholism treatment. *Journal of Studies on Alcohol, 47,* 459–467.

McCrady, B., Stout, R., Noel, N., Abrams, D., & Nelson, H. (1991). Comparative effectiveness of three types of spouse involved alcohol treatment: Outcomes 18 months after treatment. *British Journal of Addiction, 86,* 1415–1424.

Miller, P. (1976). *Behavioral treatment of alcoholism.* New York: Pergamon Press.

Noel, N., McCrady, B., Stout, R., & Nelson, H. (1987). Predictors of attrition from an outpatient alcoholism couples treatment program. *Journal of Studies on Alcohol, 48,* 229–235.

Noel, N., Sobell, L., Cellucci, T., Nirenberg, T., & Sobell, M. (1982). Behavioral treatment of outpatient problem drinkers: Five clinical case studies. In W. Hay & P. Nathan (Eds.), *Clinical case studies in the treatment of alcoholism.* New York: Plenum Press.

Orford, J., Guthrie, S., Nicholls, P., Oppenheimer, E., Egert, S., & Hensman, C. (1975). Self-reported coping behavior of wives of alcoholics and its association with drinking outcome. *Journal of Studies on Alcohol, 36,* 1254–1267.

Paolino, T., & McCrady, B. (1977). *The alcoholic marriage: Alternative perspectives.* New York: Grune & Stratton.

Sobell, M., Maisto, S., Sobell, L., Cooper, A., Cooper, T., & Sanders, B. (1980). Developing a prototype for evaluating alcohol treatment effectiveness. In L. Sobell, M. Sobell, & E. Ward (Eds.), *Evaluating drug and alcohol abuse treatment effectiveness: Recent advances.* New York: Pergamon Press.

Zitter, R., & McCrady, B. (1993). *The Drinking Patterns Questionnaire.* Unpublished questionnaire, Rutgers University, Piscataway, NJ.

Chapter 9

Systemic Couples Therapy for Alcohol-Abusing Women

Joseph L. Wetchler
Eric E. McCollum
Thorana S. Nelson
Terry S. Trepper
Robert A. Lewis

OVERVIEW

Systemic Couples Therapy (SCT) is a brief, couple-focused treatment approach designed as an addition to individual alcohol treatment for women. As such, it attends specifically to the relationship context in which women alcoholics live and the impact of that context on their alcohol use. Although similar models have been successful with male alcoholics (e.g., McCrady, 1990; O'Farrell, 1992; O'Farrell, Cutter, & Floyd, 1985) and a few studies have included females (e.g., McCrady et al., 1986), less is known about couple-focused treatment with women (Vannicelli, 1984).

The primary goal of SCT is to help women clients abstain from alcohol use and otherwise meet their treatment goals. In this regard, SCT aims to integrate its approach with the themes and messages clients receive in individual alcohol therapy. It is not designed to be a replacement for such treatment.

The SCT model is an integrative one, drawing on aspects of several family therapy schools. The basic treatment dynamic is the identification and modification of present couple behavior patterns that maintain alcohol use. This process is given further power by locating the present patterns in their historical context—in other words, the couple comes to see that their way of relating now is a legacy of what they learned in their families of origin (Boszormenyi-Nagy & Krasner, 1986; Bowen, 1978). This link serves to expose and "detoxify" the influence of the past while making actions in the present more understandable.

236

SCT also aims to help clients find the strengths they have taken from their families of origin and how those strengths can help them in the present.

SPECIAL CONSIDERATIONS

SCT is currently one treatment modality in a large outcome study that is testing the usefulness of adding couples therapy to individual drug and alcohol treatment of women. This project provides an opportunity to test for the conditions under which SCT will be most effective. However, at present we can make some statements about who we believe would benefit most from SCT.

Obviously, SCT is aimed at women clients who are currently in a committed relationship. Relationship, however, is defined broadly. Partners may be married or unmarried, of the same or different sexes, living together or separated, as long as they define themselves as having a committed, emotional bond with one another. Despite SCT's focus on relationship issues, we do not feel that maintaining the relationship is necessarily the best outcome of therapy. Clinical experience already suggests that some women will choose to end their relationships as a result of participating in SCT. When those relationships have been physically abusive, emotionally corrosive, or a factor in maintaining alcohol abuse, ending them can be a sign of therapeutic progress.

SCT assumes a therapist with a moderate level of family therapy training. Although SCT is teachable and specific, it is not a rigidly defined treatment contained in a "cookbook" manual that could be used by a therapist with no family therapy experience. SCT depends on the therapist's ability to flexibly apply its principles to varied client situations and, as such, should be readily transmittable to the "real world" of clinical practice.

As noted in the overview, SCT is not designed to replace individual alcohol and drug treatments, but to work in concert with them. It should not be thought of as the only aspect of a woman's treatment but rather as one component of it. Current testing of SCT is in an outpatient setting. It is not clear how useful it would be during the inpatient phase of treatment because SCT depends on clients having access to their partners in order to work on changing interactional dynamics. It seems doubtful that this interaction could occur in the more restrictive atmosphere of an inpatient treatment setting. However, SCT could likely be an important part of the aftercare program for women who begin their efforts to recover with hospitalization.

Other special considerations have less to do with SCT and more to do with the clients we wish to treat—women. Far less is known about female alcoholics than male alcoholics because men have traditionally been more likely to come to treatment whereas women's alcoholism has frequently been minimized and kept out of the public eye (Beckman & Amaro, 1984; Fillmore, 1984). Counseling centers wishing to treat women must make efforts to help them come to therapy, including providing such seemingly obvious things as child-care services while women attend sessions and making transportation arrangements for those women who need it (Beckman & Amaro, 1984). Many women will be expected by their male partners to continue their childcare duties even while getting treatment and will be denied the use of a car if treatment conflicts with the man's schedule. In addition, the power dynamics of the relationship in which the woman lives must be understood (Goodrich, Rampage, Ellman, & Halstead, 1988). Many male partners will be drug or alcohol abusers themselves and may actively or passively resist their female partner's efforts to recover (Beckman & Amaro, 1984; Dahlgren & Myrhed, 1977; Wanberg & Horn, 1970). Therapists must be ready to help women clients make use of shelters, the police, and the court system to protect themselves if the need arises (Goodrich et al., 1988). SCT, with its focus on relationship issues, is in a good position to monitor and work with the resistance of partners but reliance on brief, weekly therapy sessions alone to support and protect women clients is unwise.

DESCRIPTION OF THE TREATMENT MODEL

Philosophy

The fundamental principle underlying SCT is that family and other relationship contexts play an important role in maintaining alcohol and other substance abuse (e.g., Stanton & Todd, 1982; Steinglass, Bennett, Wolin, & Reiss, 1987; Todd & Selekman, 1991). Although we do not deny the possible importance of individual factors, it is our contention that to ignore the relational context of alcohol abuse is to not offer our clients as powerful a treatment as they deserve.

In order to understand and change family influences on our clients' alcohol use, SCT looks at both present and historical family processes, and at the connection between the two. In doing so, SCT integrates aspects of Structural (Minuchin, 1974), Strategic (Haley, 1987; Watzlawick, Weakland, & Fisch, 1974), and Bowen Family Systems (Bowen, 1978) approaches to family therapy. At present, it is our contention that alcohol use occurs as part of interactional sequences that must change if the behavior embedded in them is to change — a Strategic family therapy concept. Changes in interactional sequences will help to convert the relationship from an alcohol-abuse-maintaining system to an abstinence-maintaining system.

From the Structural school, we take the idea that dysfunctional behavior results from dysfunctional structures. Relationship structures are broader and more pervasive patterns of interaction than the specific behavioral sequences just described. Particularly germane to women's lives and relationships is the structural issue of power. Traditional gender role arrangements give men a disproportionate amount of power in ways that are sometimes subtle and hard to recognize but that still exert tremendous power within a relationship (Goodrich et al., 1988; Goldner, 1991). Does the women's partner consistently have more influence over what happens in the relationship than does the woman? Are threats of violence, abandonment, or economic witholding used to control the woman's behavior? Can the couple compromise when there are disagreements in a way that doesn't always result in the woman subjugating her individual needs to keep the peace (Hare-Mustin, 1980)? All of these issues are important to address.

From the multigenerational family therapists, especially Bowen (1978; Kerr & Bowen, 1988), we have taken the idea that relationship patterns are repeated across generations. Alcohol use, marital conflict, and coping strategies are included in these repeated patterns. In addition, strengths can be found in how one's forbears coped with difficulties, managed anxiety, and forged identities in the face of adversity. Tracking the recurring patterns of both strength and difficulty over generations serves to give couples a new perspective on their difficulties. Whereas the present-focused lenses of structural and strategic approaches answer the question, "What is going on in the present that maintains alcohol use?," the multigenerational lens answers the question, "Why does the present pattern make sense to this couple?" It is not uncommon for couples to abashedly describe their present pattern of relating as "crazy" or "weird" until the multigenerational context is examined. What heretofore seemed crazy suddenly comes to make perfect sense against the background of what each member of the couple learned about such things as marriage, intimacy, conflict, and alcohol use in their families of origin. Realizing that one is repeating a pattern that has existed in one's family for generations can relieve the sense of personal failure that often accompanies examining one's own difficulties. This can be a freeing experience — not relieving the couple of responsibility for their actions but, instead, changing their perspective on their difficulties and offering new alternatives.

Stages of Treatment

SCT is a brief therapy model encompassing twelve, 1-hour sessions. We have conceptualized SCT in three broad stages. This schema provides a primarily heuristic division because the stages typically commingle during therapy. However, knowing something about the typical course of treatment provides the therapist with a cognitive map of the territory that can serve to keep therapy on track. The three stages of treatment are:

> Stage I. Creating a Context for Change
> Stage II. Challenging Behaviors and Expanding Alternatives
> Stage III. Consolidating Change

Stage I consists of assessment and planning and culminates with a treatment contract. Stage II involves direct efforts to change the dysfunctional patterns identified in Stage I. In Stage III, the couple broadens and solidifies the changes they have made. Table 9.1 outlines these stages and the elements involved in SCT.

It is important to note that SCT is not intended to be a rigidly administered treatment. Therapists should aim to adapt the principles of SCT to each individual couple, not mechanistically apply the same interventions over and over again.

Stage I: Creating a Context for Change

"Joining"

Three major tasks comprise Stage I of SCT. First, it is important to begin building a strong therapeutic relationship with the client couple in order to both create a positive context for change and to help prevent drop outs as much as is possible. We have borrowed the Structural family therapy term "joining" (Minuchin, 1974; Minuchin & Fishman, 1981) to describe this process, which entails the therapist taking an appropriately active leadership position in the therapy as well as developing a cooperative and respectful relationship with the couple. A number of skills have been proposed as avenues to developing a strong therapeutic relationship. Piercy, Laird, and Mohammed (1983) provide a useful summary of them. Our clinical experience to date, as well as research evidence (Alexander, Barton, Schiavo, & Parsons, 1976; Burton & Kaplan, 1968; Shapiro & Budman, 1973), suggests that a strong relationship with the client contributes to good outcome and also helps those clients who are ambivalent about therapy to remain in treatment

TABLE 9.1. Components of Systemic Couples Therapy

Stage I: Creating a context for change
     A. Rapport or "joining"
     B. Assessment
        1. Problem definition
        2. Individual assessment—Mental status exam
        3. Definition of interpersonal sequence surrounding alcohol use
        4. Genogram interview
     C. Contracts
        1. Link the problem to the family system
        2. Propose the negative consequences of change
        3. Agree to work together

Stage II: Challenging behaviors and expanding alternatives
     A. Alteration of dysfunctional couple sequences
        1. Use sequences defined in assessment
        2. Have couple define alternatives
        3. Enact alternatives
     B. Couple Negotiation
        1. Negotiate alcohol-free activities
        2. Negotiate partner's support for client's abstinence
     C. Neutralization of family of origin themes in the present
        1. Make explicit the replications of past patterns in present relationship
        2. Help couple plan changes in these patterns

Stage III: Consolidating change
     A. Highlight gains made in therapy
     B. Anticipation of the impact of continued change

---

during the difficult initial stages. Although we discuss joining as if it were compartmentalized in the first part of treatment, it is, in fact, an overarching endeavor that continues throughout therapy (Minuchin & Fishman, 1981).

Joining is especially necessary, yet often complicated, when clients are ordered to treatment by the court or are coerced into treatment by threats of losing their families or jobs. It is helpful to acknowledge clients' complaints about therapy and their feelings of anger about being forced to come. Therapists may remind them that they have a choice of *whom* they see (e.g., "You can choose a different agency or therapist if you don't feel I'm helping you.") or suggest that they try therapy for a couple of sessions as an experiment to see if it can be helpful. Also, "benign triangling" of whoever is forcing them to come (e.g., "Since the court is making you come here, let's do what we can to help you get something out of this and not waste your time.") can help form a therapeutic alliance.

Another part of the joining process is letting partners know why they are being included in therapy. It is important to shift the focus from fixing the alcohol-abusing woman to changing aspects of the relationship that help maintain alcohol use in order to provide a rationale for couples treatment. This change in perspective is delicate, however, because it must not go so far as to suggest that the partner is to blame for his or her partner's alcohol abuse. The entire assessment and contracting process in SCT helps make this shift because relationship processes are looked at extensively in the assessment and the treatment contract that is negotiated is interactional in nature.

Assessment

Problem Definition. The assessment begins with asking the couple to state what they see as the problem and what they would like to get from therapy. For all couples, alcohol abuse will be an important area of concern but it may not be the only problem about which they are concerned. Asking about other problems gives the couple a chance to make their concerns clear and invites them to see therapy as something about which they have a say, not something that is being imposed on them. Many clients will define relationship problems as areas of concern during this phase of treatment. It is important to ask them to be as specific and behavioral as possible in their definitions (Haley, 1987; Watzlawick et al., 1974). Although many couples in treatment say they have trouble communicating, what that actually means to them will vary greatly from couple to couple.

Individual Assessment—Mental Status Exam. The second phase of assessment is a more traditional examination of both partners' individual functioning and includes such things as potential for violence and/or suicide, health status, current medications used, past treatment history, drug-use history (for *both* members of the couple—oftentimes partners are abusing drugs or alcohol but are not identified as doing so), any legal issues or charges faced by either partner, and a history of sexual abuse (again for *both* partners—men are often not asked about sexual abuse in their past). An effort is made to examine each partner's psychiatric status to screen for gross psychiatric disorders. Should indications of psychiatric disturbance be found, referral for further evaluation is in order.

Definition of Interpersonal Sequences Surrounding Alcohol Use. A third aspect of the assessment process includes asking about the interpersonal sequences that surround episodes of alcohol use and other problems the couple have defined as their primary concerns. Asking factual, sequential questions will illuminate the behavioral pattern, as the following example illustrates:

THERAPIST: When was the last time you drank, Marsha?

CLIENT: Last night, I guess.

T: Tell me what happened.

C: What do you mean, "what happened?" I just got drunk.

T: What time was it?

C: I guess about eight o'clock.

T: Where were you and where was Danny?

C: Well, he (*points to Danny*) got home from work about 4:30 and tore right into me about the shape the house was in.

PARTNER: Yeah, the house was a *disaster*. Stuff was all over the place.

T: OK, what happened next?

C: Well, I told him I wouldn't mind having a little help keeping it clean. You know, with a three-year-old and a one-year-old, it gets dirty pretty quick.

T: What happened then?

P: I told her that I work my ass off all day and it isn't my place to keep it clean. That's her job.

T: What did you two do then?

C: Well, then it turned into a big fight. I told him what a jerk he was and he said some things and then I just left.

T: Where did you go?

C: I went over to my sister's house. She understands me, at least.

P: That no good bitch! She's ninety percent of the problem right there. She's the one that you always go drinking with.

C: You can't blame it on her. I do what I do because I want to, not because of my sister.

T: OK, slow down. It sounds like what happened is that you two had a disagreement that became a fight. Then Marsha, you left and went to your sister's house. While you were there, you started drinking. Is that how it usually happens when you drink? If I wanted to predict it, would I look for this pattern?

C: Yeah . . .

P: I guess so.

When assessing a sequence it is important not to stop with the occurrence of the problem, but to also ask what solutions the couple has tried (Watzlawick et al., 1974). This will often expose a pattern of be-

havior after drinking (e.g., nagging and withdrawing, intrusive overfunc-
tioning by the nondrinking spouse when the client drinks) that will need
to change in order for the relationship to become abstinence maintaining. In one couple we worked with, the husband, himself recovering,
tried to function as his wife's "sponsor" by giving her advice on what
to do, how to get the most out of AA meetings, and often reminding
her of AA slogans. She found his actions intrusive and less than helpful and felt his almost exclusive emphasis on her drinking ignored the
areas in her life where she was functioning well.

   Genogram Interview—Multigeneratonal Family System Assessment. The fourth
component of our assessment is an examination of the multigenerational family system and is accomplished by conducting a genogram
interview. McGoldrick and Gerson (1985) provide an excellent guide
to using the genogram for this purpose and no detailed description
of the genogram interview will be given here. Aside from factual data
about past generations and an assessment of the emotional relationships between family members (e.g., patterns of cut-off, distance, closeness, triangling), we ask specifically about three other areas: alcohol and
drug abuse, physical and sexual abuse, and family rituals. All three of
these areas may shed light on multigenerational factors that influence
alcohol abuse in the present.

   When asking about alcohol and drug use in the extended family,
it is important to assess both the occurrence of use and the function
that the alcohol or drug use served (Steinglass et al., 1987). Can the client
identify behavioral sequences in her family of origin that predictably
surrounded alcohol use such as a "nag and drink" cycle, alcohol use
as the stimulus for intimacy, or alcohol use allowing conflict to emerge?
Finally, what are the similarities and differences in the pattern of alcohol use seen in the multigenerational family versus that seen in the
couple's present relationship (Bennet, Wolin, Reiss, & Teitlebaum,
1987)?

   Because childhood sexual and physical abuse has been linked to
women's abuse of drugs and alcohol (Barrett & Trepper, in press), finding out about these experiences is an important part of the assessment.
In addition to asking if abuse occurred, the therapist should find out
who in the family knew about the abuse, what action, if any, was taken
to protect the person being abused, and what sort of emotional tone
surrounded the discovery of the abuse (anger, blame of the victim, denial) (Trepper & Barrett, 1989). Our model does not propose to directly treat the consequences of sexual or physical abuse. If the client is
in immediate and obvious pain, a referral can be made to specific abuse
treatment that may either supplant or take place concurrently with SCT.
If the issues seem not to need immediate attention, SCT can continue

and a referral for further work on abuse issues can be made at the end of the couples phase of treatment.

Family rituals include the regular, patterned ways that families spend time together both on a daily basis (e.g., mealtimes) and as markers of significant events (e.g., marriages, deaths, birthdays). We are particularly interested in the part alcohol or drug use may have played in family rituals (Bennett & Wolin, 1990; Bennett et al., 1987; Steinglass et al., 1987). Did family members predictably get drunk and fight at family weddings? Did everyone await a parent's nightly arrival home with anxiety, not knowing if the parent was going to be drunk or not? Do the current couple repeat any of the family rituals in their present relationship? Is alcohol or drug use involved in these repetitive rituals?

The genogram interview may evoke some resistance. Although asking about the past may not seem relevant to couples whose immediate problems feel overwhelming, most clients respond cooperatively to our statement that we need this information in order to help them. Also, few clients will know all of the information that we ask for. For those who can't answer completely, it is important to reassure them that we aren't expecting that they be able to answer all questions. What clients do and don't know about their family of origin will also give clues to the emotional process in the extended family—the existence of cut-offs and distant relationships between some branches of the family tree, for example. It is important to get as much information as possible, because in SCT a primary focus on the families both partners grew up in is a key element.

Contracts

The final aspect of Stage I is to contract with the clients for the goals of therapy. We include several steps in this process.

Link between the Problem and the Family. First, the findings of the assessment are summarized. Therapists should discuss the sequences around drinking in the present and how these may be echoes of sequences in past generations. If drinking and other identified concerns aren't linked to family factors, the clients have no rationale for continuing in couple-focused treatment.

Discussion of the Negative Consequences of Change. The second step in the contracting process is to articulate what the therapist sees as the negative consequences of making a change. This is not done in an attempt to paradoxically move the couple toward quick action but rather as an empathic statement of the therapist's understanding of the dilemmas the couple will face as they attempt to make a difficult change.

Predicting some of the potential difficulties down the road may make them less frightening and overwhelming if they do, in fact, occur.

Agreement to Work Together. The final step in the contracting process is to come to an agreement to work together. In SCT, the contract is not a written document but is a verbal expression of the client's permission for the therapist to work with them, a statement of what is to be worked on, and an acknowledgment of the potential difficulties that may occur on the road to change.

Stage II: Challenging Behaviors and Expanding Alternatives

There are two goals in Stage II: to change the dysfunctional couple sequences surrounding drug use that were identified in the assessment and to increase problem-solving and communication skills. These goals are aimed primarily at changing the process of a couple's relationship. The content addressed may differ from couple to couple. In this sense, the goals of Stage II function as themes that can be worked on within a variety of content areas and not as objectives that specify a particular change in a specific content area of the relationship. The therapist can move in several directions as he or she works on the twin themes of sequence change and improved communication.

Alteration of Dysfunctional Couple Sequences

Articulating a typical sequence of interaction will often suggest potential ways to change it (Watzlawick et al., 1974). For example, when couples report that conflict usually precedes episodes of drinking, methods of dealing with conflict differently make perfect sense as a way of supporting abstinence. The therapist can begin the process of planning to alter a sequence by reminding the couple of the sequence they have identified. Sometimes these sequences will occur naturally during therapy and can be used in vivo. Otherwise couples can role-play or reenact a sequence to bring it into therapy (Haley, 1987). If there is a great deal of intensity in the relationship or if the couple has the potential for violence or other destructive acting-out, the sequence can simply be described to the therapist.

After the sequence has been described or enacted, the therapist prompts the couple to think about the possible alternatives. It is best if the couple themselves find a way to alter their sequence because this makes the alternative feel chosen and not imposed. Two caveats apply, however. It is best if the couple can alter a step in the sequence that is as far from the symptomatic behavior as is possible. As the sequence moves toward the symptomatic behavior, intensity builds and the process takes on a life of its own, making it harder to alter. Interrupting a sequence by not drinking when one has already been to the liquor store and has a bottle in one's hands is much harder than interrupting the same sequence by trying to talk about a minor irritation in the relationship before it becomes a major source of conflict. The second caveat is to have each member of the couple focus on what he or she, not their partner, might do to change the sequence. Each partner should be helped to monitor him or herself to observe the earliest indication that a typical sequence is beginning (oftentimes the earliest indications will be cognitive or emotional, not behavioral) and then think about what he or she, not their partner, can do to change it. When this work has been done in session, the couple is sent home with the assignment to put into practice the plan developed. Assessing the success of the couple's effort is done in subsequent sessions and needed changes are made. Needless to say, few couples can develop a workable plan to change their behavior on the first try and several sessions are typically devoted to planning and evaluating ways to change sequences.

Couple Negotiation

Although similar to altering sequences, couple negotiation aims at broader structural themes in the relationship by helping the couple improve communication and conflict resolution skills by negotiating areas of conflict that bear directly on alcohol use and support of abstinence (McCrady et al., 1986; O'Farrell et al., 1985; Treadway, 1989). Many couples, for example, have no history of engaging in activities that do not include alcohol use. The therapist can work with the couple to generate a list of alcohol-free activities that would be acceptable to both and have them begin to experiment with these activities. They can negotiate how to keep alcohol out of the house in support of the woman's abstinence and they can plan alternative actions to take in situations where alcohol might have been habitually used in the past. One couple, for example, agreed to take several "breaks" together during an extended family gathering where the woman expected there would be pressure for her to drink. Tasks such as these will both teach negotiation skills and allow the couple to communicate more clearly about how each would like their relationship to be.

Neutralization of Family of Origin Themes and Patterns in the Present Context

This component of the treatment involves making explicit the connection between present sequences and past family patterns. As such, it is more of a cognitive and empathic intervention than a behavioral one. Although the connection between past and present may have become clear during the assessment phase, it is important for the therapist to restate it clearly as clients struggle to change the sequences identified during assessment. As noted earlier, clarifying the past–present connection has the potential to "detoxify" what's happening in the present by helping the couple to understand historical antecedents and relieving the couple's sense of personal failure. The past, in other words, makes the present more understandable. For example, the therapist may say:

> "I think I really understand why it is that conflicts with your husband usually lead you to drink. You've told me that in your family of origin whenever your parents had conflicts, your mother drank and your father got mad at her and left. The same thing seems to be happening in your relationship now. I guess you didn't learn such helpful ways of solving problems from your parents."

Changes in patterned ways of interacting do not of course, come easily or in one attempt. Stage II requires that the therapist remain focused on the interpersonal patterns that need changing and continue to guide the clients as they come back to those patterns again and again, refining their efforts.

Stage III: Consolidating Change

The last stage of therapy aims at highlighting and celebrating the gains the clients have made and helping them think of what the future might bring when therapy is over. It is helpful to have a "bragging session" where the couple tells the therapist how well they have been doing and where the therapist clearly frames that progress as coming from the couple's own hard work. Sometimes even a formal celebration may be arranged for the last session with cake and coffee or some other special activity.

It is also important in Stage III to help the couple anticipate the future. To emphasize the benefits of continued abstinence and clear communication, the couple may be asked to anticipate how life will be for them in 5 years if they continue the gains they've made in therapy. They may also be prompted to identify situations that might get them in trouble again, the earliest warning signs of these situations, and how they might cope with them. Some couples find it reassuring to role-play how they used to interact when they began treatment and contrast that with how they interact now. If the contrast is great, their confidence in the changes they have made will rise. Planning for the future may also include referrals for individual treatment of issues like a history of sexual abuse or other past trauma if the client and therapist feel it is needed.

CASE APPLICATION

The following case study is a composite of several cases seen in the project. These cases have been combined to provide readers with a clear example of how the SCT model operates with women alcoholics.

Presenting Problem

Mary and John Chambers entered SCT following a 1-month period in which Mary had consistently abused alcohol and cocaine. Mary had been involved in AA for 3 years during which time she would be sober for a period of months and then relapse. She had maintained her sobriety for 9 months prior to the current relapse.

Background Information

Mary was a 25-year-old wife and mother. She had been married to John for 2 years. She met him at an AA meeting shortly after beginning her sobriety and they were married 1 year later. She was working part-time as a waitress, managing most of the household tasks, and raising her 5-year-old son from a previous marriage. Mary previously had been married to an auto mechanic who occasionally dealt drugs. They had married after Mary discovered she was pregnant and she divorced him after he began to physically abuse her shortly after the baby was born. Both she and her first husband were alcoholics who also used marijuana and cocaine. She had not seen him since the divorce.

John was a 26-year-old factory worker and a recovering alcoholic with 5 years of sobriety who was actively involved in his AA chapter. He began abusing alcohol in high school and continued this pattern until he was fired from a job for being drunk at work. His marriage to Mary was his first.

The Therapy

Stage 1—Creating a Context for Change (Sessions 1–3)

"Joining"

The initial joining phase focused on gathering the above information from the couple. They were cooperative and easy to relate to because they were highly motivated to get Mary's drinking and drug use under control. Because John and Mary were both highly invested in their AA chapter, it was important for the therapist to adopt and use the language of AA. For example, alcoholism was referred to as a disease and statements such as "maintaining sobriety one day at a time" were often used. The therapist also commended them on their involvement and encouraged future attendance.

It should be noted that AA membership is not a component of SCT. It is seen as a viable option for some people, but not necessary for everyone. The encouragement of this couple to continue their active involvement in AA was mostly done for joining purposes. Therapists should embrace and support client belief systems whenever they have positive intent. To challenge this couple on AA membership would only have facilitated resistance to treatment. Likewise, clients who do not wish to be involved with AA should not be forced to join. The important issue in this phase of treatment is the development of a strong therapist–client relationship by joining with clients whenever possible.

Present-Centered, Problem-Maintaining Sequences

In an attempt to place Mary's drinking in context, the therapist asked present-centered interactional questions about situations that led Mary to drink and about issues in the couple's relationship. The following pattern emerged. Mary and John showed a high level of intolerance for disagreements. When they had a disagreement, Mary either quickly gave in or stopped talking to John. If she withdrew by going to her room or out with friends, John would worry about her and constantly question her about her feelings. This led to further withdrawal on her part and further questioning and lecturing by John. This pattern was also observed in session when Mary hesitated to answer the therapist's questions and John stepped in to answer for her.

Each of Mary's relapses since the marriage had been precipitated by episodes of marital conflict. In each of these situations, Mary avoided stating her opinions, John would badger her for her feelings, and Mary would further withdraw, eventually beginning to drink and use drugs again. John was frustrated because Mary would not share her feelings with him and Mary was upset because she believed that John did not really want to hear her side, but wanted to tell her how to do things. This pattern led to the hypothesis that Mary's drinking behavior and withdrawal served to keep the couple from dealing with emotional marital issues.

A second, complementary pattern emerged that helped maintain the dominant pattern of John pursuing and Mary avoiding. Mary reported that John never shared anything about himself. In all of their discussions, he focused on her refusal to share what she felt and did not share of himself. This led Mary to withdraw further because she found it hard to share much when John was not forthcoming about his own feelings. This pattern was also seen during sessions when John would avoid the therapist's questions about himself by being extremely vague and turning the conversation back to Mary and her problems. This reinforced the hypothesis that Mary's drinking and withdrawal served to regulate the amount of intimacy in the relationship.

Couple's Relationship Structure

The couple presented a stable complementary relationship (Watzlawick, Beavin, & Jackson, 1967) with John in the overadequate position and Mary in the underadequate one. John was defined as having his drinking problem under control whereas Mary did not. He was perceived as more emotionally healthy and constantly told Mary how she should handle situations at work, how she should share her feelings, and how she should raise her child.

John's perceived higher level of emotional stability was merely an illusion. Bowen (1978) states that married couples share the same level of differentiation. Both share the same issues; however, the symptom may reside in only one partner. Whereas Mary used withdrawal and drinking to deal with her fears of intimacy, John avoided these same issues by projecting all of his concerns onto her and refusing to share his own feelings. Although John had given up drinking, he became involved in a relationship with a woman who still struggled with her drinking when emotional issues arose.

Transgenerational, Problem-Maintaining Sequences

The genogram assessment showed that the couple's problems were embedded in their families of origin. Mary's older brother and father were alcoholics. Her parents avoided discussing major relational conflicts in one of two ways. One way was for Mary's mother to leave home when problems became difficult. Several times she took Mary and went to stay with her own mother during times of intense conflict. At home, she sometimes retreated to her room when less intense problems arose. A second pattern of conflict avoidance involved Mary's father's drinking. Mary was constantly told to not talk with her father about problems when he was drinking and, at times, her father would leave the house to drink during fights with her mother.

John's father and mother were both alcoholic and drug addicted.

His parents had a stormy marriage and divorced when he was 10. His mother did not remarry but had several live-in lovers whereas his father remarried within two years. The theme in the family was to avoid conflict at all costs. After the divorce, John's parents did not talk to each other and left John to relay messages to each of them. Cooperative parenting was impossible and, as he grew up, John was frequently moved back and forth between his parents. He would stay with one for a while until he got in trouble and then would be sent back to live with the other. John did not remember conflicts in his family being dealt with directly.

In addition, both families of origin had ritualized alcohol consumption at dinner and during the holidays. Both families drank during meals and both engaged in excessive drinking during the holidays. This was important information because it indicated that the couple would often be tempted to drink when they visited their families of origin.

Development of a Treatment Contract and Discussion of Consequences of Change

After all of the above information was gathered, the therapist and clients formulated a treatment contract. The contract had two primary goals: (1) to help Mary stay alcohol- and drug-free and (2) to help the couple work together to share feelings and solve problems. At this point, the couple tended to believe that John had no problems and Mary had trouble sharing feelings. Therefore, the contract focused more on Mary opening up to John rather than John having to share of himself. This opening gambit was designed as a joining move, not as an endorsement of the status quo.

As a transition to Stage II, the therapist discussed the consequences of change with John and Mary. The therapist suggested that if Mary changed her drinking behavior and shared more feelings, certain problems might develop. First, if she stopped withdrawing into alcohol and drugs, the couple might have to deal with relational issues they would rather avoid. Second, if she began to share her feelings, John might be expected to share his feelings in return. This might lead John to begin drinking again to avoid dealing with Mary's feelings.

The couple denied that they would have a problem in dealing with relational issues; however, Mary stated that John would have trouble sharing his feelings. She said she did not like the pattern of John always focusing on her and not sharing of himself. John denied that this was a problem; however, the couple's belief that Mary was the problem now began to shift to include John.

The therapist accepted the couple's denial that change would produce new problems; however, she requested that therapy not proceed too quickly to avoid a sudden rush into potential new problems. She further advised the couple that they could again discuss the consequences of change if new problems arose.

The dominant hypothesis for this couple was that Mary's alcohol abuse served the purpose of regulating intimacy for the couple as part of a larger systemic pattern in which conflict and intimacy issues were avoided in both families of origin. This pattern was manifested structurally by Mary being in a "one-down" position to John. The clinical goal was to restructure the relationship, promote an egalitarian relationship, and break the avoider–pursuer pattern between them. Specific objectives were to help Mary share her thoughts with John while blocking his attempts to direct her and, simultaneously, to work with John to be more open about his own feelings and concerns. The completed couple assessment took three sessions. The therapist was ready to implement the treatment plan in Session 4.

Stage II: Challenging Behaviors and Expanding Alternatives

Sessions 4 and 5

Sessions 4 and 5 maintained a tight symptom focus. These sessions dealt with keeping Mary from relapsing and helping her to share her feelings with John. Although the initial hypothesis included both members as maintaining the problem, to avoid engendering resistance the therapist focused on Mary, thereby using the couple's definition of the problem to work on the relationship (Haley, 1980, 1987; Watzlawick et al., 1974). In addition, Treadway (1989) states that for couples in which one is a recovering alcoholic to discuss their relationship issues too early in treatment can lead to a relapse. Engaging the couple in discussions about the presenting problem can bypass this pitfall and allow the therapist to work indirectly on changing the couple's pattern of communication at the same time. This is a less risky way to enter the marital system than an immediate focus on the relationship.

Using the frame of "helping Mary," the therapist moved to unbalance the relationship and facilitate a more appropriate structure (Minuchin & Fishman, 1981). She supported Mary's attempts to state her ideas to John while blocking him when he attempted to cut her off by suggesting that Mary needed to know that John would listen when she talked about her feelings. The couple negotiated a plan in which Mary would tell John when she felt upset and what was bothering her. She would also say whether she wanted to talk about it now or later. If John thought she was upset about something, he could ask her. Mary would then tell John what the problem was and let him know whether she wanted to discuss it or not. This plan blocked John from continuously pursuing Mary and gave her control over how much she wanted to share. By telling him what the problem was, she also kept him informed of her feelings so he could feel connected.

The couple also decided that Mary would tell John if she felt the urge to drink or get high. They developed a list of alternate drug free activities to do together when this happened (e.g., go to the movies, go for a drive, etc.). This brought the couple together and counteracted the role of alcohol and drugs to promote separateness. They now had mutually satisfying activities to do together.

Session 6

The therapist started Session 6 by asking the couple how their plans had gone. They felt that things were going well. They reported that they had had several more discussions than they typically had in the past. Mary said that she felt more in control of her life by having the option to tell John when she did not want to discuss a topic. She also said she did not need to withdraw as much because John was not pressing her to share her feelings. John confirmed that Mary did not withdraw as much and stated that they had done some of the alcohol-free activities they had discussed and had enjoyed their time together. At no time during this period did Mary feel a strong urge to drink or get high.

Based on the success of this initial intervention, a larger change began to evolve. Mary said that she was concerned that John was not being as open as he claimed to be. Although he pushed her to discuss her problems, he rarely ever discussed his and it was hard to share her problems when he was so closed. It is common, as he or she opens up, for the initially withdrawn spouse to demand more openness from the "nonproblem" spouse. As Mary began to move out of the problem role, she was able to identify how John also maintained their relationship difficulties.

John initially balked at Mary's statement. When questioned about any problems he might have in the relationship, he became vague and attempted to focus back on Mary. Anticipating a roadblock if she continued to push John directly, the therapist chose to use their family of origin information as a way to work with this aspect of their relationship.

The therapist reminded them that there was little sharing of problems in either of their families of origin and she pointed out how drinking and physical withdrawal were used to create emotional distance. She especially focused on how John's family would send him from parent to parent rather than deal directly with any problems he had.

She praised both John and Mary for being as open as they were because they came from families that had tremendous difficulty discussing problems. Seeing the pattern of emotional distance in his family of origin enabled John to say that he did have problems he felt uncomfortable discussing with Mary. Mary also was able to understand how her behavior fit into her family pattern of using alcohol and distance to avoid dealing with painful issues.

The couple was given the assignment to return to the following session with a marital problem they wanted to discuss. The therapist warned them that this could be very stressful and that either of them might feel the urge to drink. Prior to ending, the therapist reminded the couple of the alcohol-free activities they had negotiated and to remember to use them if necessary.

Session 7

The couple reported having a big fight about their sex life between sessions. Mary stated that she left the house and while away wanted to get drunk. Instead, she returned home and talked with John. They decided to save the discussion for therapy and went to the movies. The therapist complimented them for having a major breakthrough in their relationship. They avoided their old pattern of Mary leaving and getting drunk and instead stayed with each other and went to a movie.

Their sexual problem entailed Mary wanting sex more often than John. Mary said that she would make sexual passes at him and he would ignore her. John complained that he did not know when she wanted sex because she never told him directly. He also said that he felt constricted by having to sexually perform when he did not want to.

The therapist had the couple negotiate an equitable solution in session and they arrived at a compromise that suited each of them. Both would overtly tell the other when they wanted sex. Each would have the option to refuse. They also discussed alternate activities they could engage in if one did not want sex so that refusing sex did not mean withdrawing emotionally as well.

Session 8

The couple reported that they had a very good week. They did not have sex any more than usual; however they felt closer and more intimate. Mary realized that she did not want more sex with John, but actually wanted more intimate time. She liked the fact that they had spent time cuddling on the couch and watching television together.

John reported that they had sex twice that week. He initiated it the first time and Mary asked the second. Both felt freed by the option to refuse sex and to find an alternative activity.

Sessions 9 and 10

John and Mary used these sessions to deal with other marital issues. They were resolving problems on their own and were less dependent on the therapist to facilitate their process. Their relationship had become more egalitarian. Mary was able to discuss her concerns without withdrawing and John had become more open to sharing his concerns. The couple was ready to begin consolidating their changes.

Stage III: Consolidating Change

Sessions 11 and 12

The last two sessions were devoted to consolidating change. The therapist focused on the new behaviors that had led to their relationship changes. Both identified being able to talk together as the major change that had made a difference.

The therapist also asked the couple to identify potential problems that could lead to Mary again using alcohol. Mary said that John sometimes took his mother's side against hers and that this could be a potential problem. John agreed. The therapist walked the couple through the steps they had taken to solve their previous problems and reminded them that they could again use those skills when problems with John's mother arose. At the therapist's suggestion, they brainstormed about how a problem with John's mother might come up and the actions each could take to solve it before it became too conflictual. At the end of the session, both Mary and John thanked the therapist for the help she had been to them and therapy ended.

RESEARCH SUMMARY

SCT is part of a 5-year research project assessing the overall effectiveness of couple-focused therapy in the treatment of substance-abusing women. Because the project is in its first year of data collection, no outcome results are available.

The SCT model is based on previous research. Earlier studies have found family therapy to be effective with adult drug addicts (Stanton & Todd, 1982) and adolescent substance abusers (Lewis, Piercy, Sprenkle, & Trepper, 1990; Szapocznik & Kurtines, 1989). Further, behavioral marital therapy has been helpful in treating male alcoholics (McCrady et al., 1986; O'Farrell et al., 1985). However, little is known about the effectiveness of systems-based marital therapy in the treatment of alcoholics (McCrady, 1990), especially with a female population.

Our project is an add-on study comparing three treatment models. Subjects are randomly assigned to each group. The first treatment is a "12-step friendly" group therapy model. This is a coeducational group for substance abusers only that utilizes 12-step ideas without taking a strict 12-step stance. Partners are not involved in this group.

The second treatment is SCT plus the 12-step-friendly group. Comparing this model to the group treatment will allow us to assess if couple-focused therapy added to traditional group therapy is superior to group therapy alone.

The third treatment is Systemic Individual Therapy (SIT) plus the 12-step-friendly group. It utilizes the components of SCT with the individual woman. Comparing SIT with SCT enables us to discover if the couple-focused individual interventions are enough to produce change or if the actual presence of the couple is needed. Although initial research has found one-person family therapy to be as effective as conjoint family therapy in treating adolescent drug abusers (Szapocznick, Kurtines, Foote, Perez-Vidal, & Hervis, 1983, 1986), no studies have assessed individual couple-focused therapy.

CONCLUSIONS

In conclusion, little is known about the effectiveness of treatment of women alcoholics. SCT is an initial attempt to assess the effectiveness of an integrated couple-focused model with this population. This model is designed to be used in conjuction with an individual-focused alcohol treatment program.

A fundamental belief of SCT is that relationships play an important role in maintaining alcohol and other substance abuse. Treatment of the individual woman is not enough. The primary relationships in which she interacts, in this case the couple, must also change if she is to maintain her sobriety.

This chapter presented the SCT model in three stages: (1) Creating a Context for Change, (2) Challenging Behaviors and Expanding Alternatives, and (3) Consolidating Change. Specific techniques were described within each stage. All interventions were derived from existing family therapy theories.

We hope that the SCT study will provide us with more infomation on treating woman alcoholics and drug abusers. More treatment models and research are needed in this area.

ACKNOWLEDGMENTS

This chapter was supported by grant R118 DA-06932-02 from the National Institute on Drug Abuse, Robert A. Lewis, Principal Investigator. The authors are grateful to Marianne Ault-Riche and David Rosenthal for their influence in developing the therapy model described in this chapter.

NOTE

Joseph L. Wetchler and Eric E. McCollulm share equal authorship.

REFERENCES

Alexander, J. F., Barton, C., Schiavo, R. S., & Parsons, B. V. (1976). Behavioral intervention with families of delinquents: Therapist characteristics and outcome. *Journal of Consulting and Clinical Psychology, 44,* 656–664.

Barrett, M. J., & Trepper, T. S. (in press). Treating women drug abusers who were victims of childhood incestuous abuse. *Journal of Feminist Family Therapy.*

Bennett, L. A., & Wolin, S. J. (1990). Family culture and alcoholism transmission. In R. L. Collins, K. E. Leonard, B. A. Miller, & J. S. Searles (Eds.), *Alcohol and the family* (pp. 194–219). New York: Guilford Press.

Bennett, L. A., Wolin, S. J., Reiss, D., & Teitlebaum, M. A. (1987). Couples at risk for transmission of alcoholism: Protective influences. *Family Process, 26,* 111–129.

Beckman, L. J., & Amaro, H. (1984). Patterns of women's use of alcohol treatment agencies. In S. C. Wilsnack & L. J. Beckman (Eds.), *Alcohol problems in women* (pp. 319–348). New York: Guilford Press.

Boszormenyi-Nagy, I., & Krasner, B. (1986). *Between give and take: A clinical guide to contextual therapy.* New York: Brunner/Mazel.

Bowen, M. (1978). *Family therapy in clinical practice.* New York: Jason Aronson.

Burton, G., & Kaplan, H. (1968). Group counseling in conflicted marriages where alcoholism is present: Client's evaluation of effectiveness. *Journal of Marriage and the Family, 30,* 74–79.

Dahlgren, L., & Myrhed, M. (1977). Female alcoholics. *Acta Psychiatrica Scandinavica, 56,* 39–49.

Fillmore, K. M. (1984). "When angels fall": Women's drinking as cultural preoccupation and as reality. In S. C. Wilsnack & L. J. Beckman (Eds.), *Alcohol problems in women* (pp. 7–36). New York: Guilford Press.

Goldner, V. (1991). Sex, power, and gender: A feminist systemic analysis of the politics of passion. In T. J. Goodrich (Ed.), *Women and power: Perspectives for family therapy* (pp. 86–106). New York: W. W. Norton.

Goodrich, T. J., Rampage, C., Ellman, B., & Halstead, K. (1988). *Feminist family therapy.* New York: W. W. Norton.

Haley, J. (1980). *Leaving home.* New York: McGraw-Hill.

Haley, J. (1987). *Problem-solving therapy.* San Francisco: Jossey-Bass.

Hare-Mustin, R. (1980). Family therapy may be dangerous for your health. *Professional Psychology, 11,* 935–938.

Kerr, M. E., & Bowen, M. (1988). *Family evaluation.* New York: W. W. Norton.

Lewis, R. A., Piercy, F. P., Sprenkle, D. H., & Trepper, T. S. (1990). Family-based interventions for helping drug-abusing adolescents. *Journal of Adolescent Research, 5,* 82–95.

McCrady, B. S. (1990). The marital relationship and alcoholism treatment. In R. L. Collins, K. E. Leonard, B. A. Miller, & J. S. Searles (Eds.), *Alcohol and the family* (pp. 338–355). New York: Guilford Press.

McCrady, B. S., Noel, N. E., Abrams, D. B., Stout, R. L., Nelson, H., & Hay, W. (1986). Comparative effectiveness of three types of spouse involvement in outpatient behavioral alcoholism treatment. *Journal of Studies on Alcohol, 47,* 459–467.

McGoldrick, M., & Gerson, R. (1985). *Genograms in family assessment.* New York: W. W. Norton.

Minuchin, S. (1974). *Families and family therapy.* Cambridge, MA: Harvard University Press.

Minuchin, S., & Fishman, H. C. (1981). *Family therapy techniques.* Cambridge, MA: Harvard University Press.

O'Farrell, T. J. (1992). Using couples therapy in the treatment of alcoholism. *Family Dynamics of Addiction Quarterly, 1*(4), 39–45.

O'Farrell, T. J., Cutter, H., & Floyd, F. (1985). Evaluating behavioral marital therapy for male alcoholics: Effects on marital adjustment and communication from before to after therapy. *Behavior Therapy, 16,* 147–167.

Piercy, F. P., Laird, R. L., & Mohammed, Z. (1983). A family therapist rating scale. *Journal of Marital and Family Therapy, 9,* 49–59.

Shapiro, R. J., & Budman, S. H. (1973). Defection, termination, and continuation in family and individual therapy. *Family Process, 12,* 55–67.

Stanton, M. D., & Todd, T. C. (1982). *The family therapy of drug abuse and addiction.* New York: Guilford Press.

Steinglass, P., Bennett, L. A., Wolin, S. J., & Reiss, D. (1987). *The alcoholic family.* New York: Basic Books.

Szapocznik, J., & Kurtines, W. M. (1989). *Breakthroughs in family therapy with drug-abusing and problem youth.* New York: Springer.

Szapocznik, J., Kurtines, W. M., Foote, F., Perez-Vidal, A., & Hervis, O. (1983). Conjoint versus one person family therapy: Some evidence for the effectiveness of conducting family therapy through one person. *Journal of Consulting and Clinical Psychology, 51,* 889–899.

Szapocznik, J., Kurtines, W. M., Foote, F., Perez-Vidal, A., & Hervis, O. (1986). Conjoint versus one person family therapy: Further evidence for the effectiveness of conducting family therapy through one person. *Journal of Consulting and Clinical Psychology, 54,* 395–397.

Todd, T. S., & Selekman, M. D. (Eds.). (1991). *Family therapy approaches with adolescent substance abusers.* New York: W. W. Norton.

Treadway, D. C. (1989). *Before its too late: Working with substance abuse in the family.* New York: W. W. Norton.

Trepper, T. S., & Barrett, M. J. (1989). *Systemic treatment of incest.* New York: Brunner/Mazel.

Vannicelli, M. (1984). Treatment outcome of alcoholic women: The state of the art in relation to sex bias and expectancy in women. In S. C. Wilsnack & L. J. Beckman (Eds.), *Alcohol problems in women* (pp. 369–412). New York: Guilford Press.

Wanberg, K. W., & Horn, J. L. (1970). Alcoholism symptom patterns of men and women: A comparative study. *Quarterly Journal of Studies on Alcohol, 31,* 40–61.

Watzlawick, P., Beavin, J. H., & Jackson, D. D. (1967). *Pragmatics of human communication.* New York: W. W. Norton.

Watzlawick, P., Weakland, J., & Fisch, R. (1974). *Change.* New York: W. W. Norton.

Chapter 10

Family Therapy for Adolescent Alcohol Abuse

Terry S. Trepper
Fred P. Piercy
Robert A. Lewis
Robert J. Volk
Douglas H. Sprenkle

OVERVIEW

This chapter will describe the Purdue Brief Family Therapy (PBFT) model for the treatment of adolescent alcohol abusers (Lewis, Piercy, Sprenkle, & Trepper, 1990; Piercy & Frankel, 1987, 1989; Piercy & Nelson, 1989). This model is based on a series of assumptions about adolescent alcohol and drug abuse. We have assumed that adolescents' problems with alcohol and drug abuse interact with family systems dynamics and are potentially maintained and/or worsened by those dynamics. We have also assumed that interventions designed to change the family dynamics will result in more effective adolescent alcohol abuse treatment. Finally, a number of reviews and studies of drug-abusing adolescents have supported these assumptions by suggesting that clinical outcomes can be improved with family therapy either as an adjunct to or as the primary mode of therapy (e.g., Baither, 1978; Coleman & Davis, 1978; Stanton, 1979; Szapocznik, Kurtines, Foote, Perez-Vidal, & Hervis, 1983, 1986).

PBFT is an integrative model that employs theoretically compatible and teachable skills from structural, strategic, functional, and behavioral family therapies. These therapies were deemed compatible for integration because each (1) focuses on the interactional rather than the individual nature of problems, (2) is present rather than past-oriented, and (3) uses both direct and indirect interventions to change behavior and expand alternatives through the restructuring of interactions among family members (Piercy & Frankel, 1987, 1989).

SPECIAL CONSIDERATIONS

PBFT was developed and tested as part of a large research grant funded by the National Institute on Drug Abuse. The study was intended for adolescents who abused illicit drugs, but almost all of our subjects abused alcohol as well, and for many if not most, alcohol was the "drug of choice." We have found that, particularly in adolescence, drug and alcohol abuse are similar with regard to their interaction with family problems, and so our program would be appropriate for both alcohol- and drug-abusing adolescents.

PBFT was designed as an independent treatment program rather than as an "add-on" to an inpatient, residential, or other intensive program. A few of our families participated in AA, NA, Alanon, and so forth, but most did not. We have no reason to doubt, however, that PBFT would be an effective adjunct to intensive outpatient, inpatient, or residential therapy programs.

The type of client that appears to benefit most from our model is a younger adolescent (12–14 years of age), with a family whose members are invested enough to participate in short-term treatment. Most of our adolescents also were in trouble at school, at work, or with the law, and PBFT was useful in addressing those problems as well. PBFT appears to be less successful with older adolescents (17–19 years of age), and those with parents who are very difficult to engage in family therapy.

Although PBFT was intended to be highly "teachable," in reality therapists who were most successful with the model had basic training and skills in family therapy. Those who did not had more difficulty and did not have as much success.

DESCRIPTION OF THE TREATMENT METHOD

PBFT involves 12 weekly 1-hour sessions. Most sessions will include all family members, including nonabusing siblings. We occasionally split the family into generational dyads, and also may see the abusing adolescent alone for part of some sessions. Treatment is organized around the specific interventions outlined in Table 10.1, which will be described in detail below. It should be emphasized that although the program generally flows sequentially, any experienced clinician knows that families rarely allow us the luxury of sequential intervention. In practice,

TABLE 10.1. Interventions in Purdue Brief Family Therapy (PBFT) for Adolescent Alcohol Abuse

---

A. Decrease family's resistance to change
  1. Initial joining
  2. Positive connotation

B. Restrain immediate change
  1. Negative consequences of change
  2. "Go Slow" messages

C. Reestablish appropriate parental control

D. Assess dysfunctional sequences and patterns of behavior around alcohol abuse

E. Interrupt dysfunctional behavioral sequences and patterns

F. Provide assertion skills training for the adolescent

G. Conduct termination interventions
  1. Consolidation and punctuation of changes in structure and behaviors of the family
  2. Development with the family of a plan for maintaining these changes

---

the order given serves as a guideline and the therapist is encouraged to be flexible and creative within the guideline.

Decrease the Family's Resistance to Treatment

It is common for a family with alcohol-abusing adolescents to display initial resistance to treatment, especially family treatment. They are often coerced into therapy by courts or school. They usually believe that the adolescent is the one with the problem and resent being dragged into treatment. In addition, the parents may have an alcohol, drug, or some other problem that they do not wish to expose.

Initial "Joining"

Therapists can employ a number of methods to deal with initial resistance to treatment. Of course, initial "joining," or relationship skills, are needed on the part of the therapist. Piercy, Laird, and Mohammed (1983) have identified a number of essential relationship skills, which our therapists attempted to use. These therapist skills include engendering hope; communicating that the family's problem is of real importance; using self-disclosure (especially important if the therapist has experience with alcohol or substance abuse); demonstrating warmth and empathy; confirming the family's experience with the problem; and using humor to engage family members, lighten the intensity, and/or punctuate a point.

Another way to decrease a family's initial resistance to therapy is to create a "workable reality" early on whereby the family members (particularly the parents) see the problem as *changeable*. The therapist can offer such a reality in the form of: (1) positive expectations regarding the outcome of therapy, and (2) a new way of looking at their child's alcohol abuse that seems reasonable and possible.

Positive Connotation of Problem Behavior

Almost all therapists who work with substance-abusing families agree that one of the most powerful ways to create a workable reality is through the active and enthusiastic employment of "positive connotation" (e.g., Alexander & Parsons, 1982; Haley, 1987; Stanton, 1981). Positive connotation is the positive labeling of what was previously considered negative behavior. For example, "hostility" of a parent may be positively connoted as "concern and interest" by the therapist. Although alcohol abuse in and of itself would never be positively connoted, the *intent* behind its use may be. For example: "Your drinking is a dangerous way to get your family into therapy. Everyone's here now, though. And you obviously care about them. Maybe we can discover better ways to show you care."

Although positive connotation is a powerful intervention to help reduce a family's resistance to treatment, we have found that it works best if there is an underlying investment in acknowledging or solving the alcohol problem. If there is little investment by the family, then it is best to shift position and emphasize the gravity of the situation (Piercy & Frankel, 1989).

Restrain Immediate Change

Negative Consequences of Change

We have found it to be quite useful to explore with the family the question: "What will be the negative consequences of your child not drinking?" Families are often unconsciously invested in maintaining the adolescent's drinking problem, and asking the question addresses this investment directly. It is best to offer this intervention in the spirit of collaboration and benevolence, which is usually how the family hears it. An example of a possible negative consequence of an adolescent boy giving up drinking is that his parents may also lose their job of taking care of him and being involved with him.

"Go Slow" Message

The "negative consequences of change" intervention leads nicely into the next intervention, the "go slow" message. The therapist suggests that with such good reasons not to change, it is important that the family not try to change too quickly. The therapist also points out that if the family has any problems implementing directives during therapy it probably will be because those negative consequences have become overriding; at that point, the therapist tells the family, "Then we will slow down again." Paradoxically, the previously resistant family usually resists the "negative consequences of change" and "go slow" messages by committing to more intense and rapid change.

In our experience, most families with alcohol-abusing adolescents, or at least some members of those families, display significant resistance to family therapy, and these techniques are helpful with them. It should be noted, however, that some families are extremely cooperative and anxious to change. For those families these strategic interventions can be modified or eliminated.

Reestablish Appropriate Parental Influence

In a family with an alcohol-abusing adolescent, it is quite common for the hierarchical structure and boundaries to be reversed. An important task for the therapist is to help the parents establish appropriate influence. This is often complicated if the parents abuse alcohol or drugs, if it is a single-parent family, if the parents display an extremely authoritarian and rigid style, or if the adolescent is older and actually needs to become more independent from the family. Still, in most cases, it is essential that the parents are "in charge" of the family and that their power to influence their child's behavior is stronger than the adolescent's ability to continue drinking.

There are a number of techniques available to strengthen parental influence in the family. The therapist can: (1) encourage and support parents openly in session; (2) make assignments where the parents together are forced to make decisions regarding the children; (3) "mark boundaries" (Minuchin & Fishman, 1981) to ensure that the adolescent does not compromise the spousal or parental relationship of his parents; (4) see the parents without the children for portions of the sessions; (5) offer the parents an opportunity to practice their new executive skills in session, with the therapist acting as "coach"; (6) develop specific change strategies that put the parents in a cooperative, parental role; and (7) for single parents, offer help in negotiating alliances with family, friends, neighbors, and other professionals that will strengthen the single parent's influence.

Our program (being purposely limited by our research protocol) specifically focuses on the adolescent's alcohol abuse. If one or both parents abuse alcohol or drugs—and that does not impede our therapeutic progress with the adolescent—we will maintain the focus on the adolescent. However, if it appears that the parent's own drinking problem gets in the way of treatment, we attempt to use their concern for their child to get them to behave more responsibly themselves. We also encourage them to join self-help groups, such as AA, and to make use of external resources such as friends and relatives. We have found, though, that if we focus on the parent's alcohol abuse too soon when the presenting problem is the teenager's drinking, the family may quit therapy prematurely.

Assess Dysfunctional Sequences and Patterns of Behavior Around Alcohol Use

One of the most important components of therapies based on a family-systems approach is the tracking of patterns of behavior around the presenting problem. This is accomplished primarily by asking questions that elucidate the specific sequences around alcohol use. The therapist asks what happens before, during, and after the adolescent abuses alcohol, looking for consistent, predictable patterns. The therapist should explore the patterns that may involve members of the family living at home and also those not living at home. For example, in one family, every time the adolescent came home drunk, the parents would become angry, then argue with each other about "whose fault this was," but then the mother would call her mother, who would calm her down, and soon all was forgotten. In this pattern, the parents never managed to take control. Also, the intensity of the moment was diffused by a well-intentioned grandmother. Because this happened almost every time the adolescent became drunk, it was assessed as a systemic pattern.

Our therapists are particularly interested in discovering what *function* the alcohol abuse may play in the family (Alexander & Parsons, 1982). Alcohol abuse by the adolescent may serve a distance-producing function or an intimacy-producing function. It is essential to accurately assess the function (i.e., the interpersonal outcome of the drinking) so that interventions can be designed that are consistent with family members' typical style of relating to one another. For example, when alcohol abuse led to less contact between parents and adolescents (e.g., they would have a fight about his drinking and the adolescent would retreat to his room for 2 days), interventions that were "distance maximizing" could be offered (e.g., increased time with non-alcohol-abusing friends as curfews were successfully met).

Interrupt Dysfunctional Behavioral
Sequences and Patterns

Once these patterns have been identified, the therapist and family develop strategies to interrupt them. Therapists were encouraged to use both direct and indirect methods of intervention, and to use strategies that were comfortable and useful to them. We felt that this would increase the utility of our general model and would result in greater overall success.

Direct methods included behavioral contracts between the adolescent and his or her parents (particularly when a closeness function was assessed), encouraging and rewarding behaviors "antagonistic" to drinking (e.g., getting a part-time job), and interventions designed to improve parent–adolescent communication. One of the most direct methods was to outline the sequences around drinking on a blackboard, then ask the family: "What can you all do to break this sequence this week?" Strategies for interrupting the sequences and alternative behaviors are typically developed, and the family is subtly challenged to implement those strategies during the following week.

Indirect methods were also used, especially the brief-therapy interventions of de Shazer (1985), such as asking the adolescent to pay close attention to what they do to resist the temptation to drink during the week. Also, the parents might be asked to pay attention to the times they did *not* fight with their adolescents or the times they could agree on parenting strategies. Other indirect interventions include prescribing some portion of the presenting problem or the interactional sequence, as well as prescribing in-session or out-of-session family rituals (e.g., preparing the family to say good-bye to their young alcohol abuser in the event he or she goes to jail or dies).

Provide Assertion Skills Training for the Adolescent

It was understood from the onset that the family system is not the only system involved in an adolescent's alcohol use and abuse; peer involvement and pressure is perhaps equally, if not more, involved. PBFT includes a basic assertiveness training component to help the adolescent appropriately resist alcohol and drugs. One of the most effective strategies we use, after teaching the basic techniques to the alcohol-abusing adolescent, is to have him "teach" them to his younger sibling. This is particularly useful because it punctuates the adolescent's positive change and provides an opportunity for him to become an "expert" in handling peer pressure.

Conduct Termination Interventions

The last session is a full-family session where interventions are planned that will consolidate and punctuate positive changes that have occurred in the structure and behavior of the family. For example, a family might be asked to role-play how they interacted with one another prior to therapy. This is usually a funny but powerful exaggeration of their actual pretreatment style that has the effect of physically demonstrating just how different they actually have become.

At the last session the therapist also talks to the family about how they will maintain these important changes. Often specific plans for dealing with crises are outlined, including the important "What if your son/daughter abuses alcohol again?" At all times, the discussion of the future is framed in terms of the family's new skills, patterns, and strengths.

CASE APPLICATION

Background Information

The Taylor family referred themselves to our program after their 14-year-old son, Paul, came home intoxicated at two o'clock in the morning. This was the second time in 2 weeks that this had happened and the fifth time that year. Paul's mother, Joan, in her phone conversation with the intake worker said she and her husband, Bob, were upset and didn't know what to do. She said they had "tried everything." She said she loved Paul very much, but she was quite concerned that his acting out might begin to influence their 10-year-old son, Jason. The intake worker described the program to her and set up a first appointment.

During the initial assessment (which in our program was done by an intake worker), it was learned that Bob, who worked in a local steel mill, had a drinking problem, and in fact he had been arrested recently for drunk driving. He denied being an alcoholic, however, and was quite defensive about his drinking even being discussed. He said he agreed to come to therapy not for himself but to help his son with *his* problem.

Joan worked full-time at a bank and felt overwhelmed by doing her job, taking care of the house and children, and being what she considered the major one to worry about her son's problem. "Oh, Bob cares what happens to Paul, but he just doesn't see it as such a big deal as I do," she would say.

The family had never been in treatment for anything before. Bob said he did not "believe" in therapy, and that a family ought to be able to manage things on its own. But he agreed with Joan that this last incident was enough that something had to be done, although he still didn't think the problem was as severe as Joan did.

Decrease the Family's Initial Resistance to Treatment

Initially the therapist found it difficult to join with the family. She found Bob to be cold and distant and Joan to be overbearing, speaking for everybody, and somewhat dramatic. She also found Paul to be easily provoked by his mother, at which times he would become enraged and curse at her. Jason, the youngest, stayed quiet.

Through the use of basic joining skills, the therapist was able to "put the problem aside" long enough to be able to talk about things other than Paul's drinking, and even to joke with them a bit. She was able to positively connote the intent behind each family member's behavioral styles. Bob was described as the strong, silent type, whose very intensity showed how much he cared for his family. Joan's yelling at Paul was an indication of just how much she loved him and worried about him. Paul was seen as carrying the "energy" for the family; it also was hinted that his drinking might be serving the family in some other way, which was not yet clear to the therapist. Jason was described as the "observer," the one who watches the family and probably understands them the best, someone the therapist would have assist her throughout treatment.

It was clear right from the beginning, in spite of what appeared to be early resistance, that the family was indeed invested in stopping Paul's drinking. Although during the first few sessions Paul did not admit his drinking was a problem (and in fact described it as something he did just a couple of times with friends), Paul also proved to be invested "in making the family better."

Restrain Immediate Change

Once the therapist felt joined with the family, she asked them to list their goals for therapy. The family identified three specific goals: (1) Paul will not drink anymore (he agreed to that goal while insisting it wasn't a problem), (2) Joan and Paul would fight less and communicate better, and (3) Bob and Paul would spend more time together. Bob's drinking was only alluded to. The therapist stated that she agreed that the parents could "make a difference in Paul's life" without dealing with Bob's drinking. If, however, change did not occur with Paul and the family, she "reserved the right" to return to the topic of Bob's drinking.

Possible Negative Consequences of Change

Once the family had their goals, the therapist discussed possible negative consequences of change. It was assumed that the family may have been unconsciously invested in maintaining Paul's drinking episodes, although in what way was not clear. This intervention was used because the family had shown some resistance, as evidenced by Bob's initial hesitation to participate in treatment.

The therapist told the family, "These are excellent goals, and there are many good reasons to want to reach these goals. For example, your family certainly will feel calmer when Joan and Paul aren't fighting so much. However, and I know this will sound strange, many families experience problems *because* of reaching their goals. If we don't talk about these possibilities now, they may be a problem later. Can you think of any ways in which reaching your goals may actually create problems for you?"

With some help from the therapist, they were able to identify some negative consequences of all three goals. For Paul, one negative consequence of his not drinking was that he might lose some friends who would think he was "uncool." A problem that could arise when Joan and Paul stopped fighting was that they, as they put it, "will have to find other things to talk about, some other way to communicate." Bob said that, although spending more time with Paul was a good goal, a "down side" might be that this time would have to come from somewhere else, like time with his friends, or time with Joan and Jason.

"Go Slow" Messages

The family was complimented for their ability to look honestly at themselves. The therapist then suggested that these negative consequences were real, that they might unconsciously impede progress, and that the therapist was inclined to go slowly in helping them attain their goals. Joan, as was characteristic, spoke for the family and was insistent that the benefits would far outweighed the negatives, and that she, for one, wanted to work toward the goals as quickly as possible. The therapist "grudgingly" agreed, but reminded the family that if things "got rough" in therapy, if they started missing appointments, not doing homework assignments, and so forth, that she would assume the negative consequences were operating, and that she would need to slow down significantly.

The beauty of this intervention is that it is both direct—that is, collaborative, straightforward, honest, benevolent—and gets the therapist out of the role of "cheerleader" pushing for change while the family resists. Instead, the therapist is in the position of actually having the family argue with her for rapid change.

Reestablish Appropriate Parental Influence

An early incident demonstrated how confused the boundaries were in the Taylor family and how much "power" the drinking episodes were giving Paul. An early in-session assignment was for the parents to come up with a set of rules for Paul and Jason to follow. Like many families, the Taylor's had few specific rules, but instead seemed to develop them as needed, on the spot. Another problem the therapist identified was that Bob and Joan rarely agreed on the family rules, or the consequences for breaking the rules. This allowed the boys, particularly Paul, to play one parent against the other. Although this happens in many families with adolescents, it can be especially problematic for families with alcohol and drug problems.

When the parents came up with their rules, Paul was noticeably angry, because most of the rules were directed at restricting his behavior. When they got to their proposed 1-week grounding for their son (which was, frankly, a bit unrealistic), Paul blew up, ran out of the office, into the parking lot, screaming at the top of his lungs, "F--- you, f--- you!" The parents became quite upset, and the therapist herself did not know immediately what to do. Staying true to her theme, to clearly establish more appropriate boundaries, she reminded the parents that this was all new to Paul. She indicated that Paul was trying to test their newfound unity and resolve to be in charge of the family. She advised them to finish the session, which lasted another 15 minutes, and to deal with Paul afterwards.

The therapist asked Jason to leave the room and then worked with the parents on what they would do together to deal with Paul's ourburst. After some discussion and compromise, both agreed on a course of action that would be different from what they usually did, and that both would support. Bob would be in charge of Paul's discipline this week, including punishment for this incident, and Joan would be supportive. They also decided that Paul would be grounded for the week as a punishment.

Paul and Jason were not in the waiting room at the next session, which surprised the therapist. Joan said they wanted the therapist to know what happened during the week without the boys there. The intervention had worked well for the first few days. When the parents left the session, Paul was still in the parking lot, although he had calmed down a lot. The family went home silently, but when they got there, Bob took Paul into his room and told him that things were going to be much different from now on, starting with that week. Paul accepted his grounding, more surprised than angry. For the first few days he tried unsuccessfully to engage Joan in an argument. Each time he tried she would, as she put it, bite her tongue, and wait until Bob got home from work; then Bob would talk with Paul.

A few days before the session, Paul had sneaked out of his room at night. The next morning, his parents found him hungover. There was a big blowup, and Joan again "took over" by yelling at and threatening Paul, this time with sending him to a residential treatment center. Bob argued with Joan, telling her she was making too big a deal about it all; and then Joan threatened to leave if things didn't change. In other words, each had assumed their part in the pattern they knew so well.

The parents were clearly distressed. The therapist reminded them that change was hard, and that this might be a very good reason to spring back to old patterns when they got close to their goals (i.e., the "negative consequences of change"). She asked if they needed to slow down a bit, but they said no, they wanted to go on with the program. She reassigned Bob to be in charge of discipline and then spent the rest of the session troubleshooting about what could go wrong. The main thrust was to unite the parents by giving them the message that *they* were in charge of the family from now on.

Assess Dysfunctional Sequences and Patterns of Behavior Around Alcohol Use

The family seemed to adapt to the changes, and the next few sessions were not difficult. The 1-week grounding came and went, and Paul had no more drinking episodes. The therapist next began to track the behavioral sequences around Paul's drinking. A number of patterns were identified, but the most important pattern occurred in the following manner: Bob would have a couple of weeks when he would work double-shifts, and Joan would work harder around the house to make up for his not being there more. Everyone would be under stress. Then Paul would do something to get into trouble, which often included staying out late and coming in drunk. Joan would yell at Paul. This would turn into a bigger argument with a lot of name calling, and then Bob would try to calm things down, usually by telling Joan it wasn't that big a deal. Joan would become equally angry at Paul and Bob, and a 2-day period would ensue in which she and Bob "sparred." Bob eventually would withdraw by volunteering to work more overtime. Paul and Joan would eventually make up, with Paul being especially helpful around the house. Jason, during all of this, would stay in his room to keep away from the yelling and conflict.

The therapist assessed that the drinking and misbehavior were serving intimacy-producing functions for Paul. It was clear that he wished for more time with his father, and also seemed to enjoy time with his mother after their fights (at least as much as could be expected for a 14-year-old). The fact that his drinking seemed to occur only after a period of time when his parents were not home, and that they tended to respond with increased attention to him supported this hypothesis.

Interrupt Dysfunctional Behavioral Sequences and Patterns

The family was generally cooperative thus far in therapy. Paul even seemed to enjoy the time, and the therapist made a point to have some time alone with him where she could work with him "as an ally." The family themselves came up with many of the insights while assessing their sequences. Because of all of this, the therapist felt it best to "go direct" in developing strategies for interrupting those sequences.

Besides putting the parents in charge of the rules and consequences, and having Bob more directly involved with his son's progress, the therapist suggested that rather than focus on Paul's bad behavior the parents should focus on his good behavior. Because there were consequences for his drinking, she thought it important that there be positive consequences for his not drinking. She suggested that every week that Paul didn't drink, he and Bob should do something fun together, of Paul's choosing. A number of specific ideas were generated (such as fishing trips, ball games, etc.). The purpose of this was to stop the dysfunctional sequences by introducing an intimacy–producing contingency for appropriate behavior.

The therapist also worked with the parents to develop ways to reduce their work-related stress. The recognition that the stress of their jobs was a critical link in the dysfunctional sequence led them, on their own, to decide that, "Although the money is nice, we need to put our kids first." Joan decided to go from full- to part-time at the bank (something she had wished to do for a long time). The therapist also assigned the parents time alone once a week, a "date night." The purpose of this was to help them reduce stress and to accentuate the need for parents to be "spouses first." Structurally, of course, this punctuated the spousal dyad as separate from the parental dyad.

Provide Assertion Skills Training

The family progressed well from that point on. Paul had no further drinking episodes, nor was he involved in any other trouble. His grades were beginning to pick up, and the parents reported that he was doing much better. The initial interventions that were imposed on the family were now largely part of their new style. Both parents were now almost equally involved with the boys' discipline, although there was less emphasis on punishment in the family. Paul reported he could communicate better with his mother, " . . . now that she was trying harder."

Paul was taught the basic assertiveness techniques in individual sessions with the therapist, and then practiced them. The main thrust was to learn to resist drinking with friends. After he mastered various "lines" to use with his friends, the therapist had a session where she had Paul teach the drink refusal skills to Jason. Paul enjoyed being in the role of teacher, and was quite effective at it.

Conduct Termination

During the last session, the family was asked to describe how they saw themselves as different. Each member described the family as "feeling better"; that is, there were fewer arguments, more "open communication," and less fear of the future. Building upon that, the therapist asked the family to look into their future, as with a crystal ball, to see what new challenges the family might have, and how they might overcome these challenges. The family members each framed their answers in terms of their perceived feelings of family strength and unity. It was clear to the therapist by the end of the session that the family's positive changes were clearly experienced as an improvement over when they first presented for therapy.

Track Outcome and Follow Up

At the 6-month follow-up, the Taylors reported no further drinking episodes. Paul had a girlfriend who did not drink or do drugs, and he was involved with high-school basketball. The structural changes in the family had been maintained, although the parents admitted that it was easy for them to fall back to Joan being overconcerned and Bob withdrawing into work. Joan was working part-time and enjoying her free time, as well as more time with Bob. Bob still said he would drink "occasionally" with buddies after work, but that he saw the need to cut down so as to provide a better model for his children. Bob and Joan maintained their "date night" at least twice a month. All four family members reported that their goals had been obtained and that they were satisfied with treatment.

RESEARCH SUMMARY

PBFT was one of three intervention programs tested in our research project. The second was a family drug education program, in which the family saw a drug educator for 1 hour per week for 12 weeks. No formal therapy was offered in that condition. The third condition was individually-oriented treatment-as-usual (TAU) counseling offered at a number of ongoing adolescent drug treatment facilities. Therapy in that condition lasted "as long as needed" according to the therapist, but averaged 19 sessions.

The design of the study called for an initial screening to determine eligibility followed by random assignment to one of the three treatment modes. Eligibility criteria for inclusion in the study were: (1) An adolescent (with an observed age range of 11–22) had to be using an illicit drug or alcohol sometime during the past 6 months; (2) The adolescent had been in some sort of trouble because of drug or alcohol use; and (3) The family (including both parents if there were two, or the one parent if it were a single-parent family) was willing to participate in assessment and treatment.

After assignment to one of the interventions, and before the first treatment session, each adolescent and his or her family participated in an assessment session. The assessment included completion of self-report measures, projective-family sculpting tasks, and videorecorded problem-solving tasks. With the exception of the demographic data, the same measures were repeated after termination of treatment, and then at intervals of 6 months, 1 year, and 2 years after termination.

The initial sample included 151 (121 male, 30 female) adolescent identified patients (IP) and their families. The age range for the IP's was 11–22, with a mean of 16.1. The sample may be said to be "typical" of adolescents who are referred to local agencies because of alcohol- and drug-related problems. When compared to national norms for high school-seniors (Johnston, O'Malley, & Bachman, 1991), these adolescents reported higher use of all drugs or drug classes, with 35% reporting use of an illicit drug in addition to alcohol over the previous 30-day period.

Preliminary analyses of the postintervention alcohol- and drug-use data are reported here. These data are limited to comparisons of preintervention with reported use after the completion of treatment. Fourteen of the adolescents received no treatment (that is, they and their families refused to participate in any intervention). Of the 151 families, 87 participated in the postintervention assessment (57.6%). With the 14 nonparticipants excluded from the initial sample, the adjusted retention rate is 63.5%. This disappointing attrition rate must be remembered when considering the present results.

Paired t tests were used to test for mean differences between preintervention and postintervention alcohol and drug use for each of the three treatment modes. Alcohol and marijuana use were measured with the Poly-drug Use History Questionnaire (Lewis, Conger, McAvoy, & Filsinger, 1979). For both alcohol and marijuana use, a decline in use after intervention was observed for adolescents in the PBFT group and in the TAU group. No reduction in alcohol or marijuana use was observed for adolescents in the family drug education condition. These preliminary data suggest that both PBFT and TAU were effective in reducing alcohol and marijuana use, whereas family drug education was not.

The preliminary results from our study, along with much clinical and anecdotal information, indicate that PBFT can be effective in reducing adolescent alcohol abuse. What is most promising is that this can be accomplished for many families through the use of family therapy as the primary mode of therapy. Also, fewer sessions were necessary for the PBFT group than for TAU. Therefore, PBFT appears to be more cost-effective than typical outpatient therapy, which is far more cost-effective than other modes of intervention, such as residential or inpatient treatment. That is, even though the TAU condition also showed significant decline in alcohol and marijuana use, it did so with a greater number of sessions. At the same time, it is clear that some adolescents may benefit from individually oriented therapy over family therapy. Further studies will be needed, both with our sample and other similar projects, to determine what factors predict the type of therapy mode that is best for different types of families with an adolescent alcohol abuser.

CONCLUSIONS

This chapter has described PBFT, a cost-effective model for the treatment of adolescent alcohol abusers and their families. PBFT is an integrated model that was derived with theoretically compatible and teachable skills from structural, strategic, functional, and behavioral family therapies. PBFT was designed as a 12-session, 1-hour-a-week outpatient program, but may be useful as an adjunct to intensive outpatient, inpatient, or residential therapy programs.

PBFT includes specific interventions designed to: (1) reduce a family's initial resistance to change, (2) restrain immediate change, (3) reestablish appropriate parental control, (4) assess dysfunctional behavioral sequences and patterns, (5) interrupt these sequences and patterns, (6) provide assertion skills training for the adolescent, and (7) consolidate and punctuate positive therapeutic changes. These interventions were described in detail and a case example was offered that exemplified the program.

ACKNOWLEDGMENT

Preparation of this chapter and the research project described herein were funded by grant DA/MH 03703-04 from the National Institute on Drug Abuse, Robert A. Lewis, PhD, Principal Investigator.

REFERENCES

Alexander, J. F., & Parsons, B. V. (1982). *Functional family therapy*, Monterey, CA: Brooks/Cole.

Baither, R. C. (1978). Family therapy with adolescent drug abusers: A review. *Journal of Drug Education, 8,* 337–343.

Coleman, S. B., & Davis, D. I. (1978). Family therapy and drug abuse: A national survey. *Family Process, 17,* 21–29.

de Shazer, S. (1985). *Keys to solutions in brief therapy.* New York: W. W. Norton.

Haley, J. (1987). *Problem-solving therapy* (2nd ed.). San Francisco: Jossey-Bass.

Johnston, L., O'Malley, P., & Bachman, J. (1991). *Drug use among American high school seniors, college students, and young adults, 1975–1990* (DHHS Publication No. ADM 91–1813). Washington, DC: Government Printing Office.

Lewis, R. A., Conger, R. D., McAvoy, P., & Filsinger, E. E. (1979). *Poly-drug Use History Questionnaire: An unpublished instrument.* Unpublished manuscript, Arizona State University, Center for Family Studies, Tempe, AZ.

Lewis, R. A., Piercy, F. P., Sprenkle, D. H., & Trepper, T. S. (1990). Family-based interventions for helping drug-abusing adolescents. *Journal of Adolescent Research, 5,* 82–85.

Minuchin, S., & Fishman, H. C., (1981). *Family therapy techniques.* Cambridge, MA: Harvard University Press.

Piercy, F. P., & Frankel, B. R. (1987). *Training manual: Purdue Brief Family Therapy.* West Lafayette, IN: Media Based Services, Purdue University.

Piercy, F. P., & Frankel, B. R. (1989). The evolution of an integrative family therapy for substance-abusing adolescents. *Journal of Family Psychology, 3,* 5–25.

Piercy, F. P., & Nelson, T. (1989). Adolescent substance abuse. In C. Figley (Ed.), *Treating stress in families* (Vol. 3). New York: Brunner/Mazel.

Piercy, F. P., Laird, R., and Mohammed, Z. (1983). A family therapist rating scale. *Journal of Marital and Family Therapy, 9,* 49–59.

Stanton, M. D. (1979). Family treatment approaches to drug abuse problems: A review. *Family Process, 18,* 251–280.

Stanton, M. D. (1981). An integrated structural–strategic approach to family therapy. *Journal of Marital and Family Therapy, 7,* 427–439.

Szapocznik, J., Kurtines, W. M., Foote, F. H., Perez-Vidal, A., & Hervis, O. (1983). Conjoint versus one person family therapy: Some evidence of the effectiveness of conducting family therapy through one person with drug-abusing problems. *Journal of Consulting and Clinical Psychology, 51,* 889–899.

Szapocznik, J., Kurtines, W. M., Foote, F. H., Perez-Vidal, A., & Hervis, O. (1986). Further evidence of the effectiveness of conducting family therapy through one person with drug-abusing problems. *Journal of Consulting and Clinical Psychology, 54,* 395–397.

Part III

MAINTAINING LONG-TERM RECOVERY AND PREVENTING RELAPSE

Chapter 11

Behavioral Contracts Between Alcoholics and Family Members
Improving Aftercare Participation and Maintaining Sobriety After Inpatient Alcoholism Treatment

Deborah J. Ossip-Klein
Robert G. Rychtarik

OVERVIEW

Aftercare treatment following inpatient programs has typically been viewed as critical for preventing relapse in chronic alcoholics. Available evidence consistently suggests that maintenance of aftercare involvement is associated with improved outcome following treatment (e.g., Ito & Donovan, 1986; Svanum & McAdoo, 1989; Vannicelli, 1978). Unfortunately, attrition rates are high, with posttreatment dropout rates of at least 50% commonly reported in aftercare programs (Ossip-Klein, VanLandingham, Prue, & Rychtarik, 1984; Pokorny, Miller, Kanas, & Valles, 1973; Strack, Carver, & Blaney, 1987). This presents a twofold problem. First, if alcohol aftercare programs do, indeed, improve long-term treatment outcomes, a significant portion of the alcohol treatment population is not making use of this modality. Second, the fact that aftercare attendees are typically a self-selected population limits the ability of treatment programs to experimentally evaluate the effects of aftercare on treatment maintenance.

A number of variables that appear to predict a greater likelihood of aftercare attendance have been identified. These include closer proximity to the aftercare facility (Prue, Keane, Cornell, & Foy, 1979), patients' perceptions of greater autonomy during inpatient treatment

(Pratt, Linn, Carmichael, & Webb, 1977), greater dispositional optimism (Strack et al., 1987), and a cognitive style indicative of field-independence and abstract thinking (Erwin & Hunter, 1984). However, few experimental attempts to actually increase aftercare attendance have been reported. This chapter presents an easily implemented contracting procedure that has been shown to increase aftercare attendance (Ossip-Klein et al., 1984) and improve treatment outcome (Ahles, Schlundt, Prue, & Rychtarik, 1983) in a chronic alcoholic population.

The contracting procedure is introduced to patients during the last portion of inpatient treatment. The alcohol counselor presents patients with an appointment calendar for aftercare and assists in negotiating an attendance contract between patient and spouse. This contract involves the patient's agreeing to: (1) post the appointment calendar in a prominent location at home, (2) attend all scheduled aftercare sessions, and (3) call to reschedule if an appointment must be missed. In exchange for adhering to the above items, the spouse agrees to provide a mutually negotiated incentive within 1 week of the appointment. The contract is then referred to at each subsequent aftercare session. Special considerations for implementing this procedure are discussed below, followed by a more detailed description of the contracting, two composite examples of cases with whom this procedure was used, and a summary of research results supporting the effectiveness of this approach.

SPECIAL CONSIDERATIONS

Therapist Characteristics

This program has been implemented by both alcoholism counselors and PhD-level professionals. Training time is minimal (we recommend one inservice session with role-plays and follow-up supervision at routine weekly or monthly case meetings), and procedures are straightforward.

Program Characteristics

The contracting procedure was developed and tested on participants in an Alcohol Dependence Treatment Program (ADTP) at the Department of Veterans Affairs Medical Center in Jackson, Mississippi. This program included a 28-day inpatient treatment with a cognitive–behavioral focus and an outpatient aftercare program. A key advantage of the contracting procedure is that it interfaces extremely well with such an existing program. The contract is negotiated during a routine inpatient counseling session, and the implementation of the contract can be incorporated into standard aftercare sessions. Further, the small amount of paperwork required for the contract can be coordinated by either the program secretary or by the counselors themselves. Additional staffing or program changes are generally not necessary.

Because the contracting procedure has been tested in aftercare following inpatient care only, it is not possible to comment on its effectiveness for participants in pure outpatient programs. Clinically, the second author has used variations of this procedure with a range of outpatient clients, and there are no obvious logistic deterrents to applying the program in this type of setting. It should be noted, however, that the majority of our experience has been with clients who have already successfully participated in residential treatment. Under such circumstances the counselor has already had time to develop a trusting relationship with both the client and the spouse. The spouse also has experienced considerable hope because the alcoholic partner has, after all, successfully completed inpatient treatment. These factors may facilitate acceptance and implementation of the current contracting procedure. We should also note that the contracting procedure was tested in a comprehensive inpatient and aftercare treatment program. Inpatient counselors who implemented the contract continued to follow the patient in aftercare. Many residential programs do not have this luxury. Aftercare is often provided in a setting different from the inpatient setting and by different staff. Under these circumstances, variations in the procedures described here would be required. Specifically, we suggest that an initial appointment between the aftercare therapist, patient, and spouse be conducted in the aftercare setting before the end of inpatient treatment for negotiation of the contract.

Finally, we have not yet attempted to implement this procedure, which is based on cognitive–behavioral models, in aftercare that is based on AA, 12-step program models. We suspect that implementation may be enhanced by using 12-step terminology in introducing, negotiating, and following the contract.

Patient Characteristics

Patients with whom we have used this procedure have typically been male, white, in their mid-40s, and have averaged just below a high-school education. In addition, they have generally had a primary diagnosis of alcohol dependence, typically were free of psychiatric disorders and other drug problems, and scored in the moderate to severe range of alcohol dependence as measured on the Alcohol Dependence Scale

(ADS) (Skinner & Allen, 1982). We, therefore, feel very comfortable in recommending using this program with populations who share the above patient characteristics. To our knowledge, this procedure has not been tested with female patients (and, thus, patients will be referred to as "he" in this chapter), nonwhite patients, or poly-drug-abusing populations. Nevertheless, we believe that the contracting procedures presented here may be appropriate for use with these populations, as well.

Marital Relationship

Two issues that merit consideration are the patient's marital status, per se, and the nature of that relationship. In cases where patients are not married and do not have a significant other, a self-contract has been used in which the patient delivers the incentive to himself following each attended aftercare session. In terms of the nature of the marital relationship, it is likely that the contracting would be most effective in cohesive marriages in which the spouse is supportive of the treatment program and the patient's efforts to remain sober. The goal of the contracting is to provide positive conditions for aftercare attendance; in disruptive relationships in which the parties have secondary agendas and control issues, contracting could become manipulative.

There are at least four situations in which the contracting may be less appropriate and difficult to implement. The first is when members of the couple have little in common and have developed parallel lives. An example is the case of a patient who had been a wealthy businessman, but lost his business due to drinking. At entry into treatment, he was unemployed and in debt. His wife, on the other hand, had become highly successful in her own career, was very involved in the community, and maintained an active social and business calendar. Although the couple still shared a home, they had little emotional investment in each other, and the wife was not willing to participate in her husband's treatment program.

A second difficult situation for implementing the contract is when alcohol serves a stabilizing function in the marital relationship. From a systems perspective (e.g., Steinglass, 1987), treatment participation and sobriety may force a change in family roles and disrupt equilibrium in the family system. In an attempt to restore equilibrium, the spouse may attempt to sabotage treatment efforts and undermine the contract (e.g., by failing to provide the scheduled incentive). Although in our own experience in implementing the contracting procedure, this scenario has been rare, awareness of this possible obstacle is important.

A third difficulty in implementing the contract could come when both partners have a drinking problem. We do not know whether couples would do better or worse in this situation, or whether a co-contract would be advisable. There is some indication from the cigarette smoking literature that couples who attempt to quit smoking together are less successful than are other groups (McIntyre-Kingsolver, Lichtenstein, & Mermelstein, 1986); whether these findings apply to alcoholic couples is unknown.

Finally, a fourth situation that may limit the success of the contract is when there is such a high degree of marital discord that even negotiating a simple contract becomes a major obstacle. In such cases, preliminary marital work may be necessary before implementing the contract. In general, although spouses are involved, the contracting procedure is not intended to replace other marital/family therapy; rather, it can be incorporated into these other treatments and may even be more effective in this context.

DESCRIPTION OF TREATMENT METHOD

The importance of aftercare attendance is stressed routinely throughout the course of inpatient treatment, and significant others are routinely invited to attend and participate in aftercare sessions. Significant others may include a spouse, relative, or friend, but may not be another person in the alcohol treatment program so as to avoid the potential problem of mutual relapses. For purposes of this chapter, the wife will be used as the example of the significant other. Aftercare sessions are conducted by inpatient staff to maintain continuity of therapeutic relationships. Aftercare sessions involve individual counseling that focuses on problem solving, coping skills, and support. Following discharge from inpatient treatment, patients are scheduled for aftercare appointments at 2-week intervals for the first 2 months posttreatment, at 4-week intervals for the next 6 months, and at 3-month intervals thereafter for a period deemed necessary by the counselor, patient, and spouse.

An overview of the contracting procedure is provided in Table 11.1. During the last week of inpatient treatment, the contracting procedure is introduced by the alcoholism counselor during a routine meeting with the patient and spouse. This procedure is discussed as a standard part of the treatment program. An example of how this might be presented is as follows:

"You deserve to feel very good about your success in the inpatient program. The next challenge is to be able to remain sober when you get back to your own daily activities. We know that aftercare is extremely important in this process, and so we use a contracting

TABLE 11.1. Overview of Aftercare Contracting Procedure

Steps	Actions
A. Negotiating the contract (last week of inpatient treatment)	1. Alcoholism counselor introduces contracting procedures to patient and spouse.
	2. Counselor provides appointment calendar and aftercare contract.
	3. Patient agrees to responsibilities listed on contract and specifies where appointment calendar will be posted.
	4. Spouse agrees to provide incentives to patient for meeting responsibilities.
	5. Patient and spouse list four incentives on contract.
	6. Patient, spouse, and counselor sign and date contract. Patient takes one copy of contract and calendar, and counselor puts one copy in patient's file.
B. Reviewing the contract at aftercare session	1. At each attended session, patient selects one incentive from contract.
	2. Patient and spouse decide when incentive will be provided.
	3. Counselor notes chosen incentive and delivery time in patient chart.
	4. Counselor confirms with patient that attendance calendar is posted in planned location.
	5. At end of session, counselor reminds patient and spouse of next appointment date and planned incentive.
	6. At subsequent sessions, counselor begins by checking on delivery of incentive for previous session. Counselor then follows Steps B1–B5 above.
C. Dealing with a missed session	1. At next attended session, counselor *briefly* comments that last session was missed, so no incentive could be provided.
	2. Counselor shifts to a positive focus on incentive from previous attended session and incentive for current session (Steps B1–B5 above).

procedure to help make aftercare attendance a positive part of your routine."

The patient is then given a calendar prompt and an aftercare contract. The calendar prompt consists of a single page on which all 12 months appear (such as might appear at the front of a date book or a month-by-month wall calendar), with aftercare appointments for a minimal 6-month period circled in red (beyond 6 months, dates are negotiated between counselor and patient and can be added to the calendar). The contract is set up so that each time the patient attends one of the scheduled appointments, the spouse will provide the patient with an agreed-upon incentive. The spouse is asked to attend all aftercare sessions. A sample contract form is provided in Figure 11.1.

Terms of Contract

Alcohol Dependence Treatment Program

1. I,_____ , agree to the following:
    (Patient's Name)

    (A) Post the appointment calendar in a prominent place. Specify where:

    _____

    (B) Attend scheduled appointment (even if I have been drinking).
    (C) If an assigned appointment cannot be kept, call ADTP (*telephone number listed here*) at least 1 hour in advance to reschedule. Then keep this new appointment.

    (D) _____

2. In return,_____ agrees to the following:
    (Significant Other)

    (A) _____

    (B) _____

    (C) _____

    (D) _____

3. Effective dates of the contract: _____

4. Signatures: _____
    (Patient)

    _____
    (Significant Other)

    _____
    (Treatment Coordinator)

FIGURE 11.1. Aftercare contract—sample form.

The contract consists of the following four sections: (1) patient responsibilities, (2) incentives from significant other, (3) effective dates, and (4) signatures. Each is described below, followed by a discussion of follow-up sessions.

Patient Responsibilities

In this section, the patient prints his name on the specified line and reads the list of what he needs to do to receive the incentives. The first responsibility is for the patient to be sure to post the appointment calendar in a *prominent* place and specify the planned location. Examples of prominent locations commonly used are the refrigerator door, a kitchen cabinet, the inside of frequently used doors in the patient's home, the bedroom wall, and the bathroom mirror. The goal is for this calendar to be highly visible, so that it serves as a reminder of aftercare. In addition, prescheduling the 6-month block of appointments may help patients conceptualize treatment as a long-term process.

The second responsibility is that he attend scheduled appointments, even if he has been drinking. Guilt is a common component of relapse (e.g., Marlatt & Gordon, 1980) and may interfere with the patient's attending the aftercare sessions that could help him regain sobriety. It is therefore important to encourage patients to attend aftercare even if they have not been abstinent. To support this belief in the importance of aftercare, the contract specifically deals with attendance only and not drinking. This means that attendance in and of itself is viewed as a positive step, and the patient receives the incentive for attendance alone, regardless of drinking status. Our recommendation is to contract for the tools for maintaining sobriety (i.e., aftercare attendance), rather than sobriety itself, because contracting for sobriety could result in deceptive reporting of drinking status and/or treatment avoidance for patients who slip or relapse.

The third patient responsibility on the contract specifies that if an assigned appointment cannot be kept, the patient is to call the treatment program at least 1 hour in advance to reschedule and to keep this new appointment. When patients call to reschedule, they are also asked to circle the new appointment date on their aftercare calendar before hanging up the telephone. Finally, space is provided on the contract for listing an additional responsibility if deemed necessary by (and agreeable to) the counselor, patient, and spouse. An example of an additional responsibility would be for the patient to arrange transportation for the scheduled aftercare appointment.

Incentives from Significant Other

In exchange for the patient's attending an aftercare session, the significant other agrees to provide an incentive from this list of incentives agreed to by all. Presenting the incentives in a positive light and choosing appropriate incentives are critical to the success of the contracting procedure. The incentives might be presented in the following way:

> "These should be things that you [the patient] would enjoy. They can serve two purposes for you. First, they will give you something extra to look forward to after each aftercare session—and you deserve that treat, because by coming to aftercare you are taking positive steps to maintaining sobriety. Second, they can give you that extra motivation to come in if it happens to be one of those days where it is tough to get going, and it would be tempting to just stay home and skip your aftercare appointment."

The patient and spouse are then asked to brainstorm a list of possible incentives. Next, they are asked to choose the four that are the most desirable, feasible, and agreeable to both. The spouse then prints her name on the contract and fills in these four incentives on the appropriate lines.

The following guidelines are given to patient and spouse for choosing incentives. First, incentives should be things that can be provided soon after the patient comes in for each follow-up session. It is best if the incentive can be provided that day (e.g., making favorite dinner that night). If it is not provided that day, the incentive should be provided as soon as possible within a week after the attended aftercare appointment (e.g., go to a movie the Saturday night immediately following the aftercare session). Second, incentives should not include things that are necessary for health, such as food, per se, or medicine. Finally, incentives may only be given if the patient attends an aftercare session. It is critical to the success of this program that the incentives not be given at any other time. For example, if the incentive is to go to a movie with the spouse, then the only time the patient may go to a movie is after an attended aftercare appointment. If the patient misses an appointment, he and the spouse may not go to any movies at all until the patient does attend an assigned (or rescheduled) aftercare session. If incentives are given even if the patient does not meet his responsibilities, then the incentives will no longer be effective in motivating the patient to come to follow-up. *Therefore, in choosing incentives, they must be ones that both patient and spouse would agree to only use when the patient has attended aftercare.*

Examples of possible incentives include:

1. Giving the patient something he likes. This may include making a favorite meal or purchasing something for patient (e.g., particular—and preferably reasonably low cost—fishing equipment).

2. Doing something the patient likes. This may include going to a specific restaurant, going to a movie, play, or other performance, going for a drive in the country, going on a special trip, having specified friends or relatives over for an evening, or having spouse give patient special praise and/or attention (be specific about type of praise/attention).

3. Not doing something that the patient dislikes. For example, the patient may not have to do dishes for that week, or may be able to avoid other specific household chores for that week.

Examples of unacceptable incentives include: (1) Going on a trip next year—this cannot be provided immediately following aftercare attendance; or (2) Food for a week—clearly, the patient needs some food for survival.

Effective Dates

The counselor or patient fills in the date on which the contract is negotiated and the date of the last scheduled follow-up.

Signatures

The contract must be signed by the patient, the significant other, and the alcoholism counselor. It is important that all sign, to indicate that the content of the contract is agreeable to all. This consensus is critical to the success of the program and it is important to generate a sense of teamwork and mutual involvement.

After filling out the contract, the patient is given the contract to keep, and one copy each of the contract and appointment calendar prompt are put into the patient's chart. The date of the first aftercare appointment is noted. Patient and spouse are told that at that session, the contract will be referred to, and the patient will be able to select one item from the incentive list to be delivered by the spouse as soon as possible within one week of that appointment.

Follow-Up Sessions

Both patient and spouse are scheduled for aftercare sessions. Reviewing the contract and selecting and discussing incentives are incorporated into the aftercare session protocol. At the first aftercare session, the alcoholism counselor takes the copy of the patient's contract and calendar prompt from the patient's chart. The patient then selects one of the incentives, and the patient and spouse decide when this incentive will be provided. The counselor notes the incentive choice and planned time of delivery in the patient's chart. The counselor also checks on whether the calendar prompt is posted in the patient's home and notes any change in location in the patient's chart. These chart notations are useful in reinforcing the importance of the calendar and contracting procedure for the patient and spouse and in facilitating follow-up at subsequent sessions.

At each subsequent attended aftercare session, the counselor first checks on delivery of the incentive for the previous session. Referring to the patient's chart, the counselor asks whether the planned incentive was provided, when it was provided, and whether it was pleasurable. Counselors have noted that this typically provides a positive beginning for the aftercare session and facilitates positive interaction between patient and spouse. The counselor also asks if any changes need to be made to the incentive list. Typically, changes are not needed, and a single contract will suffice for the entire period. However, there may be cases where modifications are appropriate. For example, if a particular incentive was not enjoyable, it may be eliminated or replaced by another mutually agreed-upon incentive. Alternately, new incentives may arise. For example, as spring or fall approach, patients may want to add attending a baseball or football game to the incentive list. If any changes are made, the counselor makes a new copy of the contract for the patient and the patient's chart. The counselor also confirms that the incentives are only being provided in response to attending aftercare sessions and not at any other time. Next, as described above, the patient selects one of the incentives for the current aftercare session attendance, along with a time when the spouse will provide the incentive. Again, this information is noted in the patient's chart. If the spouse is not present at an aftercare session, the patient and counselor discuss how the patient will inform his spouse of the chosen incentive and attempt to find a time when the patient thinks it will be possible for the spouse to provide the incentive. If possible, a telephone call can be made to the spouse to confirm these plans. At the end of the session, the counselor confirms the next aftercare appointment as listed on the calendar prompt and briefly reminds the patient and spouse of the chosen incentive (e.g., "I will see you again on November 12. Enjoy your special dinner this evening.").

It is important that the contract be discussed in a positive, supportive manner, and that the counselor focuses on the patient's successful experiences in coming to aftercare (e.g., "By coming here today, you are showing how important it is to you to stop drinking. I'm glad you have something enjoyable to do to celebrate your efforts."). If the patient misses an appointment, at the next session, the counselor briefly, and in a matter-of-fact manner, notes the missed session ("You missed last session, so you did not get anything from your incentive list.") and then shifts to a positive focus on the incentive from the previous attended session as well as the incentive for the current session.

At the end of the 6-month period, a new aftercare contract may be negotiated using the same procedures described above for negotiating a new contract. This can provide an opportunity for reevaluating patient progress, determining a new aftercare appointment schedule and calendar prompt, and reviewing the incentive list.

CASE APPLICATION

The following case descriptions represent composite cases that include typical characteristics observed across a range of patients with whom the contracting procedure was first tested. In general, our experience with married patients in this program was that they tended to either remain abstinent throughout a 1-year period, or have late slips (around month 9) followed by further relapses. Interestingly, these late slips tended to occur after the contracting procedure was completed (6 months in this study) and aftercare sessions had decreased in scheduled frequency (from a monthly to a once every 3 months schedule). This suggests the importance of formally renegotiating a contract by the 6-month point and individualizing subsequent follow-up scheduling.

Case I

Background and Descriptive Information

B.T. was a 45-year-old white male who reported a 25-year history of drinking problems. He scored in the moderate range of alcohol dependence on the ADS and showed a relatively low level of marital conflict caused by his drinking, as measured by the Alcohol Use Inventory (AUI) (Wanberg, Horn, & Foster, 1977). He had completed high school, had married for the second time 2 years prior to entry into the ADTP, and was a former salesman who was currently unemployed. He was originally from a small town in Illinois and had been relocated to a small town outside of Jackson, Mississippi through his previous sales job. He met his current wife while living in Illinois, and they moved to Mississippi following their wedding. They had participated in premarital counseling through their church in Illinois. During the course of counseling, B.T. expressed a sincere desire to stop drinking, and his wife reported going into the marriage being fully aware of B.T.'s drinking problem and being supportive of his attempts to stop drinking. B.T. had made several attempts to stop drinking on his own with varying periods of success, but had a history of relapsing during stressful periods. B.T. and his wife finally made the decision to seek inpatient care, and they were referred to the Jackson VA Medical Center ADTP by their local pastor in Mississippi.

B.T. had a stereotypic "salesman personality." He was articulate, energetic, liked being around people, and had a friendly, outgoing interpersonal style. He was often optimistic and enthusiastic about his future and had ideas and plans for job opportunities. However, this general optimism was tempered by periods of despair over his lack of progress. He had two children from his first marriage, both of whom lived in Illinois. B.T.'s wife had an even-keeled, quiet, determined manner. She was employed as a part-time music teacher in the local high school and was active in the local church. This was her first marriage, and she had no children. She clearly believed in B.T.'s ability to stop drinking and was quite willing to attend sessions with B.T. during both inpatient and aftercare treatment.

The 28-day inpatient program was conducted with groups of approximately eight participants. Treatment was based on a cognitive–behavioral/social learning approach that advocated an abstinence goal (Miller & Mastria, 1977). Treatment components included alcohol education, self-management skills training, problem solving, leisure skills development, assertiveness training, vocational counseling, and individual and couples counseling. Treatment was conducted daily in both individual and group sessions. The importance of aftercare was underscored throughout the 28-day program as a means of maintaining treatment gains and avoiding or reversing relapse.

Negotiation of the Aftercare Contract

In the final week of the inpatient program, B.T. and his wife met with their alcoholism counselor to negotiate their aftercare contract. They seemed to be excellent candidates for this program and agreed to work together on "anything that would help." They decided to post the appointment calendar prompt on the refrigerator door, so that it would be clearly visible and would remind them of the appointments. B.T. chose the following incentives: (1) dinner at one of his favorite restaurants in Jackson, (2) going to a movie, (3) going for a drive in the country on the weekend, and (4) having dinner with specific nondrinking friends from church. B.T., his wife, and the alcoholism counselor all signed the contract, then the counselor made a copy of the calendar prompt and aftercare contract for B.T.'s patient chart and gave the originals to B.T. and his wife to take home. A sample of this contract is provided in Figure 11.2.

Aftercare Sessions

At the first aftercare session 2 weeks postdischarge from the inpatient program, B.T. reported that the calendar prompt was hung on their refrigerator door. As his incentive, he selected dinner at his favorite

---

Terms of Contract

Alcohol Dependence Treatment Program

1. I,_____ *B.T.* _____, agree to the following:
   (Patient's Name)

   (A) Post the appointment calendar in a prominent place. Specify where:
   _____ *Refrigerator door* _____

   (B) Attend scheduled appointment (even if I have been drinking).
   (C) If an assigned appointment cannot be kept, call ADTP (*telephone number listed here*) at least 1 hour in advance to reschedule. Then keep this new appointment.

   (D) _____

2. In return,_____ *S.T.* _____ agrees to the following:
   (Significant Other)

   (A) _____ *Dinner at favorite restaurant* _____
   (B) _____ *Movie* _____
   (C) _____ *Weekend drive in country* _____
   (D) _____ *Dinner with R.M. & K.M.* _____

3. Effective dates of the contract: *1/14/92 – 7/14/92*

4. Signatures: _____ *B.T.* _____
                        (Patient)

   _____ *S.T.* _____
                        (Significant Other)

   _____ *A.O.* _____
                        (Treatment Coordinator)

FIGURE 11.2. Aftercare contract—sample completed form.

restaurant. He and his wife decided to run some errands immediately following their aftercare session, and then stop at the restaurant for dinner before returning home that day. B.T. reported being totally abstinent during this period, and both B.T. and his wife were hopeful that "this time would be it" for remaining abstinent. He reported several mild alcohol cravings, so coping strategies developed during inpatient treatment were reviewed.

B.T. was enthusiastic about his success at the second aftercare session, and he was beginning to look into job opportunities. He and his wife both reported enjoying their dinner after the last session and chose the same incentive for this session. His wife continued to express her support for B.T.'s efforts.

B.T. skipped the third session. At the fourth session, he reported that he had felt that he was doing so well, that he wanted to try it on his own. However, although he had not lapsed, he had experienced several strong cravings during periods of concern about his lack of employment. He and his wife, therefore, agreed that he would "stick with this program until the end." B.T. and his wife reported enjoying their incentive from the previous attended session. March 17, St. Patrick's Day, was several days away, and as his incentive for the current session, B.T. and his wife decided to celebrate by having a St. Patrick's Day dinner with nondrinking church friends. During the remainder of the session, the counselor focused on B.T.'s job efforts, as well as coping strategies for dealing with alcohol cravings under periods of stress. At the end of the session, both B.T. and his wife reported feeling comfortable about moving to monthly aftercare appointments.

B.T. attended all four remaining monthly sessions during the period of the contract, and both subsequent 3-month sessions. During this 7 month interval, he made the decision to work towards an insurance license, a plan that he had attempted in the past. He was able to follow through with this current plan, and ultimately he began to build his own business by selling insurance to friends he had made in the area, primarily through the church and his wife's school.

Results 12 Months After Inpatient Discharge

At 1 year postdischarge from the inpatient program, B.T. and his wife were asked to rate changes in their lives since entering the ADTP. Both rated home/married life, relationships with B.T.'s children, health, and employment opportunities as "much better," and friends/social life and financial situation as "better." B.T. reported that his wife's belief in him and pride in his accomplishments, the support from their pastor, his own determination, and the support from the ADTP all were important to his getting through the year without drinking. He expressed confidence in his ability to remain abstinent. B.T. and his wife agreed to come for at least one more session at the 3-month interval, with the option of subsequently moving to 6-month sessions.

B.T.'s counselor also expressed confidence in B.T.'s ability to remain abstinent and echoed the contributions of family, church, program, and B.T.'s personal determination. The counselor also expressed satisfaction with the contracting procedure. She reported that, in addition to its intended purposes of motivating and reinforcing attendance, it served at least three additional purposes. First, it reinforced positive communication between B.T. and his wife, who both appeared to enjoy planning and participating in the shared activities that comprised B.T.'s incentive list. Second, focusing on the contract helped structure the aftercare session and gave a predictable beginning and ending point for both the couple and the counselor. Last, for patients such as B.T. who were doing well (but for whom aftercare was still important), counselors sometimes experienced difficulty in finding sufficient topics to discuss that would make the sessions meaningful. The counselor reported that the contract provided a way to structure the session in a positive way, by serving as a springboard for further discussions of pleasurable activities and successful experiences during the follow-up period.

Case 2

Background and Descriptive Information

L.J. was a 25-year-old white male with a 7 year history of problem drinking. He scored at the low level of alcohol dependence on the ADS, and in the highest quartile for drinking causing marital problems, based on the AUI. He had a G.E.D. level of education, was separated from his wife after 3 years of marriage, and had no children. L.J. had worked sporadically on oil rigs in Louisiana for several years, and it was typical for him to go out with his "work buddies" on weekends for drinking binges. He appeared gaunt and weathered and was reserved in expressing or discussing emotions when sober. When drinking, he was reportedly boisterous and had become involved in several fist fights. His drinking had escalated in the months prior to treatment. As a result, his wife had asked him to leave their home; the couple had been separated for 3 months at the time of his entry into treatment. His wife demanded that he seek treatment for his drinking as a condition for his moving back to their home. He also seemed to have personal concerns about his drinking, which he expressed more clearly at a later time in inpatient treatment, and he was clearly motivated to save his marriage. L.J. was referred to the ADTP by a friend.

L.J.'s wife was a high-school graduate who worked as a cashier at a supermarket in Louisiana. She had met L.J. through friends, and married him soon after she finished school. Both came from families with problem drinkers. She stated that she was not willing to live her life with a drunk husband, but she was agreeable to helping him deal with his drinking if he went into treatment.

Negotiation of the Aftercare Contract

L.J. completed the inpatient program described above. In the final week of the program, he and his wife met with their alcoholism counselor to negotiate the contract. L.J. decided to post the appointment calendar on the inside of his back door, so that he would see it each time he left the house. Two issues arose in negotiating the contract. The first issue dealt with presenting the contract to the wife. Given the nature of the marital relationship, the counselor was careful to describe the contract in a way that would allow it to be used in a positive, and not proscriptive, manner. The counselor stated:

> "Sometimes knowing how to deal with aftercare sessions is especially challenging for the wife, who wants the best for her husband and knows how important these sessions are for him. It can be really tempting for some wives to nag or threaten their husbands as a way of making sure they will come to the sessions. I don't want you to be in that position, and the contract can help. When L.J. attends the sessions, you have a very positive way to support that step to success. If he does miss a session, you do not need to say anything; he simply will not get anything from the incentive list until he attends the next appointment."

The second issue dealt with the incentives themselves. L.J. wanted to use moving back home as an incentive for attending aftercare sessions. This was not acceptable to his wife, who wanted abstinence, and not just attendance, to be a criteria for his moving back. This was also not acceptable under the guidelines of the contract, which specified that the incentive was to be something that could be delivered immediately after attending an aftercare session, and at no other time. The counselor explained that the incentives were meant to be smaller and specific items or activities that L.J. would enjoy after attending a session, and that the larger issue of moving back home could be a topic to be discussed in aftercare sessions. L.J. and his wife had a productive and positive discussion of ideas for incentives. L.J. selected the following for his contract: (1) dinner together for barbecued ribs at a local restaurant, (2) his wife would bake his favorite pie, (3) his wife would purchase him a particular piece of hunting equipment, and (4) he would go fishing with a nondrinking buddy. L.J. identified one friend who was not a drinker with whom he had occasionally gone fishing in the past. L.J. agreed to prearrange the fishing date with the friend prior to a planned aftercare appointment and to schedule the date for the weekend immediately following the appointment. Thus, at the time of the aftercare appointment, he would be confident that he would be able to get this incentive for attendance. If he missed that aftercare session, he agreed to cancel the fishing date. L.J.'s wife agreed to pack sandwiches for this outing.

L.J., his wife, and the counselor all signed the aftercare contract, and the counselor made a copy of the calendar prompt and contract for L.J.'s file and gave the originals to L.J.

Aftercare Session

L.J. returned to work on the oil rigs after discharge. L.J. and his wife both attended the first aftercare session. The counselor took the contract from L.J.'s chart, and L.J. selected dinner with his wife from the incentive list. L.J. reported that he was "doing well" and had not had a drink since discharge. His wife stated that she was "real proud" of him so far, and that she hoped that he could "keep up the good work." The counselor then focused on strategies that L.J. had used to avoid drinking, particularly on weekends, and on conflicts in the marriage. At the end of the session, the counselor confirmed the next aftercare date, referring to the calendar prompt from L.J.'s chart, and again cued the couple on the chosen incentive by wishing them a pleasant dinner.

L.J. and his wife both attended the second aftercare session. L.J. reported enjoying the dinner with his wife after the last session, and she seemed somewhat surprised that she had enjoyed it as well. For this session's attendance, L.J. and his wife decided to stop at a sporting store in Jackson to purchase L.J.'s piece of hunting equipment. The counselor asked if L.J. wanted to fill in a new item on the incentive list because the hunting equipment would be purchased after the current session. As spring was approaching, L.J. and his wife decided to list attending a local baseball game as the new incentive. The counselor made the change on the contract and gave a copy of the new contract to L.J. L.J. reported some difficulties resisting the urges to drink since the last session. This was a particular problem when his work buddies tried to talk him into going out drinking with them on the weekends; he still felt uncomfortable saying no and then had difficulty finding things to do during those times when he otherwise would have been out drinking with friends. The counselor reviewed coping strategies developed during inpatient treatment, and the counselor, L.J., and his wife brainstormed new coping strategies for dealing with these cues to drink. In addition, L.J.'s wife agreed to discuss a plan for L.J.'s moving back home on a trial basis at the next aftercare session, if he remained abstinent. At the end of the session, the counselor confirmed the next aftercare appointment from the calendar prompt and cued the couple again about their visit to the sporting store.

L.J. attended all 8 aftercare sessions during the 6-month period of the contract and remained abstinent throughout the period. During this time, he moved back home with his wife, and he maintained his employment on the oil rigs. At the 9-month postdischarge aftercare session (the first appointment at a 3-month interval), L.J. reported having a lapse for a 6-day period during which he drank a six-pack of beer each day. He reported that the setback was due to an injury to his wrist. As a result of the injury, he had been out of work and, with nothing to do, went back to drinking. The session focused on problem-solving ways of coping with this time off from work and on marital issues that had arisen as a result of his drinking. An extra aftercare session was scheduled for the following month, and L.J. did not attend, nor did he respond to mailed reminders/offers to reschedule.

Results 12 Months After Inpatient Discharge

At his 12-month session, he reported having had another 6-day lapse in the 10th month, during which he again drank a six-pack of beer each day, and a 6-day lapse in the 11th month, during which he drank a fifth of whiskey each day. By the 12-month appointment, he reported having resumed abstinence for the past 30 days. During this time, he was able to start working again, and his marital relations had improved. L.J. reported feeling confident about getting through the relapse period and being able to get himself back on track. His wife was supportive of his efforts, but was fearful about stopping aftercare sessions. The couple agreed to continue attending aftercare sessions, and a schedule was negotiated.

Overall, the couple was pleased with the skills that L.J. had developed during the course of the program. The period prior to relapse was his longest period of abstinence since he had developed the drinking problem. Following the relapse, he had been able to resume abstinence and begin working again more quickly than in the past. L.J. was pleased to be living with his wife again, and maintaining his marriage continued to be a strong motivator for him to stay sober. The counselor noted that the aftercare contract provided a positive means for interactions between L.J. and his wife and facilitated the marital counseling and reconciliation process. During the period that L.J. was seen, the aftercare contracts were in place for the first 6 months only. This appears to have been an example of a case where continued contracting may have been beneficial, particularly to support him through the unexpected crisis and subsequent lapses following his wrist injury and to encourage attendance in the year following the lapses.

RESEARCH SUMMARY

Two studies were conducted on this contracting procedure. The first (Ossip-Klein et al., 1984) examined the effects of contracting on aftercare attendance. Consecutive groups of patients in the inpatient alcohol treatment program at the Jackson VA Medical Center were randomly divided into contracting or usual care conditions. A total of 50 male patients were evaluated (25 subjects/condition). Participants ranged in age from 20–66 years (M = 45.4 and 42.9, SD = 9.4 and 12.2 years for the contracting and usual care conditions, respectively). Educational levels were 11.3 (SD = 2.4) and 11.2 (SD = 2.8) years for contracting and usual care, respectively. In the study, 50% of contracting subjects and 43% of usual care subjects were married, and 36% of contracting and 28% of usual care subjects were employed at entry into treatment. Subjects reported that drinking had been a problem for 12.6 (SD = 10.8) and 9.5 (SD = 6.1) years for contracting and usual care groups, respectively. Subjects did not differ statistically on any of the above characteristics.

Subjects in both conditions participated in the 28-day inpatient program, which routinely emphasized the importance of aftercare. Additional interventions for subjects in the contracting condition were identical to those described in this chapter. Counselors involved in negotiating and following the contracts included three BA-level alcohol rehabilitation counselors, one MSW-level counselor, and two PhD interns. Subjects in the usual care condition were scheduled for aftercare sessions at the same intervals as contracting subjects, but were not asked to contract for aftercare attendance and were not given appointment calendar prompts.

Attendance was calculated as the number of patients attending each aftercare session at the scheduled or rescheduled day and time. Results are presented in Table 11.2. Attendance at the first seven sessions was roughly twice as high for contracting subjects as compared to usual care

subjects. These differences were both statistically and clinically significant. These results demonstrate the effectiveness of the contracting
procedure in increasing aftercare attendance. Although it is not possible to identify specific components of treatment that were critical to
the effectiveness of the program, it is possible that the program was
most powerful in increasing attendance at the first aftercare session,
which, in turn, led to elevated attendance rates at subsequent sessions.
The dropoff in attendance at the final 6-month appointment for contracting subjects may indicate a need to renegotiate the contract prior
to the 6-month visit.

The second study (Ahles et al., 1983) examined the effects of this
contracting procedure on treatment success. From the above study, 36
subjects (18 subjects/group) were contacted at 12 months postdischarge
for assessment of drinking status. Verification of patient's self-reported
drinking status by a significant other was available in 72% of the cases.
Data were analyzed in terms of abstinence, functioning days, employment, and attendance. Abstinence data are presented in Figure 11.3.
Results are presented in terms of both the percentage of patients abstinent at each month (solid circles) and cumulative months of abstinence
per group (open squares). Group differences were analyzed (using χ^2
tests) at 3, 6, and 12 months. For both measures, abstinence rates were
consistently higher in the contracting compared to the usual care control group; these differences were statistically significant at all three analysis points for the monthly abstinence measure ($p < .01$ or better) and
at all points except 12 months for the cumulative abstinence measure.
In addition, the contracting group was significantly more likely to be
abstinent during the first 6 months, as compared to the second 6 months
(77.8% vs. 38.9% abstinence, respectively, $p < .05$). This pattern was not
seen for usual care controls, suggesting that the enhanced abstinence

TABLE 11.2. Percentages of Patients Attending Scheduled Aftercare Sessions[a]

Group	n	1	2	3	4	5	6	7	8
		\multicolumn{8}{c}{Session}						
Calendar/contract	25	72*	60*	56*	68*	48**	48*	44*	24***
Control	25	36	36	28	36	28	16	20	24

From Ossip-Klein, VanLandingham, Prue, and Rychtarik (1984, p. 88). Copyright 1984
by Pergamon Press. Reprinted by permission.
[a]Simple χ^2 tests ($df = 1$) performed for each between group comparison.
*$p < .001$
**$p < .005$
***not significant

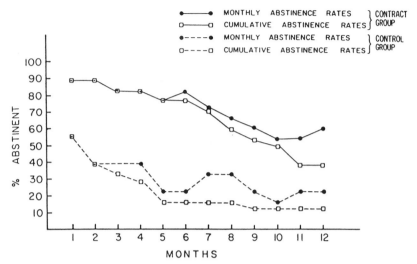

FIGURE 11.3. Monthly and cumulative abstinence rates for contract and control group participants. From Ahles, Schlundt, Prue, and Rychtarik (1983, p. 57). Copyright 1983 by Pergamon Press, Ltd. Reprinted by permission.

in the contracting group was a result of the contracting condition, which was in place for the first 6 months only.

Subjects in the contracting group also had more functioning days over the entire 12-month follow-up period, with functioning days defined as days in which the patient was abstinent or drank less than two ounces of absolute alcohol (M = 316.72 and 238.69 days for contracting and usual care, respectively, p < .05). When functioning days were combined into a measure of treatment success (defined as having 90% of the days in the 12 months postdischarge as functioning days), treatment success was significantly higher in the contracting group (77.8% and 38.9% of contracting and usual care subjects, respectively, were treatment successes; p < .05). Finally, patients in the contracting group were significantly more likely to be employed at the 1-year follow-up (46.7% vs. 13.3% of contracting and usual care subjects, respectively; p < .05).

A final set of analyses were conducted to examine the relation between aftercare attendance, per se, regardless of intervention condition, and abstinence. Results showed that subjects who attended at least 6 aftercare sessions were significantly more likely to be abstinent at both 6 months (100% and 30.4% of attendees and nonattendees, respectively; p < .001) and 1 year (58.3% and 12.5% of attendees and nonattendees respectively; p < .005).

Overall, these results demonstrate the effectiveness of the contracting procedure in improving treatment outcome with this population. Further, they support the key role of aftercare attendance in mediating this positive effect on long-term abstinence.

Additional investigations of the contracting procedure may lead to further improvements in our ability to help alcohol-dependent patients maintain abstinence and/or survive relapse crises. Specifically, studies are needed that: (1) replicate our own research; (2) extend application of the contract to a variety of settings and populations; (3) analyze the relative importance of the components of the technique (i.e., signed contract, calendar prompt, and incentives to attend); (4) examine the differential effects of contracting based on client and relationship factors (e.g., couple cohesiveness); and (5) explore the effects on outcome of renegotiating a second extended contract prior to the 6-month aftercare session.

CONCLUSIONS

In summary, the contracting intervention presented in this chapter is a simple procedure that can be easily implemented in a variety of treatment settings by a wide range of treatment professionals. This procedure interfaces well with "usual care" aftercare sessions and provides a structure for the beginning and ending of these sessions.

The aftercare contract is negotiated between the patient and spouse, under the guidance of an alcoholism counselor. The contract involves having the patient: (1) post an aftercare appointment calendar in a prominent location at home, (2) attend aftercare sessions, and (3) call to reschedule if an appointment must be missed. In exchange for adhering to these terms, the spouse agrees to provide an agreed-upon incentive within one week of the appointment. The spouse is invited to attend and participate in all aftercare sessions. The counselor begins each session with a discussion and selection of an incentive from the contract by patient and spouse and ends with verbal reminders of the next appointment and the chosen incentive. The remainder of the sessions proceeds in the usual manner for the aftercare facility, which typically involves problem-solving discussions with patient and spouse regarding temptations to drink, social adjustment, marital issues, and others. This contracting procedure has been shown to be effective in increasing aftercare attendance and improving maintenance of treatment success.

Overall, this approach provides a straightforward means of enhancing aftercare programming. Specific suggestions are offered for research to further refine and extend this procedure.

REFERENCES

Ahles, T. A., Schlundt, D. G., Prue, D. M., & Rychtarik, R. G. (1983). Impact of aftercare arrangements on the maintenance of treatment success in abusive drinkers. *Addictive Behaviors, 8,* 53–58.

Erwin, J. E., & Hunter, J. J. (1984). Prediction of attrition in alcoholic aftercare by scores on the Embedded Figures Test and two Piagentian tasks. *Journal of Consulting and Clinical Psychology, 52,* 354–358.

Ito, J. R., & Donovan, D. M. (1986). Aftercare in alcohlism treatment: A review. In W. R. Miller & N. H. Heather (Eds.), *Treating addictive behaviors: Processes of change* (pp. 435–456). New York: Plenum Press.

Marlatt, G. A., & Gordon, J. R. (1980). Determinants of relapse: Implications for the maintenance of behavior change. In P. O. Davidson & S. M. Davidson (Eds.), *Behavioral medicine: Changing health lifestyles* (pp. 410–452). New York: Brunner/Mazel.

McIntyre-Kingsolver, K., Lichtenstein, E., & Mermelstein, R. J. (1986). Spouse training in a multicomponent smoking-cessation program. *Behavior Therapy, 17,* 67–74.

Miller, P. M., & Mastria, M. A. (1977). *Alternatives to alcohol abuse: A social learning model.* Champaign, IL: Research Press.

Ossip-Klein, D. J., Van Landingham, W., Prue, D. M., & Rychtarik, R. G. (1984). Increasing attendance at alcohol aftercare using calendar prompts and home based contracting. *Addictive Behaviors, 9,* 85–89.

Pokorny, A. D., Miller, B. A., Kanas, T., & Valles, J. (1973). Effectiveness of extended aftercare in the treatment of alcoholism. *Quarterly Journal of Studies on Alcohol, 34,* 435–443.

Pratt, T. C., Linn, M. W., Carmichael, J. S., & Webb, N. L. (1977). The alcoholic's perception of the ward as a predictor of aftercare attendance. *Journal of Clinical Psychology, 33,* 915–918.

Prue, D. M., Keane, T. M., Cornell, J. E., & Foy, D. W. (1979). An analysis of distance variables that affect aftercare attendance. *Community Mental Health Journal, 15,* 149–154.

Skinner, H. A., & Allen, B. A. (1982). Alcohol dependence syndrome: Measurement and validation. *Journal of Abnormal Psychology, 91,* 199–209.

Steinglass, P. (1987). *The alcoholic family.* New York: Basic Books.

Strack, S., Carver, C. S., & Blaney, P. H. (1987). Predicting successful completion of an aftercare program following treatment for alcoholism: The role of dispositional optimism. *Journal of Personality and Social Psychology, 53,* 579–584.

Svanum, S., & McAdoo, W. G. (1989). Predicting rapid relapse following treatment for chemical dependence: A matched-subjects design. *Journal of Consulting and Clinical Psychology, 57,* 222–226.

Vannicelli, M. (1978). Impact of aftercare in the treatment of alcoholics: A cross-lagged panel analysis. *Journal of Studies on Alcohol, 39,* 1875–1886.

Wanberg, K. W., Horn, J. L., & Foster, F. M. A. (1977). A differential assessment model for alcoholism: The scales of the Alcohol Use Inventory. *Journal of Studies on Alcohol, 38,* 512–543.

Chapter 12

Couples Relapse Prevention Sessions After a Behavioral Marital Therapy Couples Group Program

Timothy J. O'Farrell

OVERVIEW

Given the high rate of relapse among alcoholics, maintaining recovery and preventing or minimizing relapse is an extremely important goal in the treatment of alcoholism and other addictive behaviors (Marlatt & Gordon, 1985). Concerns about maintenance and relapse are just as important after marital or spouse-involved treatment as they are after other types of alcoholism treatment.

We have been concerned about maintenance and relapse among cases treated in the Counseling for Alcoholics' Marriages (CALM) Project behavioral marital therapy (BMT) couples group program directed by the author at the Brockton-West Roxbury (Massachusetts) Veterans Affairs Medical Center, a Harvard-affiliated hospital in the greater Boston area. Research showed that adding the Project CALM BMT couples group program to individual alcoholism counseling produced better marital and drinking outcomes during and immediately after treatment. In the 2 years after treatment, the added BMT still produced better marital outcomes, especially fewer and shorter separations, but no longer produced better drinking outcomes (O'Farrell, Cutter, & Floyd, 1985; O'Farrell, Cutter, Choquette, Floyd, & Bayog, 1992). These results suggested that a logical next step in our research on BMT would be to add a maintenance intervention after BMT to maintain the gains produced by BMT, especially for drinking and related behaviors. Planning this next BMT study required a choice about the type of maintenance intervention to be used. We chose a couples-based maintenance interven-

305

tion because, in our earlier BMT research, events in the marriage and factors involving the spouse were the reasons most frequently cited by the alcoholics as the cause of relapse and as reasons for ending a relapse episode (Maisto, O'Farrell, Connors, McKay, & Pelcovitz, 1988).

The purpose of the present chapter is to describe the couples relapse prevention (RP) sessions developed for use after the Project CALM BMT couples group program. As described in Chapter 7, this volume, this BMT couples group program consists of six to eight weekly pregroup sessions conducted conjointly with each couple and 10 weekly BMT couples group sessions. The couples RP sessions consist of fifteen couple sessions scheduled at gradually increasing intersession intervals over the 12 months after the end of the BMT couples group. The goals of the couples RP sessions are to maintain gains achieved during the BMT couples group program, deal with problems that are still unresolved or that emerge later, and prevent or minimize relapse.

SPECIAL CONSIDERATIONS

Most of the comments about client and therapist characteristics that were discussed for BMT couples groups (in O'Farrell, Chapter 7, this volume) also apply to the couples RP sessions described in this chapter. Two additional considerations need to be mentioned.

Other Concurrent Recovery Assistance

The first consideration is that the combined program of BMT couples group followed by couples RP sessions generally has been the only alcoholism counseling patients have received. However, participation in AA for the alcoholic and Al-Anon for the spouse has been frequent. In fact, we have encouraged our clients to use AA and Al-Anon. For those who have chosen these self-help recovery programs, the therapist in the RP sessions tries to get the couple to make specific commitments to attending AA and Al-Anon meetings. These commitments are reviewed at each therapy session and the therapist verbally reinforces attendance at AA and Al-Anon. We view these self-help programs as an excellent method for maintaining sobriety and preventing relapse. A major advantage is that patients can continue to use AA and Al-Anon after the RP counseling sessions have been completed.

The Drop Out Problem in Long-Term RP Sessions

The second consideration is that the combined BMT group and couples RP sessions involve maintaining clients in outpatient treatments for almost 18 months. In a recent study approximately 20% of the couples who started the program dropped out prior to completing the program. Some dropped out before completing the BMT group. Others refused the additional RP because they felt they didn't need it, or discontinued the RP sessions soon after they started. Couples who dropped out had more severe problems prior to starting treatment and worse outcomes in the 18 months after treatment entry. Specifically, before treatment entry, drop outs (when compared with treatment completers) were younger, had been married fewer years, experienced more marital violence, and reported an earlier onset of alcohol problems and more alcohol-related arrests and job losses. In the 18 months after starting treatment, drop outs (when compared with completers) had fewer abstinent days and more light and heavy drinking days, were more likely to have been separated and to have suffered withdrawal symptoms, were less likely to have been totally abstinent, and were more likely to have drunk heavily with serious impairment. Thus, drop outs had some poorer prognostic features before treatment (e.g., younger, earlier onset, more arrests and job losses) and worse outcomes than completers.

The drop out problem should be remembered when considering the BMT plus couples RP program. The quite positive outcomes described in the cases and research summarized in this chapter apply only to cases that could be retained for the substantial course of outpatient couples therapy required by the BMT plus RP program. Nonetheless, the importance of these positive outcomes should not be minimized because those we have been able to retain in treatment have had quite serious and chronic alcoholism problems. Finally, future work is needed to develop methods of retaining the younger, earlier-onset, more antisocial alcoholics and their spouses in treatment longer so they can have the opportunity to receive the benefits of the additional couples RP sessions noted here.

DESCRIPTION OF THE TREATMENT METHOD

Table 12.1 provides an outline of the couples RP sessions developed for use in the year after a BMT couples group. In our work, the couples RP sessions consist of fifteen 50–75 minute couple sessions that are scheduled to occur every 2 weeks for the first 3 months, then every 3 weeks for the next 3 months, every 4 weeks for the following 3 months, and every 6 weeks for the last 3 months. Therapists may use up to three additional crisis sessions at anytime during the 12-month period. RP sessions are conducted conjointly with one couple at a time by one of the therapists who has led the couple's BMT group.

The RP sessions, which follow recent recommendations for booster

TABLE 12.1. An Overview of Couples Relapse Prevention Sessions
Used After a BMT Couples Group

A. Maintenance of changes achieved in BMT group program
    1. Formulate Continuing Recovery Plan that specifies behaviors from BMT
       group program and other activities to continue
    2. Monitor use of Continuing Recovery Plan activities

B. Use of skills learned in BMT Group
    1. Deal with marital and other issues still unresolved
    2. Handle new problems that emerge later in recovery

C. Relapse prevention plan
    1. Identify possible high-risk situations for and early warning signs of relapse
    2. Formulate and rehearse plan for
       a. Preventing relapse
       b. Minimizing duration and negative consequences of drinking if it occurs

D. Frequency and scheduling of sessions
    1. 15 sessions 50–75 minutes long during 12 months after the BMT Group
    2. Six sessions every 2 weeks for the first quarter
    3. Four sessions every 3 weeks for the second quarter
    4. Three sessions every 4 weeks for the third quarter
    5. Two sessions every 6 weeks for the final quarter

E. Quarterly follow-up contacts for 18 months after the RP sessions end
    1. Therapist schedules and reminds of appointment
    2. Couple calls for unscheduled meeting if needed
    3. Provide ongoing support and problem solving
    4. Collect data for outcome monitoring

maintenance interventions (Whisman, 1990), have three major components. The first is to help the couple maintain the marital and drinking gains achieved in the BMT group. The second is to use the therapist's
assistance and the skills learned in the BMT group to deal with marital
and other issues still unresolved or that emerge in the year after the
couples group. The third is to develop and cognitively and behaviorally rehearse a Relapse Prevention Plan. The treatment manual used for
the RP sessions specifies the methods to be used but does not prescribe
a rigid session-by-session format. After the highly structured BMT couples group sessions, the RP sessions are an opportunity for the therapist to individualize these sessions to the needs of each couple. Finally,
in our research practice setting, couples have quarterly follow-up contacts for the 18 months after the RP sessions end.

Maintenance of Changes Achieved in the BMT Group

Continuing Recovery Plan

The first goal of the RP sessions is to help the couple maintain the marital and drinking gains achieved in the BMT group. To this end, each couple completes a "continuing recovery plan" (see Figure 12.1) at the final BMT couples group meeting. This plan specifies what interventions or behavior changes accomplished during the group the couples would like to continue after the group ends. To note their importance, behaviors directly related to maintaining abstinence are discussed first. To this end, therapists often urge couples to continue the Antabuse Contract for at least the first 6 months after the BMT group. In addition, those who had chosen AA and/or Al-Anon as part of their recovery plan before or during BMT are encouraged to continue these activities on a regular basis. Specific couple behaviors related to the procedures of the BMT group also are considered as possible components of the continuing recovery plan. Continuing regular "shared rewarding activities" and "communication sessions" (see O'Farrell, Chapter 7, this volume) are frequently mentioned maintenance goals. Specific behavior change agreements that were negotiated in the group also often are mentioned. Agreements pertaining to the couple's handling of their finances and their children are among the more frequently chosen goals for maintenance after the group.

Initial Couples RP Sessions

The first RP session is held with the couple 2 to 3 weeks after the last BMT couples group meeting. The session begins with a brief review of events that have occurred since the end of the BMT group to determine if there have been any drinking episodes or serious conflicts or problems. Serious problems, although rare at this point in treatment, are given priority when they do occur. In most cases, the session quickly turns to considering the three purposes of this initial RP session, namely orienting the couple to the RP sessions, reviewing the continuing recovery plan, and considering issues to address in upcoming RP sessions.

Orienting the Couple to the RP Sessions

This section involves explaining the purpose and schedule of these sessions. A handout that contains the information in Table 12.1 is used. The availability of phone or in-person crisis contacts between regular-

PROJECT CALM CONTINUING RECOVERY PLAN

Select which of the activities listed below you have decided to do to maintain sobriety and recovery of your marriage after the end of the Project CALM BMT couples group program.

1. Antabuse *with* Antabuse Contract
2. Antabuse *without* Antabuse Contract
3. AA meetings (specify day, location, and type of meetings): _____

_____

4. Al-Anon meetings (specify day, location, and type of meetings): _____

_____

5. Specific activities from CALM group:
   a. "Catch your spouse doing something nice"
   b. "Caring days"
   c. "Shared rewarding activities"
   d. "Communication sessions" to discuss constructively using listening response ("What I heard you say was . . . Is that right?") and expressing your feelings in a respectful, non-blaming manner.
   e. Agreement negotiated during group (specify) _____

_____

_____

6. Other (specify): _____

_____

_____

FIGURE 12.1. Form on which couple specifies plan for maintaining gains after the BMT couple group program.

ly scheduled sessions also is explained. The therapist emphasizes that the goal of the RP sessions is to prevent or minimize drinking relapse and serious marital deterioration. Thus, the couple is urged to use the opportunities for crisis contact as early in the development of a drinking or marital crisis as possible so that further deterioration can be avoided.

Reviewing and Refining the Couple's Continuing Recovery Plan

Discussion of the continuing recovery plan formulated at the last BMT group meeting occupies most of the initial RP session. The extent of success and any problems in adhering to the plan since the end of the BMT group are examined. Any additional items that either partner feels should be added to the plan also are discussed. The couple's continued commitment to the plan is obtained. The expectation is conveyed that compliance with the plan will be reviewed at the start of each subsequent RP session, immediately after reviewing any drinking or strong urges to drink that may have occurred.

Discussing Issues to Address in Upcoming RP Sessions

Issues to be addressed in the upcoming sessions are the final focus of the first RP session. Often this topic is deferred or at least not completed until the second RP session. Dealing with such issues and problems will be considered in more detail next.

Unresolved and Emergent Problems

The second goal of the RP sessions is to use the therapist's assistance and the skills learned in the BMT group to deal with marital and other issues that are still unresolved or that emerge in the year after the couples group. During the initial RP sessions, the therapist tries to help the couple identify unresolved problems either in the marriage or related to maintaining sobriety that they wish to discuss in the RP sessions. If simple questioning fails to produce unresolved issues to address in the RP session, the therapist may review the couple's responses to the assessment battery completed prior to the BMT group and determine whether any of the problems identified then may need further attention. The therapist may also explain that many couples use the RP sessions to discuss sensitive and/or long-standing problems that they felt uncomfortable raising during the BMT group meetings.

Although a wide variety of issues are discussed in the RP sessions, certain concerns and problems predominate. The RP sessions often deal with difficulties in role readjustment that occur when the spouse and other family members resist the alcoholic's efforts to regain important roles in the family (e.g., disciplinarian, equal partner and parent) that were lost through drinking. Nearly all families with a seriously alcoholic member face this problem in the recovery process and, although some resolve it on their own, many need help. Problems with children, especially communication and behavior management with adolescents, frequently become a focus for intervention during the RP sessions. Substance abuse problems of other members of the couple's immediate and extended family often become a focus of some of the RP sessions. Couples often address problems of sex and intimacy (O'Farrell, 1990) somewhat later in the RP sessions, when many of the most severe hardships due to alcohol abuse have been repaired and family roles have started to restabilize. Sexual problems do not usually develop later in recovery, but rather the couple becomes willing and able to consider confronting such issues only after a period of sobriety when more pressing problems have been resolved. Finally, couples and families during the recovery process seem particularly vulnerable to stresses created by critical transitions in the family life cycle (e.g., children leaving home), external life-change events (e.g., job loss), and/or developmental changes in any of the family members (e.g., mid-life crisis). Problems related to such issues frequently emerge during the 12 months of RP sessions and become an important focus.

A number of methods are used to help couples deal with unresolved problems or problems that emerge during the RP sessions. One important emphasis is having couples apply many of the skills they were taught during the BMT group (see O'Farrell, Chapter 7, this volume). Communication and negotiation skills are used frequently. The therapist often will ask the couple to have a communication session about the problem under consideration during the meeting with the therapist. During this discussion, spouses speak one at a time without interruptions using the listening and speaking skills learned in the BMT group to discuss possible ways to deal with the problem. Negotiations and compromising also are used to reach agreements about continuing conflicts.

A second emphasis in the RP sessions is the use of new methods not covered in the BMT group. Problem-solving skills training can be used to help the couple learn skills to solve problems stemming from both external stressors (e.g., job, extended family) and relationship conflicts. In solving a problem, the couple first lists a number of possible solutions. Then, while withholding judgment regarding the preferred solution, the couple considers both the positive and negative and the short-term and long-term consequences of each solution. The therapist also provides input to generate and evaluate potential solutions. Finally the spouses rank the solutions from most to least preferred and agree to implement one or more of the solutions. Use of problem-solving procedures can help spouses avoid polarizing on one solution or another or the "yes, but . . . " trap of one partner pointing out the negative aspects of the other partner's solution.

We have used an approach called "dating sessions" to deal with some couples' sexual problems during the course of RP treatment (Annon, 1976). The procedure involves each partner alternately being responsible for setting and arranging social "dates" in conjunction with sexual "sessions." The latter involve a series of sessions devoted to verbal and physical communication about sexual likes and dislikes, nondemand pleasuring, and sexual experimentation. The dating sessions are designed to help a couple improve their sexual relationship by increasing communication about sex and removing performance pressure and bickering from their sexual interaction.

Relapse Prevention Planning

The third goal of the RP sessions is to develop and cognitively and be-haviorally rehearse an "RP plan." Formulation of the RP plan has three parts. The first is to provide a framework for discussing relapse. The second is to identify high-risk situations and early warning signs for relapse. The third is to plan how to prevent drinking and how to minimize the length and negative consequences of any drinking that should occur (Marlatt & Gordon, 1985).

Providing a framework for discussing relapse is very important be-cause such discussions can be upsetting to many alcoholics and their spouses. Often, couples will be concerned that talking about relapse implies that relapse is inevitable or subtly gives permission for drink-ing. This is particularly the case when discussion turns to what to do to minimize drinking after the first drink has been taken. Use of Marlatt and Gordon's (1985) "fire drill" analogy can be particularly helpful in providing a reassuring framework for discussing relapse. Taking steps to prevent a fire (e.g., removing oily rags or old paint cans stored near the furnace) does not mean a fire is inevitable. Having a fire drill to practice what to do in case of fire is designed to save lives by being pre-pared for quick action. Once a fire has started, the goal is to put out the fire as quickly as possible to minimize damages. None of these aspects of fire prevention and fire safety imply that fires are inevitable or in any way desirable. In fact, just the opposite is the case. The fire drill analogy, when combined with normalizing statements that most couples become anxious at first when discussing relapse, can be used successfully in most cases to manage the initial resistance to discussing relapse.

After establishing a framework for discussing relapse, the next step is to identify high-risk situations and early warning signs for relapse. To begin this process, the husband and wife complete a worksheet (shown in Figure 12.2) for homework, adapted from a section of Marlatt's Drinking Profile (Marlatt, 1976), designed to help specify high-risk sit-uations and early warning signs for relapse to drinking. During the next session, the worksheet is reviewed and a list of high-risk situations and early warning signs is formulated. Situations that have been associated with urges to drink during the BMT group and the RP sessions also may be added to the list of possible high-risk situations.

Finally, the RP plan is formulated. This plan has two parts. In the first part, the alcoholic and spouse determine their planned course of action if they encounter one of the high-risk situations or "danger signs" that they have considered to be likely precursors of a drinking episode. Care must be taken to ensure that planned actions to be taken by the spouse to deal with perceived danger signs and fears do not produce

PREVENTING A RELAPSE

If you are in the Project CALM program, drinking has become a serious problem in your life. But you don't start drinking again for no reason at all. For each person, there are certain times when he or she is most likely to start drinking. We call them HIGH-RISK SITUATIONS—situations when *you* are more likely to drink.

Answering the following questions carefully may help you to identify HIGH-RISK SITUATIONS that can cause a relapse. If extra space is needed to answer any of the questions, please continue on the reverse of this sheet.

1. In your own words, what is the *main reason* why you drank? _____

_____

_____

2. Are there other important reasons? If yes, what? _____

_____

_____

3. Do you have inner thoughts or emotional feelings, or things *within you* as a person, that could "trigger off" your need or desire to take a drink at a particular moment in time?

_____

_____

4. Are there particular situations or events, things that happen to you in the *outside world*, that would be most likely to make you feel like having one or more drinks?

_____

_____

5. When do you feel *least* like drinking? _____

_____

_____

6. *When you drank*, what did you like *best* about alcohol? _____

_____

_____

7. Try to break down into steps the things that lead to drinking in your family. Try to pinpoint when it really started. Do not be afraid to state situations that involve family members.

_____

_____

8. On the back, please write what you think you and your spouse should do if either of you fears a relapse may be going to happen. Also if the alcoholic should take a drink, what do you think the two of you should do?

FIGURE 12.2. Worksheet used to begin discussion of "relapse prevention plan."

couple interactions (e.g., nagging, accusing) that can unwittingly lead to relapse. In the second part, the couple decide what each of them will do to deal with any drinking that might occur in order to minimize the length and negative consequences of the drinking. Here the techniques suggested by Marlatt and Gordon (1985) are very useful, including allowing a delay after the first drink, calling the therapist, and engaging in realistic and rational thinking about the slip. A specific couple "relapse episode plan" is written and rehearsed. Early intervention at the beginning of a relapse episode is important and must be stressed with the couple. Often spouses and alcoholics wait until the drinking has reached dangerous levels again before acting. By then, much additional damage has been done to the marital and family relationship and to other aspects of the drinker's life.

Typical Format of RP Sessions

Certain aspects are part of all RP sessions whereas other aspects change over the course of the 12 months during which the couple completes the 15 RP sessions. Nearly all sessions begin with a review of any drinking or strong urges to drink that have occurred since the last session. The extent of continued compliance with the couple's continuing recovery plan, with an emphasis on activities to prevent drinking and promote sobriety, generally is reviewed at each session. Other parts of each session depend on the specific items that are the focus of that phase of the RP sessions (e.g., problem-solving, RP plan) and on significant events in the couple's lives at the time. The RP sessions are considerably less structured than the BMT group so that the therapist can individualize the therapy to each couple's specific needs. In later sessions the therapist gradually reduces the control and structure he or she provides to the sessions and the time between sessions gets greater so that the couple becomes less dependent on the therapist. The final few sessions are spent reviewing the lessons that have been learned and considering what the couple plans to do to maintain their progress.

Quarterly Follow-Up Contacts for 18 Months After RP Sessions End

Couples have in-clinic or at-home quarterly follow-up visits for 18 months after the RP sessions end. This ongoing contact with the couple is a very useful method to monitor progress, to assess compliance with planned maintenance procedures, and to evaluate the need for additional preventive sessions. The therapist takes responsibility for scheduling and reminding the couple of these follow-up sessions because this is necessary if continued contact is to be maintained successfully. The therapist also instructs the couple to call for an unscheduled meeting if needed to prevent or deal with problems. The following rationale is given to couples for the continued contact. Alcoholism is a chronic health problem that requires active, aggressive, ongoing monitoring by the therapist and family members to prevent or to quickly treat relapses after an initial stable pattern of recovery has been established. The follow-up contact also provides the opportunity to deal with additional marital and family issues that appear after a period of recovery.

CASE APPLICATION

Background and Presenting Problem

Gerald and Cathy Quinn were referred to the Project CALM BMT program while Gerald was hospitalized for a 7-day detoxification program. Mrs. Quinn had told her husband she was considering a divorce, and that she had obtained the name of a divorce attorney from one of her daughters-in-law. Mr. Quinn did not want a divorce. He requested Antabuse and a referral to Project CALM as part of his discharge plan from the detox program. Gerald and Cathy were both in their mid 50s. They had been married 29 years and had five children ages 24 to 35, none of whom were living at home. Gerald had completed the eighth grade, and Cathy was a secretarial school graduate. Gerald was unemployed, having lost his job of over 20 years as a security guard due to drinking. Cathy was working full-time as a secretary at the same large insurance company where Gerald had been employed.

Gerald's drinking had been a problem for many years. Cathy felt his drinking had been heavy and caused problems at home for the past 20 years. Gerald did not think drinking had been a problem for so long, but both spouses agreed that for the past 5 to 6 years, Gerald's drinking definitely had been "getting the best of him." The previous 2 years had been the worst in that Gerald's drinking had caused serious health, domestic, and work problems. Medical problems included a "slight heart attack" and seizures on two occasions in the past 2 ½ years. He had been hospitalized for 10 days for pneumonia less than a month before admission to the detoxification program. Gerald's physician felt these medical problems were either directly caused (e.g., the withdrawal seizures) or seriously exacerbated (e.g., heart and lung problems) by his drinking. Embarrassing incidents at home when intoxicated included a situation in which Gerald had made suggestive comments to a visiting daughter-in-law. Unplanned sick or vacation days due to drinking or hangovers had become more and more frequent in the previous 2 years and he had missed nearly all Mondays for the previous 18 months. Then Gerald was caught drinking on the job for the second time. Because he had already been on probation at work, he was terminated from the job that he had held for over 20 years. The stress of the job termination was compounded by the embarrassment that Cathy felt about this event. Because she and Gerald worked at the same company, Cathy's coworkers knew about Gerald's drinking problem and his dismissal. Further, her favorite daughter-in-law had been visiting when Gerald was caught drinking on the job and terminated.

When Gerald admitted himself to the detoxification program about a week after his job loss, his marital future was uncertain because his wife was discussing divorce and sounded serious this time. In addition, his employer had not decided whether his termination would be considered early retirement (with a modest pension) or fired for drinking on the job (with no pension or other benefits). While in detox, Gerald received an Antabuse prescription at his request and an appointment 2 weeks later for Cathy and him with a Project CALM therapist. Cathy agreed not to contact the divorce attorney until after the initial CALM appointment.

Initial Assessment and BMT Group Program

The initial Project CALM meeting with the Quinns occurred 4 days after Gerald's 55th birthday. This was a stormy session because Gerald had drunk a half pint of vodka to celebrate his birthday, having stopped the Antabuse a week before his birthday. He had restarted the Antabuse the day after his birthday. In fact, he could not quite understand why Cathy was so upset over this drinking because he had planned it as a 1-day celebration. Cathy was furious. She had placed a call to the divorce attorney's office the day before the initial CALM meeting but had not received a return call yet. After explaining the Project CALM BMT program, the therapist asked if the Quinns still wished to try the program. Although Gerald was very interested, Cathy was angry and skeptical. After a careful review by the therapist of a number of alternative courses of action (e.g., file for divorce, trial separation, trial of Project CALM), Cathy agreed to try the couples counseling program. However, Cathy stated clearly that any further drinking would result in separation and probable divorce. An Antabuse Contract (O'Farrell & Bayog, 1986) was negotiated and practiced in this initial meeting: Gerald took the Antabuse dissolved in liquid while Cathy observed and both thanked each other. The Quinns agreed to continue the Antabuse Contract and not to discuss separation/divorce or negative past incidents for the next week until their next couple session.

Pregroup sessions over the next 2 months consisted of reviewing the Antabuse Contract, conducting a detailed assessment, and preparing the Quinns to enter a BMT group. The Antabuse Contract was done faithfully and Cathy gradually became less angry as she became convinced that Gerald was sincerely interested in sobriety. Assessment of Gerald's drinking problem showed that he had been abstinent while living in the community for only 20 days (6%) of the previous year, having drunk a pint or more of vodka daily either alone at home in his room or with friends and acquaintances at the Elk's Club to which he had belonged for many years. Gerald's score of 21 on the Alcohol Dependence Scale (Skinner & Allen, 1982) and his history of blackouts, severe shakes, and withdrawal seizures indicated he had developed a significant degree of physical dependence on alcohol. Negative consequences from drinking included heart problems, enlarged liver, two job losses, five prior hospitalizations for detox or rehab, and serious marital problems and family embarrassment. Gerald's elevated score of 43 on the Michigan Alcoholism Screening Test (MAST) (Selzer, 1971) was consistent with these negative consequences. Both of Gerald's parents had been alcoholics. Gerald indicated that his goal was to give up drinking even though he was not sure this was possible. Assessment of the marital relationship showed Gerald's drinking had led to Cathy's score of five on the Marital Status Inventory (MSI) (Weiss & Cerreto, 1980) indicating she had taken a number of steps toward divorce, including establishing an independent bank account, discussing divorce with trusted friends, and calling a lawyer to discuss her options concerning divorce. Gerald's MSI score was zero indicating no desire to end the marriage. Responses to the Conflict Tactics Scale (Straus, 1979) about the year prior to starting BMT revealed no violence and elevated levels of verbal aggression in the top 10% for U.S. couples for both Gerald and Cathy because of their frequent, heated arguments. Cathy's responses to the Marital Adjustment Test (MAT) (Locke & Wallace, 1959) indicated serious marital problems (score of 53) although Gerald was less unhappy with the marriage (MAT score of 97).

The Quinns attended 10 weekly 2-hour BMT couples group sessions. Three other couples, all with newly sober alcoholic husbands, also participated in the couples group. With only a few minor exceptions, Gerald and Cathy completed all the homework assignments for each group session. At the end of the BMT group, both Gerald and Cathy were considerably happier with their marriage (MAT score of 126 for Gerald and 111 for Cathy) and Gerald had been abstinent 5 months. As part of a research project, the Quinns were assigned to receive 15 RP sessions in the 12 months after the BMT group ended.

Elements of the RP Sessions

The female therapist who had been a coleader of the BMT group conducted the RP sessions with the Quinns. Each RP session lasted 50–75 minutes and was a conjoint session with just the Quinns and the therapist.

Continuing Recovery Plan

When the benefits of the BMT group were discussed in the initial RP session, the Quinns indicated there were four aspects that had been particularly helpful and that they wished to continue. The first was the Antabuse Contract, which made Cathy less fearful of a relapse and helped Gerald with his sobriety. An additional 6-six month extension of the Antabuse Contract was negotiated at the first RP session. The second was the planning of weekly enjoyable activities together, including going to the movies, watching television or a video together at home, visiting their children, going for walks, and eating out. The third was improved communication due to use of the communication sessions they had done during the BMT group and the fact that they were talking more. Finally, the focus on the present and future was something they wished to maintain. Both agreed that after many years of marriage, it was all too easy to destroy their hopes for happiness now by dwelling on the hurts and disappointments of the past.

Unresolved Problems

Two problem areas were the focus of the RP sessions. The first was Gerald's continued unemployment. The second was the serious cocaine problem of their 28-year-old daughter. The way in which these problems were addressed is described below.

RP Plan

Discussions about relapse prevention were accepted readily by both Gerald and Cathy. The fire drill analogy made sense to them. An earlier extended period of sobriety had ended with a serious relapse after which problematic drinking had continued for over 5 years. Thus, preventing relapse was important to the Quinns.

Identification of high-risk situations and early warning signs of relapse presented some initial difficulties. At first Gerald insisted he could not identify any potential relapse triggers. He indicated that the relapse that had ended an earlier period of sobriety happened for no particular reason at all. After more than a year of sobriety, while walking down the street that he had traversed many times, he "just turned around and went into a bar." Recalling this earlier relapse evoked a sense of vulnerability on Gerald's part that was heightened by his description of the unpredictability of relapse and the futility of trying to plan ahead to prevent relapse.

The worksheet for identifying relapse triggers (see Figure 12.2) was completed during two therapy sessions with considerable therapist assistance. This was done rather than the usual procedure of assigning the worksheet as homework because of Gerald's resistance to the procedure and his reading difficulties. The worksheet and discussions surrounding it proved fruitful. Gerald was eventually able to identify an internal feeling state that put him at risk of relapse. He described this state as a feeling of "walls closing in" that was often accompanied by sweating, stuttering, and a desire to escape from this feeling. Situations that led to his feeling nervous, irritable, angry, frustrated, confused, or helpless were related to this feeling.

The RP plan was formulated without much difficulty once the internal feeling state of agitation was identified as the most likely relapse trigger. The plan had three parts. First, Gerald was to remain alert to the feelings of agitation and any urges to drink. These were reviewed at each session. Second, if he experienced the feelings or urges, he would try to decrease them by going for a brisk walk outside. Third, if the walk was not successful or not feasible, he would call someone to discuss his feelings and to get encouragement not to drink. A list of persons to call in order of priority included his wife, his son, a neighbor, or the Project CALM therapist. He agreed to keep calling until he reached someone or until the risk of drinking had passed.

Course of the Relapse Prevention Sessions

The Antabuse Contract was the part of the Quinn's continuing recovery plan that was maintained most fully over the 12 months of RP sessions. Gerald and Cathy were consistently compliant with the Antabuse Contract with the exception of an occasional Sunday on which they missed due to a change in their regular daily schedule. They continued the Antabuse Contract for the entire 12 months and at the final RP session, Gerald planned to continue for as long as Cathy felt some benefit from it. The Quinns also remained relatively consistent in avoiding recriminations about the past and in talking regularly together. Continued joint fun activities were less frequent and less than planned due to work schedules and other family problems.

The RP plan described above took gradual form over the first 3 months of RP sessions. Urges to drink related to various problems initially were dealt with by taking a walk. Later the further step of calling a supportive person was added. The plan was completed and formalized at the eighth RP session. It was reviewed at each subsequent session while discussing any urges to drink that had occurred since the last visit. Gerald reported using the plan successfully on six different occasions.

Detailed discussions of the successful use of the RP plan decreased fears of relapse and increased confidence in continued sobriety for both Gerald and Cathy. They had more difficulty establishing a plan to minimize drinking if it started. Neither wanted to consider this possibility. Finally, after a number of attempts to consider a variety of alternative courses of action, the therapist suggested that the best plan was to call the therapist as quickly as possible after any drinking started so that the crisis intervention could be started at that time.

Concerns about Gerald being unemployed were the focus of many of the RP sessions in the first three months. Gerald was avoiding looking for work because of his embarrassment over having lost his last job due to drinking and his fear that no one would hire him at his age. Cathy was angry that she was working full-time while Gerald stayed home. Gerald started looking for work after considerable discussion and problem solving. The therapist wrote a letter documenting his recovery program for Gerald's use if an employer questioned his job loss. Job-hunting effort was reviewed at each session. Eventually Gerald found a part-time, temporary job as a security guard. The rotating shifts and unpredictable paychecks were a source of stress that was discussed frequently in the RP session. Fortunately, Gerald's persistence was rewarded with a full-time, permanent, day-shift position after his initial probationary period.

The Quinns started to discuss problems with their 28-year-old daughter at the fourth RP session. At first, the complaints centered on the daughter's practice of dropping her two preschool children at the Quinn's house unexpectedly so she could visit her friends. A few sessions later, they revealed the full extent of the daughter's problems. A single mother living in a nearby public housing project, the daughter had a serious cocaine abuse problem. She often did not have money for food or utility bills and occasionally left her children unsupervised or without adequate food. The Quinns, especially Cathy, felt torn between wanting to ensure the welfare of their grandchildren and not wanting to enable their daughter's substance abuse by giving her money or taking care of the children. This problem was an important focus of most of the remaining RP sessions. Two crisis sessions were held with the Quinns and their daughter who accepted a referral for outpatient substance-abuse counseling. The daughter moved back home at the start of the counseling but soon discontinued treatment and resumed occasional cocaine use. Cathy pushed the daughter to get residential treatment but the daughter did not enter a program despite repeated promises to do so. After considerable discussion with the RP therapist, Cathy told the daughter she planned to file charges of child neglect with the state child welfare agency unless the daughter sought treatment. The daughter entered detox the next day. A week later she entered a 21-day rehab program followed by a weekly aftercare program for cocaine abuse. At the time of the last RP session, the daughter had been clean for 2 months. She and her children were still living with the Quinns. An application had been made for a government sponsored rental subsidy program that would allow the daughter to leave the housing project permanently. The Quinns were hopeful that their daughter would remain abstinent and find housing that was more conducive to her continued recovery and the welfare of their grandchildren.

Outcome and Follow-up Information

At the end of the RP sessions a little over a year after the end of the BMT couples group, ongoing regular treatment sessions were terminated. Quarterly check-up sessions to monitor progress were scheduled at this time for the next 18 months (the extended follow-up was part of the research project in which they participated). When the Quinns ended formal treatment, it had been nearly 20 months since Gerald's last drink.

Information obtained during the follow-up contacts showed continued positive outcomes for drinking and marital adjustment. Gerald had been abstinent 3 years at the time of the final follow-up. He had continued daily Antabuse for 12 months after the RP sessions. At the final follow-up, he was still taking Antabuse occasionally when either he or Cathy felt a strong need to do so. Urges to drink had become less frequent, but he still used the plan of taking a walk or calling a supportive person if he became very emotionally upset or had a strong desire to drink. He had continued full-time employment at the job he had started during treatment, and the couple's financial concerns had decreased significantly. The couple's marital relationship also had stabilized. There had been no further talk of separation. Scores on the Locke-Wallace MAT had risen to 126 at the end of the BMT group and fluctuated between 102–123 at the various follow-up contacts with all scores in the range for nondistressed couples.

Unfortunately, their daughter had not been able to establish a sustained recovery from her cocaine problem or to find affordable housing. By the time of the last follow-up contact, the Quinns had obtained custody of their two grandchildren who were now in school. Gerald and Cathy reported being pleasantly surprised that despite the problems involved, their shared caring for their grandchildren had brought a renewed sense of purpose and closeness to their relationship.

RESEARCH SUMMARY

A BMT couples group program (as described in chapter 7, this volume) produces important short-term gains in drinking and marital adjustment (O'Farrell et al., 1985). However, by two years after treatment, the more severe problem cases had suffered serious relapses (Maisto et al., 1988; O'Farrell, Cutter, Choquette, Floyd, & Bayog, 1992). Therefore, couples RP sessions were added after the BMT couples group to maintain gains and prevent relapse.

A recent study (O'Farrell, Choquette, Cutter, Brown, & McCourt, in press) evaluated whether alcoholics who received couples RP sessions in the year after BMT did better than those not receiving the additional RP. The study also examined a purported mechanism of change in maintenance sessions, namely that such sessions improve outcome by getting patients to make greater continued use of treatment-targeted behaviors. Finally the study also examined whether problem severity predicted differential benefit from the couples prevention sessions.

In this study, couples with an alcoholic husband, after participating weekly for 5 months in a BMT couples group program, were assigned randomly to receive or not receive 15 additional couples RP sessions over the next 12 months. Outcome measures were collected before and after BMT and at quarterly intervals for the year after BMT. Four predictions were tested: (1) Couples who received RP in the year after a short-term BMT couples group would have better drinking and marital outcomes than couples who did *not* receive the additional RP; (2) Couples who received the additional RP, when compared with those who did not, would show greater use of the behaviors targeted by BMT; (3) Greater use of the behaviors targeted by BMT would be associated with better outcomes irrespective of the amount of maintenance treatment received; and (4) Couples with more severe alcohol and marital problems at study entry would show the greatest additional benefit from receiving the additional RP sessions.

Results showed that significant improvements in male alcoholic's drinking and marital adjustment occurred from before to after BMT thus replicating results of our own and other's earlier studies of BMT with alcoholics. Furthermore, outcomes remained significantly improved through the 12-month follow-up independent of the amount of aftercare received. Given these favorable outcomes overall, the study provided a stringent test of the hypothesized utility of RP.

As predicted, alcoholics who received RP after BMT had more days abstinent and fewer light and heavy drinking days, maintained their improved marriages better, and used behaviors targeted by BMT more than did those who received BMT alone. The prediction that greater continued use of behaviors targeted by BMT would be associated with better outcomes irrespective of the amount of aftercare received also was supported. The final prediction that couples with more severe alcohol and marital problems at study entry would show the greatest additional benefit from RP was not supported.

These results indicate that adding couples RP sessions improved drinking and marital outcomes for alcoholics and their wives in the year after BMT. As predicted, behaviors targeted by BMT were associated with better outcomes overall, and the superior outcomes observed for RP subjects appeared to be mediated at least in part by greater continued use of treatment-targeted behaviors in the year after BMT. These results are for the first year after BMT when the RP sessions were conducted. Longer-term follow-up currently in progress will reveal whether superior RP results continue and whether the severity of patient's problems becomes a significant predictor of differential benefit from RP. Work in progress also will determine whether the additional cost of providing RP is offset by monetary benefits of reduced health and legal system costs and increased productivity after treatment.

CONCLUSIONS

This chapter has described the couples RP sessions developed for use after the BMT couples group program that was described in Chapter 7. The RP sessions have three major components. The first is to help the couple maintain the marital and drinking gains achieved in the BMT group. The second is to use the therapist's assistance and the skills learned in the BMT group to deal with marital and other issues that are still unresolved or that emerge in the year after the couples group. The third is to develop and cognitively and behaviorally rehearse a relapse prevention plan. The treatment manual used for the RP sessions specifies the methods to be used but does not prescribe a rigid session-by-session format. After the highly structured BMT couples group sessions, the RP sessions are an opportunity for the therapist to individualize these sessions to the needs of each couple. Finally, in our research practice setting, couples have quarterly follow-up contacts for the 18 months after the RP sessions end. A case description of the successful application of the RP sessions was provided. Finally, research was summarized that indicates that the addition of couples RP sessions improved drinking and marital outcomes for alcoholics and their wives in the year after BMT and that the superior outcomes observed for RP appeared to be mediated at least in part by greater continued use of treatment-targeted behaviors.

ACKNOWLEDGMENTS

Preparation of this chapter was supported by grant R01 AA08637 to the author from the National Institute on Alcohol Abuse and Alcoholism and by a grant from the Smithers Foundation. The research and treatment program described in this chapter was supported by the Office of Research and Development, Medical Research Service, of the Department of Veterans Affairs.

REFERENCES

Annon, J. S. (1976). *Behavioral treatment of sexual problems: Brief therapy.* New York: Harper & Row.

Locke, H. H., & Wallace, K. M. (1959). Short marital-adjustment and prediction tests: Their reliability and validity. *Journal of Marriage and Family Living, 21,* 251–255.

Maisto, S. A., O'Farrell, T. J. Connors, G. J., McKay, J., & Pelcovitz, M. A. (1988). Alcoholics' attributions of factors affecting their relapse to drinking and reasons for terminating relapse events. *Addictive Behaviors, 13,* 79–82.

Marlatt, G. A. (1976). The Drinking Profile: A questionnaire for the behavioral assessment of alcoholism. In E. J. Mash & L. G. Terdal (Eds.), *Behavior therapy assessment: Diagnosis and evaluation* (pp. 121–137). New York: Springer.

Marlatt, G. A., & Gordon, J. R. (Eds.). (1985). *Relapse prevention: Maintenance strategies in the treatment of addictive behaviors.* New York: Guilford Press.

O'Farrell, T. J. (1990). Sexual functioning of male alcoholics. In R. L. Collins, K. E. Leonard, B. A. Miller, & J. S. Searles (Eds.), *Alcohol and the family* (pp. 244–271). New York: Guilford Press.

O'Farrell, T. J., & Bayog, R. D. (1986). Antabuse contracts for married alcoholics and their spouses: A method to insure Antabuse taking and decrease conflict about alcohol. *Journal of Substance Abuse Treatment, 3,* 1–8.

O'Farrell, T. J., Choquette, K. A., Cutter, H. S. G., Brown, E. D., & McCourt, W. (in press). Behavioral marital therapy with and without additional couples relapse prevention sessions for alcoholics and their wives. *Journal of Studies on Alcohol.*

O'Farrell, T. J., Cutter, H. S. G., Choquette, K. A., Floyd, F. J., & Bayog, R. D. (1992). Behavioral marital therapy for male alcoholics: Marital and drinking adjustment during the two years after treatment. *Behavior Therapy, 23,* 529–549.

O'Farrell, T. J., Cutter, H. S. G., & Floyd, F. J. (1985). Evaluating behavioral marital therapy for male alcoholics: Effects on marital adjustment and communication from before to after therapy. *Behavior Therapy, 16,* 147–167.

Selzer, M. L. (1971). The Michigan Alcoholism Screening Test: The quest for a new diagnostic instrument. *American Journal of Psychiatry, 127,* 1653–1658.

Skinner, H. A., & Allen, B. A. (1982). Alcohol dependence syndrome: Measurement and validation. *Journal of Abnormal Psychology, 91,* 199–209.

Straus, M. A. (1979). Measuring intrafamily conflict and violence: The Conflict Tactic (CT) Scales. *Journal of Marriage and the Family, 41,* 75–88.

Weiss, R. L., & Cerreto, M. C. (1980). The Marital Status Inventory: Development of a measure of dissolution potential. *American Journal of Family Therapy, 8,* 80–85.

Whisman, M. A. (1990). The efficacy of booster maintenance sessions in behavior therapy: Review and methodological critique. *Clinical Psychology Review, 10,* 155–170.

Chapter 13

Relapse Prevention
A Couples-Therapy
Perspective

Barbara S. McCrady

OVERVIEW

In recent years, the focus of addictions treatment has shifted from attaining to maintaining change. The high rate of relapse after attempts to change any addictive behavior led to the development of models for conceptualizing relapse and treatments to prevent relapses or diminish the seriousness of relapses (e.g., Marlatt & Gordon, 1985). This chapter will discuss a behavioral approach to relapse prevention (RP) that includes both the alcoholic and his or her partner.

RP is applicable to a wide range of addictive behaviors. The RP model assumes that there are at least two distinct phases in changing drinking behavior–initiation of change and maintenance of change. Different treatment techniques and strategies are appropriate to the two phases of change, and the treatment model presented in this chapter introduces a number of treatment elements for each phase.

Several elements are hypothesized to contribute to success or relapse (Marlatt & Gordon, 1985). Alcoholics are exposed to a variety of situations that can be considered "high risk" for drinking. The situations are high risk because of conditioned autonomic responses to environmental cues or because of a strong association between reinforcement for alcohol consumption and these environmental cues. In response to a high-risk situation, the alcoholic may engage in successful coping responses, which would reduce the probability of relapse. If successful, the alcoholic's self-efficacy for coping with future high-risk situations is enhanced, and the probability of future relapses is reduced.

A number of elements interfere with the alcoholic's ability to cope successfully, including positive expectancies about the reinforcing effects of alcohol and low self-efficacy for coping. If the alcoholic consumes alcohol in a high-risk situation, a cognitive process, the abstinence violation effect (AVE) (Marlatt & Gordon, 1985) is hypothesized to occur. The AVE involves both an affective and a cognitive reaction to the ingestion of alcohol and is tied to the person's recognition that he or she has violated a personal commitment to abstinence. The AVE sets the stage for further drinking.

Basic RP treatment includes: (1) identification of high-risk situations for drinking, (2) development and implementation of coping skills, (3) recognition of cognitive factors associated with drinking, (4) education on ways to modify cognitions, (5) development of a more balanced lifestyle to decrease the frequency with which high-risk situations occur, and (6) development of skills to avoid or manage relapses.

Including the spouse or cohabiting partner in RP treatment is a logical extension of the model (McCrady, 1989b). Both partners are involved with and affected by the individual's drinking, and positive family involvement is associated with positive treatment outcome. Clinically, it appears that at times clients have difficulty recognizing high-risk situations, or underestimate the potential impact of a situation. The high arousal that clients experience in high-risk situations (e.g. craving, anxiety) may also interfere with their ability to implement a coping response learned in a low-arousal situation. Thus, the spouse may help the drinker identify high-risk situations and may be able to prompt or cue coping responses if the drinker is having difficulty doing so. Additionally, a positive conjugal relationship may provide a powerful incentive for the drinker to maintain positive changes in drinking, and anticipation of the loss of these reinforcers may facilitate coping.

SPECIAL CONSIDERATIONS

Providing RP treatment to couples requires particular therapeutic skills and is best suited for certain kinds of couples. We have implemented our model in an outpatient treatment setting, drawing referrals from inpatient treatment programs, direct referrals to outpatient treatment, and responses to newspapers announcements of the availability of couples therapy within a clinical research program. Although elements of the treatment program probably could be modified for inpatient or intensive outpatient treatment programs, it has not been tested in such settings. We have used our program only with a goal of abstinence, although modification for a moderation goal would be possible if the client was an appropriate candidate for controlled drinking, and if the spouse or partner supported that goal.

Client Characteristics

The model was designed for clients who are married (living together or separated) or, if not married, have been living with the same partner for at least 6 months. Couples are most appropriate if they hope to stay together, if the client's drinking problem can be treated successfully. The treatment requires active change attempts on the part of both partners and is most easily implemented if the drinker has a stated intent to stop drinking and the spouse is willing to change his or her own behavior as well. Clinically, the treatment seems most difficult to implement with couples in which the drinker does not want to change the drinking behavior, in couples in which the spouse strongly subscribes to an Al-Anon philosophy, and in couples who have a severely dysfunctional, hostile relationship. Spouses who are actively involved with Al-Anon have difficulty with the aspect of the relapse prevention treatment that actually focuses on relapses, how to manage them, and what the spouse's role should be. Our experience has been that the Al-Anon-involved women perceive this aspect of the treatment as endorsing renewed drinking and also believe that the treatment places too much responsibility on them for their partner's abstinence. Excluded from our treatment have been couples where both have problems with alcohol or drug use, and drinkers who show evidence of other drug dependence (moderate to severe), psychosis, or organic brain syndrome.

Therapist Characteristics and Approach

The therapist does not need any special characteristics beyond those required to implement other behavioral treatment approaches with alcoholics and their partners (for an extended discussion, see McCrady, 1991; McCrady & Epstein, in press). The therapist should have basic positive therapeutic skills, including an ability to provide empathy and positive regard to both partners, despite differences in their apparent "blame" for problems, interpersonal styles, and degree of compliance with treatment. Ideally, therapists should have knowledge of and skills in the implementation of behavioral therapy with persons with drinking problems and experience working with couples. The therapist generally takes the role of expert consultant and teacher and supports both partners' attempts to change. Each partner is seen as responsible for changing his or her own behavior. Change is conceptualized as a gradual process, during which both partners are learning new behaviors and ways of thinking, and during which both are likely to make mistakes and have difficulties in implementing new behaviors.

DESCRIPTION OF THE TREATMENT METHOD

A number of the basic elements of the RP couples treatment approach are drawn from our earlier, alcohol-involved behavioral marital therapy (ABMT) program, described elsewhere in this volume (Noel & McCrady, Chapter 8). Elements of the treatment common to both approaches will be mentioned briefly, and the reader is referred to Chapter 8 for further details. Table 13.1 provides an outline of the content of the treatment sessions.[1] Our treatment is provided in the context of a clinical research program, so assessment is somewhat more extensive than in usual clinical practice, and the treatment program is more highly structured. Readers should adapt the aspects of the assessment and treatment that are most applicable to their own clinical settings and circumstances.

Assessment

Assessment is conducted in two sessions. The first, a clinical screening interview,[2] assesses the suitability of the couple for the treatment program. Alcohol and drug use of both partners, severity of alcohol dependence, presence of other psychopathology, and cognitive functioning are evaluated in an interview that lasts approximately 1 ½ hours. If couples are appropriate, they are provided with a packet of questionnaires to complete at home and bring back with them when they come for a second evaluation session. During the second assessment, a detailed interview is conducted to assess drinking and drug use, history of use, and consequences of use, and couples are videotaped so that we can formally assess their communication patterns using a standardized interactional coding system. During treatment, both partners use self-recording cards to report on alcohol use, drinking urges, and relationship satisfaction.

Alcohol and Drug Use

To assess the severity of the client's drinking problem, a number of structured measures are employed. The Alcohol Dependence Scale (ADS) (Skinner & Allen, 1982) is a self-report measure of severity of alcohol dependence. The Drinking Patterns Questionnaire (DPQ) (Zitter &

TABLE 13.1. Topical Outline of Couples Relapse Prevention Therapy

Therapy orientation
  1. Therapy overview
  2. Introduction to functional analysis
  3. Introduction to self-recording

Common elements of all treatment sessions
  1. Review of self-recording cards
  2. Review of homework
  3. Anticipation of high-risk situations in upcoming week
  4. Assignment of homework

Skills training for the alcoholic
  1. Functional analysis of drinking situations
  2. Development of hierarchy of high-risk situations
  3. Stimulus control techniques
  4. Self-reinforcement techniques
  5. Methods for coping with urges to drink
     a. Covert rehearsal of positive coping
     b. Urge imagery
  6. Drink-refusal training
  7. Assertiveness training

Techniques for influencing the alcoholic's cognitive and motivational factors
  1. Decisional matrix
  2. Alcohol autobiography
  3. Enhancement of self-efficacy through coping skills review
  4. Challenge to positive expectations of positive outcomes of drinking
  5. Cognitive rehearsal of negative consequences of drinking
  6. Cognitive restructuring techniques

Lifestyle Balance
  1. Want–should balance assessment
  2. Want–should balance modification

Focus on Relapses
  1. Identification of warning signs for relapse
  2. Plan for coping with relapse warning signs
  3. Ways to handle relapses

Maintenance Issues
  1. Integration of the relapse prevention treatment—the relapse roadmap
  2. Maintenance planning
  3. Therapy follow-up sessions—four sessions over next 12 months

Spouse-Focused Treatment Techniques
  1. Spouse self-recording
  2. Spouse functional analysis
  3. Spouse alcohol autobiography
  4. Spouse high-risk hierarchy
  5. Spouse decisional matrix about partner's drinking
  6. Spouse reinforcement for sobriety
  7. Education in new responses to drinking situations—ignoring and decreasing protection

(cont.)

TABLE 13.1. (cont.)

8. Challenge to spouse positive expectancies about alcohol
9. Spouse role in coping with urges to drink
10. Spouse role in drink-refusal situations
11. Expression of feelings about drinking and drinking-related situations

Conjoint Couple-Focused Treatment Techniques
1. Marital "fun" activity
2. "Love days"
3. Communication Skills Training
4. Problem-Solving Training

McCrady, 1979) assesses client and spouse perceptions of high-risk situations for drinking. The Time-Line Follow-Back (TLFB) interview (Sobell, Maisto, Sobell, Cooper, & Saunders, 1980) is used to evaluate the amount of alcohol consumed for each day of the 6 months prior to treatment. The alcohol section of the Composite International Diagnostic Interview–Substance Abuse module (CIDI–SAM) (Robins et al., 1988) is used to assess symptoms and establish a formal diagnosis of alcohol abuse or alcohol dependence. A structured baseline interview assesses past treatment history, as well as occupational and legal consequences of alcohol use. The structured clinical interview described above is used to assess drug use, including classes of drugs used, quantity and frequency of use, and recency of use. During treatment, clients self-record any drinks consumed and drinking urges (rated on a 1–7 scale). Spouses also record daily estimates of their partner's alcohol consumption (none, light, moderate, or heavy) and estimate the intensity of their partner's urges to drink (on a 1–7 scale).

Marital Relationship

The quality of the marital relationship is assessed with self-report questionnaires, structured videotaped observation of couples, and self-recording of relationship satisfaction during treatment. The Dyadic Adjustment Scale (Spanier, 1976) assesses satisfaction with the relationship, areas of disagreement, and commitment to improving the relationship. The Areas of Change Questionnaire (ACQ) (Margolin, Talovic, & Weinstein, 1983) assesses the degree of change desired by each partner. Each couple is videotaped during a 10-minute discussion of a relationship problem, and the tape is coded using the Communication Skills Test (Floyd & Markham, 1984) to evaluate the quality of the couple's interactions. During treatment, each partner rates his or her daily relationship satisfaction on a 1–7 rating scale.

Other Areas of Life Functioning

General distress level is assessed using the SCL-90 (Derogatis, Lipman, & Covi, 1973). The structured baseline interview assesses occupational status, health status, residential situation, legal problems, and relationship status.

Cognitive Variables

A number of measures assess expectancies and beliefs about drinking. The Alcohol Expectancy Questionnaire (AEQ) (Brown, Goldman, Inn, & Anderson, 1980) assesses positive expectancies about alcohol's effects in six major areas: global positive changes, changes in social and physical pleasure, enhanced sexual experiences, increased arousal with facets of power and aggression, increased social assertiveness, and relaxation and tension reduction. Both partners' perceptions are evaluated to assess the degree to which beliefs are congruent or incongruent. The Situational Confidence Questionnaire (SCQ) (Annis, 1987) assesses self-efficacy for coping with different alcohol-related high-risk situations. The original SCQ assessed the client's confidence in his or her ability to resist drinking heavily in each high-risk situation. The SCQ was modified for our program to ask about self-confidence for resisting drinking at all. Spouses' self-efficacy for coping with alcohol-related situations is assessed with a modification of the Spouse Behavior Questionnaire (Orford et al., 1975). The Drinking-Related Locus of Control Scale (Donovan & O'Leary, 1978) is administered to assess the degree to which subjects view their drinking as internally or externally determined. A Relapse Ideology Questionnaire (Reid, McCrady, & Zwick, 1982) assesses the degree to which the client subscribes to a disease model or behavioral view of alcohol problems and relapse.

Orientation to Treatment Philosophy

In the first treatment session, couples are provided with a formal orientation to the RP philosophy of treatment. The therapist informs the couple that treatment will include four major elements: (1) identification of high-risk situations for drinking and development of skills to manage these situations without drinking, (2) development of spouse skills to cope with alcohol-related situations, (3) development of skills to improve the couple's relationship, and (4) a focus on skills to prevent relapses. The therapist uses a modified version of Marlatt and Gordon's "journey" metaphor to describe the treatment (McCrady, 1989a):

The three of us are starting a journey in this therapy. Like all journeys, we will need to do some planning before we start, and like all journeys, we have a destination in mind. The destination of the journey is "Sobriety Hill,"[3] where the two of you will have a happier life together. Before you leave on the journey, you have to be sure that you want to go, and we will spend some time in the next couple of sessions with helping you reaffirm that decision. To get to your destination, you will need a roadmap that shows you all the routes and detours that you will have to choose from. You will have to plan out your best route, using the roadmap. You'll have to figure out how far you can go each day and where to stop each night. You will also need tools for emergencies. In therapy, we will develop a "roadmap" during this and the next couple of sessions. The roadmap will show us what kinds of situations are *high risk* for you to drink. Some of these situations will involve things in your environment like drinking haunts. Other situations may involve certain thoughts and feelings that you associate with drinking. Other situations may involve the two of you as a couple. We will develop a plan for you to learn good skills to get through these situations, just like a good route plan. You won't reach your destination *immediately*, so we will be breaking up our journey into day by day and week by week changes. Each week, we'll look at what kinds of situations are coming up during the week, so that you'll be ready to handle them. And, we'll throw in some "emergency flares" in case you run into unexpected problems.

In one way, the journey that we're beginning is different than a vacation. You always expect to come home after a vacation. On this journey, hopefully you'll like the destination you reach and will want to stay there. To do so, you'll need to figure out how to turn your visit into a permanent home. To do this, we'll work on skills to help you *maintain* the changes that you've made. One way that we'll do this will be by scheduling some additional treatment sessions after the end of the first 15-week block of treatment. We'll spread these additional few sessions out over the next year, to make sure that you're settling in, and to help you with any problems you might have in your new neighborhood. The other way that we'll help you stay in your new home is by using techniques called "relapse prevention" to help you avoid relapses, and also to handle any relapses, if they should occur. (pp. 3–4)

High-Risk Situations and Coping Skills

Our model for identification of high-risk situations and the teaching of coping skills closely parallels that in our ABMT approach (see Noel & McCrady, Chapter 8, this volume). One major addition to the treatment is the development of high-risk hierarchies for client and spouse. The client and therapist develop a list of high-risk situations, based on responses to the DPQ, information from the self-recording cards, and interviewing. The client then takes the list home and assigns ratings to each major situation. Clients rate the difficulty of each drinking antecedent, using a 0–100 rating scale. Situations are targeted for change based on these ratings, with the therapist helping the client to develop coping skills for situations rated less difficult before situations rated more difficult. Spouses also develop high-risk hierarchies for alcohol-related situations with which they have difficulty coping (drawn from the Spouse Behavior Questionnaire, self-recording cards, and interviewing), and the selection of targets for behavior change is also based on this hierarchy. Additionally, techniques for managing urges to drink are introduced. These include the use of urge imagery (developing imagery to help cope with the urge, such as surfing over the urge like a wave or attacking it with a sword [Marlatt & Gordon, 1985]), and helping the couple brainstorm for creative ways that they could work together to manage drinking urges. A third addition to the basic ABMT skills training is a weekly discussion of the upcoming week, with a focus on identifying potential high-risk situations. The weekly attempt to identify future high-risk situations is intended to teach couples how to anticipate and plan rather than being reactive to events as they occur.

Enhancement of Motivation

A third important element in our treatment is a focus on motivation to change. Although all clients agree to an abstinence goal at the beginning of the treatment, motivation is conceptualized as a fluid state, rather than a stable trait of the individual (e.g., Miller, 1985). As such, continued efforts to enhance motivation are used to facilitate compliance.

Alcohol Autobiography

A first intervention designed to affect motivation is the use of an alcohol autobiography (Marlatt & Gordon, 1985). Each partner writes an autobiography, describing their earliest experiences with alcohol, perceptions of their families' attitudes about alcohol, positive and negative experiences they had with alcohol during their lives, and expectations about their future relationship with alcohol. Couples are given a handout with suggested questions to consider in the autobiography. Instructions begin (McCrady & Niles, 1989):

> A good place to start your story may be when you were a child. Did your parents drink? Was there a lot of drinking in your household? Was drinking considered a "grown-up" thing to do? Did you look forward to having your first drink?
>   Then you might want to move on to your own first experiences with drinking. How old were you when you had your first drink? What were

the circumstances? Did you get drunk? Did you think it was funny? Did your friends and/or family think it was funny? How did your parents react to you drinking? Did it cause any problems? Did you get into trouble because of your drinking?

When you began drinking regularly, did drinking allow you to be more social? Was drinking always part of a dating situation? Did you think that you needed a drink to help you relax after work? After school? Did drinking allow you to feel more accepted by your friends? (p. 2)

In addition to the historical aspects of the autobiography that we ask each partner to consider, we also pose individual questions to each. Questions for the drinker (McCrady & Niles, 1989) include: When did you first . . . realize that drinking was a problem for you? What embarrassing or upsetting things happened? How did your drinking affect your marriage, your work, your relationships with your children, parents, friends? The drinker is also asked to write about his or her life without drinking, considering such questions as: What do you think about yourself as a nondrinker? How do you feel in social situations . . . ? How do you think others view you now? Questions posed to the partner include: How do you feel about your own drinking? What will it be like to socialize with your husband when he is not drinking? How will you feel if you drink when you know that he cannot? In our structured treatment program, the autobiography is assigned as homework in the second treatment session.

Decisional Matrix

In a second intervention to increase motivation, the client and spouse each complete a decisional matrix about drinking and abstinence. Each partner independently lists their views of positive and negative consequences of drinking and of abstinence. Consequences are divided into short-term and long-term consequences. The therapist reviews their completed decisional matrices, discusses them, and adds to them as appropriate. In discussing the decisional matrices, the therapist acknowledges that there may be positive aspects of drinking and negative aspects of not drinking. However, the therapist helps the client and spouse consider how important these reasons for not changing are when compared with the many positive reasons to stop drinking and the negative consequences of continued drinking. Similar to the ABMT approach, as homework clients are asked to review the matrix frequently, in association with a frequently performed behavior (such as looking at the matrix each time the client makes a telephone call). The matrix is completed after the third treatment session, then reviewed and added to during the sixth session.

Change in Positive Alcohol Expectancies

Two other interventions are designed to affect motivation and change expectancies about the reinforcing effects of alcohol. About halfway through the treatment, clients are given two assignments to challenge their positive expectancies about alcohol's reinforcing effects. First, the couple is told to find a way to observe intoxicated behavior. They could complete the assignment by watching a movie or videotape or by going to a drinking environment. Following the observation, each partner writes down observations and reactions. We developed this assignment to enhance the common client negative reaction to viewing others' drinking after a period of abstinence. To build on this assignment, we also review the results of the AEQ and list for the client what he or she had perceived as the strongest positive effects of alcohol. The client and spouse together develop counterarguments for each of these perceived positive effects, and the client is asked to review these frequently between therapy sessions.

The net effect of these motivational interventions is to enhance the perceived positive benefits of abstinence and decrease the perceived positive benefits of drinking. These interventions include the spouse, both so that he or she can add to the client's assessment of the effects of drinking and abstinence and to counter any ambivalence that the spouse may have about the partner's stopping drinking.

Creation of Positive Incentives to Maintain Change

The fourth major element of the treatment involves the development of positive incentives for maintenance of change. These fall into three types: client-generated incentives, partner-provided incentives, and relationship-related incentives. The treatment interventions for each of these incentives parallel those from the ABMT approach (see Noel & McCrady, Chapter 8, this volume, for details). Clients are helped to identify ways to provide self-reinforcers for changes in drinking, and spouses are taught ways to reinforce abstinence using both verbal and behavioral reinforcers. A number of procedures to enhance positive interactions are introduced, including shared recreational activities, use of the Fun Deck (Gottman, Notarius, Gonso, & Markman, 1976) to identify new shared activities, and use of "caring days" (Stuart, 1980). Finally, couples are taught positive communication and problem-solving skills.

Lifestyle Change

Couples are helped to examine the overall balance in their lives between required and enjoyable activities. This "lifestyle balance" assessment

(Marlatt & Gordon, 1985) is used to guide their choices about behavioral alternatives to drinking and shared recreational activities, and each partner is assigned homework to help make adjustments in lifestyle balance.

Interventions Focused Directly on Relapse

All of the elements of treatment described above are part of the relapse prevention program — identifying high-risk situations, learning alternative coping skills, developing a more positive and balanced lifestyle, changing expectancies about the reinforcing effects of alcohol, and maintaining positive motivation to change. In addition to these treatment elements, the couples approach to relapse prevention introduces several techniques that focus directly on the issue of relapse.

Couples are told that relapses are common after alcohol treatment, and that major concerns in treatment are learning ways to avoid relapses and knowing how to manage relapses if they do occur. An initial assignment toward this goal is to ask each partner to list possible "warning signs" for relapse. The warning signs may include changes in behavior or affect, or shifts in thinking about alcohol (usually toward revaluing alcohol in a more positive light). The partners develop their warning signs lists independently, then discuss the lists in the treatment session. A joint "warning signs" list is then developed.

The couple then negotiates a contract for each partner's behavior should any of the identified warning signs occur. The contract specifies each partner's role, and both sign the agreement. Role-play rehearsal of the contracted roles is intended to help them learn the skills necessary to implement the agreement.

After the discussion of ways to prevent relapses, the couple also discusses what steps to take should a relapse occur. Guidelines suggested by Marlatt and Gordon (1985) are provided by the therapist, but each couple develops their own unique agreement. Signing an agreement and behavioral rehearsal are used to facilitate use of the plan.

Maintenance Planning

Three major treatment elements directly address maintenance of the gains made during the treatment. First, the therapist and couple review the treatment program and identify what aspects of the treatment were most helpful, underscoring the importance of using these elements after treatment. Changes in the use of these skills may also be signs of impending relapse and such changes may be added to the list of warning signs for relapse. Second, the therapist has each partner draw a "relapse roadmap" (Marlatt & Gordon, 1985) to define the major high-risk situations for them and the coping skills they found most helpful. Finally, the treatment program includes follow-up visits after the initial, weekly treatment is completed. Follow-up visits can be provided on a flexible schedule, and clients are encouraged to call the therapist to schedule additional sessions as a way to avoid or manage relapses. If the client does not schedule sessions, the therapist will arrange follow-up visits at 1 month, 3 months, 6 months, and 1 year after the end of weekly treatment. The therapist uses each of these sessions to assess the couple's current status, their use of coping skills learned during treatment, and new problems they have encountered. The therapist may schedule one to three additional sessions, if necessary.

CASE APPLICATION

Background and Presenting Problems

Frank and Mary[4] are an unmarried couple, self-referred after seeing a notice in the paper about the availability of couples alcoholism treatment. Frank was 37 at the time of admission; Mary was 32. Both had been married previously. He had two children from his previous marriage; she had one. Both were Irish Catholic, and although Mary went to Mass regularly, Frank was not observant of his religion. Frank worked as a milkman, and Mary was a secretary at a law firm.

Frank began drinking in high school. He quickly increased his intake to a minimum of two six-packs of beer or a pint of bourbon each time he drank. He entered the military when he graduated from high school and became a daily drinker during his military service. He also began to use other drugs, including marijuana, cocaine, and heroin. He married after his discharge from the military. He continued to drink every day, drinking a fifth of hard liquor each weekday and adding two six-packs of beer per day on the weekend. His drug use decreased, although he smoked marijuana at least twice weekly and used cocaine one to two times per month. He experienced repeated blackouts from his drinking, lost several jobs because of his intoxicated state on the job, and began to become violent towards his first wife. She eventually divorced him, and he continued to drink. At the age of 34, Frank decided that he could not continue to drink as he had, went through a detoxification program, stopped all use of alcohol and drugs, and became involved with Alcoholics Anonymous. He met Mary through a friend in AA, and they began to date and then live together about a year prior to his seeking treatment with our program. After they lived together for 6 months, he relapsed, quickly returning to daily drinking and intermittent drug use, and he began to become violent towards Mary. He became increasingly despondent about his life and made a veiled suicide attempt by walking onto a major highway while intoxicated. Luckily, he was not struck by a car, but was instead picked up by the state police, who transported him to a psychiatric unit where he was detoxified and treated for his depression. He and Mary came to our couples treatment program consequent to this hospitalization.

Frank and Mary presented themselves as a very attractive couple, well-dressed, articulate about their problems as well as their affection for each other. In the intake, they smiled at each other often, touched each other affectionately, and answered questions clearly. Frank still appeared to be somewhat depressed and indicated that he felt he had been depressed his entire life. Their primary concerns were: Frank's being able to maintain abstinence from alcohol and drugs, Frank's depression, Mary's uncertainties about Frank's commitment to their relationship, Frank's violence toward Mary, Mary's distrust of Frank's actions (she suspected that he still had contact with drug dealers), and Mary's discomfort with discussing feelings and problems. They were also concerned about Frank's relationship with his ex-wife, who made it difficult for him to see his children.

Assessment

As described earlier in the chapter, our assessment includes a screening interview, completion of a variety of questionnaires, and a structured interview to assess drinking history.

Alcohol Use

On the Michigan Alcoholism Screening Test (MAST) (Selzer, 1971), Frank scored 41, indicating that while drinking he had experienced fights, blackouts, loss of control, and relationship problems, that he had received treatment previously and been involved with AA, and that he did not perceive himself as a normal drinker. He denied medical or legal consequences of his drinking. The structured interview using the alcohol section of the CIDI–SAM (Robins et al., 1989) revealed that he showed a strong pattern of dependence-style drinking — morning drinking, drinking throughout the day, feeling dependent on alcohol, experiencing loss of control. The TLFB interview (Sobell et al., 1980) revealed that he had drunk every day for the past 6 months, being abstinent only for the 3 weeks prior to the intake.

On the DPQ (Zitter & McCrady, 1979), Frank indicated that the most important antecedents to his drinking were emotional (anger, sadness, depression), interpersonal (feeling hurt or lonely), physiological, financial, and environmental (seeing others drinking, payday).

Emotional Domain

Although our assessment of the emotional domain is limited, Frank's responses on the SCL-90 (Derogatis et al., 1973) indicated significant depression and some continued suicidal ideation, although he was quite specific that he felt hopeful that things would change now that he was sober and that Mary was still with him. He also indicated a fair degree of social isolation. On interview, he indicated that he trusted no one and expected that people usually were out to get what they could from other people. He felt that the only persons he trusted were Mary and his children.

Relationship

On the Dyadic Adjustment Scale (Spanier, 1976) they both indicated a high degree of commitment to each other. On the ACQ (Margolin, Talovic, & Weinstein, 1983) they both indicated a number of areas of dissatisfaction: Frank wanted to spend more time together, have a more frequent sexual relationship, have fewer arguments, and have Mary be more emotionally expressive. Mary wanted Frank to stop hitting her, wanted them to spend more time with friends and relatives, and wanted to have more time to herself.

Course of Treatment

Frank and Mary came to all treatment sessions on time and completed the majority of homework assignments. Frank remained abstinent from alcohol and other drugs throughout the treatment and attended AA regularly even though that was not an explicit part of the treatment.

Sessions I–4

In the first treatment session, we discussed the violence, and the sequence of events surrounding it became clearer. Usually, the sequence began when Mary was angry at Frank, or when she was feeling distrustful of his actions, thinking that he was spending time with drug dealers and being afraid that he was buying or using drugs. These thoughts were usually triggered by his calling her later than usual when he got home from work, or being later than she expected when he had taken his children out for the day. She would make a nasty, sarcastic comment to him, and he would grab her arm. He would be extremely angry that she did not trust him and would tell her to retract her statement. She would continue to be negative, and the violence would then escalate to hitting or pushing. At times he would grab an object and throw it against a wall.

I decided to treat the couple together, despite the presence of domestic violence. Although many clinicians would disagree with that decision, I based it on their strong commitment to each other, the fact that the violent acts were very distressing to Frank, and the links between the substance abuse and violence. However, I made it clear that if the violence continued we would have to reconsider the contract for conjoint treatment.

We developed an initial contract around the violence that included the following elements: (1) Frank would leave the house if he felt angry and felt like grabbing Mary; (2) Mary would tell Frank if she was upset, tell him that she needed to calm down, and set a time for later in the day to discuss her upset; (3) Frank would leave Mary alone until the agreed-upon time; (4) discussion of "hot topics" would occur only when they were sitting down at the kitchen table; and (5) if at any time during the discussion Frank felt himself getting upset, he would get up and go for a walk until he felt he had regained control. I also asked whether Mary had some place to go if she felt unsafe, and she indicated that she had gone to her parents' home in the past. Frank did not bother her there unless he was intoxicated. I stressed the importance of her safety, and that if I did not believe she was safe that we would have to take immediate steps to assure that.

After developing the initial agreement about how to avoid violence, Frank and Mary had no further episodes of physical violence during the treatment. They had a number of rather intense verbal arguments, and Frank took many walks, but they were able to use the simple behavioral self-control strategies outlined above to avoid actual physical abuse.

The other major focus of the first few sessions was developing a functional analysis of Frank's drinking, developing a hierarchy of drinking and drug-use situations, and focusing on enhancing motivation to continue to be abstinent. Frank indicated the most important high-risk situations for his drinking and rated how difficult each would be to deal with without alcohol (0–100 scale, with 100 being most difficult): seeing beer commercials on television (5); paydays (20); when his ex-wife would not let him see the children (50); when Mary was upset and yelled at him (75); when he felt sad (90); when Mary was upset but would not talk (95); when he was alone for extended periods of time (100). This hierarchy guided the development of strategies to deal with major high-risk situations.

Additionally, I used two of the techniques described previously to attempt to enhance their motivation to continue in treatment and continue to abstain. The alcohol autobiographies that they each wrote were very detailed discussions of their personal histories and the ways that alcohol had affected their lives. They were somewhat self-conscious about discussing the autobiographies in the therapy, indicating only that they were very personal and helped them to think about how much alcohol and drugs had made their lives different from their hopes and aspirations. The decisional balance sheets that they completed were also informative and gave me a strong indication of their current motivation. A copy of Frank's decisional balance sheet is included as Figure 13.1.

Frank saw many short-term disadvantages to abstinence, but many long-term benefits. He felt that, with time, he would experience "peace and serenity" with abstinence, that he and Mary would stay together and marry, and that he would respect himself more. Short-term, he felt that he missed alcohol, had no way to cope with bad feelings, and felt irritable and depressed. However, he did not see alcohol as providing any positive benefits, short- or long-term. Mary also completed a decisional balance sheet and wrote almost the identical items on hers, even though they did them independently.

Decisional Matrix

	Consequences of Continuing Drinking	Consequences of Quitting Drinking
Immediate Negative	Psycho ward Hate myself Mary will leave	Irritable Depressed No way to get rid of bad feelings Miss drinking
Immediate Positive	None	Not dead

Delayed Negative	Death	None
Delayed Positive	None	Peace and serenity Mary will marry me Self-respect

FIGURE 13.1. Frank's decisional balance sheet.

From the two motivational enhancement techniques, as well as discussion in the therapy sessions, it was clear that Frank had a very strong desire to reattain a comfortable abstinence, but that he was struggling with his own emotional pain at the present time, as well as with missing alcohol. I encouraged him to keep the decisional matrix with him and to look at it any time he experienced an urge to drink. Along with some other urge techniques (discussed below), he found this to be a helpful approach to dealing with drinking urges.

Sessions 5–8

In the next four sessions, we focused primarily on enhancing Frank's cognitive and behavioral skills for staying abstinent. In addition, we introduced treatment elements to enhance positive, reciprocal exchanges between Frank and Mary and began to focus on the couple's communication.

To enhance cognitive skills related to abstinence, we focused on enhancing awareness of negative consequences of drinking, challenging positive expectancies about alcohol, and developing imagery to use when experiencing urges to drink. As noted above, Frank attended AA meetings regularly. He also devoted 15 minutes a day to reading AA literature and saw this activity as important to maintaining his awareness of the negative consequences of drinking. Although he completed a decisional matrix, he did not feel that reviewing it was as helpful as reading the AA literature. I also suggested that he might need skills to cope with positive expectancies about alcohol, but Frank flatly stated, "There is nothing good about it. If I drink, I'll be in the nuthouse or dead. Anything I thought was good about alcohol was an illusion. It's not worth it." I did examine his responses to the AEQ (Brown et al., 1980), but he indicated that none of the positive responses applied. Given his adamance, I did not pursue this topic further. To cope with urges to drink, he developed a vivid image of the psychiatric unit where he had received treatment. When experiencing urges, he would imagine the unit, the intense anxiety he experienced at being confined, and two patients who had been acutely psychotic and hallucinating. He commented, "I would *never* want to go back there, and I know that if I started drinking again I'd be right back there unless I was dead." He used this image whenever he had an urge to drink.

Treatment also focused on behavioral coping skills. Frank's high-risk hierarchy revealed several situations in which behavioral coping skills were important. We spent considerable time on ways to handle loneliness. He began to keep a journal, planned to read the AA literature when he was alone, and began weight lifting for exercise. He called

Mary at work each day when he got home, and she decided to call him again, later in the afternoon, if he seemed "down." He also decided to do some household chores (e.g., laundry, vacuuming) during his time alone. We discussed the possibility of his going out in the afternoons when he was finished with work, but Mary's intense anxiety about his past associations with drug dealers made this possibility remote. She indicated that she could not stand being uncertain about where he was, and Frank indicated that he did not want to deal with Mary's anxiety, so he would rather stay home and learn to deal with being lonely.

Other environmental cues for drinking, such as payday or beer commercials, Frank experienced as "trivial" and felt that his overall ways of staying sober were sufficient. He suggested that the only two things that still generated urges were when he was lonely and when he and Mary had an argument. Mary became very upset at this comment, stating that she felt she was being held responsible for his sobriety, and that she did not want that burden. Frank attempted to assure her that he was not blaming her, and we spent considerable time discussing the difference between identifying a high-risk situation and blaming the situation for drinking. I emphasized that we were identifying high-risk situations so that Frank could learn skills to cope differently with them, and that they had wanted to come to treatment together to change their communication patterns and decrease the angry outbursts. Frank said, "I've learned to handle a lot of these other situations, I'll learn how to handle this too." Mary was not able to accept the cognitive reframing that I suggested and walked out of the treatment session. Frank attempted to follow her, but she ran into the parking lot and started walking up the road. He returned, visibly shaking, and discussed how much he wanted to drink when she behaved that way. Although a very difficult treatment session, it did provide an opportunity to practice, *in vivo,* some of the coping skills we had been discussing. Mary returned 10 minutes later, saying "It's too far to walk." She refused to talk further, but during the week they discussed the issue several times, and she was better able to understand the distinction between identifying a situation and blaming the situation.

The third focus of these sessions was the couple's relationship. I suggested to Frank and Mary that the more they were able to identify positive aspects of their relationship and have positive experiences together, the easier it would be for them to cope with the times they were angry and for Frank to stay sober. They were both able to discuss many positive feelings they had about each other and were enthusiastic about implementing love days and increasing the activities that they shared. The love days included fairly sensual activities, as well as bringing each other breakfast in bed and writing each other tender notes.

They began to go to a local diner on Friday nights, and Frank found out about some "AA dances" where they could dance (an activity they both enjoyed) without alcohol and drugs being present. Frank had suggested going to a club where they used to enjoy dancing, but Mary refused to go because some of Frank's old drug-dealing crowd frequented the club. The AA dances were a positive compromise for them. They also continued some other activities that they had enjoyed, watching certain favorite television programs together, doing the laundry together if Frank did not do it during the week, and taking baths together.

Sessions 9–12

As treatment progressed, Frank became increasingly comfortable with being abstinent, and we began to attend to some general behavioral coping skills and communication skills. Assertiveness and cognitive restructuring were closely interwoven skills for this couple. I introduced both concepts to them and emphasized their interdependence through examples. For Frank, his ex-wife's arbitrary behavior about visitation was paralyzing. He would alternately yell at her, feel hurt and angry, and give up on attempting to see the children. We analyzed two major skills that could be helpful. First, Frank practiced ways to discuss his concerns about visitation in a calm, clear, firm manner. He developed specific requests that he wanted to make and practiced ways to speak with his ex-wife that she was likely to be receptive to. Concomitantly, he had to focus on his cognitions about the situation, challenging his immediate reaction that the ex-wife was trying to retaliate for past wrongs from their marriage and challenging his all-or-nothing thinking ("if she's going to give me a hard time, then I'll just cut off my ties").

For Mary, we directed attention to her feelings and concerns about Frank's past associations with drug dealers. He had lied to her repeatedly in the past, and she still anticipated that he was lying whenever there was any deviation from his usual schedule. She suggested spontaneously that she needed to "let go of the past" and recognize that Frank's behavior was different now that he was not drinking or using drugs. However, there still were certain situations that aroused her previous anxiety, situations that she had coped with previously by either exploding in angry accusations, or fuming and refusing to talk. She began to practice being more assertive in such situations. For example, one day Frank had less cash than Mary thought he should have. In the past, she would have assumed that he spent it with the dealers, but she instead said to him, "Seeing you short of cash gets all my old fears going. Could you tell me what happened to the money so that I can feel reassured? It would help me." Frank responded positively to her request, and detailed a number of small purchases (e.g., auto supplies, shoelaces, new sunglasses, contribution to a person collecting door-to-door for a charity).

As is apparent from these examples, the focus of these sessions turned increasingly to Frank and Mary's relationship. I provided them with some readings on good communication, and they found the concept of intent–impact (Gottman et al., 1976) particularly helpful to them. Early communication skills that we rehearsed included: asking what the other person meant rather than mind-reading, expressing negative feelings in an assertive manner, expressing positive appreciation for the other's actions, and suspending a conversation when either began to feel angry. (This is not a skill that I teach to all couples, but given their history of violence, it was an important skill for them to develop.) They practiced these skills at home, with some success. We had one additional treatment session during which they became quite angry at each other and alternately left the office and yelled at each other.

Sessions 12–15

The final segment of therapy focused specifically on relapse prevention and problem solving. The couple was able to identify a number of warning signs for relapse: increasing arguments, not using the communication skills they had been practicing, Frank getting depressed, Frank discontinuing his involvement with AA, and Frank beginning to think about positive aspects of drinking. Mary also indicated that he was "different" before he relapsed previously, and she recalled the change quite vividly, although she could not articulate in what ways he was different. They developed an agreement about how to handle these warning signs that both felt comfortable they could implement. However, when we began to discuss how to handle a relapse, they reacted very intensely. Frank firmly believed that, for him, a "slip" was impossible—if he drank he would drink heavily and uncontrollably. He indicated that he drank only to get drunk and had not had a moderate drinking day since he went into the Navy. Mary also indicated that she did not want to take a chance and be with Frank if he drank at all—that she was not willing to make herself vulnerable to violence, or the intensely emotional times she had experienced when he last relapsed. They flatly refused to negotiate any sort of moderate contract to deal with relapses, saying instead that the relationship would be over.

The other focus of the last few sessions was on teaching the couple specific problem-solving skills. I taught them a basic step-by-step approach to problem solving (identify the problem, collect information, brainstorm solutions, evaluate solutions, select solutions), and we used it first with easy problems, such as their disagreement about whether or not to get a dog. Eventually, they used the problem-solving approach to develop a plan for managing money and for handling Mary's continued anxiety that Frank might still associate with drug dealers.

Termination and Follow-Up

After the end of the weekly treatment, I saw Frank and Mary three times over the next 6 months. They are also followed monthly for our research. Frank has remained abstinent from alcohol, they have gotten married, and are expecting a child. The last time I saw them, there was some tension between them during the session, and they indicated that they felt that coming to see me made them feel as though they had to talk about problems, so they did not want to schedule any more follow-up sessions.

RESEARCH SUMMARY

Research on the effectiveness of conjoint approaches to treating alcoholics has been reviewed in other chapters in this volume and will not be repeated here. Currently, two research groups are examining the effectiveness of relapse prevention approaches to couples treatment, and the two approaches differ substantially. In our own research, we are comparing different approaches to maintenance of change after outpatient, conjoint alcoholism treatment. Male alcoholics and their partners are randomly assigned to one of three treatment conditions—ABMT (described in Chapter 8, this volume), ABMT plus relapse prevention, or ABMT plus AA/Al-Anon. Subjects receive 15 sessions of conjoint treatment and are followed for 18 months after the treatment. The research is currently in progress, and no results have yet been reported. O'Farrell and his colleagues have detailed their own research in Chapter 12, this volume. Thus, although there is substantial support for the superior effectiveness of conjoint alcoholism treatment, there are as yet no published studies to support the expanded approach described in this chapter.

CONCLUSIONS

This chapter presents a comprehensive model for the treatment of drinking problems. The model, expanded from our previous work with behavioral approaches to conjoint alcoholism treatment, addresses individual coping skills and deficits of both the drinker and the partner, as well as interactional problems. The model does not assume intrinsic personality disorders or severe psychopathology of the partners, as do popularized, disease-model approaches that focus on "the family disease" or "codependency." Instead, we assume that couples have strengths and weaknesses, that they must learn new skills to be able to successfully change the drinking and the marital relationship, and that these skills are difficult to learn and sustain over extended periods of time. The program explicitly teaches the couple how to apply skills learned in therapy to the natural environment and spans an extended period of time to facilitate maintenance. Whether the treatment is more effective than earlier approaches to behaviorally based, conjoint alcoholism treatment can only begin to be answered when current research is completed.

ACKNOWLEDGMENT

Preparation of this chapter was supported in part by grant AA 07070 from the National Institute on Alcohol Abuse and Alcoholism.

NOTES

1. A complete copy of the treatment manual is available from the author. A charge will be made for photocopying and mailing costs.
2. A copy of the clinical screening interview is available from the author.
3. The term "Sobriety Hill" was created by Barbara Niles, one of the many talented graduate students who contributed to the development of this research study.
4. Identifying information has been changed to protect the privacy of the couple.

REFERENCES

Annis, H. M. (1987). *Situational Confidence Questionnaire (SCQ-39)*. Toronto: Addiction Research Foundation of Ontario.

Brown, S. A., Goldman, M. S., Inn, A., & Anderson, L. R. (1980). Expectations of reinforcement from alcohol: Their domain and relation to drinking patterns. *Journal of Consulting and Clinical Psychology, 48,* 419–426.

Derogatis, L., Lipman, R., & Covi, L. (1973). SCL-90: An outpatient psychiatric rating scale—Preliminary report. *Psychopharmacology Bulletin, 9,* 13–28.

Donovan, D. M., & O'Leary, M. R. (1978). The Drinking-Related Locus of Control Scale. Reliability, factor structure and validity. *Journal of Studies on Alcohol, 39,* 759–784.

Floyd, F. J., & Markham, H. J. (1984). An economical observational measure of couples' communication skill. *Journal of Consulting and Clinical Psychology, 52,* 97–103.

Gottman, J., Notarius, C., Gonso, J., & Markman, H. (1976). *A couple's guide to communication.* Champaign, IL: Research Press.

Margolin, G., Talovic, S., & Weinstein, C. D. (1983). Areas of Change Questionnaire: A practical approach to marital assessment. *Journal of Consulting and Clinical Psychology, 51,* 920–931.

Marlatt, G. A., & Gordon, J. (1985). *Relapse prevention: Maintenance strategies in the treatment of addictive behaviors.* New York: Guilford Press.

McCrady, B. S. (1989a) *Manual for relapse prevention treatment for couples alcohol treatment.* Unpublished manuscript.

McCrady, B. S. (1989b). Extending relapse prevention models to couples. *Addictive Behaviors, 14,* 69–74.

McCrady, B. S. (1991). Behavioral marital therapy with alcoholics. In P. A. Keller & S. R. Heyman (Eds.), *Innovations in clinical practice: A source book* (Vol. 10, pp. 117–139). Sarasota, FL: Professional Resource Exchange.

McCrady, B. S., & Epstein, E. (in press). Marital therapy in the treatment of alcohol problems. In N. Jacobson & A. Gurman (Eds.), *Clinical handbook of marital therapy* (Vol. 2). New York: Guilford Press.

McCrady, B. S., & Niles, B. (1989). *Relapse prevention. Handout #3. Your alcohol autobiography.* Unpublished manuscript.

Miller, W. R. (1985). Motivation for treatment: A review with special emphasis on alcoholism. *Psychological Bulletin, 98,* 84–107.

Orford, J., Guthrie, S., Nicholls, P., Oppenheimer, E., Egert, S., & Hensman, C. (1975). Self-reported coping behavior of wives of alcoholics and its association with drinking outcome. *Journal of Studies on Alcohol, 36,* 1254–1267.

Reid, P., McCrady, B. S., & Zwick, W. (1982). *Relapse Ideology Questionnaire.* Unpublished questionnaire.

Robins, L., Wing, J., Wittchen, H. U., Helzer, J. E., Babor, T. F., Burke, J., Farmer, A., Jablenski, A., Pickens, R., Regier, D. A., Sartorius, N., & Towle, L. H. (1988). The Composite International Diagnostic Interview: An epidemiologic instrument suitable for use in conjunction with different diagnostic systems and in different cultures. *Archives of General Psychiatry, 45,* 1069–1077.

Selzer, M. L. (1971). The Michigan Alcoholism Screening Test: The quest for a new diagnostic instrument. *American Journal of Psychiatry, 127,* 1653–1658.

Skinner, H., & Allen, B. A. (1982). Alcohol dependence syndrome: Measurement and validation. *Journal of Abnormal Psychology, 91,* 199–209.

Sobell, M. B., Maisto, S. A., Sobell, L. C., Cooper, A., Cooper, T., & Saunders, B. (1980). Developing a prototype for evaluating alcohol treatment effectiveness. In L. C. Sobell, M. B. Sobell, & E. Ward (Eds.), *Evaluating alcohol and drug abuse treatment effectiveness: Recent advances* (pp. 129–150). New York: Pergamon Press.

Spanier, G. (1976). Measuring dyadic adjustment: New scales for assessing the quality of marriage and similar dyads. *Journal of Marriage and the Family, 38,* 15–28.

Stuart, R. (1980). *Helping couples change.* New York: Guilford Press.

Zitter, R., & McCrady, B. S. (1979). *The Drinking Patterns Questionnaire.* Unpublished questionnaire.

Part IV

FUTURE DIRECTIONS AND CONCLUDING COMMENTS

Chapter 14

Brief Couples Treatment for Alcohol Problems

Allen Zweben

David Barrett

OVERVIEW

The brief couples treatment approach described in this chapter is based on the assumption that alcohol-abusing behavior can be altered through interventions that involve the client in decision-making processes. For certain clients, the decision to modify their drinking patterns is based on a calculation of the perceived costs versus the benefits of continuing these patterns. The costs include the financial, medical, and social consequences incurred when alcohol abuse threatens supportive relationships, personal values, ideals, and beliefs. The benefits include the belief or expectation that alcohol use can significantly improve social performance, enhance pleasurable events, and reduce stress and anxiety.

The treatment model discussed in this chapter assumes that external factors play a major role in decision-making about the drinking. Individuals who experience emotional conflict over their drinking patterns because of external pressures (e.g., separation from partner) will be more amenable to treatment than those who lack such pressures (Pearlman, Zweben, & Li, 1989). Thus, to the extent that the individual resides in a socially stable environment, he or she may be more susceptible to external pressures and consequently may be more likely to benefit from treatment (Finney & Moos, 1986; Orford & Edwards, 1977; Zweben, Pearlman & Li, 1983).

The brief couples treatment approach also assumes that the spouse or partner can play a salient role in the decision to alter alcohol-abusing behaviors. The nonalcoholic partner can provide valuable information, constructive feedback, and support to the client while he or she is making a decision about the severity of the problem and what action needs to be taken. In addition, having the partner play an active role in the sessions can help to minimize his or her negative influence on the treatment process.

In this context, brief couples treatment provides an opportunity for the client and partner to work together to assess the costs and benefits of the drinking behavior and to work cooperatively in carrying out the necessary actions for change.

SPECIAL CONSIDERATIONS

Within the past 10 years there has been a reexamination of the scope and nature of alcohol problems. It is recognized that individuals with alcohol problems are a heterogeneous population ranging from those with mild or moderate consequences stemming from the hazardous drinking pattern (e.g., family and economic problems) to those with severe difficulties (e.g., medical and psychiatric problems) (Skinner & Allen, 1982). At the same time, professionals have become more cognizant of the interrelationship between drinking problems and various social, medical, and psychological concerns including accidents, crime, trauma, and domestic violence. Consequently, a substantial number of individuals with alcohol problems are now being treated in general health-care and social-service settings. These include outpatient services of general hospitals, family service agencies, employee assistance programs, and community mental health centers (Weisner & Room, 1984; Room, 1985).

Given the diverse needs and capabilities of problem drinkers, professionals in the field have recommended that a menu of treatment options be made available to alcohol client groups in order to address the varying medical and psychosocial needs, coping capacities, and external resources in this at-risk population (Institute of Medicine, 1990). Brief couples treatment (less than six sessions) is one approach recommended by professionals for inclusion in the repertoire of treatment modalities offered to alcohol clients (Institute of Medicine, 1990). Such an approach is considered to be a suitable (and less costly) alternative to conventional alcoholism treatment strategies, particularly for those individuals with mild to moderate alcohol problems (Institute of Medicine, 1990). This latter population, termed "early-stage problem drinkers," have a significant number of psychosocial difficulties stemming from their consumption pattern without the accompanying physiological and medical complications generally observed in a chronic alcoholic population (Holt et al., 1980). Within this context, the brief treatment approach is consistent with the trend in the alcohol treatment field toward providing a continuum of treatment approaches responsive to the differing characteristics, environments, and circumstances of alcoholic client groups.

DESCRIPTION OF TREATMENT METHOD

Introduction: Drinking Check-up Project

The present treatment approach has been employed at a regional community mental health center with clients having low-to-moderate alcohol problems in a program called the Drinking Check-Up Project. These clients are usually referred to the program from health maintenance organizations and employee assistance programs. This program is based on an earlier model developed at the Addiction Research Foundation in Canada. Data generated from the project have been encouraging as evidenced by the number of individuals who complete the program and feedback received in the follow-up interviews. Our experiences with the project have been incorporated into this chapter. Table 14.1 outlines the content of brief couples treatment described in detail below.

Assessment Interview and Screening

To determine eligibility for the brief treatment approach, brief screening is conducted prior to the assessment interview. To be considered eligible, the clients should: (1) be at least 18 years old; (2) have alcohol abuse as the primary issue of concern; (3) have no major medical or psychiatric disabilities requiring hospitalization; (4) score between 5 and 20 on the Michigan Alcoholism Screening Test (MAST) (Selzer, 1971), a score that indicates low-to-moderate alcohol problems; (5) have experienced alcohol-related difficulties within the past 12 months as revealed on the Alcohol Dependence Scale (ADS) (Skinner & Horn, 1984); and (6) have a partner willing to participate in all phases of treatment. Screenings are usually scheduled on the same day as the assessment interview.

After the screening is conducted, the client and partner are oriented to the nature of the brief treatment approach. Efforts are made to reinforce attitudes and beliefs about change. Activities focus on affirming the client's efforts to change both now and in the past. Techniques such as complimenting, pacing, joining, and eliciting self-motivational statements are used throughout this initial session in order to enhance attitudes of self-responsibility and empowerment, factors that appear crucial for the success of the program. Any ambivalence the client expresses about change is normalized, and labelling is strictly avoided.

TABLE 14.1. Outline of Brief Couples Treatment for Alcohol Problems

A. Assessment interview and screening (one session)
  1. Preparing the client for change
  2. Owning the change process
  3. Gathering information
     a. Michigan Alcoholism Screening Test
     b. Time-Line Follow-Back Drinking Interview
     c. Alcohol Dependence Scale
     d. Inventory of Drinking Situations
     e. Situational Confidence Questionnaire
     f. Revised Marital Happiness Scale
     g. Spouse Hardship Scale

B. Team conference (one meeting of professional team)
  1. Reviewing assessment data and preparing personalized feedback and advice to the couple
  2. Formulating drinking goal based on individualized assessment
  3. Preparing strategy for use by counselor in feedback session

C. Feedback session (one meeting)
  1. Identifying the severity of the alcohol problem and issues associated with alcohol use
  2. Establishing a consensus about change
  3. Setting drinking goals
  4. Requesting a period of abstinence
  5. Delaying a commitment to change
  6. Enhancing a commitment to change
  7. Maintaining a commitment to change

D. Follow-up session 2–4 weeks later (one or two sessions)

E. Emergency session (if necessary)

Preparing the Client for Change

The session usually begins with a summary of how the client was referred and a description of what will occur in each of the sessions. In describing the program, attention is paid to using terminology and language relevant to the partners' sociocultural background and previous treatment experience. A rationale is offered for their involvement in the brief couples-treatment program. They are advised that the short-term nature of the program is based on the assumption they have the problem-solving and decision-making capacities to deal with the drinking problem on their own. They are told that extensive involvement in treatment may cause them to place too much reliance on the counselor for change and thus reduce their own ability to work on the alcohol problem.

The partner is presented with a rationale for his or her participation in the sessions and is complimented for being involved. The program philosophy is that any changes resulting from the client's participation in treatment will have a direct impact on the partner, which in turn may influence (positively or negatively) the treatment process. The partner is advised that by working cooperatively and supportively with one another to implement treatment goals, each partner can become a valuable asset for positively affecting change.

Owning the Change Process

Discussion is centered on the reasons for entering treatment at this time. The client is asked about efforts to change the drinking currently and in the past. All change efforts are affirmed throughout the session. In this way, the personal problem-solving and decision-making capacities are reinforced.

Discussion is then focused on the costs and benefits of continuing the current pattern of drinking. At this time any discrepancies between the partners concerning the severity of the drinking problem and the need for treatment are acknowledged and normalized. The counselor avoids taking sides with either of the partners. He or she affirms that each partner's perspective or position regarding the drinking behavior has merit. The goal here is to have both of the partners take "ownership" of the change process by allowing them the opportunity to present their own views about the drinking behavior.

Gathering Information

After this orientation, information is gathered on a variety of dimensions associated with the presenting problem. Along with alcohol use, data are gathered on medical history, social support, life events, immediate stressors, and other matters related to the pattern of alcohol use. The Time-Line Follow-Back (TLFB) Alcohol Use Interview (Sobell, Maisto, & Sobell, 1979) and the Alcohol Dependence Scale (ADS) (Skinner & Horn, 1984) are employed, respectively, to measure the client's recent consumption pattern and degree of psychological or physical dependence on alcohol. Such information is used primarily in the feedback session for the purposes of "consciousness-raising" about the level of severity of alcohol problems and to set suitable drinking goals.

The Inventory of Drinking Situations (IDS) (Annis, Graham, & Davis, 1987) and the Situational Confidence Questionnaire (SCQ) (Annis & Graham, 1988) are administered to the client to identify potential situations associated with heavy drinking episodes and to determine client's ability to cope with these high-risk situations. Taken together, these measurements identify the probable circumstances that might lead to the continuation or cessation of problematic drinking. Both measurements are useful in formulating a treatment plan to stabilize drinking behavior and forestall relapse.

The Revised Marital Relationship Scale (RMRS) (Azrin, Naster, & Jones, 1973) is given to both partners to assess the degree of cohesiveness in the marriage, a factor positively related to treatment outcome (Orford & Edwards, 1977). The Spouse Hardship Scale (SHS) (Orford & Edwards, 1977) is administered to the partner to assess the perceived level of social support available to the client. The SHS deals with the hardships experienced by the partner as a consequence of residing with or being in a relationship with the problem-drinking partner. The non-problem-drinking partner's role in treatment is determined by a number of factors. In circumstances where the partner evidences a low commitment to the marital relationship and/or little investment in changing the drinking behavior, she or he is requested to play a minimal ("witness") role in treatment (Zweben, 1991). In these cases, partner involvement is usually limited to sharing relevant information about the drinking and related problems without participating in decision-making about drinking goals and implementing change activities. In contrast, in situations where the marital relationship is satisfactory and the partner demonstrates a high commitment to change, extensive involvement of the partner in the sessions is encouraged—that is, the partner is asked to play an active role in planning and carrying out treatment goals. However, in order to play a constructive role in the sessions, many of these partners may need to attend to their own difficulties stemming from the drinking (e.g., financial and legal difficulties, trouble with children, social isolation) while helping the problem drinker cope with the abuse. Consequently, partners may be referred for further assistance while participating in the brief couples treatment in order to maintain their constructive involvement in the sessions.

Team Conference

The brief intervention team is composed of counselors participating in the program. The team conference is used to review assessment data and prepare personalized feedback and advice to the couple. The team assists the counselor in structuring the feedback and advice to reflect the client's and partner's perceptions of the drinking behavior and degree of commitment toward change. The team format removes the counselor from playing a confrontational role in the sessions. In this model the counselor is an agent of change insofar as he or she delivers the message from the team. Such a process helps promote a sense of autonomy, self-direction, and commitment to treatment goals on the part of the client and partner. The team also monitors the performance of the counselor to ensure that his or her behavior is consistent with the brief treatment model employed in the program.

At the team conference drinking goals are formulated based on such factors as medical history, history of sustained control, scores on the assessment battery, client's perceptions/expectations about the drinking behavior (e.g., the client wants moderate drinking), partner's perceptions/expectations of the drinking (e.g., the partner believes alcoholism is a disease), and stability of the client's social environment. For example, if an individual reports a high degree of marital stress over the drinking, shows little evidence that he or she can drink moderately, and maintains a strong belief in the disease model of alcoholism, he or she is considered a poor candidate for a moderate drinking goal.

A feedback strategy is then constructed with other members of the team. In preparing the strategy, the client's goals and his or her motivation to engage in the change process are carefully considered. The team offers recommendations and suggestions for change based on the information collected in the assessment interview. Specific factors that may have contributed to the drinking episodes, termed "high-risk" situations (Annis, Graham, & Davis, 1987), are explored. In addition, the client's coping capacities for dealing with these high-risk events are examined (Annis & Graham, 1988). A potential plan of action to deal with these difficulties and/or improve client's coping capacities is developed. The final plan is presented to the client in the form of a message from the team being delivered by the counselor. The client's language, unique frame of reference, and world view are incorporated in the particular message developed by the team.

Feedback Session

In this session, the counselor facilitates discussion and interaction about each of the goals and strategies proposed. He or she takes a neutral stance with the couple, summarizing or clarifying issues, avoiding arguments, using reflective listening, and examining alternatives. Differences between the team and the couple concerning goals and strategies are mediated by the counselor. The feedback session is usually held within 1 week following the assessment interview. The session includes the activities listed in Table 14.1 above (under Feedback session) and is described in detail below.

Identifying the Severity of the Alcohol Problem and Issues Associated with Alcohol Use

The session begins with a review of how the client was referred and a reorientation to the nature of the treatment approach. The counselor then reviews with the couple relevant material from the assessment battery, such as extent and pattern of alcohol use, potential high-risk situations, and coping capacities with respect to risk situations. Any discrepancy between client and partner is usually met with a request for more information. When identifying high-risk situations, the information from the assessment is checked against the couple's own perceptions of the event.

Discrepancies between the counselor and couple concerning potential high-risk situations are explored. If agreement with the couple about the interpretation of the event cannot be achieved, it may be necessary to have the client and partner elaborate further on the areas in question. Such an exploration may help reveal the client's underlying ambivalence about changing the drinking problem or the partner's ambivalence about the proposed goals. For example, a client asserted, "I accept the fact that the information I gave you says I have a problem. Yet I can't get past the fact that most people I know drink even more than I do." Such ambivalence was reflected back to the couple by the counselor. He stated, "Despite the evidence, you still do not *feel* ready to make any changes. Is that right?"

By externalizing the ambivalence, the counselor provides the couple with the opportunity to explore various "benefits" or "rewards" from current alcohol use. At the same time, the benefits are weighed against the potential costs of continuing the drinking behavior. Efforts are then made to elicit self-motivational statements from the client and partner using tactics such as scaling and prioritizing. For example, the partners may be asked to rate their desire to change on a scale of 1–10.

Establishing a Consensus about Change

The goal is to formulate a treatment contract between the counselor and the couple about how to address the presenting problems. The assumption here is that such an agreement is essential to facilitate compliance with the treatment recommendations that emerge from the team conference.

In addition, different ways of coping with the situation are examined. The counselor outlines various alternatives and explores the pros and cons of undertaking specific action, including the notion of "doing nothing."

Setting Drinking Goals

If the client and partner appear to be committed to change, specific action steps should be negotiated, beginning with setting clear and reachable goals with respect to the drinking. The counselor begins by asking the couple about their concerns and expectations regarding the use of alcohol (e.g., whether or not moderate drinking is desired or reasonable). The counselor presents the team's consensus about drinking goals based on its review of the assessment data and other material mentioned earlier. The couple is encouraged to express their views on the goal recommended by the team.

The counselor always presents abstinence as the safest goal for anyone with a history of problem drinking. Abstinence is never opposed or discouraged, even if the data suggest that the client might be successful with moderation. If the team believes that the client may change his or her goal in light of continuing experience with abstinence, the counselor may raise that for discussion and planning.

The partner's input is particularly important for reaching an agreement about drinking goals. Clients may be more amenable to accepting a recommended drinking goal when such a recommendation is positively or negatively reinforced by the partner. In one case agreement was reached on abstinence after the wife mentioned that she would be more amenable to spending weekends at their cottage if her husband "gave up" drinking. In another case the client became committed to abstinence after hearing his wife talk about her plans for leaving the household in order to protect herself and children from the weekend binge-drinking episodes. In these cases the input from the partner was valuable in resolving the client's ambivalence about the drinking goal. There was a shift on the part of the client regarding the perceived costs and benefits of the drinking behavior, which in turn helped to facilitate a commitment to abstinence.

In contrast, if agreement is reached that moderate drinking is a suitable goal, the counselor negotiates with the couple specific amounts, frequency, and circumstances for drinking. Strategies for maintaining moderate drinking goals are reviewed. These might include sipping drinks, spacing drinks, and alternating alcoholic with nonalcoholic beverages. The couple is encouraged to plan ahead when they know that a particular event may involve the serving of alcohol beverages. In this way appropriate safeguards to maintaining satisfactory drinking levels can be employed. Relapse prevention techniques (to be discussed later) are also reviewed in the event that a moderate level of drinking cannot be maintained.

Requesting a Period of Abstinence

Regardless of drinking goals, all clients are expected to maintain, at a minimum, a 3-week period of abstinence (Sanchez-Craig, Annis, Bornet, & MacDonald, 1984). The rationale for maintaining an initial period of abstinence is presented to the couple. The counselor informs them that experience has shown that a period of abstinence can be an important factor in resolving the drinking problem, especially in situations where there has been long-standing conflict between client and partner about the drinking behavior. This period of abstinence provides the client with the opportunity to become more sensitive to high-risk situations, develop and improve confidence in his or her coping capacities, and discover alternative behaviors for dealing with situations that in the past have led to hazardous drinking. The counselor should emphasize that the length of the abstinence period needs to be decided on a case-by-case basis. Those clients having a greater number of alcohol-related difficulties will need a longer period of abstinence.

Based on the data gathered in the assessment interview, the treatment team sets a specific time period for the client to remain abstinent. Requests by the couple to forego the abstinent period or to negotiate a different time period are reviewed by the team following the feedback session. A client's request to change the suggested timeframe for the abstinent period will not be opposed by the team unless data indicate otherwise, namely that serious consequences (loss of job or marriage, incarceration) may result if the client resumes heavy drinking. In this case, the client is advised that he or she may need to adopt an abstinence goal if he or she can not adhere to moderate drinking goals.

Delaying a Commitment to Change

There may be situations where one or both partners remain uncommitted to the action plan, despite the counselor's attempt to explore and resolve underlying ambivalence. In such cases, rather than attempt to achieve closure with the couple, the counselor encourages the couple to postpone the decision making to a later time. The counselor compliments the couple for their willingness to reveal their differences and cautions the couple about prematurely committing themselves to a particular plan of action. The counselor "normalizes" the couple's misgivings and underscores the importance of fully exploring the consequences of different options for changing the drinking behavior (Zweben, Bonner, Chaim, & Santon, 1988). The counselor reveals his or her optimism about the couple's ability to resolve the matter at hand.

The concern here is that the client and partner may undertake a plan of action before they feel confident about or committed to carrying out the proposed change plan. As a consequence, the problem drinker may return to drinking over his or her inability to follow the recommended plan. This offer to delay the decision is often met with a "sigh of relief" by one or both partners. The focus then shifts to how long of a period of time (generally 1–2 weeks) they will need to decide. Client's are often willing to negotiate an intermediate plan while exploring the potential costs and benefits of change.

Enhancing a Commitment to Change

Where both partners evidence a willingness or readiness to change, strategies for realizing drinking goals and other objectives are discussed. This may entail choosing alternative behaviors for dealing more effectively with risk situations, such as avoiding certain companions or settings, learning how to enjoy leisure-time activities without resorting to alcohol, using relaxation techniques to manage stress instead of drinking, and using natural helping relationships (namely, family, relatives, and friends) to gain support in overcoming the alcohol problem.

The partner is also given the opportunity to explore options for helping the client address the drinking problem. He or she can identify others in the support network who can encourage and strengthen the client's commitment to change. He or she can show the client useful ways of informing family and friends about the alcohol problem in order to elicit their support. Emphasis is placed on providing support to one another. Evidence from the assessment data is used to reinforce relationship cohesion and to generate activities that can improve and sustain the quality of the relationship, for example, finding time for intimate conversations, spending a weekend without the children, rewarding each other for successfully abstaining from alcohol, and so on. Every effort is made to maintain a mutuality between the partners about these action steps. The assumption is that such agreement is essential if the couple is to implement change.

Maintaining a Commitment to Change

The aim here is to sustain the accomplishments derived in the session and prevent relapse from occurring after leaving the session. The counselor needs to be sensitive to anxieties and fears that have been generated from issues that appear to be "resolved" in the feedback session. For example, a client's partner experienced a "panic attack" following the feedback session after she realized that her husband had agreed to dining at home every evening instead of socializing with "drinking buddies." The counselor can attend to these secondary reactions by exploring and identifying anticipated difficulties, normalizing them, and preparing the couple to deal with them if and when they occur outside a session. A counselor may ask the couple to note ideas that may arise out of their involvement in treatment and discuss such thoughts with each other at home. In this way the couple is "immunized" against reacting negatively to second thoughts and is better prepared to deal with the change process (Marlatt, 1985).

The session is concluded with a discussion of relapse prevention. The counselor attempts to normalize relapse by explaining that "slips" or "setbacks" are common and not unexpected, especially during the early stages of change. In addition, the counselor notes that feelings of guilt and self-blame usually accompany a slip. A discussion of relapse prevention techniques is conducted in order to prevent a slip from becoming a total relapse. The counselor should emphasize the importance of examining these potential problems in order to reduce the client's susceptibility to further setbacks (Marlatt, 1985).

Follow-Up Session

This session is used to firm up the couple's earlier commitment or to resolve a couple's ambivalence about carrying out the recommendations offered in the feedback session. It is not unusual for the partners to remain hesitant about undertaking an action plan after receiving feedback from the counselor. This interview usually occurs between 2 weeks and 1 month after the feedback session. In cases where the couple continues to remain uncommitted to previously negotiated goals and strategies, an additional follow-up session may be scheduled.

The following activities are performed by the counselor in these sessions: (1) confirming decision-making capacities of the clients by reinforcing their ability to carry out recommended goals and strategies, and (2) determining whether the previously established goals are viable and formulating new goals if necessary.

A primary interest of the counselor in these sessions is to determine what has been useful (or not useful) in helping the client adhere to the treatment goals. The counselor explores with the client and partner what has happened (or "what is different") since the previous visit. The goal here is to sensitize the partners to specific factors or situations that are helping sustain improvement and, conversely, those that are interfering with improvement. Again, the counselor attempts to reinforce the client's sense of autonomy and self-direction rather than creating dependency.

Emergency Session

Consistent with the notion of self-direction discussed earlier, the counselor informs the client and partner that they have the responsibility for initiating contact if there is a worsening of the drinking problem during the posttreatment period. In the emergency session, the counselor needs to determine whether, based on the client's condition, further treatment is warranted. For example, is the client experiencing serious medical, psychiatric, and social problems resulting from ongoing, excessive drinking behavior? Or, for that matter, is the "crisis" more related to the client's concern about having to cope with the alcohol problem on his or her own rather than an actual change in medical status. For instance, one client called the counselor to tell him she was in a "panic" after taking just one drink. If the counselor concludes that the "crisis" is not serious, then he or she should reaffirm previously established goals and strategies and reinforce client's willingness and ability to handle the drinking problem on his or her own. In addition, problem-solving strategies should be employed to identify and resolve issues that continue to interfere with the recovery process.

CASE APPLICATION

Background and Reason for Seeking Help

The client, Bob, was a 32-year-old male referred by an employee assistance program because of his concern about his drinking. He had been married for 6 years to Kay and they had a 6-month-old child. Bob, who had an undergraduate degree in business administration and was self-employed, reported that he had been drinking since age 14. Bob stated that his drinking pattern had worsened when he graduated from college and started his own business. He had become more of a weekend drinker, averaging 4–15 drinks per occasion depending on the situation. He liked to drink in social situations because alcohol helped him feel more sociable.

Bob had been concerned about his drinking for over a year. He had noticed that he had a hard time stopping once he started and was embarrassed by his behavior when intoxicated. He reported several attempts to cut down or control his drinking. He was worried because he no longer could predict what would happen once he started drinking. He feared that his drinking was beginning to look a lot like his father's, who had been a self-described "alcoholic" prior to his death. Bob's seeking treatment seemed to have been prompted by the recent

birth of a child and his consideration of what kind of a father he wanted to be.

Assessment Interview

Below is an excerpt from the assessment interview with Bob and Kay.
After completing the standard questionnaires on alcohol use and related
issues, the client was asked about his own perceptions about the severity of the alcohol problem.

BOB: I feel I have some problems with alcohol that I have to deal with.

COUNSELOR: What happens that tells you that you have a problem?

B: I can't control it. Sometimes, when I start, I just don't stop, even
though I know I should. I feel bad the next day, hungover, and I
wonder why I do it.

C: What happens when you try to control it?

B: Normally I can control it. A lot of times, I stop at three or four beers,
because I have to do something the next day or because the people
I am with aren't drinking very much. But once or twice a month
I get into a situation where people are drinking a lot; then I drink
a lot too.

C: What's different about those situations?

B: The main difference is that I'm with people I know who drink a lot.
They expect me to drink a lot, too. I get uncomfortable in prolonged
social situations if I'm not drinking. I've tried it before, to go to a
party and have a couple. But I spend all my time wishing I was drinking and thinking about how much more fun I'd be having if I was
drunk. I always end up drinking more.

Comment: Bob is aware that the loss of control over his drinking
has a situational component. The counselor then talks with Kay to obtain more information and her perspective on the problem.

KAY: Why does he do this to me? He says he is only going to have a
few, and then he gets drunk. It's very irresponsible. I've done just
about everything I can think of to help him. When we go out I find
myself paying more attention to his drinking than I am to what I'm
doing. It's like I want to show him it's possible to have just two or
three.

C: You're feeling hurt that your attempts to help Bob have failed. Is
that right?

K: Yes.

C: Why do you think that is?

K: I think it's inherited, alcoholism. His father, grandfather, and brother are all alcoholic. I see the same thing with Bob; he can't stop. Once he starts, he drinks faster and longer than his friends. He seems uncomfortable being around people unless he is drinking. He has a hard time saying "no," if other people are drinking, he inevitably starts, and if they stop, he keeps right on going.

C: Are there ever times when he doesn't drink that way?

K: He's different when we are at home. We rarely have a drink at home, but if we do, he is much more relaxed about it, like it's no big deal. It's mainly a problem when we're with other people. Then Bob has a hard time stopping.

Comment: This is our first indication that Kay sees the problem as more severe than Bob does. She labels it "alcoholism" and later she went on to elaborate on how hurt, confused, and disappointed she felt that Bob continues to drink despite the consequences. Bob is aware of the fact that his drinking is hurting the relationship, but he is also aware of the personal cost if he stops drinking. Bob talks about his goal for the drinking.

B: My goal is probably abstinence. I did that before, for a couple of months when Kay was pregnant, but I went back to drinking.

C: What happened?

B: I was out with some of my buddies. They were drinking and sort of talked me into just having a couple. I had more than a couple. I guess I really missed it, not drinking.

Comment: Kay talks about the same time period, and again demonstrates that she is more aware of what actions Bob can take to avoid drinking.

K: He did fine while I was pregnant. We would go out with our friends, and we would both just drink soda. He seemed more comfortable not drinking then because he had a good excuse for not drinking: I was pregnant. He was not drinking to do it with me.

C: What do you think he needs to tell your friends now?

K: They all see that he has a problem. He has to be assertive and just tell them that he is not going to drink. Once he's had more than two beers, it's too late to say "no."

Team Conference

The team's review of the assessment measures indicated clear evidence of an alcohol problem and a high level of marital cohesion. Situational factors presented the greatest danger of continued drinking. Concerning the IDS subscale, Bob identified social pressure to drink, pleasant emotions, and pleasant times with others as high or very high risk situations. Similarly, on the SCQ, Bob reported relatively low confidence in the following categories: testing personal control, social tension, pleasant and unpleasant emotions, and urges and temptations. In the team's assessment, Bob already had an awareness of how serious his drinking had become, but he lacked an understanding of how to overcome it. Kay, on the other hand, had a clear agenda for Bob to follow to make the necessary changes. Developing a consensus about change was the counselor's primary task in the next session. It was hoped that focusing on the costs and benefits of change would help Bob decide it was time for action. The team developed a strategy that included focusing on the strengths of the partners, eliciting self-motivational statements, normalizing slips, and strengthening the client's social supports for not drinking.

Feedback Session

The feedback session occurred 12 days after the initial session. Bob reported that he had not been drinking despite the fact that he had been in three high-risk drinking situations. He reported feeling more confident about his ability to be in social situations without drinking. He reported that deciding not to drink and knowing Kay was pleased were the most important factors in his success.

Because one of the goals for this session was to build Bob's confidence in his ability to succeed, the counselor needed to both convey a sense of optimism about Bob's potential for success and highlight his success to date. The team sent compliments to set a positive tone and to help Bob and Kay see that they had many of the characteristics common to successful changers.

Kay's role was seen as crucial to Bob's success. Her concern had prompted much of his self-evaluation. She was not only clearer about what Bob needed to do (abstinence), but had a clear sense about what steps he needed to take in order to be successful. The discrepancy between Bob and Kay about telling their friends was a major concern and needed to be addressed in the feedback session. Bob's ambivalence and limited confidence to deal with the drinking situations in his life made him a high risk for relapse. The counselor hoped that normalizing slips and preparing him to deal with thoughts about drinking would increase the likelihood that he would stick with the change process. Presenting this self-help approach as one of several different change strategies introduced the idea of a more intensive intervention if circumstances warranted.

The following excerpt illustrates how the counselor delivered the feedback from the team, in this case giving compliments and asking for more information from the couple about an area of concern.

C: Bob, the team is impressed by your recognition that you are unable to stop once you've started drinking. That awareness usually comes later, after significant trouble has occurred in a person's life. The team thinks you have a strong sense of responsibility to yourself and your family and believes that you really want to do the right thing. They are impressed by your ability to talk about your awareness that your drinking is not normal. Kay, the team thinks that you are Bob's strongest supporter and most important ally. They are impressed that even with the drinking problem, both of you report no conflict on the Revised Marital Relationship Scale. We think that you are both together on wanting to catch this problem at an early stage. In our last meeting, Kay, you said you thought that Bob is becoming an alcoholic, like his father. The team is wondering what it would mean to you to have a husband who is alcoholic?

K: It would mean he can't drink. I already know that. I just want him to be able to see it.

C: You want him to decide to stop drinking. Is that it?

K: Yes, and he would tell our friends so that they would understand what he's doing and leave him alone.

C: Do you think he is ready to do that, stop drinking and tell your friends?

K: He already has. He's gone three weeks without drinking, and he told several people that he is stopping. I'm really proud of him.

Comment: Eliciting self-motivational statements from both Bob and Kay was a way of building motivation. Clarifying what steps he took to successfully avoid drinking would help Bob to see that he has a great deal of influence over the outcome of his efforts.

C: Taking the first step of coming in for some help gave you enough confidence to begin talking about your problem with the important people in your life. Is that right?

B: Yes. And it really wasn't so hard not drinking. We had three situations where I normally would have drunk, and I did great.

C: What did you do to avoid drinking?

B: Thursday night is our bowling league. Kay and I talked before we went and figured out what I would say to people if they offered me a drink. Last Friday we had a cook-out at our house, and this Friday was Kay's birthday. Both times I made sure I had something else to drink, like sparkling water. It also helped to stay busy.

C: How was it for you, not drinking?

B: I was real aware of it all the time, not drinking. But I felt proud of myself, like I'm doing what's best for me and my family.

C: How did you think he handled it, Kay?

K: I think he did great, too! I think it's really important that he tell his friends.

B: She thinks I should tell everyone. That's just not my style. I know I have a problem, but it's hard for me to tell people.

Comment: Bob and Kay both agreed that progress had been made. He had experienced some success to date with the initial goal of stopping drinking and identifying what action needed to be taken in order to maintain his change. Because there was still a discrepancy between Bob and Kay in terms of their readiness to tell their friends, the counselor had to deal with the different points of view. The counselor hoped that clarifying the choices and normalizing ambivalence would help both Bob and Kay see Bob's reluctance as a problem to be dealt with rather than as a failure. The following excerpt labels the problem as "normally occurring" and externalizes the ambivalence by asking the client to consider what will happen if no change takes place.

C: That's pretty typical, worrying about the future. The good part about recognizing a problem at an early stage is that you are able to do something before it really causes trouble for you. The bad part is that it is harder to commit yourself to a course of action that seems so radical and so permanent. I think it says a lot about your integrity and your courage, being able to admit you have a problem and doing what you're doing. One of the questions that the team had for you, Bob, is "What do you think will happen if you continue drinking the way you have been?"

B: Well, for one thing it would cause more trouble between Kay and I. I also think it would hurt me on my job. It's like my drinking problem causes me to lose confidence in myself. That hurts me in more ways than one. I just have a hard time thinking about what might happen if I don't change.

C: So, on the one hand, you like the immediate effects of alcohol, and miss it when you're not drinking. On the other hand, you see it is poisoning your life, the longer you drink. That's a tough situation.

Comment: This captured Bob's dilemma. He would give up something valuable if he stopped, but he would hurt everyone if he continued. In an effort to shift the client towards a commitment, the counselor shared with both Bob and Kay the results of the objective assessments. Because both parties recognized and freely talked about the problem, the counselor was in the position of using the data to support their perceptions rather than convince them that there was a problem.

C: You scored a 9 on the Michigan Alcoholism Screening Test, a test that measures the kinds of consequences that you have experienced from your drinking over your lifetime. This is "clear evidence" of a drinking problem and supports your own impression that you have a significant problem. When we consider that along with your score of 14 on the Alcohol Dependence Scale, we get a picture of psychological dependency on alcohol, with some developing physical dependency. This fits with your concern about loss of control and Kay's concern about your developing alcoholism. These scores are slightly higher than average for individuals in this self-help program, but we still think you are a good candidate because you have a great deal of support from people for what you are trying to do. At the same time these scores suggest that you may think about drinking again, especially if circumstances in your life change. So the team thinks that we have to do some careful planning for how you will deal with drinking situations and how you will handle a "slip" or a lapse, if it occurs.

Comment: Once agreement was obtained on what the drinking goal would be, in this case abstinence, the objective data could be used to plan for high-risk situations that would occur in the near future. Bob and Kay discussed how he would handle a "stag party" that he would attend. In the following excerpt the counselor talked about high-risk situations and the menu of options.

B: I have a hard time relaxing, and the more drunk other people get, the more I notice how different I feel. It's not exactly that I want to drink, but it's just hard for me to imagine doing this for a long time, not drinking.

C: This fits with the information that you gave us in the final two forms you completed in the assessment, the ones that measure risk and confidence to succeed. The Inventory of Drinking Situations shows that social pressure to drink, pleasant times with others, and pleasant emotions are all high-risk situations for you. At the same time you reported only low-to-moderate confidence about handling a range of situations without drinking. So it seems like you will have to develop some very specific plans if you are going to be successful in the next month, before our follow-up meeting. Let's talk about how you can handle the stag party. One option would be to just not go. That is how some people would handle a situation that is so obviously a risk for you. Of course, you could also just go and "wing it." By that I mean figure out how to deal with it once you are there. But then, you have tried that in the past and it didn't work for you. I'm not sure you would have any more success now. What else do you see that you could do?

B: I don't think either of those two options you just mentioned will work. I'm going to go. I'm standing up in the wedding. But if I don't do something ahead of time, I'm sure I'll end up drinking. I guess I could call John and talk with him before the party and tell him why I'm not drinking.

Comment: This client-generated alternative, from a menu of less desirable options, was more likely to be followed up on. Kay supported the problem solving and the solution decided upon. Both Bob and Kay agreed that if he could get through the stag party, he would have passed the biggest immediate obstacle to success.

Follow-Up Session

The purpose of the follow-up is to evaluate the client's progress in the stated drinking goal, to consolidate the client's motivation for change, and to involve the partner in any problem solving that needs to occur in order to continue the change process.

One month after the feedback session Bob reported that no drinking had occurred and that he was committed to abstinence. He indicated that relations between him and Kay were "better than ever." He reported a greatly increased awareness of people and events that could trigger his desire to drink. He was also aware of how other people act when intoxicated and was attaching a negative value to that behavior for the first time in his life.

Bob and Kay were obviously pleased with his success to date. He had handled a number of difficult situations, including several parties in his own home, without drinking. He had told his mother and some friends about his problem. And he was seeing drinking in a new light: as a much less desirable lifestyle. The next step the counselor initiated, relapse prevention, was a strategy aimed at slowing down the pace of change, anticipating what might go wrong, and planning for how the client would like to behave in the event that a slip or a change of heart occurred.

C: Let me share with you some problems that people sometimes experience when they get to the point where you are. One thing is, people get overconfident. They think because things are going so well, they don't have to worry about the problem any more. Generally when that happens they stop doing the things that were working for them, like planning ahead or being assertive. Sometimes they slip and have an unplanned drinking episode. Do you think it's possible that might happen to you?

B: It's possible, but I don't plan to let down my guard.

C: Sometimes, people are confronted with a new situation that they don't have any experience with or they don't have a chance to plan for. That can also lead to a slip. The other thing, is that people can experience "second thoughts." By this I mean they stop seeing abstinence in the same positive light. They begin to remember the good things about drinking, and their motivation to not drink goes down.

K: I can't imagine that happening to Bob. We both can see how much better things are going now that he's not drinking.

B: I can't see it either. I think if I can just keep doing what I'm doing now, it will get easier over time.

C: I agree, it will get easier over time. I'd like you to think about how you should handle it if you do slip or you have "second thoughts." Our experience is that, even if it never happens, it helps people to think this through ahead of time.

Emergency Session

Three weeks later the clients called to request a session. Bob had drunk heavily over the weekend, was feeling very discouraged, and didn't know what to do. Despite the setback, the counselor was encouraged that the couple did not give up or drop out. It appeared that Bob had picked himself up after a slip and was in the position to learn from his experience. It was essential that the counselor maintain a neutral posture toward the drinking and an attitude of optimism about overcoming the problem. It was anticipated that Bob may have been questioning his drinking goal. He may have lost confidence in the program or in his ability to make the program work for him. If so, the counselor would have to work to restore confidence for Bob and Kay.

Reviewing the Drinking Episode

The counselor's attempt in the last session to immunize the clients to the possibility of trouble had failed. Now he had to evaluate in the course of this emergency session whether Bob was ready to recommit himself to the change plan or whether a more intensive intervention was needed. In this excerpt Bob talks about what went wrong.

B: It was a trip to a ball game with about 15 guys from work. We met at the Park and Ride and then all went together to a pizza place before the game. It was a planned thing. Originally I was going to drive myself, but when I came out of the office and a couple of the other guys called and said, "why don't we drive together." I said, "OK." I guess I picked the easy way out. We sat down and I didn't assert myself.

C: What would you have said if you had asserted yourself?

B: I would have asked for something else to drink.

C: How much did you have to drink?

B: Three or four beers at the pizza place, four more at the game, and at least eight drinks at the bar after the game.

C: So we're talking sixteen drinks over about eight hours. (*pause*) Say something about what's happened since that night.

B: Well, obviously Kay is very upset. She felt let down, and I feel guilty because I let her down. I feel embarrassed that I screwed up.

C: Is he right, Kay, that you feel let down?

K: Yes! I can't believe he did this to me!

C: Kay, it feels like a personal hurt when Bob drinks. What did you do when you realized he had been drinking?

K: I waited up for him. When he wasn't home by midnight, I began to think something was wrong. About 2:00 A.M. I called the wife of one of the guys he was with and she said her husband wasn't home either. Then I started to get angry. By the time he got home I couldn't even look at him. The worst part is he got sick in the middle of the night, and I had to clean him up. I never want to go through that again.

C: It caused a real disruption for you that night. What have you done since then?

K: I don't know what to do. I'm not sure I can trust him anymore. He was doing so well, and then this happened.

Comment: Having clarified the consequences of the drinking, it was important to move the discussion to "what he might have done differently." This helped set the stage for planning for future high-risk situations. It was unclear to what extent this drinking episode had eroded Kay's support for Bob's efforts. It was important that Bob and Kay both see that he was still doing many things right. Compliments, eliciting positive self-statements, and positive reframing would help them regain the self-confidence necessary for future success.

C: Looking back on it now, what do you think happened? How did it happen that you made the decision to start? Because it seems that once you started drinking, you were not going to stop.

B: Right, it is critical for me to say "no" first. What I've done in the past is once I said "yes," I continued to say "yes." Once I have a certain amount, I increase and I drink until I'm drunk. It's my normal pattern.

Comment: Bob saw clearly what he needed to do differently and then engaged in some problem solving.

B: I was thinking about this. I think I have to feel more comfortable with myself and not worry that I am going to appear different. I need to assert myself instead of just taking the easy way, you know, letting whatever happens, happen. I am going to have to take action in some situations in order to not fail like this. I just didn't give much thought when I went out there. And instead of doing something, I did nothing, which is stupid.

C: I think what you are saying is that you see you are going to have to be more proactive . . .

B: More aggressive!

C: And take charge like you did early in the program, like around the stag party. You got together with your friend before the party and told him what you were doing. You also did some planning around other events; you were planning ahead. Am I right about this? (*Bob shakes his head "yes"*) You were planning about that first drink, which for you is the crucial one.

B: Right, because if I can start out with something nonalcoholic, I don't have a problem continuing with that.

C: What do you think about what he is saying, Kay?

K: I think he is right, he has to plan ahead, and he has to tell people, so they can help him instead of offering him drinks.

C: How do you think you can help Bob.

K: I know he feels bad about what he did. I guess I need to forgive him and give him support to try again.

C: So, you need to keep working on your end of the bargain, which is supporting Bob. Just like he needs to keep working at saying "no" and managing his discomfort with not drinking.

Recommitting to the Change Plan

The counselor reviewed with them the menu of options. The options ranged from the realistic to the absurd.

C: Let's talk about where you go from here. It's obvious that you've had a setback. The good part is that you haven't given up, and you're both still working together to find a solution. The bad part is that you're both feeling some discouragement about this working out. That's to be expected. It seems to me that there are a number of things you might do. You could just decide to forget this whole thing. You could decide it's not worth the effort or the disappointment to try and address the problem. You could decide you want to keep trying, but not within the framework of a program. Some people say, "If I'm in a program and I fail, it's just one more person I let down." You might also decide that you need more help than what you can get in this program. Perhaps meeting like this, once every few months, just doesn't help you when you're faced with so many temptations and drinking situations in your life. Do you know what I mean?

B: Yes, but I know I can't do it on my own. I tried that and it didn't work. I can't go back to that.

C: What about the other option, a more structured program?

B: I don't know if I really need that. It's so much time. I was doing okay until last weekend. I guess I'm not ready to say that this didn't work out.

C: What about you Kay. What do you think?

K: I think he can do it in this program, if he sets his mind to it.

Comment: Both Bob and Kay agreed to proceed with the change plan. The counselor took this opportunity to talk about where additional support was available on a day-to-day basis. They indicated that there were other individuals in Bob's life who knew and supported what he was attempting. The counselor asked them if they thought that AA would be helpful. Bob and Kay discussed what support he needed and what other problem situations might be anticipated.

Progress Report

As part of the Drinker Check-Up research and demonstration project, Bob was seen at various intervals over a 12-month period after entering treatment in order to evaluate his progress. Bob's final evaluation was conducted 12 months after the assessment interview. At the final evaluation, Bob reported no drinking except for one episode on New Year's Eve. He was disappointed in himself but not devastated as he had been with his first lapse. The incident reinforced his belief that abstinence was the only reasonable goal for him. He was able to see his mistaken thinking and lack of effective planning for a high-risk situation. He sought additional support through AA, as had been suggested in the emergency session, and resumed his efforts at abstinence.

Bob reported continued progress in establishing a lifestyle that was incompatible with problem drinking. Kay stated that many of their friends were starting families and that social gatherings now included children, which seemed to exclude heavy drinking. Bob reported that these social gatherings were much easier to handle because there were other people not drinking. He stated that there had been a fundamental change in how he viewed himself.

B: I no longer feel "different" when I am with other people. I look at how I was able to be there and there and there, and not drink. I realize that I am just being myself and doing what I want to do. It seems entirely possible that I won't drink for the rest of my life.

RESEARCH SUMMARY

From a cost-benefit standpoint, partner-involved brief treatment has been as successful as more intensive, multimodal therapies across a variety of outcomes dealing with drinking behavior and related consequences for individuals with low-to-moderate alcohol problems. Beginning with the work of Orford and Edwards (1977), individuals with a moderate degree of alcohol problems fared better with a partner-involved brief advice approach, consisting of a single counseling session, than with a more intensive package of conventional treatments that also involved partners. Subsequent studies have supported the potency of brief couples treatment. Chick, Lloyd, and Crombie (1985), studying problem drinkers in a hospital setting, found that a single counseling session produced better outcomes than routine medical care. The sample consisted of men admitted to a medical unit who were subsequently identified as problem drinkers. The brief approach employed by Chick and his colleagues involved partners if they were available and willing to participate in the feedback sessions. The authors concluded that brief interventions for problem drinkers within a hospital setting appeared to be very promising, especially for patients with some degree of social support. Finally, Zweben, Pearlman, and Li (1988) compared a single session of partner-involved brief advice with an eight-session, systems-based conjoint therapy approach. The brief approach provided couples with feedback and advice about the severity of drinking problems and issues related to changing the drinking behavior. The study included individuals who had a low-to-moderate degree of alcohol problems and whose partners were willing to be involved in the treatments. Approximately 60% of the subjects in both treatment groups were rated as "much improved" at 18 months after the assessment interview. However, there were no between-group differences with respect to the alcohol-related outcomes employed in the study.

A major question arising from the above studies is whether the same outcomes could be obtained without partner involvement. That is, could the apparent success of the brief intervention be attributed primarily to other dynamics occurring in the session (e.g., counselor empathy) rather than to the active involvement of the nondrinking partner? None of the aforementioned studies were designed to compare a brief approach with and without partner involvement. Therefore, it is difficult to determine what the actual impact of the partner's involvement was on the effectiveness of the brief approach. Nonetheless, the findings generated in the above research, at the very least, support the need to continue to refine, standardize, and evaluate rigorously brief couples treatments with individuals deemed suitable for such approaches.

CONCLUSIONS

The brief couples treatment approach has been successfully employed with individuals having mild to moderate degrees of alcohol problems. Many of these individuals have the necessary coping capacities and support system to effectively utilize the present approach. The model requires that a comprehensive assessment interview be employed to determine the severity of alcohol problems, the situations associated with the drinking behavior, the presence or absence of a support system, and the commitment on the part of the client and partner to deal with the alcohol abuse. The treatment team evaluates the information gathered and helps prepare a feedback strategy relevant to the issues, concerns, and idiosyncracies of each couple. At the feedback session relevant material derived from the assessment battery is utilized for purposes of raising the couple's awareness of the severity of the problem and exploring potential solutions to resolving the alcohol problem. Emphasis is placed on maintaining or enhancing a mutuality between the couple. Motivational counseling techniques are employed throughout the session to buttress the coping capacities of the couple. Follow-up and emergency sessions can be used to strengthen or sustain the couple's resolve to change the drinking behavior. Strategies and goals can be revised in light of the client's experience. Recent findings have revealed that brief couples treatment may be an appropriate intervention to include in the menu of options offered to persons with low-to-moderate alcohol problems. However, further research will be necessary to ascertain the circumstances and conditions under which the present approach is more suitable than individually-focused brief treatment approaches in treating early-stage problem drinkers.

REFERENCES

Annis, H. M., Graham, J. M., & Davis, C. D. (1987). *Inventory of drinking situations user's guide.* Toronto: Addiction Research Foundation.

Annis, H. M., & Graham, J. M. (1988). *Situational confidence questionnaire user's guide.* Toronto: Addiction Research Foundation.

Azrin, N. H., Naster, B. J., & Jones, R. (1973). Reciprocity counseling: A rapid learning-based procedure for marital counseling, *Behavior Research and Therapy, 11,* 365–382.

Chick, J., Lloyd, G., & Crombie, E. (1985). Counselling problem drinkers in medical wards: A controlled study. *British Medical Journal, 290,* 965–967.

Finney, J. W., & Moos, R. H. (1986). Matching patients with treatments: Conceptual and methodological issues. *Journal of Studies on Alcohol, 47*(2), 122–134.

Heather, N. (1987). Psychology and brief intervention. *British Journal of Addiction, 84,* 357–370.

Holt, S., Steward, I. C., Dixon, J. M. J., Elton, R. A., Taylor, T. V., & Little, K. (1980). Alcohol and the emergency service. *British Medical Journal, 281,* 638–640.

Institute of Medicine. (1990). *Broadening the base of treatment for alcohol problems.* Washington, DC: National Academy Press.

Marlatt, G. A. (1985). Relapse prevention: Theoretical rationale and overview of the model. In G. A. Marlatt & J. R. Gordon (Eds.), *Relapse prevention:*

Maintenance strategies in the treatment of addictive behaviors (pp. 3–70). New York: Guilford Press.

Orford, J., & Edwards, G. (1977). *Alcoholism: A comparison of treatment and advice, with a study of the influence of marriage* (Institute of Psychiatry Maudsley Monographs, No. 26). New York: Oxford University Press.

Pearlman, S., Zweben, A., & Li, S. (1989). The comparability of solicited versus clinic subjects in alcohol treatment research. *British Journal of Addiction, 84,* 523–532.

Room, R. (1985). Dependence and society. *British Journal of Addiction, 80,* 133–139.

Sanchez-Craig, M., Annis, H., Bornet, A. R., & MacDonald, K. R. (1984). Random assignment to abstinence and controlled drinking: Evaluation of a cognitive–behavioral program for problem drinkers. *Journal of Consulting and Clinical Psychology, 52,* 390–403.

Selzer, M. (1971). The Michigan Alcoholism Screening Test: The quest for a new diagnostic instrument. *American Journal of Psychiatry, 127,* 1653–1658.

Skinner, H. A., & Allen, B. A. (1982). Alcohol dependence syndrome: Measurement and validation. *Journal of Abnormal Psychology, 91,* 199–209.

Skinner, H. A., & Horn, J. (1984). *Alcohol dependence scale user's guide.* Toronto: Addiction Research Foundation.

Sobell, L. C., Maisto, S. A., & Sobell, M. B. (1979). Reliability of alcohol abusers' self-reports of drinking behavior. *Behavior Research and Therapy, 17,* 157–160.

Weisner, C., & Room, R. (1984). Financing and ideology in alcohol treatment. *Social Problems, 32*(2), 167–184.

Zweben, A., Bonner, M., Chaim, G., & Santon, P. (1988). Facilitative strategies for retaining alcohol-dependent clients in outpatient treatment. *Alcoholism Treatment Quarterly, 5*(1/2), 3–24.

Zweben, A., Pearlman, S., & Li, S. (1983). Reducing attrition from conjoint therapy with alcoholic couples. *Drug and Alcohol Dependence, 11,* 321–331.

Zweben, A., Pearlman, S., & Li, S. (1988). A comparison of brief advice and conjoint therapy in the treatment of alcohol abuse: The results of the Marital Systems study. *British Journal of Addiction, 83,* 899–916.

Zweben, A. (1991). Motivational counseling with alcoholic couples. In W. R. Miller & S. Rollnick (Eds.), *Motivational interviewing, preparing people to change addictive behavior* (pp. 225–235). New York: Guilford Press.

Chapter 15

Family Intervention with the Alcoholic After Major Injury in the Trauma Center Setting

Larry M. Gentilello
Patrick Duggan

Make not thyself helpless drinking in the beer shop ... falling down, thy limbs will be broken and no one will give thee a hand to help thee up.

—EGYPTIAN PAPYRUS, 1,000 B.C.

OVERVIEW

Trauma is the single leading cause of death for alcoholics. Treating the injuries of traumatized alcoholics and ignoring the underlying alcoholism amounts to little more than preparing these patients to be involved in another accident, where they may permanently disable or fatally injure themselves or others. Alcoholics often enter treatment as a result of a crisis. The crisis of a major injury significantly impacts upon both the alcoholic and the family, providing the health-care team with a unique opportunity to address alcoholism and alcohol abuse.

This chapter describes a method that identifies alcoholism among patients admitted to a trauma center, and uses the Johnson Institute Intervention approach (e.g., Johnson, 1986; see also Liepman, Chapter 3, this volume) with the patient's family to influence the alcoholic trauma patient to enter treatment. Prior to describing this family treatment method in detail, background information on the relationship between alcohol and trauma will be presented.

Scope of the Trauma Problem

Trauma-related fatality and disability have become a priority issue in public health and are recognized as a "neglected epidemic," (Baker, 1987).

Twenty-five years ago, in the report *Accidental Death and Disability: The Neglected Disease of Modern Society*, the National Academy of Sciences (1966) pinpointed trauma as the number one public health problem facing the United States. Little has changed to this day. At present, there are over 150,000 deaths and 3,600,000 hospital admissions secondary to trauma each year, and the cost to society is estimated to be over $180 billion dollars annually (National Academy of Sciences, 1985).

Due to the relatively young age of most trauma victims, more than 4,100,000 years of potential life are lost each year (Institute of Medicine, 1985). To put this in perspective, 2,100,000 years of life are lost each year to heart disease and stroke, and 1,700,000 years of life are lost to cancer. Thus, more years of life are lost each year to trauma than to the next three leading causes of death combined.

The National Academy of Sciences (1966) report gave impetus to the development of regional trauma systems. These systems have contributed to a decline in the fatality rate associated with major injury (Cales, 1984; Trunkey, 1982). However, the underlying causes of nearly half of our nation's trauma, alcoholism and alcohol abuse, are routinely ignored in the care of patients at these trauma centers (Gentilello et al., 1988; Soderstrom & Cowley, 1987).

Alcohol Use and Trauma

Alcohol plays a major role in such traumatic events as suicides, fires, gunshot wounds, stabbings, falls, drowning, domestic violence, accidents in which autos hit pedestrians and motor vehicle accidents (Baker, O'Neil, & Karpf, 1984; Noble, 1978). The U.S. National Institutes of Health (Haberman & Natarajan, 1986) reported that 64–70% of homicides, 75% of stabbings, 69% of assaults, and 56% of cases of domestic violence involve alcohol. Motor vehicle accidents are the single leading cause of traumatic death and injury (Zuska, Trunkey, & Hering, 1983), and these accidents account for more quadriplegia and paraplegia than all other causes combined.

During the Vietnam war approximately 63,000 U.S. soldiers were killed in action. In that same time span 274,000 Americans died in alcohol-related motor vehicle accidents. Over 1,000,000 Americans who were alive in 1980 will eventually die as a result of alcohol-related traffic accidents (Whitfield, Zador, & Fife, 1985). Alcohol use results in an estimated 60,000 fatal injuries annually, making trauma the leading cause of death attributable to alcohol use (Center for Disease Control, 1990). Stated another way, more alcoholics die from injury than from any other single cause. The trauma death rate of alcoholics is, in fact, more than twice the death rate for other long term alcoholic problems (cirrhosis, hepatitis, pancreatitis, etc.) and results in the loss of over 1,000,000 years of potential life each year (Rice et al., 1989).

Alcoholism and Trauma Recidivism

Most drivers involved in an alcohol-related accident have a long history of arrests and social and medical problems related to alcohol (U.S. Department of Transportation, 1968; Waller, 1990). Due to the prevalence of alcohol use in trauma patients, an admission to a trauma center should be considered a possible marker for alcoholism.

Israel (1987) found a 16-fold greater prevalence of prior fractures in alcoholics than in hospitalized nonalcoholic controls. Oppenheim (1977) also studied the relationship between trauma recidivism and alcoholism in patients admitted with fractures and found the incidence of alcoholism in patients admitted with their first episode of fracture to be 17%. Alcoholism was present in 33% of patients admitted with a second fracture and, for patients admitted with a third fracture episode, the incidence of alcoholism was 62%.

Sims et al., (1989) performed follow-up of 263 patients admitted to a Level 1 trauma center and found a trauma readmission rate of 44% within 5 years. Despite the relatively young age of this population sample (32 yr), the 5-year mortality rate of these patients was 20%, with 77% of these deaths being attributable to continuing substance abuse. This study also found that as an individual's number of trauma admissions increased, the probability that substance abuse was present rose precipitously.

Reed, Miller-Crotchett, & Fischer (1991) analyzed the economics of trauma recidivism and failure to treat alcohol abuse in trauma patients. In that study, 23 of 55 intoxicated trauma patients were readmitted for a second alcohol-related injury. The hospital charges for the first 55 admissions totaled $242,564, of which $126,033 (52%) was written off as bad debt. The subsequent 23 readmissions had hospital charges totaling $628,752, of which $492,146 (78%) was absorbed as bad debt. Although 36% of patients had hospitalization insurance at the time of their first admission, only 23% had coverage at readmission. This suggests that failure to treat alcohol abuse in trauma centers places a significant financial burden on trauma centers. Also, because of their deteriorating financial status, untreated alcoholics are less likely to have insurance during subsequent admissions. For some patients, the first admission may, therefore, be the only opportunity to afford therapy.

Need for Alcoholism Intervention in Trauma Centers

In an editorial to the Journal of the American Medical Association, Waller (1988) noted that "identifying potential areas for successful patient counseling to prevent or reduce high-risk behavior is one of the ongoing goals of the medical profession" (pp. 2561–2562). Nonetheless, despite the strong relationship between alcohol and trauma, the opportunity to address alcoholism as a risk factor for injury is ignored in most trauma centers (Lowenfels & Miller, 1984). A survey by the Maryland Institute of Emergency Medical Services (Soderstrom & Cowley, 1987) found that half of U.S. trauma centers do not assess patients' blood alcohol level. The most frequent reason given by survey respondents was "the test has little clinical importance."

In another study of 346 trauma patients (Chang & Astrachan, 1988), the median blood alcohol level for patients testing positive was 200 mg% (legal intoxication is defined as having a blood alcohol concentration $\geq$ 100 mg%); not one patient was referred for alcohol abuse evaluation and treatment. The only counseling observed was given to two patients whose blood alcohol levels were 245 mg% and 368 mg%, who at the time of discharge were told "not to drink and drive."

Because alcoholism and alcohol abuse are leading risk factors for trauma, Intervention and treatment initiated in the trauma center may reduce the risk that these patients will inflict future injuries upon themselves or others. Because the typical trauma patient is less than 31 years of age, a trauma-related hospital admission may also provide an opportunity to identify and treat alcoholics at an early stage, possibly diminishing the long-term consequences of alcoholism upon these patients.

SPECIAL CONSIDERATIONS

Trauma centers do not possess the facilities or personnel necessary to carry out alcoholism treatment. The appropriate role of the trauma center is to screen patients for potential alcohol problems and to diagnose, intervene, and refer the alcoholic patient to persons able to provide such care.

There are constraints in trauma centers that are not apparent in the more traditional Intervention settings that must be addressed if this is to be accomplished. Most trauma centers admit hundreds, if not thousands, of patients each year, and the volume of potential alcohol-abusing patients could potentially overwhelm all but the most streamlined system for addressing alcohol problems. Furthermore, many patients have only a brief hospital stay. Mental status changes caused by alcohol use can complicate the diagnosis of head injury, or mask symptoms of significant abdominal injury. Therefore, patients who are intoxicated in the emergency room after an accident are often admitted on a precautionary basis and are discharged when the effects of alcohol are no longer present. In such cases, time constraints may severely limit the screening, evaluation, and intervention process.

Identification of promising candidates for Intervention and referral should take place at admission. Personnel capable of initiating this process must be fully integrated into the trauma team activities if Intervention is to be made available to such patients. The integration of alcohol counselors as part of the trauma team should be considered as routine as is the use of physical therapists, occupational therapists, and speech therapists to address the ongoing disabilities of the patient.

Given the large number of alcoholic patients admitted to trauma centers, it is also important to classify the severity of patients' problems with alcohol. Because most trauma victims are relatively young, a large number of patients with early alcohol problems are likely to be identified. By referring such patients to a level of treatment that is matched to their level of problem severity, overutilization of more costly intensive treatment services, which many patients cannot afford, may be avoided. Patients with higher levels of alcohol dependence can then be referred to more intensive treatment with less risk of overwhelming such treatment facilities with unnecessary and costly referrals.

An additional factor affecting many trauma patients is a lack of medical insurance, or the absence of financial ability to pay for treatment. Many of these patients also will not qualify for public alcohol treatment funding. Thus, the trauma center must be capable of assessing the socioeconomic status of the patient and must make suggested treatment relevant not only to the level of alcohol dependence, but also to the patient's financial ability to participate in it. Feasible treatment referrals may range from brief in-hospital counseling provided by the alcohol counselor affiliated with the trauma center, to 12-step programs (AA, etc.), private outpatient and inpatient programs, publicly funded treatment programs, and others. Social-services departments in most trauma centers routinely make socioeconomic assessments that can be incorporated into the alcoholism referral plan.

The referral process also must take into account any ongoing physical disabilities that the patient may have. For example, patients confined to a wheelchair or crutches, or who have large lower extremity casts may not be appropriate candidates for daily outpatient therapy sessions if they must rely on public transportation.

DESCRIPTION OF THE TREATMENT METHOD

Preparations for family intervention in the trauma center involve a number of sequential steps as outlined in Table 15.1. The first step is screening and identification followed by discussion of the alcohol problem with the patient's family. Unlike settings where the family is already motivated to intervene, family members of the patient may be unaware of the need for or the possibility of intervening in the trauma center. The interventionist must be prepared to educate the family about the process of Intervention, and to present it as a viable option. This will involve meeting with the family and other significant persons and informing the group about the impact of alcoholism on families and other important alcohol-related issues.

The next step involves training the participants for the Intervention and conducting a rehearsal or practice Intervention. The family also must receive guidance in selecting a form of treatment that is appropriate to the patient's alcohol problem severity and financial and physical condition. Each of these steps will be presented in detail next.

Identification of Alcoholism Among Trauma Patients

Determine Blood Alcohol Level

We believe that all patients admitted to a trauma center should have a blood alcohol level drawn in the emergency room as an initial screening test. This is important because clinical assessments of intoxication have been shown to be inaccurate (Maull, Kinning, & Hickman, 1984).

At Harborview Medical Center, blood alcohol testing was performed on 2,823 patients admitted to the trauma service over a 2-year period (Jurkovich et al., 1992). A full 47% of patients had a positive blood alcohol test. Nearly 36% of patients were legally intoxicated upon arrival to the emergency room (blood alcohol concentration $\geq$ 100 mg%, and 20% had a concentration of 200 mg% or more. The mean blood alcohol concentration (BAC) for those who were legally intoxicated on admission was 187 mg%. Alcohol use was so common that the mean BAC for all admitted males was 98 mg% and 49 mg% for all admitted females.

Routine blood alcohol testing facilitates the diagnosis of pathophysiologic conditions associated with alcoholism, such as hepatic disease, electrolyte abnormalities, coagulation defects, and nutritional deficiencies. It also helps identify patients who are at risk for developing delirium tremens or withdrawal syndromes, and it facilitates the evaluation of patients with an altered mental status. Intoxicated patients are also prone to make inappropriate medical decisions, such as leav-

TABLE 15.1. Outline of Steps in Using Family Intervention with the Alcoholic After Major Injury in the Trauma Center Setting

A. Identification of alcoholism among trauma patients and screening
  1. Determine blood alcohol level on admission
  2. Administer screening questionnaires
    a. Short Michigan Alcoholism Screening Test (SMAST)
    b. CAGE
  3. Establish the diagnosis
    a. Interview the patient
    b. Interview the family

B. Family meeting
  1. Request attendance of all members of immediate family
  2. Indicate meeting is at physician's request and vital to patient's well being
  3. Do not inform family in advance that meeting is about patient's drinking problem
  4. Present results of screening tests and other evidence for diagnosis of alcoholism
  5. Elicit family member's reactions to screening and diagnostic information and their views of patient's drinking
  6. Obtain family member's agreement with diagnosis and need for patient to receive treatment for alcoholism

C. Preparation for and conducting the family Intervention
  1. Prepare the family to intervene
    a. Orient family to process of Intervention
    b. Select the Intervention team
    c. Educate the team about alcoholism briefly
    d. Each person lists specific instances of patient's abusive drinking and how they were negatively affected
    e. Rehearse the Intervention meeting
  2. Conduct the family Intervention meeting
    a. Meet at the hospital before patient is discharged from the trauma center
    b. Each family member describes in a concerned, supportive, nonaccusatory manner the specific drinking episode from their list and how the drinking made them feel
    c. The family request the patient to enter alcoholism treatment and (if necessary) state their response if patient refuses
    d. Transfer patient to alcoholism treatment

ing the hospital against medical advice and refusing important diagnostic or therapeutic procedures. When this occurs, blood alcohol testing is vital in helping the health-care provider to make informed judgments about the patient's competence.

Failure to measure a patient's BAC can potentially lead to civil liability on the part of the physician caring for the patient. In a recent survey, Simel and Feussner (1989) found that a majority of lawyers said they would recommend filing a negligence suit against a physician if an intoxicated patient were allowed to leave the emergency room without documented advice to the contrary and was subsequently involved in another accident. What has not been clarified is the physician's responsibility towards the patient with alcoholism who is discharged without having the diagnosis and need for treatment explicitly pointed out, and who is subsequently disabled or fatally injured in another alcohol-related accident.

The blood alcohol level may also provide an estimate of the patient's future risk of death from fatal injury. A study by the Center for Disease Control (Anda, Williamson, & Remington, 1988) examined the relationship between the usual number of drinks consumed per occasion and the incidence of fatal injuries. The injury risk was found to be related to the peak BAC attained at each drinking episode. Persons who consumed five or more drinks per occasion were nearly twice as likely to die from injuries than persons who drank fewer than five drinks per occasion. A clear dose–response relationship was observed between number of drinks consumed per drinking episode and the risk of fatal injuries, with persons consuming nine or more drinks per occasion being 3.3 times more likely to die from injuries than those drinking less than that amount.

Because most trauma patients admitted with a positive blood alcohol test are not merely social drinkers, but have diagnosable problems with alcoholism or alcohol abuse, we feel that the most important use of the blood alcohol test is its utility as a screening tool to initiate the process of Intervention and treatment. A markedly elevated blood alcohol level serves as objective information with which to confront patients who deny excessive alcohol consumption. It also may identify patients with chronic alcohol abuse by indicating tolerance in patients with very high levels who otherwise appear sober.

Administer Screening Questionnaires

Although the prevalence of alcoholism in the trauma center population is high, not all trauma victims with diagnosable alcohol problems will be intoxicated at the time of injury. Therefore, in the trauma patient population, where there is a 40–50% incidence of alcohol-related injuries, initial screening with both a blood alcohol level and the Short form of the Michigan Alcoholism Screening Test (SMAST) (Selzer, Vinkor, & Van Rooijen, 1975) should be viewed as a routine part of care.

At Harborview Medical Center, Jurkovich, et al. (1992) administered the SMAST to 2,823 trauma victims. The SMAST was considered positive if two or more questions were answered affirmatively. The majority of patients (57.4%) scored two or more positive responses on the SMAST, with higher SMAST scores being associated with higher blood alcohol levels. Approximately 25% of patients with no detectable blood alcohol on admission tested positive on the SMAST. Among patients who tested positive for any amount of blood alcohol, 75.6% tested positive on the SMAST.

A high degree of concordance was found when the SMAST was administered to both the patient and the patient's surrogate (usually spouse). This may be a potential advantage in the trauma center, where the patient initially may be unable to take the SMAST because of the residual effects of anesthesia, head injury, or medications. Thus, by obtaining the SMAST about the patient from a relative or other knowledgable informant, the need for further evaluation and possible treatment can be anticipated earlier than would otherwise be possible.

The SMAST has been widely used as a screening tool in the areas of alcoholism and drug abuse treatment, psychiatry, and primary care medicine. Morse (1987) found that the SMAST identified about 90% of known problem drinkers, compared to about 30–50% for such laboratory assays as the GGT (gamma glutamyl transpeptidase) or MCV (mean corpuscular volume). A small but appreciable level of false negatives is a limitation of a simple test such as the SMAST, but missing a few cases may be a small price to pay for an easily administered test that stands up well against other available tests, particularly when utilized in a busy trauma center environment.

A variety of other screening tests in addition to the SMAST are available. Each institution may wish to determine the test that works best in their particular clinical environment. A few of these tests are described below.

The CAGE test (Mayfield, McLeod, & Hall, 1974) is a simple four-question screening tool with its name derived from key words from each of the four questions: Have you ever tried to *Cut down* on your drinking? Are you *Annoyed* when people complain about your drinking? Do you ever feel *Guilty* about your drinking? Do you ever drink *Eye-openers?* The brevity of the CAGE test is a potential advantage. It also does not require the use of a questionnaire. Staff can be trained easily to incorporate these four questions into an admission history or interview.

Personnel may not be always available to administer a screening test, particularly on weekends, and trauma patients admitted for observation may have only a brief hospital stay. Self-administered tests are therefore an option worth considering. In a study performed at the Mayo Clinic, the Self-Administered Alcoholism Screening Test (SAAST) was found to have a 95% sensitivity and 96% specificity (Morse, 1987). An additional advantage of the SAAST when administered to a surrogate is a 90% agreement with the results obtained from the patient. A potential drawback of self-administered tests is the need on the part of the staff to be sensitive to the problem of illiteracy in the alcohol-abusing trauma patient population.

Establish the Diagnosis

The purpose of screening is to alert the physician that a potential problem exists. Patients who test positive on their screening test simply may be intoxicated, or they may be alcoholics or alcohol abusers. A full diagnostic assessment is needed to determine if an alcohol problem requiring treatment is present, and if so, to determine the optimal treatment referral. It is important to provide an accurate assessment, as the decision of whether or not to intervene will be based upon it.

An in-depth, face-to-face interview for each patient by a certified psychiatrist or counselor trained in diagnosing alcohol problems would be ideal. Face-to-face interviews allow for probing of information in detail, ensure that the patient understands the questions being asked, and encourage the establishment of rapport. However, time, financial, and personnel constraints may make face-to-face interviews of every possible substance-abusing trauma patient impossible.

An alternative (Lettieri, Sayers, & Nelson, 1985) is to train nurse practitioners or social workers in the use of one of the many available structured interview tools. For example, a variety of personnel have been trained to reliably administer the Addiction Severity Index questionnaire (Fureman, Parikh, Bragg, & McLellan, 1990). The potential advantages of a structured interview are that data can be collected by people other than highly trained professionals, the interviewer may paraphrase the questions being asked until the patient understands them, and a supportive interviewer can help establish rapport with the patient.

Questionnaires in the self-report style have been developed to provide a comprehensive assessment of alcohol problems. Those with proven validity and reliability include the Severity of Alcohol Dependence Questionnaire (Stockwell, Murphy & Hodgson, 1983) and the Alcohol Dependence Scale (Skinner & Allen, 1982). There are valid concerns with the use of self-reporting as a sole means of diagnosis. These include "too much sensitivity," with the inadvertent inclusion of nonalcoholics into the Intervention process, and the fact that some patients will be missed due to intentional misrepresentations by the patient.

In our experience, however, there is a difference between attempting to diagnose the alcoholic patient who is blending in with the general population (case-finding) and diagnosing alcohol problems in patients drinking at levels that result in trauma center admission. As a result of the injury, family members often begin to see the patient's alcohol use as a life and death issue and overwhelmingly corroborate data obtained by the screening process. The frequent concomitance of legal charges, employment problems resulting from the accident, and the physical injuries themselves can provide objective evidence to the health-care team and the family that the patient is drinking at problematic, if not dangerous, levels.

Guidelines for Dealing with Family Members

Determine When Family Intervention Is Necessary

Occasionally, trauma patients realize that they are risking their health, career, marriage and family life, and so forth, and this is sufficient incentive for them to seek and ask for help. Such patients will respond positively to suggestions from their health-care providers regarding participation in alcoholism treatment. In most cases, this does not happen. Family-focused Intervention is designed for trauma patients who do not desire treatment, and who believe that either they do not have an alcohol problem, or that they could quit any time on their own.

Studies of recovering alcoholics have revealed that crises are the most common events enabling alcoholics to see through their denial and seek treatment. This knowledge has led to the use of crises to weaken denial and lead to acceptance of treatment. To the alcoholic, the prospect of treatment creates greater pain and anxiety than does the pain of alcoholism itself. However, the pain of alcoholism is greatly increased when the patient is suffering from the acute physical, psychological, and emotional pain associated with an alcohol-related injury. This moment can be seized and utilized to induce the patient to accept help. Families that previously were too frightened and too confused to act may also be so affected by the circumstances of the accident that they are motivated for the first time to confront alcoholism on behalf of their family member.

Interact with Families in the Trauma Center

If the screening and diagnostic procedures indicate that the patient might benefit from treatment, the patient's closest family members are approached. They are asked to convene a meeting to involve all family members and are told that information vital to the patient's well-being will be discussed. The seriousness of the situation is conveyed by the physician's expectation that all involved members of the family will come to this meeting, despite personal inconvenience. The purpose of the meeting is to inform the family that the patient has signs of alcoholism or alcohol abuse, and that professional treatment is recommended.

We have taken the approach that notifying individual family members of the diagnosis and need for treatment should not be performed prior to this meeting. We found that discussing this issue with individual family members beforehand usually resulted in private family discussions regarding alcoholism. Frequently a family member, often one who does not live with the patient, will convince the others that the patient does not have an alcohol problem because they are employed, only drink on weekends, drink only beer, and so forth. In addition, such families often have other members with alcohol problems, and there is an inability on the part of the family to have an honest discussion. These factors may cause the family to notify the health-care team that they do not wish to discuss the alcohol issue any further.

By bringing all significant family members together when the alcohol problem is first discussed, the health-care team is able to provide the entire family with the results of screening tests and medical and historical evidence to support the diagnosis. Questions can be asked out in the open, and those who have misconceptions about alcoholism can be responded to at that time. At this meeting, family members being most affected by the alcoholism will have a chance to be heard without intimidation by other, more dominant family members.

We feel that discussing the patient's alcoholism with the family does not require previous release from the patient. An injury requiring hospitalization provides sufficient medical justification to permit thorough history taking and documentation of underlying illnesses. The injury itself frequently makes the patient unable to provide such information, and family members of trauma patients are a traditional source of needed medical background information. Active attempts at locating next of kin after an injury is standard practice, and the accident, surrounding circumstances, and the patient's condition are routinely discussed with family members whether or not alcohol was a factor in the accident.

An injury requiring admission to a trauma center may indicate alcoholism or alcohol abuse at a stage that can be considered a serious health risk. Diagnosis and recommendations regarding synchronous, life-threatening medical conditions found to be present in a trauma patient are not normally withheld from family members. This information, however, should be confined to immediate family members and should not be available to employers, legal personnel, insurance companies, or other parties. Anonymity is a traditional aspect of treatment, and it is an important factor in inducing patients to accept therapy. Each hospital must, therefore, ensure strict confidentiality of alcohol and drug information in order to prevent future discrimination in employment, and insurance status.

Deal with Family Concerns

The most common question the family will have at this meeting is "How can you help someone who does not want to be helped?" The family is informed that because of denial, the patient is incapable of help himself or herself at this point. He or she either can't or won't go for help. In such cases, if the patient is to be helped, the helping process must take place outside of the patient. It must be initiated by concerned family members.

The family is told that they do not have to wait until the alcohol problem destroys its victim before obtaining professional help. They are told that they do not have to stand by helplessly, but can use the crisis of trauma to intervene. They must be convinced that if they wait for the patient to get help on his or her own, most likely it will never happen. They are told that the purpose of the Intervention is to enable them to show the patient how much they care, how much they hurt, and what they see this disease is doing to the patient and the family. It is a way for the family to say that their love for the patient will not allow them to stand by and do nothing.

Family members are often emotionally or psychologically disabled as a result of living in an alcoholic household. For many, this will be the first time that the alcoholism has been brought out into the open and discussed with a health-care professional. When attempting to address the trauma victim's alcohol problem, families also can be brought into the treatment process and provided with counseling, or brought into contact with appropriate support groups. The opportunity to include the patient's family in the therapeutic process should not be missed. It is also important, however, to realize that the family is already under a significant emotional burden as a result of the accident. An attempt should be made to convince them that alcoholism is a disease, not a disgrace, and that their loved one is a sick person trying to get well, not a bad person trying to be good.

The Intervention

Prepare the Family to Intervene

If the family has agreed with the diagnosis and the need for intervention and treatment, a meeting between the interventionist and the family is arranged. The purpose of this meeting is to provide the family with relevant information and knowledge essential to motivate them to intervene successfully and to provide them with the necessary skills to accomplish this goal.

The family must be taught that the Intervention is not a humiliating event, but rather it is a loving, caring, nonjudgmental process designed to penetrate denial and enable the alcoholic to accept professional help. The family members may be scared, frightened, or concerned because they do not expect the Intervention to work. The interventionist must be prepared to address these fears and to convince the family that the person they are concerned about needs them to care enough to intervene.

The interventionist helps the family to select and choose the strongest possible Intervention team by asking for a list of possible participants, which may include friends, neighbors, coworkers, and others. It is important to respect the patient's right to privacy by not considering the Intervention as a means to expose the patient's drinking problem. Participation should be limited to people who have significant impact on and meaning in the patient's life. Such people already will be well aware of the patient's drinking problem.

Once the team is selected they are provided with information about addiction, denial, the defense mechanisms of alcoholics, and the purpose of intervening. The educational process may include written as well as video material. Each participant is given a worksheet to help him or her recall and develop a list of several specific instances during which he or she witnessed the patient's loss of control over alcohol. This list should describe specific drinking behaviors that caused pain, hurt, embarrassment, or distress.

A day or two before hospital discharge a meeting of the participants is reconvened. Each individual brings his or her list and reads aloud the observations. To initiate a caring rather than a blaming atmosphere the interventionist reflects the family's concern about the patient's drinking. At this meeting the family must learn how to state in a positive and affirming way how much they care about the patient, and how much they are personally affected by the damage and pain caused by the alcoholism. The interventionist must convince the family not to look upon the Intervention as an unpleasant duty or obligation that has been thrust upon them, but as a way of letting the patient know how much they care and their concern about the damage they see resulting from the alcoholism.

At this meeting, with input from the counselor, the family also will decide upon an appropriate treatment plan for the patient's alcoholism. The Intervention team then proceeds with a dress rehearsal in which they become fully prepared. Does each one know where he or she will be sitting? Are there enough seats for everyone? Does everyone know the order of presentation? There is no eating, drinking, smoking, or joking allowed during the Intervention.

Conduct the Intervention

On the day of hospital discharge, the patient is brought to a meeting room where the intervention takes place. The patient is advised that the participants have gathered together for his or her welfare, and that they have information crucial to his or her well-being. During the Intervention each participant in turn speaks to the patient in a concerned, supportive, nonaccusatory manner. They describe in detail the episode during which they witnessed the alcoholic's loss of control over alcohol, sharing as effectively as they can how they felt during that episode, and how it affected those involved.

Each family member must speak with conviction and be sincere, affirming, and determined to reveal his or her feelings. If the family cannot relate to the patient on an emotional level, the alcoholic is unlikely to go into treatment. The emotions that are most likely to reach the alcoholic are love and pain. In our experience, a patient is likely to ignore intellectual persuasion, but will agree to enter treatment only because he or she cannot stand to see the family so hurt as a result of his or her disease.

The role of the interventionist is to motivate, encourage, and unite the family group into a solid, united force, committed to be the most effective they can be at convincing the alcoholic that, today, they will settle for nothing less than professional help. After each participant has spoken, the group urges the alcoholic to accept treatment. If the patient accepts, they should be transferred directly from the trauma center to a treatment facility capable of providing appropriate therapy. It is important to seize this moment. Possible objections to immediate transfer must be anticipated and dealt with beforehand. This may mean anything from delaying court appearances to taking care of pets, and so forth.

CASE APPLICATION

Admission to the Trauma Center and Screening for Alcoholism

A.B. was admitted to the trauma center with multiple facial lacerations, rib fractures, and lung contusions after a single-car motor vehicle accident. Empty beer cans were found in the car. In the emergency room a strong odor of alcohol was noted on his breath, and he was combative, threatening, and abusive to the emergency room staff. His blood alcohol level on admission was 208 mg%.

On questioning, he was found to be 42-years-old, married, and employed as a successful photographer. His injuries were serious but not life-threatening. The following morning, when told of his blood alcohol level and emergency room behavior, he accused the hospital staff of jeopardizing his career. He was told that his situation was a result of his own behavior, but he remained unconvinced. CAGE questions were asked, and the patient did admit to previous attempts at cutting down on his drinking, that his drinking angered his wife, and that he occasionally felt guilty about certain embarrassing consequences of his drinking, such as the present accident. When a formal evaluation and possible treatment was suggested, he stated that admission to an alcohol treatment center would be too disruptive of his work schedule.

Initial Meeting with Patient's Family

His immediate family included a wife, two daughters, a son, and a son-in-law. At a family meeting the patient's trauma physician described the patient's condition as serious and stated that based upon his blood tests, his behavior, and the circumstances of the accident, alcohol appeared to be involved. The family exchanged knowing glances.

They were told that although he would recover from his injuries, there were serious concerns about his overall health. Although the patient refused to meet with an alcoholism counselor for formal evaluation, discussion with the family confirmed a long-standing history of problematic drinking that was associated with significant marital problems, as well as increasing difficulties at work. The physician stated that help was available, but that the psychological state of the patient was such that the he might not be capable of accepting such help right now without the support and concern of his family. An Intervention was recommended, and the family agreed.

Preparation of the Family for the Intervention

The family was provided with detailed information about alcoholism and about how denial often prevents patients from receiving help until irrevocable damage to health, relationships, and career has occurred. At follow-up sessions with the interventionist, plans were solidified and the Intervention rehearsed.

The Family Intervention Meeting

On the day of hospital discharge the patient was brought into a private conference room on the hospital ward. His family, his physician, his assigned nurse, and the interventionist were present. He was told by his physician that everyone had gathered to talk to him because they cared and were concerned about what was happening to him.

His wife said:

> "I love you more today than you can imagine. I feel that because of alcohol you are not the person I knew. I feel that you have a serious drinking problem. We are here to try to help you to realize that there is a problem, and that together we can deal with it. I am afraid of the person that you become when you are drinking. I would give anything I have for us to regain our friendship. When the police came to the house and told me you had been in an accident, I cried so hard. This last week has been the worst time of my life. The fear and loneliness were like a nightmare. I believe that with professional help, and with the support of your family and friends, you can get well."

His son stated:

> "Dad, I want to' say that I love you and that I really care about you. As I grew up you were always my best friend. But in the last few years that all seems so different. I know that all of the terrible things that are happening to you would not be happening except for your drinking. It hurts me to see you in that kind of shape. Your drinking problem is killing you on the inside. I only wish you knew how much I respect you. I am scared to death about being here today, but it would be so disrespectful not to be here, and not to say anything about this. This may sound hard to you, but I would be so happy if you would please get professional help today for your drinking problem."

From his son-in-law, he heard:

> "You have accepted me into your family. I love you, and I know you have a serious drinking problem. It hurts me to see such a loving and caring man end up being drunk. It hurts me to see this happening to the only father I have to look up to, and the only grandfather my children have. I know that what happened is not you, but is what this disease is doing to you. Please get professional help today for your drinking problem."

His older daughter added:

> "Dad, you know I love you. In the past I have talked to you about
> your drinking, and I sounded like a lecturer. But now I have to say
> these words straight from the heart. You always seemed so in con-
> trol, you knew your priorities, and were a wonderful father. I felt
> that security would never leave me, and I felt so safe. But as your
> drinking behavior changed it pained me so much to witness it. Now,
> I have to say that you do have a drinking problem. Please know
> that I know you are in pain and that I love you. Dad, it doesn't have
> to be. Please get professional help today for your drinking problem."

And his younger daughter finished up by saying:

> "Daddy, I love you. I know that you have a drinking problem and
> it is taking you a little bit, day by day. Only someone who didn't
> love you could sit back and watch you suffer and watch you dying.
> I want you back in my life. I have suffered deep sorrow at the loss
> of my dad to alcohol. Daddy, please get professional help for your
> drinking problem today."

After each family member had spoken, the physician reinforced
the opinion of the family members and counseled the patient to accept treatment. During the Intervention the patient's defensive posture
changed to one of acceptance. He agreed to accept treatment and was
transferred directly from the trauma center to an inpatient alcoholism
treatment facility.

RESEARCH SUMMARY

At the University of Texas Health Science Center we tested the application of the above approach in the trauma-center setting (Gentilello et
al., 1988). The goal was to induce injured alcoholic patients to accept
transfer to an alcoholism treatment facility during the rehabilitative
phase of their alcohol-related injuries.

All patients admitted to the trauma service had a blood alcohol
level drawn in the emergency department. Patients found to have a blood
alcohol level of 100 mg% or greater were identified and assessed for
alcohol problems. Each patient's physician conferred with his or her
family, and a drinking history was obtained. Diagnostic instruments were
used if the diagnosis could not be clearly established with face-to-face

patient questioning or with family corroboration. If a diagnosis of alcoholism was established and the patient was not receptive to treatment, a member of the team met with the family and provided information about alcoholism. Written and video materials were utilized, and Intervention and treatment were recommended.

If the family agreed, a meeting with a professional alcoholism counselor was arranged. When the patient was ready for hospital discharge the family Intervention occurred. If the patient agreed to treatment, he or she was transferred directly from the trauma service into an inpatient alcoholism treatment facility.

We identified 19 consecutive, nonselected patients with a blood alcohol level of greater than 100 mg% who were admitted following alcohol-related trauma. All 19 patients met DSM III-R criteria for alcoholism, and 17 families agreed to intervene. All of the 17 Interventions resulted in immediate transfer of the patient into a treatment facility (medically uninsured patients had the costs of treatment supplied to them).

No attempt at follow-up was made, as the purpose of this pilot study was to develop a model for screening, diagnosis, and family Intervention for alcoholism in the trauma center setting. This study demonstrated that injured patients can be motivated readily to accept intensive treatment for underlying alcohol problems, and that family-focused Interventions are feasible within a trauma center setting.

CONCLUSIONS

Family-focused Intervention performed after injury and during trauma center admission is an effective means of instituting treatment for alcoholics. Crises are the most common events that enable alcoholics to see through denial and to accept help. Trauma centers, as gatekeepers to crises, are uniquely situated to carry out a program of Intervention through close interaction with alcoholism treatment facilities.

Although a trauma center is a unusual setting for an Intervention, we believe there is a significant benefit to be achieved from the incorporation of this technique into the care of injured patients. Trauma centers should have an individual on staff who is capable of assessing patients for alcohol problems, and who can help families initiate and carry out the Intervention process. Such care addresses alcohol problems in patients who are drinking at dangerous levels, reduces the risk of future life-threatening injuries in such patients, and provides a unique opportunity to creatively use a crisis to effect therapy.

REFERENCES

Anda, R. F., Williamson, D. F., & Remington, P. L. (1988). Alcohol and fatal injuries among U.S. Adults. *Journal of the American Medical Association, 260,* 2529–2561.

Baker, S. P. (1987). Injuries: The neglected epidemic. *Journal of Trauma, 27,* 343–348.

Baker, S. P., O'Neill, B., & Karpf, R. S. (1984). *Injury fact book.* Lexington, MA: Lexington Books.

Cales, R. H. (1984). Trauma mortality in Orange County: The effect of implementation of a regional trauma system. *Annal of Emergency Medicine, 13,* 15–24.

Center for Disease Control. (1990). Alcohol-related mortality and years of potential life lost: United States. *Morbidity and Mortality World Report, 39,* 173–178.

Chang, G. & Astrachan, B. (1988). The emergency department surveillance of alcohol intoxication after motor vehicle accidents. *Journal of the American Medical Association, 260,* 2533–2536.

Fureman, B., Parikh, G., Bragg, A., & McLellan, A. T. (1990). *Addiction Severity Index* (5th ed.). Philadelphia: University of Pennsylvania/Veterans Administration Center for Studies of Addiction.

Gentilello, L. M., Duggan, P., Drummond, D., Tonneson, A., Degnel, S. E., Fisher, R. P., & Reed, R. L., II. (1988). Major injury as a unique opportunity to initiate treatment in the alcoholic. *American Journal of Surgery, 156,* 558–561.

Haberman, P. W., & Natarajan, G. (1986). Trends in alcoholism and narcotics abuse from medical examiner data. *Journal of Studies on Alcohol, 47,* 316–321.

Institute of Medicine, Committee on Trauma Research, Committee of Life Sciences, National Research Council. (1985). *Injury in America: A continuing public health problem.* Washington, DC: National Academy Press.

Israel, Y. (1987). Trauma as a marker of alcoholsm and a guide to diagnosis. In *Screening for alcoholism in primary care settings* (pp. 29–30). Rockville, MD: National Institute of Alcohol Abuse and Alcoholism.

Johnson, V. E. (1986). *Intervention: How to help someone who doesn't want help.* Minneapolis, MN: Johnson Institute Books.

Jurkovich, G. J., Rivara, F. P., Gurney, J. (1992). Effects of alcohol intoxication on the initial assessment of trauma patients. *Annal of Emergency Medicine, 21,* 704–708.

Lettieri, D. J., Sayers, M. A., & Nelson, J. E. (1985). *Summaries of alcoholism treatment asessment research* (DHHS Publication No. ADM 85–1379). Washington, DC: U.S. Government Printing Office.

Lowenfels, A., & Miller, T. (1984). Alcohol and trauma. *Annals of Emergency Medicine, 13,* 1045–1060.

Maull, K. I., Kinning, L. S., & Hickman, J. K. (1984). Culpability and accountability of hospitalized injured alcohol-impaired drivers. *Journal of the American Medical Association, 252,* 1880–1883.

Mayfield, D., McLeod, G., & Hall, P. (1974). The CAGE questionnaire: Validation of a new alcoholism screening instrument. *Amerian Journal of Psychiatry, 131,* 1121–1123.

Morse, R. (1987). The Short Michigan Alcoholism Screening Test: Update and comparison with other techniques. In *Screening for alcoholism in primary care settings* (pp. 7–10). Rockville, MD: National Institute of Alcoholism and Alcohol Abuse.

National Academy of Sciences of the National Research Council, Committee on Trauma and Committee on Shock. (1966). *Accidental death and disability: The neglected disease of modern society.* (Public Health Service Publication 1071-A-13). Washington, DC: National Academy Press.

National Academy of Sciences (1985). *Injury in America: A continuing public health problem.* Committee on Trauma Research, National Research Council and the Institute of Medicine. Washington, DC: National Academy Press.

Noble, E. P. (1978). *Third special report to the U.S. Congress on alcohol and health.* Washington, DC: Secretary of Health, Education and Welfare.

Oppenheim, W. L. (1977). The battered alcoholic syndrome. *Journal of Trauma, 17,* 850–856.

Reed, R. L., II, Miller-Crotchett, P., & Fischer, R. P. (1991). *Economic consideration of failing to treat alcohol abuse in trauma patients.* Paper presented at the meeting of the American Trauma Association, Washington, DC.

Rice, D. P., MacKenzie, E. J., & Jones, A. S. (1989). *Cost of injury in the United States: Report to congress.* San Francisco, CA: Institute for Health and Aging, U. of California and Injury Prevention Center, and the Johns Hopkins University.

Selzer, M. L., Vinkor, A., & Van Rooijen, L. (1975). A self-administered Short Michigan Alcoholism Screening Test (SMAST). *Journal of Studies on Alcohol, 36,* 117–126.

Simel, D. L., & Feussner, J. R. (1989). Does determining serum alcohol concentrations in emergency department patients influence physicians civil suit liability? *Archive of Internal Medicine, 149,* 1016–1018.

Sims, D. W., Bivins, B. A., Obeid, F. N., Horst, H. M., Sorenson, V. J., & Fath, J. J. (1989). Urban trauma: A chronic recurrent disease. *Journal of Trauma, 29,* 940–947.

Skinner, H. A., & Allen, B., (1982). Alcohol dependence syndrome: Measurement and validation. *Journal of Abnormal Psychology, 91,* 199–200.

Soderstrom, C. A., & Cowley, R. A. (1987). A national alcohol and trauma center survey: Missed opportunities, failures of responsibility. *Archives of Surgery, 122,* 1067–1071.

Stockwell, T., Murphy, D., & Hodgson, R. (1983). The Severity of Alcohol Dependence Questionnaire: Its use, reliability and validity. *British Journal of Addictions, 78,* 145–155

Trunkey, D. (1982). The value of trauma centers. *Bulletin of the American College of Surgeons, 67,* 5–7.

U.S. Department of Transportation. (1968). *Alcohol and Highway Safety* (Rep. to Congress). Washington, DC.

Waller, J. R. (1988). Editorial. *Journal of the American Medical Association, 260,* 2561–2562.

Waller, J. A. (1990). Management issues for trauma patients with alcohol. *Journal of Trauma, 30,* 1548–1553.

Whitfield, R. A., Zador, P., & Fife, D. (1985). Projected mortality from injuries. *Accident Analysis, 17,* 367–71.

Zuska, J. J., Trunkey, D. D., & Hering, A. C. (1983). Treating the trauma victim; alcohol abuse, road trauma, and the role of medical professionals. *Bulletin of the American College of Surgeons, 68,* 22–124.

Chapter 16

Conclusions and Future Directions in Practice and Research on Marital and Family Therapy in Alcoholism Treatment

Timothy J. O'Farrell

This final chapter has two goals. First, we will review each of the earlier sections of the book. These concluding comments will consider the clinical methods and research outcomes described by the authors in the preceding chapters. Second, given the current state of marital and family therapy in alcoholism treatment revealed in the preceding chapters, this final chapter will end with a consideration of future directions that go beyond the good beginnings presented here.

CONCLUDING COMMENTS

The following comments will consider, for each section of the book, the similarities and differences among the methods in each chapter and the extent of research support currently available for each of the methods.

Part I: Initiating Change and Helping the Family when the Alcoholic is Unwilling to Seek Help

The chapters in Part I describe treatment methods that address the common clinical problem posed by the spouse or other family member who contacts a therapist or treatment program seeking advice on how to deal with an alcoholic who is unmotivated for treatment. Part I describes four methods. Three of these methods try to motivate the alcoholic to change and also try to help family members to cope better. The fourth method provides group therapy to help alcoholics' wives cope with their emotional distress and to concentrate on their own motivations for change rather than trying to motivate the alcoholic to change. This latter approach borrows many concepts from Al-Anon, by far the most widely used source of support for family members troubled by a loved one's alcoholislm. Al-Anon advocates that family members detach themselves from the alcoholic's drinking in a loving way, accept that they are powerless to control the alcoholic, and seek support from other members of the Al-Anon program (Al-Anon Family Groups, 1981). Thus the major difference among the methods presented in Part I is whether they advocate that family members actively intervene to attempt to motivate the alcoholic to change or conversely that family members should detach and focus on themselves. The major similarity among the aproaches is the common attempt to help the family reduce emotional distress and improve coping. Other similarities and differences among these approaches are considered next.

Similarities and Differences Among Methods Described in Part I

Three Methods to Motivate Change in the Alcoholic

Unilateral Family Therapy (UFT) (Chapter 1), Community Reinforcement Training (CRT) for Families (Chapter 2), and the Johnson Institute Intervention approach (Chapter 3) are each described in detail in Part I. These three methods to motivate change in the resistant alcoholic have a number of goals in common. These common goals include educating the spouse and family about alcoholism, reducing spouse and family emotional distress, decreasing spouse and family behavior that enables drinking, and, of course, facilitating abstinence and treatment entry by the alcoholic. The importance of these common goals as well as other aspects of the three methods vary from one approach to the other.

The type and importance of confrontation in motivating the alcoholic to seek help varies considerably for the three approaches. The Johnson Institute Intervention relies heavily on an "Intervention" session in which a counselor aids family members (and other members of the alcoholic's social network) in confronting the alcoholic about the negative effects of the drinking and requesting the alcoholic to enter treatment. A programmed confrontation by the spouse at home with the alcoholic is the last part of the extensive multifaceted UFT method; the confrontation is used when previous steps in this therapy have failed to change the alcoholic's drinking. The CRT approach does not use confrontation. Rather the spouse is taught to request that the alcoholic seek counseling at a time when the alcoholic is motivated to stop drinking (generally after a specific occasion when drinking has caused a serious problem).

These three approaches also differ with respect to certain other methods and goals. Both CRT and UFT provide methods to change the spouse's response to the alcoholic's drinking and to improve the marital relationship as a way to increase the influence potential of the spouse, whereas the Johnson Intervention approach does not include such methods. The goals and the time spent in the Johnson approach are somewhat more limited than in CRT and UFT. The Johnson approach focuses almost exclusively on preparing the family for and conducting the confrontation. Counselors averaged four to five 2-hour sessions with families in the study of the Johnson approach. Contrast this with an average of 7.2 sessions over a 2-month period for CRT and weekly UFT visits by the spouse for 6 months in the studies of these two methods. The number of family members or significant others involved in each method varies also. The Johnson approach targets multiple persons including employers, friends, and other relatives not living with the drinker in addition to immediate family members. As Liepman noted in Chapter 3, difficulty engaging these social networks can lead to premature termination of the Johnson method. Only one person, usually the spouse, is seen in the other approaches.

The approaches also differ in how they deal with cases in which domestic violence is a concern. UFT excludes such cases. The Johnson approach suggests caution with such cases but does not provide specific guidelines for dealing with violence. CRT, on the other hand, was developed with domestic violence in mind. CRT specifically teaches the spouse how to avoid violence. The risk of violence is reduced further because CRT does not use a confrontation to promote treatment entry.

The type of treatment the alcoholic enters is not specified by either UFT of the Johnson approach, whereas CRT is a prelude to a specific type of treatment based on the Community Reinforcement Approach (CRA). Thus, a counselor who plans to use CRT must learn and practice CRA. The CRT counselor also must be available when needed and be able to arrange a quick prescription for Antabuse.

Finally, the extent to which a specific conceptual or theoretical model underlies each of the approaches varies. CRT is clearest with its basis in a learning and behavioral approach. In fact, the behavioral analysis of the actions of alcoholics' family members provided by CRT (Chapter 2) is an important normalizing alternative to the potentially stigmatizing focus of disease model concepts such as "codependency."

UFT is somewhat eclectic because it uses some elements of a behavioral approach as well as the Johnson confrontation, and earlier social case-work approaches to wives of alcoholic (Cohen & Krause, 1971). Although the Johnson approach often is identified with a disease model approach to treatment, it is an essentially pragmatic method that does not necessarily require adherence to any specific ideology. In fact, the Johnson approach represented an attempt to go beyond some limitations of earlier disease model treatment notions that had encouraged family members to disengage, take care of themselves, and wait until the alcoholic "hit bottom" and sought help.

Group Therapy for Wives of Alcoholics

Dittrich's group program for wives of treatment resistant alcoholics (Chapter 4) is not designed to influence the alcoholic to change. The goals of this professionally led program are to educate the wife about alcoholism, to assist the wife to become less emotionally distressed by the alcoholism, and to help the wife consider her own options for change. Such a program would seem to be an extremely valuable resource for wives who are not ready or do not wish to try to force the alcoholic to change. Dittrich's program has all the benefits of Al-Anon plus the added opportunity to receive support from the group members and group leader in considering specific lifestyle choices she can make in response to the husband's alcoholism. It also is time limited and more focused than Al-Anon. As the case example and research presented by Dittrich illustrates, wives benefitted greatly from the program. Interestingly, nearly half of the husbands decided to enter treatment.

Extent of Research Support for the Methods Presented in Part I

Clearly, enough research has been done to show the promise of each of the methods presented in Part I. Nonetheless the studies generally were characterized by relatively small sample size, limited outcome measures, and other methodological problems. Further, the extent of research support for the different methods does vary somewhat.

UFT has been subjected to the most scrutiny and has the strongest support based on two studies with a total of 94 subjects. The first compared completers and dropouts from a demonstration project pilot study on UFT. The second study was a randomized clinical trial comparing UFT with a waiting-list control group. In the initial pilot study of 25 spouses, Thomas and colleagues (Thomas, Santa, Bronson, & Oyserman, 1987) randomly assigned 15 spouses of alcoholics to receive

either immediate or delayed UFT treatment and studied 10 other untreated nonrandom comparison cases who dropped out after little or
no treatment. Using cases with available outcome data, treated cases
after 4–6 months of UFT were compared with the untreated dropouts.
From 13 (of 15) treated cases with usable data, 8 drinkers (62%) had
entered treatment and/or reduced drinking by at least 53%, whereas
none of the 6 (10) untreated cases with available data had done so (p
= .02 by Fisher's Exact Test). Results also showed a decrease in spouses'
emotional distress and increases in marital satisfaction after UFT. In
a second UFT study of 69 spouses (Thomas, Yoshioka, Ager, & Adams,
1993), spouses were randomly assigned to either an immediate (N =
27) or delayed (N = 28) UFT treatment, and an additional nonrandom,
untreated comparison group consisted of 14 spouses whose alcohol-
abusing partners did not give the required consent for their spouses'
participation. Results showed reductions after UFT in certain spouse
behaviors including enabling, attempts to control the alcoholics' drinking, psychopathology and life distress, and improvements in marital adjustment and satisfaction. Significant changes in drink-related outcomes
were noted with treatment entry of the alcohol abuser being significantly higher immediately following spouse treatment than at comparable time periods for the delayed and untreated cases. At the final
follow-up assessment, which occurred 12 months after the immediate
treatment and 6 months after the delayed treatment, 73% of the alcohol abusers had become abstinent or "achieved clinically meaningful
reductions in their drinking" and 57% had entered treatment. Considering both change criteria, 79% had either entered treatment, reduced
their drinking, or both. Unfortunately, only preliminary reports
(Thomas et al., 1987, 1992) have appeared to date of the results of these
two UFT studies. These preliminary reports present positive outcomes
for UFT. A more complete report of the findings of these two studies
is needed.

CRT and Dittrich's group program for wives each have one randomized clinical study supporting their efficacy. In their study of CRT,
Sisson and Azrin (1986) randomly assigned 12 family members (usually wives) to either the CRT program described in Chapter 2 or to a traditional disease model program consisting of alcohol education,
individual supportive counseling, and referral to Al-Anon. Six of seven
alcoholics entered treatment after relatives had received CRT for a mean
of 58.2 days and an average of 7.2 sessions. During the 5 months after
their relative started CRT, the alcoholics showed more than a 50% reduction in average consumption prior to treatment entry and nearly total
abstinence in the 3 months after entering treatment. None of the five
alcoholics whose relatives received the traditional program (mean of

3.5 sessions) entered treatment and their drinking was not reduced during the 3 months for which outcome data were available. A number of comments can be made about the impressive results obtained in the Sisson and Azrin study. The small sample size argues strongly for the need to replicate the results. Further, proponents of a traditional disease model approach could argue that a number of factors may have biased the results in favor of CRT over the traditional program. The traditional program, compared to CRT, consisted of fewer sessions, had a shorter follow-up period so possible delayed effects could not be observed, was conducted by therapists who were less experienced in and less enthusiastic about the approach, and was evaluated using outcomes that may not be considered relevant to the traditional program that (like Al-Anon to which traditional program clients were referred) targeted decreased enabling and increased serenity and well-being of the family member, not the alcoholic's sobriety. Nonetheless in considering these criticisms, the intent of the Sisson and Azrin study must be kept in mind. This study sought to evaluate a new, behaviorally oriented method by comparing it to an existing method frequently used for the same purpose. Only larger, better-designed studies can determine whether the promise of CRT is sustained.

Dittrich and Trapold (1984) evaluated an 8-week program for wives of treatment-resistant alcoholics consisting of group therapy with a primarily disease-concept focus (as described in Chapter 4). Using measures of the wives' enabling behavior and well-being as the primary outcome variables, 23 wives were randomly assigned to the group therapy program ($n = 10$) or a waiting-list control condition ($n = 13$). Results indicated a significant reduction in enabling behaviors at the end of treatment for the experimental group relative to the waiting-list control; a similar reduction in enabling behaviors occurred for those on the waiting list once they had completed treatment. Reductions that occurred after treatment in enabling behavior, depression, and anxiety and increases in self-concept were maintained at the 2- and 4-month follow-up. Related outcomes during the 12 months after intake showed that 48% of the husbands had entered some form of treatment for their alcoholism and 39% of the wives had either separated from or divorced their husbands. Like the other methods in Part I, the findings from this relatively modest sample, presumably all treated and assessed by the first author for her master's thesis, require replication. Anecdotal information provided by Dittrich and Trapold indicated that, in addition to the group therapy, some of the wives used methods from other approaches including the Johnson Intervention and confrontations at home reminiscent of UFT; and many belonged to Al-Anon. Finally, the substantial proportion of alcoholics who entered treatment and of wives who left alcoholics who continued drinking point to the readiness for change apparent in this sample and the motivating conditions created by this group therapy program that explicitly focused wives on their options and choices for change.

Ironically, the counseling method described in Part I that has the least empirical support—the Johnson Institute Intervention approach described in Chapter 3—is by far the most widely used method in treatment centers in the United States. Research support for the Johnson approach comes from a demonstration project (Liepman, Nirenberg, & Begin, 1989) in which less than 30% (7 out of 24) of families given the Intervention training completed the confrontation. Of the seven alcoholics who were confronted by their families and social networks, six (86%) entered treatment as compared with 17% of those not confronted. The confronted alcoholics had longer periods of abstinence on average (11 months versus 3 months) than those not confronted. Unfortunately, given the self-selected rather than random assignment to confronted and nonconfronted groups, this study provides only very modest support for the efficacy of the Johnson Intervention. Perhaps the most striking finding was the low rate of performing the confrontation. This finding was unexpected and had not been reported in clinical materials on the Intervention method. Only further study can determine the extent of this problem and the efficacy of the Johnson approach.

Al-Anon, as already mentioned above, is by far the most widely used source of support for family members troubled by a loved one's alcoholism. Although Al-Anon is not considered in detail in the present volume, it is interesting to examine the research support available for this self-help method. A small number of correlational studies have shown that, among wives of alcoholics, Al-Anon membership is associated with (1) fewer ineffective ways (e.g., covering up for the alcoholic, nagging, trying to control the drinking) of coping with their husbands' drinking (Gorman & Rooney, 1979; Rychtarik, Carstensen, Alford, Schlundt, & Scott, 1988) and (2) better abstinence rates for alcoholics whose wives are receiving outpatient counseling (Wright & Scott, 1978). No controlled research is available concerning the effectiveness of Al-Anon.

Two related conclusions seem apparent after considering these various methods to assist the family when the alcoholic is unwilling to seek help. The most popular and most frequently used methods—the Johnson Intervention approach and Al-Anon—have little or nor research support for their effectiveness. Conversely, methods that have at least some research support for their effectiveness—UFT, CRT, and Dittrich's group therapy program—are used infrequently, if at all. The concern raised by this state of affairs will be considered further when future directions for research and practice are examined below.

Part II: Stabilizing Sobriety and Relationships when the Alcoholic Seeks Help

Most research and practice of marital and family therapy with alcoholics occurs after the alcoholic seeks help. The chapters in Part II describe methods for stabilizing sobriety and marital and family relationships when the alcoholic has sought help at a detoxification or treatment center, clinic, or practitioner's office. Part II chapters include methods for use in both inpatient and outpatient settings and methods drawn from a variety of theoretical approaches. Inpatient programs include an eclectic approach to family treatment in short-term detoxification (Chapter 5) and the Hazelden psychoeducational disease model program for family members of alcoholics in a residential rehab program (Chapter 6). Outpatient approaches include two behavioral marital (BMT) programs, an Antabuse Contract plus BMT couples group program (Chapter 7), and work combining BMT with alcohol-focused spouse involvement to change spouse behaviors that trigger or reinforce drinking by the alcoholic (Chapter 8). Two final chapters in this section from the Purdue University Family Therapy Program present outpatient methods drawn from a family systems approach for use with women alcoholics (Chapter 9) and with adolescent alcoholic abusers (Chapter 10). Concluding comments about the chapters in Part II will consider similarities and differences among these methods and the extent of research for each of these therapeutic programs.

Similarities and Differences Among the Methods Described in Part II

The Hazelden disease model program (Chapter 6) is quite different from the other methods described in Part II. The disease model approach sees the family member(s) separately from the alcoholic, tries to get the family member to give up any attempts to influence the alcoholic's drinking, does not focus directly or extensively on improving family relationships, and puts a primary emphasis on the family member's increased well-being. The other methods described in Part II see the alcoholic and family member(s) together to promote interactions that reduce abusive drinking, improve relationship cohesion and communication, help solve relationship problems, and increase the well-being of the individuals involved. Of course, the nature and extent of methods devoted to each of these goals varies considerably as described in Table 16.1.

TABLE 16.1. Comparison of Marital and Family Therapy Approaches Described in Part II for Use when the Alcoholic Has Sought Help

Treatment Approach	Setting and Intensity	Extent of methods devoted to three goals		
		Alcohol reduction focus[a]	Relationship improvement focus[b]	Individual well-being focus[c]
Family treatment in detox (Chapter 5)	Two 2-hour family meetings with and without alcoholic during detox stay	High	Low	Low
Hazelden disease model program (Chapter 6)	Family member(s) alone for 5-day residential program	Low	Low	High
BMT couples group program (Chapter 7)	Spouses together for 16 to 20 outpatient 1- to 2-hour sessions	High	High	Low
Alcohol-focused spouse involvement with BMT (Chapter 8)	Spouses together for 12 to 17 90-minute out-patient sessions	High	High	Low
Systemic couples therapy for women alcoholics (Chapter 9)	Spouses together for 12 1-hour out-patient sessions	High	Moderate	Low to Moderate
Family system therapy for adolescents (Chapter 10)	Parents and teen together with separate meetings as needed for 12 1-hour outpatient sessions	High	Moderate	Low to Moderate

[a]Focus is on methods to change behavior of family member(s) in order to promote reduced drinking by the alcoholic. Interactions between the alcoholic and family member(s) may be the target of the interventions but the interactions are directly related to drinking and not to broader nondrinking aspects of the relationship between the alcoholic and family.
[b]Focus is on interactions between the alcoholic and family member(s) that are *not* primarily related to drinking. Goals may include improved relationship cohesion, communication, and problem solving.
[c]Focus is on increasing the well-being of the family member and/or alcoholic directly through methods other than promoting abstinence or improving relationships.

Table 16.1 provides a comparison of the six approaches described in Part II in terms of treatment setting and intensity and of the extent to which each approach uses methods devoted to alcohol reduction by the alcoholic (abstinence), relationship improvement, and individual well-being. As already discussed, the Hazelden disease model residential program for family members of alcoholics is the only approach that puts a primary emphasis on increasing the well-being and serenity of the individual family members with no direct focus on the alcoholics' abstinence or relationship improvement. The other inpatient approach — the eclectic approach to family treatment during short-term detoxification — is limited to attempts to promote abstinence in the alcoholic by getting family member(s) to discontinue emotional and financial support unless the alcoholic pursues sobriety and continues alcoholism treatment. This short-term inpatient approach does not deal with other aspects of relationship or individual functioning.

The remaining behavioral and systems approaches, described in Chapters 7 through 10, have a number of commonalities. All consist of 12 to 20 outpatient sessions. All involve the alcoholic and spouse or other family members together in therapy with an emphasis on promoting abstinence by the alcoholic and improved relationship functioning. The two BMT approaches are quite similar in the methods used to increase caring and communication in the relationship. They also are similar in their attempt to decrease conflict about drinking and provide spouse reinforcement of abstinence, although the specific drinking-focused components differ (Antabuse Contract vs. individualized spouse behavior change to reduce triggering or reward drinking). The format of the two BMT approaches differs (conjoint sessions only vs. conjoint plus couples group sessions), however. A final similarity between the two BMT approaches is the relatively low emphasis on directly promoting the individual well-being of the alcoholic and family member except for indirect effects obtained through abstinence and relationship improvements.

The Purdue group's family systems approaches for women and adolescent alcohol abusers put the greatest emphasis on promoting abstinence through identifying and altering dysfunctional sequences of couple and family behavior that are associated with problematic alcohol use. Such sequences include specific behaviors (like those dealt with in a behavioral approach) by the spouse or family member(s) that may trigger or reward drinking as well as larger patterns of behavior. A moderate emphasis is placed on improving the relationship(s). It seems to be assumed that abstinence and changes in interpersonal behavior related to drinking will provide important gains in relationship functioning for many couples and families. The high emphasis on a structured, consistent set of interventions to promote cohesion and communications (such as those seen in BMT) are not evident in the system approaches presented here. Finally, individual issues are given some emphasis in the two systems approaches. Assertion-skills training is included for the adolescent. Analyzing and neutralizing family of origin themes and patterns as they affect the present context for each member of the couple is part of the couples therapy for women alcoholics.

Extent of Research Support for the Methods Presented in Part II

Most of the research examining marital and family therapy in alcoholism treatment has focused on alcoholics who have sought help in a treatment setting. Many other studies not included in the present volume have been covered in available reviews of the literature (McCrady, 1989b; O'Farrell & Cowles, 1989; Steinglass, 1976). The methods included in Part II of this book were chosen to provide current methods that represent the major existing types of approaches (i.e., 12-step disease model, family systems, and behavioral), have at least some research support, and are designed for use in a variety of settings. The extent of research support varies considerably for the methods presented in Part II.

Research support is strongest for BMT, based as it is on randomized clinical trials with state-of-the-art outcome measurement and long-term follow-up data for two somewhat different BMT approaches. In an initial study of the BMT couples group program described in Chapter 7, 36 married male alcoholics, who had recently begun individual outpatient alcoholism counseling, were randomly assigned to a no-marital-treatment control group or to 10 weekly sessions of either a BMT or an interactional couples therapy group. Results showed that the addition of BMT to individual alcoholism counseling produced better marital and drinking outcomes during and immediately after treatment than individual counseling alone or the addition of an equally credible, nonbehavioral interactional couples group. In the 2 years after treatment, the added BMT still produced better marital outcomes, especially fewer and shorter separations, than individual counseling alone but no longer produced better drinking outcomes (O'Farrell, Cutter, Choquette, Floyd, & Bayog, 1992; O'Farrell, Cutter, & Floyd, 1985). It was interesting that alcoholics who received the interactional couple group in addition to their individual counseling also had less time separated. A second study of this BMT couple group program has replicated the clinically and statistically significant improvement in marital and drinking outcomes observed in the initial study and has demonstrated that drinking outcomes at follow-up can be significantly enhanced by adding relapse prevention sessions after BMT (O'Farrell, Choquette, Cutter, Brown, & McCourt, in press).

In a study of the BMT program described in Chapter 8, treatment was provided to 53 alcoholics and their spouses who were randomly assigned to one of three outpatient spouse-involved treatments: (1) Minimal Spouse Involvement (MSI) in which only individual behavioral drinking interventions for the alcoholic were used and spouses were present as observers; (2) Alcohol-Focused Spouse Involvement (AFSI) that included the drinking interventions for the alcoholic in addition to interventions to change spouses' behaviors that trigger and reinforce the alcoholic's drinking, or (3) Alcohol-Focused Spouse Involvement plus Behavioral Marital Therapy (ABMT) to improve communication and enhance the marital relationship (McCrady et al., 1986; McCrady, Stout, Noel, Abrams, & Nelson, 1991). ABMT subjects had better drinking and marital outcomes during, and in the 18 momths after, treatment. ABMT subjects showed gradual improvement in number of days abstinent whereas those in the other two treatment conditions showed gradual deterioration in days abstinent over much of the 18-month follow-up period. Subjects assigned to the ABMT condition were less likely to experience marital separations and reported greater improvement in marital satisfaction and subjective well-being than did the other experimental groups.

Additional support has been found for BMT beyond that which has been summarized in Chapters 7 and 8 of the present volume. Three other randomized clinical trials not detailed here also reported positive outcomes for variations of BMT that were superior to various individual therapy approaches (Azrin, Sisson, Meyers, & Godley, 1982; Hedberg & Campbell, 1974; Stout, McCrady, Longabaugh, Noel, & Beattie, 1987). Earlier less controlled studies of BMT also reported positive outcomes (e.g., O'Farrell & Cutter, 1977). Finally, behavioral methods have been effective in maintenance and relapse prevention (Chapters 11 to 13 in Part III of this volume as discussed below).

A systems approach receives some support in preliminary results from the Purdue study with adolescents in which 151 alcohol-abusing adolescents were randomly assigned to family systems therapy, family drug education, or individual counseling as described in Chapter 10. Significant decreases in adolescents' alcohol and marijuana use occurred from before to after the family systems therapy, and a similar improvement was noted among those who received individual counseling. Although the potential impact of these initial results is weakened by reliance on posttreatment substance-use outcomes (without follow-up data or measures of family functioning) from only a subsample (i.e., about 60%) of study participants, presumably the full report of findings from this first randomized clinical trial of family systems therapy will contain additional needed information including statistical comparisons of outcomes among the different treatment conditions. The systemic couples therapy study for alcoholic women described in Chapter 9 and currently in progress at Purdue has the potential to provide much-needed outcome information on two topics about which data are scarce—a family systems approach to alcoholism treatment and couples therapy for women alcoholics. Given the impact that family systems concepts have had on alcoholism treatment professionals (e.g., Bowen, 1978; Steinglass, Bennett, Wolin, & Reiss, 1987), data on the effectiveness of systems approaches is long overdue.

The two approaches with the least strong research support are the eclectic approach to family treatment in detoxification and the psychoeducational disease model program for family members during inpatient rehab. Support for the detox program was based on an observed 57% increase in the rate of treatment continuation after detox by the alcoholic, when a comparison was made of the 6 years before and 2 years after the family program was introduced (Thomas, Weaver, Knight & Bale, 1986). Further research evaluation of the detox family treatment method would be important because its potential applicability is high and is likely to increase as concerns about health care costs reduce many inpatient treatment programs to detoxification only. Further, as increased use is made of outpatient (e.g., Alterman, Hayashida, & O'Brien, 1988) or home (Stockwell, Bolt, Milner, Pugh, & Young, 1990) detoxification, the potential for family treatment to use the crisis of detoxification as an opportunity to promote further recovery can only grow. The significance of a family-focused method to promote continued treatment after detoxification is clear because alcoholics with greater physical dependence (e.g., those who need detox to stop drinking) have better outcomes with longer and more intensive treatment (Orford & Edwards, 1977).

Finally, it must be noted that the most widely used method—a disease model psychoeducational approach—does not have strong research support. Laundergan and Williams are to be commended for their large-scale program evaluation and follow-up studies of the Hazelden Family Program that have examined more than 1,500 participants. These studies have shown that participants report satisfaction with various program elements, attitude changes targeted by the program, and Al-Anon involvement by about half (e.g., Laundergan & Williams, 1979). Given the influence of this type of approach on the field, stronger research designs are needed to provide support for its effectiveness. This is important because the widespread use of the psychoeducational disease model approach is not limited to residential programs accompanying inpatient rehab treatment; the approach is offered on an outpatient basis as the "family program" component for many treatment agencies.

Two related conclusions, reminiscent of concerns about Part I methods for families of resistant alcoholics, seem apparent after considering these various marital and family therapy methods to stabilize sobriety and relationships after the alcoholic has sought help. The most popular, most influential, and most frequently used methods—family systems and disease model approaches—have relatively weak research support for their effectiveness. Conversely, methods that have the strongest research support for their effectiveness—various BMT methods—enjoy little popularity and are used infrequently, if at all. This conclusion does not appear to be a function of the set of studies included in Part II of the present volume because similar conclusions were reached by other recent reviews of the broader literature (McCrady, 1989b; O'Farrell, 1992).

Part III: Maintaining Long-Term Recovery and Preventing Relapse

Given the high rate of relapse after treatment for alcoholism, Part III describes methods for maintaining long-term recovery and preventing relapse. Three chapters in this volume describe methods to maintain recovery after the alcoholic has completed an intensive treatment program: behavioral contracts between alcoholics and family members after an inpatient rehab program (Chapter 11), couples relapse prevention (RP) sessions after a BMT couples group program (Chapter 12), and couples therapy based on Marlatt and Gordon's (1985) model of the relapse process after an initial BMT program (Chapter 13).

Similarities and Differences
Among the Methods Described in Part III

All three approaches in Part III pursue the common goal of preventing or minimizing relapse albeit in somewhat different ways. Behavioral contracts between the alcoholic and family member are devoted to maintaining the alcoholic's attendance at scheduled aftercare sessions following an inpatient rehabilitation program. Given the better outcomes for longer treatment among more severe alcoholics (Orford & Edwards, 1977), these behavioral contracts serve a very important goal.

The goals and methods of the other two relapse prevention approaches are not limited to maintaining treatment attendance. The couples RP sessions after the BMT couples group program attempt to maintain behaviors targeted toward sobriety, relationship cohesion, and communication that were begun during BMT. These RP sessions also help the couple plan to prevent or minimize relapse and deal with life problems and challenges to sobriety.

Perhaps the most ambitious and comprehensive approach to relapse prevention is McCrady's attempt to translate Marlatt and Gordon's (1985) model of the maintenance and relapse process for use in a couples therapy format (as described in Chapter 13, this volume). According to this model, alcoholics are exposed to a variety of situations that can be considered "high risk" for drinking because of conditioned autonomic responses to environmental cues or because of a strong association between reinforcement for alcohol consumption and these environmental cues. In response to a high-risk situation, the alcoholic may engage in successful coping responses that enhance the alcoholic's self-efficacy for coping with future high-risk situations and reduce the probability of future relapses. Alternatively, positive expectancies about the reinforcing effects of alcohol and low self-efficacy for coping can lead to drinking. If the alcoholic drinks, the abstinence violation effect, an affective and a cognitive reaction to the person's recognition that he or she has violated a personal commitment to abstinence, sets the stage for further drinking.

Including the spouse or cohabiting partner in RP treatment is a logical extension of the RP model (McCrady, 1989a). At times alcoholics have difficulty recognizing high-risk situations, or they underestimate the potential impact of a situation. The high arousal that clients experience in high-risk situations (e.g., craving, anxiety) may also interfere with their ability to implement a coping response learned in a low-arousal situation. Thus, the spouse may help the drinker identify high-risk situations and may be able to prompt or cue coping responses if the drinker is having difficulty doing so. The development of a more balanced lifestyle to decrease the frequency with which high-risk situations occur and development of skills to avoid or manage relapses are also part of McCrady's program.

Extent of Research Support
for the Methods Presented in Part III

Relatively little research evidence is available currently to support the methods presented in Part III. Although some promising results are available to suggest that maintenance interventions improve outcomes when the interventions are being delivered, adequate data are not available on the utility of such methods to maintain gains once the intervention has been discontinued. This is due largely to the fact that research on marital and family therapy to maintain recovery and prevent relapse has only begun recently. Although a well-designed study is currently in progress, no data are available on McCrady's relapse prevention program. Preliminary outcome data are available from O'Farrell's RP after BMT couple troups. Only behavioral contracts to maintain aftercare participation have a completed randomized clinical trial that examined their effectiveness.

After completing a 4-week VA inpatient alcoholism program, 50 male alcoholics were randomly assigned to receive a calendar prompt and behavioral contract with a family member to reinforce aftercare attendance (as described in Chapter 11) or standard aftercare arrangements. During the 6 months after hospital discharge, while the contracts were in effect, results showed significant aftercare attendance differences between groups, with nearly twice as many contract subjects as standard control subjects attending aftercare sessions (Ossip-Klein, Van-Landingham, Prue, & Rychtarik, 1984). Of the 50 subjects, 36 (18 subjects per condition and 72% of total sample) were contacted 12 months after hospital discharge and the aftercare conditions were compared on outcomes during the year after discharge. Results showed that subjects in the contract condition, when compared with the standard aftercare control group, had significantly more months abstinent and were more likely to be employed and classified as a treatment success (abstinent or nonproblem drinking for at least 90% of the year) (Ahles, Schlundt, Prue, & Rychtarik, 1983). These results are impressive given the simple, cost-effective, and rather limited nature of the aftercare contract intervention and the clear pattern of results favoring this method. Confidence is much stronger in the results for the aftercare attendance findings based on the entire sample than it is for drinking and related outcome results based on an incomplete sample. Thus, only future research can determine whether aftercare contracts lead to better drinking outcomes once the contract is no longer in force.

Preliminary results from a study in progress provide some information on the effectiveness of the couples RP sessions after a BMT couple group program (as described in Chapter 12). In this study, 59 couples with an alcoholic husband, after participating weekly for 5 months in a BMT couples group program, were assigned randomly to receive or not receive 15 additional couples RP sessions over the next 12 months. Outcome measures were collected before and after BMT and at quarterly intervals for the 2½ years after BMT. Results during the 12 months after BMT showed that alcoholics who received RP after BMT had more days abstinent and fewer light and heavy drinking days, maintained their improved marriages better, and used behaviors targeted by BMT more than those who received BMT alone (O'Farrell, Choquette, Cutter, Brown, & McCourt, in press). These results are for the first year after BMT during the time when the RP sessions were conducted. An addi-

tional 18 months follow-up currently in progress will reveal whether superior RP results continue and whether the severity of patient's problems becomes a significant predictor of differential benefit from RP.

FUTURE DIRECTIONS

After considering the current state of research and practice of marital
and family therapy (MFT) in alcoholism treatment as revealed in the
chapters of the present volume and the wider literature, certain general conclusions can be drawn that set the stage for future directions in
this field. Research has produced promising data supporting MFT to
initiate change and help the family of the resistant alcoholic. Well-
established findings support the effectiveness of MFT when the alcoholic has sought help. Research on MFT to promote long-term recovery and prevent relapse has begun but has not yet produced many
results. The most popular and frequently used MFT methods have little research support for their effectiveness, whereas methods that have
research support are used infrequently in practice. There is a need for
improved research studies that encompass a wider variety of clinical
challenges. These conclusions provide the basis for recommending future directions that would (1) consolidate and apply the work of the
past three decades and (2) expand to include additional conceptualizations, target populations, outcome measures, treatment settings, and
treatment methods.

The following four recommendations are described below for the
future direction of research and practice of marital and family treatment of alcohol problems. First, a pressing need exists to narrow the
gap between practice and research. Second, studies of family treatment
for serious alcohol problems in alcoholism-specific settings need to be
broadened considerably. Third, marital and family approaches need
to be expanded beyond alcoholism-specific treatment settings; the
methods described in Chapters 14 and 15 of the present volume will
be considered as examples of the proposed expansion. A final recommendation for the future is that an identified area of practice and
research focused on "families and addictions" might be developed. Many
of these recommendations have been made elsewhere as well (O'Farrell, 1992).

Narrowing the Gap Between Research and Practice

Narrowing the gap between research and practice requires developing
a sound knowledge base of research-tested therapy methods, disseminat-

ing research-tested methods to clinicians to facilitate their application, and evaluating currently popular, but as yet untested, methods.

Replication of Results of Promising Approaches

Research is needed to provide larger-scale replications of family treatment methods that have shown promise in previous, controlled, comparative outcome studies. Many of the methods that deserve replication have been described in the concluding comments above and in the earlier chapters of the present volume.

UFT (Thomas & Santa, 1982, Thomas et al., 1987), Sisson and Azrin's program (1986), and the Johnson Institute Intervention (Johnson, 1986); Liepman et al., 1989) are all methods that initiate change in the alcoholic and that deserve further research. Dittrich's group program for wives of alcoholics also deserves careful replication. Such replication should include a requirement to develop procedures and methods to assess the severity of the alcohol abuser's drinking problem accurately through family member's reports and should include safeguards to prevent coercing the alcohol abuser into overly restrictive treatment goals and programs.

Two alcohol-focused methods that deserve replication and further study are disulfiram contracts (O'Farrell & Bayog, 1986) and Alcohol-Focused Spouse Involvement (McCrady et al., 1986). These methods, which have been used along with BMT to instigate positive activities and teach communication and conflict resolution skills, could be compared with each other and with an individual behavioral treatment. Finally, a replication study is needed of family-mediated aftercare attendance contracts that have improved aftercare attendance and recovery rates after inpatient alcoholism treatment (Ossip-Klein et al., 1984).

Further work needs to be done or completed to provide initial controlled outcome studies of Bale's eclectic approach to family treatment in detox and of behaviorally oriented RP therapy with couples.

As will be discussed further below, these recommended replication and other studies should attempt to identify patient characteristics that predict differential response to family treatment versus other methods. In this regard investigators could relax subject selection criteria to study the generality of family treatment effects.

Application of Research-Tested Methods to Clinical Practice

Concern has been expressed repeatedly in recent years that most alcohol treatment programs in the United States generally use treatment methods that lack empirical support and do not use research-tested methods, many of which are more cost effective than commonly used methods (Holder, Longabaugh, Miller, & Rubonis, 1991; Institute of Medicine, 1990; Miller & Hester, 1986). McCrady (1989b) has expressed these same concerns about family treatment methods:

> The discrepancies between the research and clinical practice communities are striking in terms of both the theoretical models that underlie the treatment, and in the settings for the delivery of family-involved treatment. The bulk of the controlled couples alcoholism treatment research has been conducted by behaviorally oriented clinicians. Fairly well-controlled studies with adequate measures, well-described treatments, and appropriate controls are most common in the behavioral literature. However, the family concepts most cited and the most common clinical practices derive from family disease models and family systems models. Clinicians working from these latter perspectives should be challenged to evaluate their work or it will be difficult for them to justify the continued use of untested practices when carefully evaluated and articulated procedures are available. Similarly, many residential alcoholism treatment programs have begun to offer short-term residential programs for family members. No data exist to support the efficacy of this practice over outpatient models of family involvement. In the current era of concern about spiraling health costs, there needs to be strong empirical support for these practices, and none exists at the present time. (p. 180)

Available knowledge about family treatment methods that are supported by research findings needs to be disseminated to and used by the practitioner community. The present volume, which provides practical guidelines for clinicians who wish to learn and use family treatment methods that show promise in outcome studies, is an initial effort in this direction.

Evaluation of Popular but Untested Methods

A pressing need exists to evaluate the popular and influential methods drawn from family disease and family systems models. These approaches have been discussed in the present volume. It is instructive to see how these approaches have been described by other authors.

McCrady (1989b) has described family disease models of treatment as follows:

> Contemporary disease model approaches describe alcoholism as a "family disease." This assumes that alcoholism is a physical, emotional/psychological, spiritual, and family disease (Cermak, 1986). Family members are seen as suffering from a disease, just as in the alcoholic. The disease of the family is labeled "codependence." Codependence is described as a

"recognizable pattern of personality traits, predictably found within most members of chemically dependent families" (Cermak, 1986, p. 1). . . . Other programs that view alcoholism as a family disease have drawn from family systems models as well as disease models (Laundergan & Williams, 1979) and stress that dysfunctional family roles, communications, and family equilibrium that is dependent on an alcoholic family member are important aspects of the family disease. Treatment programs derived from a family disease perspective usually provide separate treatment for family members, without the alcoholic present. Treatment usually includes education about alcoholism as a disease, education about dysfunctional family behaviors that characterize the family disease, referrals to Al-Anon or Adult Children of Alcoholics groups, and individual or group therapy to focus on core personal and interpersonal issues. Many inpatient alcoholism treatment programs offer short-term residential treatment programs for family members. (pp. 166–167)

Family systems perspectives have been described by McCrady (1989b), as follows:

Family systems perspectives on alcoholism have incorporated many of the core concepts of family systems theory into models of the alcoholic family system. Steinglass's (1979) model posits that all families obey the general laws of all systems including organization, homeostasis, circular causality of events and feedback. Alcoholism is seen as an organizing principle in alcoholic families, and the presence or absence of alcohol is seen as the most important variable defining interactional behavior in the family. . . . Systems-oriented treatment of alcoholic families utilizes a variety of techniques to affect interactions within the family. Therapy focuses on the interactional rather than the individual level, and discussion of the presenting problem (drinking) is directed to a collaborative, interactional approach rather than an individual approach. Attempts are made to redefine roles, realign alliances, and change patterns of communications within the family. Understanding changes in family interactional behavior when the alcoholic is drinking is crucial to the therapy. (pp. 167–168)

Finally, as McCrady (1989b) has noted, these approaches "have generated a great deal of enthusiasm in the alcoholism field . . . and have been incorporated into many treatment programs (e.g., Laundergan & Williams, 1979). However, the empirical base for evaluating the effectiveness of these approaches is lacking" (p. 176).

The coming years are likely to produce studies of the family disease and systems approaches. At least two studies in progress are evaluating a systems approach, one with women alcoholics (Chapter 9, this volume) and one comparing systems and behavioral methods with male alcoholics (T. Jacob, personal communication, December 15, 1992). Although no studies currently are examining a family disease approach, the time seems right for such studies. A major collaborative study in progress has 12-Step Facilitation Therapy for alcoholics as one of the treatment approaches being used (Nowinski, Baker, & Carroll, 1992). Professional facilitation was one method developed for studying AA; other methods also are being investigated. These methods could be applied to Al-Anon and related family disease approaches. Once studies have examined disease and systems models and presumably found some positive impact of these approaches, comparative outcome studies could be conducted. A most interesting study would compare individual therapy only for the alcoholic, separate and concurrent 12-step disease model treatment for the alcoholic and spouse, and conjoint behavioral (or systems) couples treatment. Outcomes would include drinking and relationship and individual adjustment, and predictions would include patient treatment matching hypotheses.

Broadening Research and Practice of Family Treatment in Alcoholism Specific Settings

Among serious alcoholics and their families receiving help in alcoholism-specific treatment settings, there is a need to broaden who is included in treatment and how treatment is evaluated.

Expansion of Focus on Children

In research on family treatment of alcohol problems, controlled studies have examined couples therapy or spouse-involved treatment that do not include children in the treatment or research protocol (McCrady, 1989b). One notable exception is the Purdue Brief Family therapy for adolescent alcohol abuse (Chapter 10, this volume). Practical models for involving children with their parents in whole family therapy need to be developed and studies are needed to evaluate this type of treatment (Orford, 1990). In addition, a pressing need exists for the development of brief, practical family assessment methods that can be implemented when the alcoholic seeks treatment to determine whether other members of the family, especially children, need individual assistance (O'Farrell, 1989). Such methods could be used in the many programs that will not be conducting whole family therapy.

Focus on a Wider Range of Alcoholics and the Subject Characteristics that Predict Response to Family Treatment

Most recent controlled outcome studies have targeted male alcoholics and excluded cases with more complicated problems. Future studies need to include female alcoholics, couples and families with more than one alcoholic member, alcoholics with comorbid drug abuse and other psychopathology, single-parent families, and lower-income, multi-problem families. Broadening study samples will include a wider range of alcoholics, some of whom have poorer prognoses in traditional alcoholism treatment; thus it will be important to determine if these subject characteristics also predict response to family treatment methods. It also will be important to conduct studies of patient treatment matching to determine which patients do better in individuals versus family treatment methods. For example, Longabaugh and colleagues (Longabaugh, Beattie, Noel, Stout, & Malloy, in press) found that alcoholics who were highly invested in their marital relationships and whose spouses supported abstinence did better if they received marital therapy rather than individual counseling. Conversely, alcoholics with low investment in their marriages or whose spouses did not strongly support abstinence did better with individual than marital therapy. Interestingly, many of the latter group were female alcoholics married to heavy-drinking or alcoholic husbands whose support for their wives' abstinence often was marginal (Longabaugh et al., in press). Patient treatment matching studies also should examine which patients and families do best with which type of family treatment. In this regard, Orford (1990) has distinguished between three forms of family treatment that differ in the degree of emphasis placed on three foci: "While some family treatments focus most on excessive drinking and its effects and control, others focus much more on family communication, conflict, and cohesion" (p. 139). A third focus referred to as "ecological" by Orford (1990) includes interventions that provide extensive assistance with day-to-day problems experienced by multiproblem families: "In addition to counseling on excessive drinking and family communication, they involved advice on financial, legal and welfare matters" (p. 139). Such ecological programs (e.g., Azrin, 1976; David & Hagwood, 1979; Patterson, 1965) could be potentially very helpful to some families whereas other families might not need this additional help.

Adherence to Recommended Methodological Standards and Expansion of Outcome Domains Assessed

As McCrady (1989b) and others (Emrick & Hanson, 1985; O'Farrell & Maisto, 1987; Sobell, Brochu, Sobell, Roy, & Stevens, 1987) have noted, the standards for alcoholism treatment research have become more rigorous over the past 15 years. Recommended standards include: (1) random assignment to treatments being compared; (2) well-defined treatments within each experimental condition; (3) detailed descriptions of the subjects in the study; (4) objective measures of treatment outcome with established reliability and validity; (5) outcome data collected by individuals other than treatment staff to minimize bias due to subjects wishing to please their therapists; (6) measurement of drinking behavior and functioning in other major areas of life functioning; (7) at least 12 months follow-up; (8) adequate rates of follow-up, preferably at least 90% of the sample, and careful consideration of possible bias due to missing data and subjects lost to follow-up; (9) reports from collateral informants to corroborate the alcoholic's self-reported drinking data; (10) clearly defined criteria of global outcome categories of treatment success, improvement, no change, and deterioration; and (11) appropriate statistical analyses. Furthermore, studies of family treatment should include the measure of outcome domains that go beyond the alcoholics' drinking and life adjustment. Given the broader goals of family treatment, outcome measures should include assessment of the physical, mental, and general life adjustment for spouses and children and the functioning of the family as a unit, as well as family subsystems (i.e., marital dyad, parenting, and parent–child relationships) (McCrady, 1989b; Moos, Finney, & Cronkite, 1990).

Expanding Family Approaches Beyond the Alcoholism Specialist Treatment Setting

Family involved approaches need to be applied and studied for alcohol problems of persons who seek help outside the specialist alcoholism treatment setting. These include family treatment of serious alcohol problems, family involvement in identification and brief intervention for mild to moderate alcohol problems, and family-focused prevention efforts.

Family Treatment for Serious Alcohol Problems in Nonspecialist Settings

Family treatment methods that have been shown to be effective in alcoholism specialist treatment settings should be applied and evaluated in nonspecialist settings that encounter many alcoholics. Chapter 15 of the present volume describes such an approach in which Gentillelo et al. (1988) used the well-known Johnson Institute Intervention method in a trauma setting with family members of alcoholics who had suffered a serious injury while intoxicated. Although no formal research design was used, the Gentillelo et al. program evaluation report provided descriptive information indicating that the family intervention was successful in getting recently injured alcoholics to enter an alcoholism treatment program. Clearly, controlled research studies of this approach are needed. Other settings that would seem obvious places to consider the use and evaluation of a family treatment approach would include education and counseling programs for drunken-driving offenders, especially second and multiple offenders, and liver clinics, with a high proportion of alcoholic cirrhosis patients.

Family Involvement in Identification and Brief Intervention with Mild to Moderate Alcohol Problems

A recent report form the Institute of Medicine (1990) recommends far-reaching, potentially revolutionary expansion and changes in the treatment of alcohol problems in the United States. These recommended changes are directly relevant to the expansion of family approaches. The report recommended considerable expansion of the definitions and conceptualization of alcohol problems and of the types and location of treatment for alcohol problems. The report advocates matching the type and intensity of treatment to the severity of the alcohol problem and expanding treatment for persons with mild to moderate alcohol problems. Persons with mild or moderate alcohol problems would receive brief interventions conducted in the community setting where they are identified while persons with substantial or severe alcohol problems would be referred to specialized treatment settings. Currently in the United States, many mild to moderate alcohol problems go unidentified or untreated. Further, little matching of patient needs to types of treatment goes on because most treatment occurs in specialized alcohol treatment programs that are relatively homogeneous, consisting of abstinence-oriented, 12-step, disease model programs delivered on an intensive and frequently inpatient basis.

"Alcohol problems are defined for the purpose of this report as those problems that may arise in individuals around their use of beverage alcohol and that may require an appropriate treatment response for their optimum management" (Institute of Medicine, 1990, p. 25). Figure 16.1 illustrates the expanded conceptualization and definition of the population of persons requiring treatment when the alcohol-problems perspective advanced by the committee is applied to the United States. "What the diagram suggests is that most people have no alcohol problems, many people have some alcohol problems, and a few people have many alcohol problems. This suggestion has a substantial basis in empirical data" (Institute of Medicine, 1990, p. 214) from careful population surveys (e.g., Cahalan, 1970; Hinton, 1987).

This alcohol-problems perspective significantly broadens the scope of persons targeted for treatment to include the much larger numbers of persons with mild to moderate problems and adds greatly to the al-

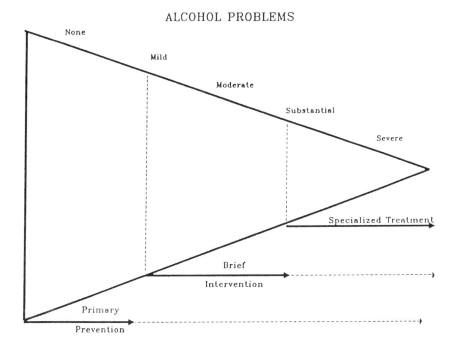

ALCOHOL PROBLEMS

A spectrum of responses to alcohol problems. The triangle represents the population of the United States, with the spectrum of alcohol problems experienced by the population shown along the upper side. Responses to the problems are shown along the lower side (based on Skinner, 1988). In general, specialized treatment is indicated for persons with substantial or severe alcohol problems; brief intervention is indicated for persons with mild or moderate alcohol problems; and primary prevention is indicated for persons who have not had alcohol problems but are at risk of developing them. The dotted lines extending the arrows suggest that both primary prevention and brief intervention may have effects beyond their principle target populations. The prevalence of categories of alcohol problems in the population is represented by the area of the triangle occupied; most people have no alcohol problems, many people have a few alcohol problems, and some people have many alcohol problems.

FIGURE 16.1. Alcohol problems and a proposal for their treatment. From Institute of Medicine (1990, p. 212). Copyright 1990 by the National Academy of Sciences. Reprinted with permission.

ready recognized heterogeneity of alcohol problems. Alcohol problems are seen as heterogeneous in where, when, and how they initially present themselves to the attention of professionals in health care, social service, work place, education, criminal justice, or other community setting. A greatly expanded role for nonspecialist community agencies and settings is proposed. This role involves identifying individuals with alcohol problems, providing brief interventions (six or fewer sessions) to reduce or eliminate alcohol consumption of those with mild or moderate alcohol problems (Heather, 1989), and referring those with substantial or severe problems to the specialized alcoholism treatment sector.

Very promising results have been found for brief interventions with mild to moderate alcohol problems (Babor, Ritson, & Hodgson, 1986; Chick, Lloyd, & Crombie, 1984; Wallace, Cutler, & Haines, 1988). Some investigators pursuing brief intervention strategies have recognized the potential value of including the spouse or a family member who lives with the patient in the brief assessment and intervention process (e.g., Chapman & Huygens, 1988; Zweben, Pearlman, & Li, 1988). Chapter 14 of the present volume provides an example of a spouse-involved method for brief treatment with mild to moderate alcohol problems in nonspecialist settings. Studies of such approaches are needed. However, no studies have examined specifically the role of family member involvement in the brief intervention. Studies are needed that compare brief intervention with and without family involvement and that compare various methods for involving family members in brief interventions to determine the optimal approach.

Family-Focused Primary Prevention Programs

Earlier articles (e.g., O'Farrell, 1989; Orford, 1990) have called for well-designed, carefully executed studies to evaluate the impact of prevention programs targeted to the family setting. A special case of prevention in the family setting is the prevention of alcohol-related damage to the unborn fetus (Orford, 1990). Although initial efforts to prevent alcohol-related fetal damage by working with expectant mothers to reduce or eliminate their alcohol consumption have appeared in the literature (e.g., Little, Streissguth, & Guzinski, 1980), considerably more work needs to be done. In developing prevention programs for the family setting, specific considerations should be given to the role of the family in educating children in responsible drinking practices and to marital/family education of high-risk groups (e.g., children of alcoholics) prior to or early in marriage.

Other Areas for Expanded Research

Two other important areas should see important advances. First, the role of alcohol and alcoholism in marital violence is just beginning to receive serious study. Research under way currently should bring greater understanding to this complex issue (Bushman & Cooper, 1990; Kaufman-Kantor & Strauss, 1987; Leonard & Jacob, 1988; Murphy & O'Farrell, 1992; O'Farrell & Choquette, 1991). Second, there is a need for greater international collaboration in the study and practice of family treatment of alcohol problems because concern about alcohol problems is worldwide. Orford's (1990) recent review of the international literature on alcohol and the family is an excellent place to begin.

Focusing on "Families and Addictions" as an Emerging Area

A final recommendation for the future is that an identified research and clinical area focused on "families and addictions" might be developed. This new area would encompass the study of the role of the family in the etiology, course, treatment, and prevention of addictive behavior problems. This would include problems with alcohol, drugs, smoking, and obesity.

Although it has long been recognized that family processes most likely were important in the development of addictive behavior problems and that family approaches to treatment and prevention of such problems were plausible and promising, it has only been in recent years that research has begun to document this importance. Furthermore, within each addictive behavior, development of treatment and prevention research has proceeded separately from research on etiology and on processes within the family that affect and are affected by the addictive behavior problem. In addition, each addictive behavior has its own set of investigators, journals, and so forth, so there has been little or no cross-fertilization among family approaches to the various addictive behavior problems.

An identified area of "addictions and the family" could bring together investigators pursuing family research on each of the addictive behaviors. This might lead to improved research as we examine the commonalities and differences in findings, methods, and conceptualizations that characterize family studies of each of the addictive behaviors. Consider, for example, the possible benefits of a closer collaboration between family treatment researchers in alcohol problems and in drug abuse. Complimentary strengths of family research on each of these two addictions might strengthen the other. As indicated above, alcohol problems research lacks the well-established tradition of studying family systems therapy approaches that has characterized drug-abuse family research from the outset (e.g., Liddle & Diamond, 1991; Stanton & Todd, 1982). Further, the rigorous experimental methodology and meticulous attention to reliability and validity of outcome measures that characterizes the recent BMT alcohol studies could benefit research on family treatment of drug abuse. In addition, family involvement in treatment currently is being studied for smoking (e.g., Cohen & Lichenstein, 1990; Cohen et al., 1988) and obesity (e.g., Epstein & Squires, 1988).

In closing, the stage is set for the development of an area focused on "families and addictions" within the field of family psychology. The work on marital and family therapy in alcoholism treatment that has been documented in the present volume will contribute to and be substantially enriched by further developments concerning "families and addictions".

ACKNOWLEDGMENTS

Preparation of this chapter was supported by grant R01 AA08637 to the author from the National Institute on Alcohol Abuse and Alcoholism and by a grant from the Smithers Foundation.

REFERENCES

Ahles, T. A., Schlundt, D. G., Prue, D. M., & Rychtarik, R. G. (1983). Impact of aftercare arrangements on the maintenance of treatment success in abusive drinkers. *Addictive Behaviors, 8,* 53–58.

Al-Anon Family Groups. (1981). *This is Al-Anon.* New York: Author.

Alterman, A. I., Hayashida, M., & O'Brien, C. P. (1988). Treatment response and safety of ambulatory medical detoxification. *Journal of Studies on Alcohol, 49,* 160–166.

Azrin, N. H. (1976). Improvements in the community-reinforcement approach to alcoholism. *Behaviour Research and Therapy, 14,* 339–348.

Azrin, N. H., Sisson, R. W., Meyers, R., & Godley, M. (1982). Alcoholism treatment by Disulfiram and community reinforcement therapy. *Journal of Behavior Therapy and Experimental Psychiatry, 13,* 105–112.

Babor, T. F., Ritson, E. G., & Hodgson, R. J. (1986). Alcohol-related problems in the primary health care setting: A review of early intervention strategies. *British Journal of Addiction, 81,* 23–46.

Bowen, M. (1978). *Family therapy in clinical practice.* New York: Jason Aronson.

Bushman, B. M., & Cooper, H. M. (1990). Effects of alcohol on human aggression: An integrative research review. *Psychological Bulletin, 107,* 341–354.

Cahalan, D. (1970). *Problem drinkers: A national survey.* San Francisco: Jossey-Bass.

Cermak, T. (1986). *Diagnosing and treating co-dependence.* Minneapolis: Johnson Institute Books.

Chapman, P. L. H., & Huygens, I. (1988). An evaluation of three treatment programmes for alcoholism: An experimental study with 6 and 18 month follow ups. *British Journal of Addiction, 83,* 67–81.

Chick, J., Lloyd, G., & Crombie, E. (1984). Counseling problem drinkers in medical wards: A controlled study. *British Medical Journal, 290,* 965–967.

Cohen, D. C., & Krause, M. S. (1971). *Casework with the wives of alcoholics.* New York: Family Service Association of America.

Cohen, S. & Lichenstein, E. (1990). Partner behaviors that support quitting smoking. *Journal of Consulting and Clinical Psychology, 58,* 304–309.

Cohen, S., Lichtenstein, E., Mermelstein, R., Kingsolver, K., Baer, J., & Kamarch, T. (1988). Social support interventions for smoking cessation. In B. H. Gottlieb (Ed.), *Marshalling social support: Formats, processes and effects* (pp. 211–240). New York: Sage.

Davis, T. S., & Hagood, L. (1979). In-home support for recovering alcoholic mothers and their families: The family rehabilitation co-ordination project. *Journal of Studies on Alcohol, 40*, 313–317.

Dittrich, J. E., & Trapold, M. A. (1984). Wives of alcoholics: A treatment program and outcome study. *Bulletin of the Society of Psychologists in Addictive Behaviors, 3*, 91–102.

Emrick, C., & Hanson, J. (1985). Thoughts on treatment evaluation methodology. In B. S. McCrady, N. E. Noel, & T. Nirenberg (Eds.), *Future directions in alcohol abuse treatment research* (National Institute of Alcohol Abuse and Alcoholism Research Monograph No. 15, pp. 137–172). Washington, DC: U.S. Government Printing Office.

Epstein, L. H., & Squires, S. (1988). *The stop-light diet for children: An eight-week program for parents and children.* Boston: Little, Brown.

Gentillelo, L. M., Duggan, P., Drummond, D., Tonnesen, A., Degner, E., Fischer, R. P., & Reed, L. R. (1988). Major injury as a unique opportunity to initiate treatment in the alcoholic. *American Journal of Surgery, 156*, 558–561.

Gorman, J. M., & Rooney, J. F. (1979). The influence of Al-Anon on the coping behavior of wives of alcoholics. *Journal of Studies on Alcohol, 40*, 1030–1038.

Heather, N. (1989) Brief intervention strategies. In R. K. Hester & W. R. Miller (Eds.), *Handbook of alcoholism treatment approaches* (pp. 93–116). New York: Pergamon Press.

Hedberg, A. G., & Campbell, L. (1974). A comparison of four behavioral treatments of alcoholism. *Journal of Behavior Therapy and Experimental Psychiatry, 5*, 251–256.

Hinton, M. E. (1987). Drinking patterns and drinking problems in 1984: Results from a general population survey. *Alcoholism: Clinical and Experimental Research, 11*, 167–175.

Holder, H. D., Longabaugh, R., Miller, W. R., & Rubonis, A. V. (1991). The cost effectiveness of treatment for alcohol problems: A first approximation. *Journal of Studies on Alcohol, 6*, 517–540.

Johnson, V. E. (1986). *Intervention: How to help someone who doesn't want help.* Minneapolis, MN: Johnson Institute Books.

Institute of Medicine (1990). *Broadening the base of treatment for alcohol problems.* Washington, DC: National Academy Press.

Kaufman-Kantor, G., & Straus, M. A. (1987). The "Drunken Bum" theory of wife beating. *Social Problems, 34*, 213–230.

Laundergan, J. C., & Williams, T. (1979). Hazelden: Evaluation of a residential family program. *Alcohol Health and Research World, 13*, 13–16.

Leonard, K. E., & Jacob, T. (1988). Alcohol, alcoholism and family violence. In V. B. Van Hasselt, R. L. Morrison, A. S. Bellack, & M. Herson (Eds.), *Handbook of Family Violence* (pp. 383–406). New York: Plenum Press.

Liddle, H. A., & Diamond, G. (1991). Adolescent substance abusers in family therapy: The critical initial phase of treatment. *Family Dynamics of Addiction Quarterly, 1*, 55–68.

Leipman, M. R., Nirenberg, T. D., & Begin, A. M. (1989). Evaluation of a program designed to help family and significant others to motivate resistant alcoholics into recovery. *American Journal of Drug and Alcohol Abuse, 15*, 209–221.

Little, R. E., Streissguth, A. P., & Guzinski, G. M. (1980). Prevention of fetal alcohol syndrome: A model program. *Alcoholism, 4*, 185–189.

Longabaugh, R., Beattie, M., Noel, N., Stout, R. & Malloy, P. (in press). The effect of social investment on treatment outcome. *Journal of Studies on Alcohol.*

Marlatt, G. A., & Gordon, J. R. (Eds.). (1985). *Relapse prevention: Maintenance strategies in the treatment of addictive behaviors.* New York: Guilford Press.

McCrady, B. S. (1989a). Extending relapse prevention models to couples. *Addictive Behaviors, 14,* 69–74.

McCrady, B. S. (1989b). Outcomes of family-involved alcoholism treatment. In M. Galanter (Ed.), *Recent developments in alcoholism: Vol. 7. Treatment research* (pp. 165–182). New York: Plenum Press.

McCrady, B., Noel, N., Abrams, D., Stout, R., Nelson, H., & Hay, W. (1986). Comparative effectiveness of three types of spouse involvement in outpatient behavioral alcoholism treatment. *Journal of Studies on Alcohol, 47,* 459–467.

McCrady, B., Stout, R., Noel N., Abrams, D., & Nelson, H. (1991). Comparative effectiveness of three types of spouse involved alcohol treatment: Outcomes 18 months after treatment. *British Journal of Addiction, 86,* 1415–1424.

Miller, W. R., & Hester, R. K. (1986). The effectiveness of alcoholism treatment methods: What research reveals. In W. R. Miller & N. Heather (Eds.), *Treating addictive behaviors: Processes of change* (pp. 131–174). New York: Plenum Press.

Moos, R. H., Finney, J. W., & Cronkite, R. C. (1990). *Alcoholism treatment: Context, process and outcome.* New York: Oxford University Press.

Murphy, C. M., & O'Farrell, T. J. (1992, November). *Factors associated with marital aggression among male alcoholics.* Paper presented at the Annual Convention of the Association for the Advancement of Behavior Therapy, Boston, MA.

Nowinksi, J., Baker, S., & Carroll, K. (1992). *Twelve step facilitation therapy manual.* (DHHS Publication No. ADM 92-1893). Washington, DC: National Institute on Alcohol Abuse and Alcoholism.

O'Farrell, T. J. (1989). Marital and family therapy in alcoholism treatment. *Journal of Substance Abuse Treatment 6,* 23–29.

O'Farrell, T. J. (1992). Families and alcohol problems: An overview of treatment research. *Journal of Family Psychology, 5,* 339–359.

O'Farrell, T. J., & Bayog, R. D. (1986). Antabuse contracts for married alcoholics and their spouses: A method to ensure Anatabuse taking and decrease conflicts about alcohol. *Journal of Substance Abuse Treatment, 3,* 1–8.

O'Farrell, T. J., & Choquette, K. A. (1991). Marital violence in the year before and after spouse-involved alcoholism treatment. *Family Dynamics of Addiction Quarterly, 1,* 32–40.

O'Farrell, T. J., Choquette, K. A., Cutter, H. S. G., Brown, E. D., & McCourt, W. F. (in press). Behavioral marital therapy with and without additional relapse prevention sessions for alcoholics and their wives. *Journal of Studies on Alcohol.*

O'Farrell, T. J., & Cowles, K. (1989). Marital and family therapy. In R. Hester & W. R. Miller (Eds.), *Handbook of alcoholism treatment approaches* (pp. 183–205). New York: Pergamon Press.

O'Farrell, T. J., & Cutter, H. S. G. (1977). *Behavioral Marital Therapy (BMT) for alco-*

holics and wives: Review of literature and a proposed research program. Paper presented at the NATO International Conference on Experimental and Behavioral Approaches to Alcoholism, Bergen, Norway. (ERIC Document Reproduction Service No. ED 155 531).

O'Farrell, T. J., Cutter, H. S. G., Choquette, K. A., Floyd, F. J., & Bayog, R. D. (1992). Behavioral marital therapy for male alcoholics: Marital and drinking adjustment during the two years after treatment. *Behavior Therapy, 23,* 529–549.

O'Farrell, T. J., Cutter, H. S. G., & Floyd, F. J. (1985). Evaluating behavioral marital therapy for male alcoholics: Effects on marital adjustment and communication from before to after therapy. *Behavior Therapy, 16,* 147–167.

O'Farrell, T. J., & Maisto, S. A. (1987). The utility of self-report and biologial measures of alcohol consumption in alcoholism treatment outcome studies. *Advances in Beahviour Research and Therapy, 9,* 91–125.

Orford, J. (1990). Alcohol and the family: An international review of the literature with implications for research and practice. In L. T. Kozlowski et al. (Eds.), *Research advances in alcohol and drug problems* (Vol. 10, pp. 81–155). New York: Plenum Press.

Orford J., & Edwards, G. (1977). *Alcoholism: A comparison of treatment and advice with a study of the influence of marriage.* London: Oxford University Press.

Ossip-Klein, D. J., VanLandingham, W., Prue, D. M., & Rychtarik, R. G. (1984). Increasing attendance at alcohol aftercare using calendar prompts and home based contracting. *Addictive Behaviors, 9,* 85–89.

Pattison, E. M. (1965). Treatment of alcoholic families with nurse home visits. *Family Process, 4,* 75–94.

Rychtarik, R. G., Carstensen, L. L., Alford, G. S., Schlundt, D. G., & Scott, W. O. (1988). Situational assessment of alcohol-related coping skills in wives of alcoholics. *Psychology of Addictive Behavior, 2,* 66–73.

Sisson, R. W., & Azrin, N. H. (1986). Family-member involvement to initiate and promote treatment of problem drinkers. *Journal of Behavior Therapy and Experiemental Psychiatry, 17,* 15–21.

Skinner, H. A. (1988). *Executive summary: Toward a multiaxial framework for the classification of alcohol problems.* Unpublished paper prepared for the Institute of Medicine Committee for the Study of Treatment and Rehabilitation Services for Alcoholism and Alcohol Abuse, University of Toronto, Department of Behavioral Science, Toronto, Ontario, Canada.

Sobell, M. B., Brochu, S., Sobell, L. C., Roy, J., & Stevens, J. (1987). Alcohol treatment outcome evaluation methodology: State of the art 1980–1984. *Addictive Behaviors, 12,* 113–128.

Stanton, M. D., Todd, T. C., & Associates (1982). *The family therapy of drug abuse and addiction.* New York: Guilford Press.

Steinglass, P. (1976). Experimenting with family treatment approaches to alcoholism, 1950–1975: A review. *Family Process, 15,* 97–123.

Steinglass, P. (1979). An experimental treatment program for alcoholic couples. *Journal of Studies on Alcohol, 40,* 159–182.

Steinglass, P., Bennett, L., Wolin, S., & Reiss, D. (1987). *The alcoholic family.* New York: Basic Books.

Stockwell, T., Bolt, L. Milner, I., Pugh, P. & Young, I. (1990). Home detoxification for problem drinkers: Acceptability to clients, relatives, general practitioners and outcomes after 60 days. *British Journal of Addiction, 85,* 61–70.

Stout, R. L., McCrady, B. S., Longabaugh, R. Noel, N. E., & Beattie, M. C. (1987). Marital therapy enhances the long-term effectiveness of alcohol treatment. *Alcoholism: Clinical and Experimental Research, 11,* 213.

Thomas, A., Weaver, J., Knight, L., & Bale, R. (1986). *Family treatment in short-term detoxification.* Paper presented at the National Council on Alcoholism Forum, San Francisco.

Thomas, E. J., Santa, C., Bronson, D., & Oyserman, D. (1987). Unilateral family therapy with the spouses of alcoholics. *Journal of Social Service Research, 10,* 145–162.

Thomas, E. J., Yoshioka, M., Ager, R. D., & Adams, K. B. (1993). *Experimental outcomes of spouse intervention to reach the uncooperative alcohol abuser: Preliminary report.* Manuscript submitted for publication.

Wallace, P., Cutler, S., & Haines, A. (1988). Randomized controlled trial of general practitioner intervention in patients with excessive alcohol consumption. *British Medical Journal, 297,* 633–638.

Wright, K. D., & Scott, T. B. (1978). The relationship of wives' treatment to the drinking status of alcoholics. *Journal of Studies on Alcohol, 39,* 1577–1581.

Zweben, A., Pearlman, S., & Li, S. (1988). A comparison of brief advice and conjoint therapy in the treatment of alcohol abuse: The results of the Marital Systems study. *British Journal of Addiction, 83,* 899–916.

Index